Spirits of the Space Age

Spirits of the Space Age

The Imagined World of Brazil's Valley of the Dawn

KELLY E. HAYES

OXFORD
UNIVERSITY PRESS

Oxford University Press is a department of the University of Oxford. It furthers
the University's objective of excellence in research, scholarship, and education
by publishing worldwide. Oxford is a registered trade mark of Oxford University
Press in the UK and certain other countries.

Published in the United States of America by Oxford University Press
198 Madison Avenue, New York, NY 10016, United States of America.

© Oxford University Press 2024

All rights reserved. No part of this publication may be reproduced, stored in
a retrieval system, or transmitted, in any form or by any means, without the
prior permission in writing of Oxford University Press, or as expressly permitted
by law, by license, or under terms agreed with the appropriate reproduction
rights organization. Inquiries concerning reproduction outside the scope of the
above should be sent to the Rights Department, Oxford University Press, at the
address above.

You must not circulate this work in any other form
and you must impose this same condition on any acquirer.

Library of Congress Cataloging-in-Publication Data
Names: Hayes, Kelly E., 1968- author.
Title: Spirits of the space age : the imagined world of Brazil's valley of
the dawn / Kelly E. Hayes.
Description: New York, NY : Oxford University Press, [2024] |
Includes bibliographical references and index.
Identifiers: LCCN 2023057232 (print) | LCCN 2023057233 (ebook) |
ISBN 9780197516409 (paperback) | ISBN 9780197516393 (hardback) |
ISBN 9780197516423 (epub)
Subjects: LCSH: Spiritualism—Brazil—Vale do Amanhecer. |
Mediums—Practice—Brazil—Vale do Amanhecer. |
Mind and body—Religious aspects.
Classification: LCC BF1242.B6 H38 2024 (print) | LCC BF1242.B6 (ebook) |
DDC 299.8/917—dc23/eng/20240117
LC record available at https://lccn.loc.gov/2023057232
LC ebook record available at https://lccn.loc.gov/2023057233

DOI: 10.1093/oso/9780197516393.001.0001

In memory of Marilyn Jule Hayes (1939–2016), who traveled to the astral plane too soon.

This book is dedicated to Jaguars and all who imagine a future of progress for themselves that depends on the wellbeing of others.

Contents

List of Illustrations ix
Acknowledgments xi

1. Introduction — 1
2. The Clairvoyant — 26
3. The Intellectual — 57
4. The Journey of the Jaguars — 78
5. A Total Synesthetic Experience — 106
6. Knights and Princesses — 144
7. The Work of Healing — 178
8. Transcendental Heritages — 216
9. A Space Age Religion for Modern Brazil — 242

Notes 261
Bibliography 285
Index 299

Illustrations

Images

1.1 Entrance to the Valley of the Dawn. — 2
1.2 Temple entrance. — 3
1.3 Solar dos Médiuns. — 4
1.4 Estrela Candente. — 5
2.1 Neiva and her truck. — 29
2.2 Brasília work force. — 32
2.3 UESB (Spiritualist Union Father White Arrow), 1959–1964. — 46
2.4 Statue of Father White Arrow. — 47
3.1 Mário Sassi 1955. — 60
3.2 Mário Sassi and Aunt Neiva. — 69
4.1 Jaguar symbol. — 79
4.2 Virachocha, Sun Gate in Bolivia. — 90
4.3 Painting of Tiãozinho from the Mother Temple. — 96
5.1 Symbol of the doutrinador (cross with draped mantle). — 116
5.2 Symbol of the apará (triangle with open book). — 117
5.3 Branquinha uniform or "little whites." — 122
5.4 Colete back (apará). — 129
5.5 Colete back (doutrinador). — 130
5.6 Colete badges. — 131
5.7 Jaguar uniform. — 133
5.8 Indumentária male and female. — 134
5.9 Radar de Centúria. — 135
5.10 Centurion Medium. — 136
6.1 Aunt Neiva. — 146
6.2 Doutrinador: Positive Polarity/Sun/Gold. — 154
6.3 Apará: Negative Polarity/Moon/Silver. — 155

6.4	Sun Nymph.	157
6.5	Moon Nymph.	158
6.6	Missionary Guide Arana Amarela.	167
6.7	Master.	169
6.8	Knight.	170
7.1	Pira.	196
7.2	Thrones.	197
7.3	Female prisoner.	205
7.4	Gathering bonuses.	206
8.1	Pyramid.	231
8.2	Nefertiti and Tutankhamon in Pyramid.	232
8.3	Moon Grega.	237
9.1	Official Illustrator of the Doctrine, Joaquim Vilela.	254

Tables

6.1	Master and Nymph.	149
6.2	Implicit Valuations of Masculinity and Femininity.	151
6.3	Mediumship.	153
6.4	The Intersection of Gender and Mediumship.	156

Acknowledgments

Writing this book took me longer, and challenged me more thoroughly, than any other writing project I have undertaken to date. Partly this was a result of the amount of detailed information that I collected over the years that I have been researching the Valley of the Dawn. Partly it was due to the complexity of the movement itself as well as the imagined world to which it gave rise. I wanted to accurately convey this rich complexity and distill it into readable prose without overwhelming the reader with detail. So, the issue of how to convey information and in what order preoccupied me. I also wanted to narrate the Valley's historical emergence without abstracting it from the human beings whose experiences, imaginations, and efforts birthed it as well as those human beings who shared their present-day experiences with me.

These goals seemed to defy the conventions of scholarly writing. So, I looked to other genres like historical fiction and long-form journalism for models. I experimented with different organizational structures before settling on this one, which moves from biographically oriented chapters to more thematically oriented ones. Of course, the story that unfolds in these pages is neither the only one possible nor the most comprehensive, but it is my attempt to be as faithful as possible to my data while organizing it in a way that I hope will be of interest to both scholars and general readers.

This book would not have been possible without funding from the Fulbright US Scholars Program as well as various grants over the years from my home institution, Indiana University. I am grateful to the IU New Frontiers in the Arts and Humanities Program; the IU Consortium for the Study of Religion, Ethics and Society; the IUPUI Arts and Humanities Institute; and the School of Liberal Arts at IUPUI for supporting my research in various ways.

The heart of this project are the Jaguars who shared their time, compassion, wisdom, and stories with me. I am grateful to the many people with whom I spent time at the Valley of the Dawn and who always received me graciously. While there are far too many to name here, I especially want to recognize Raul Zelaya, Carmem Lúcia Zelaya, Vera Lúcia Zelaya, Jairo Oliveira Junior Leite, Cristina Zelaya, Kátia Sartório, Teresinha Bastos, Lúcia

Pimentel, Seu Pimental, João Nunez Rocha, Joaquim Vilela, Neide Coelho de Assis, Geny Santana, Paulo Andrelino, Socorro, Nicolina, Tiago, Mestre Carlan, Mestre Caldeira, Mestre Lacerda, Mestre Anderson, Seu Sidney and Dona Dalva, and Dona Vera Lúcia. May those whose names I have inadvertently omitted here forgive my oversight.

At different times from 2014 to 2016, Francisco Bergamo, Mariana Martins da Costa Freitas, Luigi Farias de Lima, and Marília Sinigalia worked as my research assistants. Each helped me with the painstaking work of transcribing and translating my field interviews and I am grateful for their efforts. A special shout-out to Francisco Bergamo, whose attention to issues of translation and word choice improved this work and with whom I shared many interesting conversations about the Valley.

I would like to recognize my Indiana University colleagues Charli Champion-Shaw, David Craig, Edward Curtis IV, Matthew Condon, Thomas Davis, Andrea Jain, Peter Thuesen, Joseph Tucker Edmonds, and Rachel Wheeler for their collegiality and support as well as thoughtful comments on various iterations of this project. My dear friend Jerry Handler was a key interlocutor for me, and we spent many hours on the phone as he helped me think through and organize my material while discouraging me from getting bogged down in theory. Micah Oelze offered generous and insightful feedback on Chapter 4, and his enthusiasm for the project buoyed me. I thank Karin Wolf, Becca Hopson, KJ Mohr, and Din Bonny for listening to endless ramblings about the project and reading different chapters of the book.

Márcia Alves, whose stunning photographs are included in this book, was instrumental in this project at every stage from initial conception to end. Her joyful spirit, good humor, and love of adventure made the work fun and I treasure our friendship. My sincere appreciation and gratitude to Virginia Scotti and Rosana Pauluci, whose hospitality and generosity I enjoyed on countless occasions. To my dear friends Sérgio Carrara, Josué Laguardia, Márcio Valgas Lobo, Ana Paula Gomes, and Luiza da Silva, big love and saudades. To my family of blood and heart—Catherine Crouch, Leslie Hayes, Eric Houtkooper, Katie Houtkooper, KJ Mohr, and Karin Wolf—you sustain me.

1
Introduction

I felt like an intruder, a Peeping Tom, hesitant even to snap pictures of one of the most extraordinary places I had ever been. There was nothing there I could look at seriously, nothing he said that I could take seriously. It was all, frankly, ridiculous. I felt rotten, inwardly mocking something so clearly meaningful to these people. Before long, however, I was struck by how normal that Valley of the Dawn felt, how authentic, how homey. I couldn't imagine a cult like this in Texas, where I grew up, with our Branch Davidians and creepy child molesters dreaming of alien rapture. These people were friendly, open, and willing to share the experiences that had brought them there. Back pain, one woman said. His daughter's death, said a man. This, I thought, was the real Brazil, a place so effortlessly weird, so welcomingly friendly, and so unexpectedly fascinating that anyone, like me, who finds themselves there once keep going back, and can never quite shake it.

—Benjamin Moser (2008)

Among the greatest blessings bestowed on us by the Most High, who rules the Universe, are the freedom to act and the power of superior ideas. However, the warning I have always had from our mentors is not to waste our strength wanting to bring the light to others without the light coming to us first, inside us. Avoid the desire to enlighten, without first being enlightened within.

—Aunt Neiva

A Universal Emergency Room for a Planet on the Verge

There is little to distinguish the main road leading into the Vale do Amanhecer, or Valley of the Dawn, from any other road in this dusty stretch of the central Brazilian highlands except for the colorful wooden archway that stretches over it (see Image 1.1). Passing under it to enter the town recalls

Image 1.1 Entrance to the Valley of the Dawn. Credit Márcia Alves

the moment in the 1939 movie version of *The Wizard of Oz* when Dorothy is transported from monochrome Kansas to the vivid, Technicolor world of Oz. Unlike the drab streets of neighboring Planaltina, six kilometers down the road, the Valley of the Dawn is exuberant with color—its buildings adorned in canary yellow, sky blue, crimson, and lilac. Despite the bleaching rays of the highland sun these colors pulsate with a saturated intensity that draws the eye and finds its echo in the brilliantly hued garments of the Valley's resident mediums.

Women, known within the community as nymphs (*ninfas*), dazzle in colorful, floor-length gowns encrusted with sequined symbols that sparkle as the sun's rays catch them, their arms sheathed in full-length, fingerless lace gloves. Many wear tiara-like headdresses from which multicolored veils and velvet ribbons cascade, riffling in the breeze. A more somber color palette characterizes the attire of their male counterparts, the masters (*mestres*). Some masters wear brown pants and black shirts topped with short white vests on which are pinned numerous badges, brooches, and other insignia particular to the Valley. Others are garbed in dark, voluminous capes that rise up into stiff, Dracula-like collars framing the face. The capes fasten at the wrist so that when the masters raise their arms, as they do in certain rituals, the effect is like giant bats flapping their wings. For this reason, people in the surrounding region sometimes jokingly refer to the Valley of the Dawn as Gotham City. Like Batman's hometown, or the Emerald City of Oz, the Valley of the Dawn is its own imaginative universe, a place that visitors find at once familiar and fantastical, kitschy and quixotic.

Its center of gravitational pull is the Mother Temple, a large stone edifice whose uncharacteristically drab exterior hides a multifaceted interior of colorful rooms dedicated to different spirit-healing rituals. Dotting the plaza surrounding the Temple are other unusual architectural structures and brightly painted monuments. Among these are a two-story-high, cutout image of Jesus and a circular enclosure with a large, star-shaped table at its center (See Image 1.2). Another six-pointed star stands directly in front of the Temple, emitting sparkly shards of refracted light from the bits of mirrored glass covering its surface. In the highlands' bright sun, the visual effect of all the shimmer and polychrome surfaces is kaleidoscopic, even psychedelic. Even the air smells distinctive, like the scent of an ancient forest, musky yet clarifying. To clear negative energy and center the mind, Valley members regularly burn the dehydrated sap of the amescla tree found throughout the region.

Not far from the temple plaza is an even larger, open-air complex reminiscent of a water park called the Solar dos Médiuns or Medium's Estate[1] (see Image 1.3). Arrayed around the shores of its central body of water is a kind

Image 1.2 Temple entrance. Credit Márcia Alves

Image 1.3 Solar dos Médiuns. Credit Márcia Alves

of promenade filled with more color-coded structures and large images, including a sizeable pyramid, a multi-hued staircase crowned by a rising sun, and an elaborate platform rising from the water in the shape of a six-pointed star. The star-shaped platform is where the Ritual of the Incandescent Star (Estrela Candente), perhaps the most well known of the Valley's repertoire, takes place three times a day in accordance with the arrival of a fleet of invisible spacecraft (See Image 1.4).

This phantasmagoric town, so unlike its prosaic neighbors, is the headquarters of the "Social Works of the Christian Spiritualist Order" or OSOEC, as the Valley of the Dawn officially is called. It is the oldest and largest of the New Age communities that have sprung up in the nondescript satellite cities surrounding Brasília, the country's starkly modernist capital city.[2] Known throughout Brazil for its flamboyant aesthetics and Space Age cosmology, the Valley of the Dawn is a unique psychic ecosystem: equal parts religious movement, enchanted city, utopian project, and theatrical spectacle. Every day mediums garbed in their fairytale vestments gather to perform ceremonies for healing and karmic redemption by invoking a phalanx of invisible spirit guides. For them, the Valley of the Dawn is the visible hub of a vast cosmic power plant, and they are its technicians, harnessing and converting invisible energies in order to galvanize psychic transformation.

Image 1.4 Estrela Candente. Credit Márcia Alves.

Most days the Mother Temple's expansive grounds are abuzz with mediums and patients, each following their own itinerary. The latter come from across Brazil and even farther away to participate in the community's healing ceremonies. These are offered to the public free of charge and performed by the Valley's cadre of trained mediums. The demand is constant: in any given month thousands of people suffering from health problems, mental illness, grief, or addiction visit the Mother Temple to receive healing energies and be freed of negative spiritual influences. Any problem, regardless of magnitude, merits attention. Many patients have had unsuccessful experiences with both conventional medicine and other religions, and the Valley of the Dawn is their last resort.

Valley members consider the work of spiritual healing to be their sacred duty. "We are sworn to Christ," longtime medium Master Antônio Carlos told me in 2010 when I visited the Mother Temple for the first time.

> The Valley of the Dawn is a Spiritist doctrine based in the Gospel of Jesus Christ. Here we do not preach the gospel, we live out the gospel in practice, in our work—that's our way of preaching. Here we don't come to pray, we come to work. And that's precisely why you will see everyone here with their sleeves rolled up. The principal objective of the Valley of the Dawn is

to assist incarnate and disincarnate souls, our brothers and sisters. We don't preach physical healing. Here our concern is with spiritual healing, with the recovery of the spirit.

The Valley's healing mission was established by Neiva Chaves Zelaya (1925–1985), a visionary clairvoyant convinced that her spirit guides had brought her to the sleepy outskirts of the nation's capital to establish a capital of a different kind. Aunt Neiva, as her followers affectionately refer to her, was a young widow when she and her four children migrated to Brasília in 1957 to work in the construction of the new capital city. Not long after their arrival, Aunt Neiva began to suffer from visual and auditory disturbances that left her terrified and, at times, unable to work. Her search for answers led her away from the Catholicism of her upbringing to the spirit-mediumship traditions of Umbanda and Brazilian Kardecism. Eventually, she was persuaded that her troubling experiences were evidence of a unique spiritual sensitivity and that she had been chosen by highly evolved cosmic beings to usher humanity through the calamitous transition to a new age, known as the Third Millennium. Over some two decades, she built a spiritual metropolis that today is home to over 25,000 residents and the center of a growing international religious movement with nearly 800 affiliated temples and over a hundred thousand members worldwide.[3]

Aunt Neiva was part of a deeply rooted tradition of religious visionaries and folk healers in Brazil: otherwise ordinary individuals whose extraordinary charisma, healing abilities, or inspirational message attracted attention and, eventually, a following. Like many of her counterparts, Aunt Neiva taught an inspired synthesis that reflected the country's diverse religious milieu and addressed the pragmatic, daily challenges people faced—a doctrine that deferred to God and Jesus yet focused on spirits as vectors of supernatural assistance. Unlike most, Aunt Neiva's reputation grew well beyond a local, or even regional, circle. At the time of her death in 1985, she was one of the most famous spiritual healers in the country, sought out by the powerful and the poverty-stricken alike.

Many observers predicted that the community Aunt Neiva founded would disintegrate with her death. Instead, the Valley of the Dawn expanded worldwide. Its multinational, multiracial membership now spans divides of class, educational level, age, language, and region, and it includes people living in large cities like Brasília, São Paulo, Rio de Janeiro, Lisbon, London, and Atlanta, as well as suburban and rural settings. The Mother Temple itself has become famous in Brazil as a sacred site, center of spiritual healing, and part of the federal district's intangible cultural heritage.[4]

By any measure, the Valley of the Dawn is a successful new religion. Yet outside observers and mainstream media outlets routinely dismiss it as naive escapism or whimsical make-believe: a "poor man's Disneyland," "Fellini set," "miniature theme park," or, as a 2012 BBC article archly opined, a "fancy dress party for adults." Some have impugned the mental health of Valley members, describing the community as a "refuge for lost souls"[5] Others imagine something more malign and accuse its leaders of abusing the genuine faith of the uncultured masses: "A spectacular syncretism where the naivety of our ignorant people is exploited to the fullest."[6]

What these various descriptions share is a scarcely veiled tone of disdain that portrays the Valley as a frivolous curiosity or New Age oddity at best, and, at worst, an exploitative cult. The implication is that members of the community are credulous, unsophisticated, juvenile, or mentally infirm. Whether intended or not, the effect of such portrayals is to remove the Valley of the Dawn from the arena of authentic religion and therefore from the aegis of human cultural productions that one must take seriously or, at the very least, feign respect.

In part this reflects the persistent suspicion of, and bias against, new religious movements that is common in most societies. But it also reflects a deep-rooted discomfort with religions that are visibly different from the status quo—perhaps because these movements throw into high relief the constructed and contingent nature of all religions. As historian of religion Catherine Wessinger noted, comparative studies of religion have shown that "beliefs and practices that are regarded as strange in one religion are normative in another" (Wessinger 2000, 5). Hence, many Christians regard as nonsensical the idea of reincarnation that is taken for granted by Hindus and Buddhists even as the latter find the Christian doctrine of Jesus's bodily resurrection to be fantastic and implausible.

If we understand religion as a human construction founded on claims about a greater reality that is not completely knowable to humans and cannot be empirically demonstrated, the Valley's understanding of that reality is no more outlandish than that of other, more established religions, as I endeavor to show in this book. The conviction that human beings are born into sin or that an omnipotent God created the world are accepted as facts by many people not because there is objective, scientifically verifiable evidence supporting these claims. Rather, such claims are accepted because they have become part of the social fabric into which people are born and that gives structure to their lives.

In other words, claims about non-empirically verifiable realities function as part of a worldview: a set of mental constructs and capacities that enable humans to "make sense" of their experiences and address existential questions and concerns (e.g., What is real? How should we live? Where did we come from? What happens after death?). Answers to these questions create an orderly, meaningful world in which humans can live. Religions can be defined as intersubjectively shared webs of meaning predicated on claims about transcendent worlds and their other-than-human inhabitants—worlds that stretch beyond the conventional dimensions of space and time, worlds that are peopled by powerful beings or forces, worlds we inhabit before birth or after death.[7] What makes religions different from other intersubjectively shared ways of making sense of the human experience is their appeal to an unseen order of existence whose reality status cannot be independently verified.[8]

By providing answers to questions about the nature of the universe and human beings, religions establish structures for organizing human life around which communities form: ethical and legal systems, philosophies, doctrines, and practices. The answers they proffer typically take the form of stories about beginnings and endings; special times and places; culture heroes; and gods, deities, and supernatural powers. As anthropologist T. M. Luhrmann wrote, religions involve imaginative acts of storytelling and world-making that encourage their adherents to "imagine a world beyond the one we have before us" (Luhrmann 2020a, 76). People engage with these imagined otherworlds through sensory experiences of various kinds—iconography, imagery, scripture, sermons, hymns, music, worship, rituals, special foods and drink, forms of dress, sacred objects, and so forth—that give felt presence to otherwise intangible realities. These imagined worlds appear implausible or fantastic only to those who do not share their central precepts.

Mainstream reporting about new or alternative religions does a great disservice when it focuses only on the fantastic and fails to explain why imagined worlds like the Valley of the Dawn's are meaningful to their adherents.[9] On the one hand, such reporting prevents us from perceiving unconventional religions as complex cultural phenomena that propose alternative understandings of the universe and human beings—alternative narratives that make possible different ways of being in the world. If we took this aspect more seriously, we might learn a lot about why people choose to join these groups. And people choose to join the Valley of the Dawn, which emphasizes free will and strongly discourages proselytization and any manner of coercion.

On the other hand, it reinforces our unexamined assumptions about what constitutes an authentic religion and our prejudices against that which does not correspond. Such attitudes can slide easily into intolerance and discrimination, perpetuating the idea that alternative religious communities are not actually legitimate religions at all but rather "cults" whose members are either delusional or in thrall to some charismatic personality.

But Is It a Cult?

Scholars of religion may agree on little else, but there is overwhelming consensus that the use of the term "cult" to identify and categorize certain religious (or other kinds of) groups is problematic for several reasons. First, the term has a broad range of meanings with competing moral valences and different authors use it to mean different things. Second, it does not pick out a set of characteristics that are found only among groups so labeled. And third, because it typically is applied in a pejorative manner its usage carries negative social consequences.

In its most restricted usage, cult refers to a set of rites or organized worship directed toward a particular object of reverence, like "the cult of Dionysus." Scholars of religion continue to use the term in this neutral sense. The problem is that since the 1970s, "cult" has entered mainstream use as a negative term for groups that dominant society perceives as aberrant, suspicious, or sinister. "Whenever someone uses the word 'cult,'" scholar of new religions Rebecca Moore observed pithily, "we know they're talking about bad religion" (2018).[10]

Cult is a convenient four-letter word to put into headlines, but it is perilously distorting, warned Catherine Wessinger (2000, 3). On the one hand, labeling a group as a cult dehumanizes its members, making them seem deviant, crazy, or under the control of their leader. On the other, Wessinger noted, by splitting off the violence associated with religion from conventional religions, projecting it on to others, and then imagining that only aberrant groups engage in violence, we perpetuate a psychologically powerful but historically inaccurate fiction. This fiction shields us from confronting the uncomfortable fact that mainstream religious groups have long histories of violence (2000, 4). To take merely one example, systematic violence has been waged in the name of Christianity from Constantine to the Crusades and the Inquisition, and from anti-abortion activists to contemporary white-supremacist groups. So, violence is hardly a feature only of so-called cults.

Moreover, the characteristics commonly associated with cults are equally prevalent among groups recognized as legitimate religions. These characteristics include: (a) beliefs and practices that contravene dominant norms (often involving sexuality, marriage, and family arrangements), (b) a charismatic leader who is thought to exercise coercive control over his or her followers, (c) extraordinary dedication on the part of members, and (d) insularity or efforts to separate the group from mainstream society though communal living, forms of dress, or economic arrangements. Early forms of Christianity and Islam, among other religions, formed around charismatic leaders who influenced their followers and promoted beliefs and practices that went against the social norms of their time and place. Similarly, Hasidic Jews and the Old Order Amish rarely are described as cults despite exhibiting most or all of these characteristics. There seems to be an unspoken consensus that referring to these groups as cults would be offensive, despite the term's descriptive accuracy in these cases.

By contrast, the Valley of the Dawn does not exhibit any of these traits. Valley members are free to participate in mainstream culture as much or as little as they like—with the exception of alcohol and drug use, which is strongly discouraged. In fact, Valley members are indistinguishable from other Brazilians in terms of their employment, marital, residential, and educational patterns (Pierini 2020, 51). As I detail later in the book, in terms of sexual and family arrangements, the movement promotes a conventional understanding of gender norms and exhibits a marked preference for heterosexuality and male authority.

Because of its emphasis on free will, the Valley of the Dawn is not insular or exclusive: people can come and go as they please, participate to the degree they desire, and leave the movement at any time with no questions asked. It is not unusual for Valley members to have spouses, children, or other family members who belong to other religions. Neither is there any expectation for members to live communally or share economic or other resources. When they are not involved in rituals, Valley members wear the same clothing as, and are indistinguishable from, anyone else.

Similarly, many of the Valley's teachings and much of its ethics overlap with Catholicism, the majority religion in Brazil. Valley members believe in God and Jesus, hold the Virgin Mary in high regard, and recognize Catholic saints as exemplary models of virtue. The Valley shares the practice of spirit mediumship and its pantheon of healing spirits with the religions of Kardecist Spiritism, Umbanda, and Candomblé, which are widespread and popular in Brazil.

It is true that Aunt Neiva was a revered figure, but she was not an autocrat who exercised complete control over her followers. Both outside observers and veteran members describe her as an exceptionally warm, compassionate, and motherly figure who showed selfless dedication to others and whose example of kindness and love set a precedent. Nor have I seen evidence that present-day Valley leaders are materially exploiting members for their own financial gain. In fact, the community provides food and housing to those in need and has created a thriving local economy for entrepreneurs, small-scale vendors, and service providers. Finally, the doctrine condemns violence of all kinds and expects members to exhibit "doctrinal conduct" that exemplifies Jesus's teachings of unconditional love, tolerance, and humility. "Of all the religions I've seen, this is the one with the least prejudice," a frequent visitor named Fernando assured me.

> In addition to generating a thousand prejudices, it is the least prejudiced. The Valley does not pre-judge you, it doesn't discriminate, it leaves you at the mercy of your judgments. It doesn't tell you what to do or interfere in your life or your decisions. It is a school: it tries to show you what life is and that is what I have learned in these years with the Valley of the Dawn. Because this life is just a passage, I really believe that I am eternal. And what will guarantee my evolution is my behavior. My behavior with people, my behavior with my family.

The Doctrine of the Dawn

In response to ongoing public controversies over cults and the sharply pejorative use of this term by the mainstream media, many scholars adopted "new religious movements" (NRMs) to refer to non-mainstream religions, which they sought to understand using the tools of sociology, history, and other academic disciplines.[11] Since then, the study of NRMs has become a recognized specialization within academia and has generated a large scholarly literature.

Generally, NRMs share a number of traits. They are, by definition, new: they offer innovative religious responses to the conditions of the modern world, even as some NRMs represent themselves as rooted in ancient traditions. NRMs often are regarded as "countercultural"—that is, they are perceived (by others and by their members) to be alternatives to mainstream religions. These movements tend to be highly eclectic, freely combining doctrines and practices from diverse sources. They typically consolidate around a charismatic leader who addresses specific needs that many people cannot satisfy through more traditional religious organizations or through secular groups (Rubinstein 2019).

The Valley of the Dawn exhibits all of these traits. As indicated by its official name, Social Works of the Spiritualist Christian Order, ideas drawn from Spiritism and Christianity anchor the movement's doctrinal structure. Added to this are spirit entities venerated in Brazilian religions like Candomblé and Umbanda, vocabulary shared among various esoteric traditions, as well as the belief in extraterrestrial life forms and intergalactic space travel. For Valley members, the Doctrine of the Dawn (as they refer to it) offers a Space Age cosmology that is compatible with both the gospel of Jesus and modern science as well as a set of practices focused on spiritual evolution and healing through mediumship, self-knowledge, and karmic redemption.

From Spiritist and esoteric metaphysics, the Doctrine of the Dawn inherited an emphasis on mediumship and the conception of a universe composed of a physical or terrestrial plane that is surrounded and interpenetrated by a series of invisible planes that exist in dimensions beyond the physical. Animated by the divine principle, which Valley members identify as the Christian God, the entire cosmos (including Earth and humanity) follows a grand scheme of evolutionary and spiritual development that unfolds in sequential, millennial cycles. The transition between these cycles is said to be especially fraught and marked by social conflicts, environmental catastrophes, and increased human suffering. According to the Doctrine, we are currently in the midst of the transition to the "Third Millennium."

Driving the evolutionary process are the universal laws of karma and reincarnation. While physicality is a passing state associated with terrestrial existence, the spirit itself is "transcendental," existing both before and after the physical body and, following the laws of karma, periodically reincarnating on Earth in order to atone for past acts and learn lessons that will facilitate continued perfection. Earth is considered a place of expiation where one can either make amends for one's karmic debts, evolving into a higher moral state, or accrue new karmic debts thus extending the cycle of reincarnation into the future. Once an individual has evolved to the point that incarnation on Earth is no longer necessary, they continue their journey in the spirit world until finally returning to the source.

According to the Doctrine, some highly evolved "spirits of light" work on behalf of incarnated humans as mentors while other, lower-level spirits can provoke illness and misfortune. Much of the community's day-to-day work centers on the collective performance of different healing rituals intended to "indoctrinate" these troublesome spirits and "elevate" or guide them along the path toward evolution.

Unlike Spiritualist mediums in the United States, Valley members do not channel messages from the "beloved dead": spirits of deceased family members or individuals known to their audience in life.[12] Rather, the spirits of light cultivated by Valley members as guides or mentors have completed their own reincarnatory process on Earth and have chosen to help human beings as part of their own evolutionary trajectory. They are spirits of high rank who "have lived reincarnatory experiences over millennia, liberating themselves from . . . the Law of Karma, being, therefore, totally liberated from the physical laws of this plane" (*Manual de Instruções* 2008, 16).

While Valley members consider themselves Christian, their beliefs and practices depart significantly from those of mainstream Christianity, reflecting the strong influence of Spiritist and esoteric metaphysics on Valley cosmology. Jesus, for example, is seen as a highly evolved spirit and esoteric master sent by God to restructure both the spiritual and terrestrial worlds by establishing a system of karmic redemption. Aunt Neiva emphasized that Jesus's teachings of love, humility, and forgiveness offer humans a new path for spiritual evolution referred to as the "Christic System," or "living gospel." By emulating the example of Jesus depicted in the Gospels through the practice of love, tolerance, humility, charity, and forgiveness, Valley members believe that they can redeem the negative karma they have accrued over the course of multiple lifetimes. The task of karmic redemption is considered vital to the community's mission of addressing the spiritual roots of human suffering, which the fraught transition to the Third Millennium has intensified.

Why This Book

I first visited the Valley of the Dawn in 2010. At the time I was looking for a new project after finishing a decade-long study of Afro-Brazilian religions in Rio de Janeiro (Hayes 2011). Reportage from Brazilian and international media had given me the impression that the Valley was a kind of New Age Mecca inhabited by hippies who wore outlandish costumes and worshipped crystals. After years of attending ceremonies involving animal sacrifice and amoral trickster spirits known as exus, the prospect of hanging out with crystal-besotted New Agers sounded refreshing. So in 2010 I spent the better part of two days touring the grounds and speaking with members as part of a larger research trip comparing new religions that took me to São Paulo, Brasília, Rio de Janeiro, and several smaller cities around the country. Despite the brevity of my initial visit, the Valley of the Dawn captured my imagination. When I returned to the United States, I decided to abandon my comparative project to focus solely on the movement. That was twelve years and hundreds of hours of fieldwork ago.

Like most journalists and visitors, I was intrigued initially by the movement's theatrical sensibilities and all-enveloping aesthetics. But as a scholar of religion, I also wanted to understand the historical genesis of the movement's imagined world, what it meant to its founders, and what it means to those who currently inhabit it. I was impressed by Valley members' dedication to the work of healing, their empathy for the suffering of others, and their shared sense of a collective identity that spans past, present, and future. Without the constraints under which journalists operate, and with the luxury of time afforded to me by a sabbatical period and summers off from teaching, I was able to deeply immerse myself in the Valley's extraordinary otherworld.

What I found was far richer and more complex on every level than any popular media account could possibly convey: a cosmology that was both bewilderingly intricate and yet (in simplified form) accessible to novices; a set of teachings that adherents felt helped them understand and better their lives; ritual practices oriented toward helping others and modeling virtues; an integrated community that fostered a sense of belonging and dignity across lines of race, color, educational level, age, and socioeconomic status; a place where everyone has access to resources that lead to greater knowledge and self-mastery; and a form of work in which people feel that they achieve something positive and valuable.

I marveled at the movement's organizational structure, with its nested hierarchies, ritual *falanges* or phalanxes, working groups, healing sectors, and ranks. Through this many-leveled bureaucracy, the community deploys a massive volunteer work force to staff a bewildering array of rituals with the efficiency of a multinational corporation. Even the group's bright colors are laden with meanings linked to the Valley's system of chromotherapy, organizing everything from architectural spaces to member's vestments.

The Valley also has its own dialect. My first tour of the Mother Temple left me with a throbbing headache from the intense effort I expended trying to follow the explanations of my guide, which were salted with words particular to the group, such as Koatay 108, Simiromba, Equitumans, and Tumuchy. Today, after over a decade of study and frequent visits, the Valley no longer gives me a headache, but there is still much I do not understand. I take comfort in the fact that this is true for adherents themselves—the doctrine "is like a huge jigsaw puzzle where the pieces were delivered, distributed to all the Jaguars," veteran member José Carlos Nascimento Silva observed. "But some have the pieces that others do not . . . and we need to join the parts."[13]

With its specialized garments and built environments, as well as intricately choreographed rituals, symbols, hymns, and even its own vocabulary, the Valley engages all the senses at once. This overlapping cascade of sensory impressions helps imbue the Valley's imagined world with a palpable realness or verisimilitude. When people experience their faith vividly, anthropologist T. M. Luhrmann contended, it feels more real to them (Luhrmann 2012; Luhrmann 2020a, 26). The creation of the Valley's imagined world and the immersive combination of sensory information, embodied practices, affective relationships, and stories that enable members to experience it as emphatically real is the subject of this book.

Among other things, *Spirits of the Space Age: The Imagined World of Brazil's Valley of the Dawn* offers a narrative portrait of a new religious movement as seen in and through the lives of the founder Aunt Neiva, her most important collaborators, and contemporary adherents. Situating the Valley of the Dawn within its larger social and historical environment, I trace the movement's antecedents, the period of its founding and development, as well as the gradual materialization of its imagined world. As a result, *Spirits of the Space Age* also chronicles the place and time that provided the generative matrix for Aunt Neiva's visionary mission. This was mid-twentieth-century Brazil and more specifically the newly created federal district where, from 1957 to 1960, a brand new and daringly modern capital city called Brasília was being built in the sparsely populated central highlands. As I detail in the following chapters, the construction of Brasília and its aftermath shaped the Valley of the Dawn in fundamental ways. It supplied the immediate environment for the movement's creation, as well as the majority of Aunt Neiva's early clients and followers. But the project of Brasília also influenced the Valley in deeper, more profound ways. These involve the human capacity to imagine transformative possibilities for our lives and to make meaningful worlds through narrative, ritual action, and material objects.

Religions are more than the life stories of their founders or the historical and social contexts in which they emerged, however. Once established in institutional forms, religious ideas and practices exist outside of and apart from individuals, but it is only within people's lives that we can appreciate their world-making effects. And so, in this book I also attend to what contemporary adherents find compelling and meaningful about the Valley's imagined world, how they come to live within it, and how they are changed by their experiences. As a scholar who works ethnographically, I am interested in religion on the human scale as a means of being, doing, and living that situates the individual in relationship to a more encompassing order that is understood as transcendent, powerful, and suprasensible. I sometimes refer to this order as "superhuman" because it is perceived to both influence our trajectory as human beings while itself exceeding conventional, human ways of knowing.

I do not take a position on the truth status of the claims that my informants made about the superhuman. I am interested in how these claims first came to be, how they evolved and became institutionalized, why they attracted and continue to attract followers, and how they are adopted and adapted in ways that transform people's lives. While I treat claims about the superhuman seriously, I also recognize that such claims are contested, and that other interpretations and meanings are possible for the experiences that Aunt Neiva and my informants attributed to invisible forces outside of themselves.

Imagined Worlds

I speak of the superhuman realities that Aunt Neiva claimed were revealed to her, and subsequently institutionalized in Valley doctrine and practice, as an imagined world or an imagined order. I use this terminology not to imply that this world is a fantasy or illusion (that is, an "imaginary world" in contrast to the "real world"), but to convey the important role that the human faculty of imagination and collective acts of imagining play in creating and sustaining an intersubjectively shared social reality. "Imagined world" is my shorthand for the collectively shared representations that foster a common sense of identity, meaning, and purpose among members and structure how they pursue their collective life. Imagined worlds are expressed in and through mythical narratives, theological doctrines, ritual practices, symbolism, imagery, vestments, and other creative expressions as well as codes of conduct that encourage the development of an ideal self.

To be clear, I think that all religions propose imagined worlds that they invite their adherents to inhabit. But this is not exclusive to religion. In fact, most aspects of human culture are based on collective acts of imagination. As historian Yuval Noah Harari observed, what differentiates human beings from other animals is our ability to create imagined orders in the form of laws, entities, stories, organizational structures, and so on (2017, 150). Among other things, this imaginative ability enables us to conceive nation states, organize political parties, establish social hierarchies, devise financial markets, build economies, start wars, create corporations, enforce moral norms, and so on. "All large-scale human cooperation," Harari wrote, "is ultimately based on our belief in imagined orders" (143). We can think of imagined orders as world-making devices that generate the forms, structures, material expressions, and values of our common life as social beings.[14]

Most of us live so completely within these imagined worlds that we mistake them for objective reality, like the physical environment or the force of gravity. But objective reality exists whether we collectively believe in it or not, while imagined orders exist purely in our common imagination. This is not to say that they are not real. Quite the contrary. Imagined orders are very real, but their reality status derives from the fact that they are intersubjectively shared by groups of people who coordinate their actions in response. They have no objective reality *in and of themselves* independent of human beings.

There are several important things to note about imagined orders that derive from their status as intersubjectively shared social realities. The first is that once enough people stop believing that an imagined order is necessary or desirable, it fades away. So, while Zeus and Apollo were once powerful figures in the Greco-Roman world, able to mobilize people to build cities and wage wars, they have no authority for most people today. They are no longer part of an intersubjectively shared reality that unites significant numbers of people. To take another example, cowrie shells were once a valuable currency and a source of wealth and power, but today you cannot purchase a cup of coffee with cowrie shells no matter how many you offer.

The second thing to note is that an imagined order has no reality status at all for those who stand outside of its collective web of meanings. No matter how powerful Zeus and Apollo were for people living in Ancient Greece, they had no authority over the people living in ancient China. Similarly, while Kurdish people in Iraq consider themselves a separate nation—part of greater Kurdistan—the Iraqi government considers this territory to be part of Iraq.

The third thing to note is that imagined orders produce different kinds of what I will call "reality effects." These include material structures, like buildings and other types of physical objects, as well as ideological structures or systems of ideas and ideals that shape human behavior. Ideologies determine the distribution of social resources and shape how individuals understand their identities, capabilities, and place in the world, among other things. They also animate prejudice, discrimination, and other forms of hostility and violence against so-called others.

Intersubjectively shared realities are reinforced and reproduced through a matrix of assumptions, beliefs, stories, practices, material objects, rituals, and institutions that form a self-perpetuating loop. For the most part, we are socialized into these loops and they remain part of an invisible background that gives structure to our everyday lives. However, new religious movements like the Valley of the Dawn reveal the processes through which imagined orders are created and perpetuated. They demonstrate processes common to all religions, but which are more difficult for us to identify in mainstream religions that have become part of the taken-for-granted background or in which we have been socialized.

By presenting a more complete picture of the Valley of the Dawn as a new religious movement, this book counters the persistent media representations of the Valley as a cult. But it also illuminates patterns common to all religions: how nascent religious movements respond to their particular places and times even as they situate themselves in relationship to imagined otherworlds and times. In challenging conventional notions about religious legitimacy, alternative religions like the Valley of the Dawn force us to confront the diverse ways that human beings try to make moral, intellectual, and practical sense of the experience of being human by appealing to a more transcendent or superhuman reality.

Beyond all that, the Valley is richly fascinating in its own right. Here is a religion founded in the mid-twentieth century by a young widow and mother who worked as an itinerant truck driver before migrating with her children to participate in the construction of Brasília. Here is a religion for the Space Age that synthesizes diverse cultural influences of 1960s and 1970s Brazil into one phantasmagoric package. Here is a religion that dazzles the senses trying to convey "what life is life on other spiritual planes," as one of my informants put it, in the process developing its own visual language and architectural style now reproduced in smaller temples around the world. Here is a religion founded by a woman that sanctions women's spiritual power while denying them access to the highest levels of communal authority. Here is a religion premised on the idea of individual spiritual evolution, in which members share a collective past and must work together to bring about a common future.

In creating this portrait of the Valley of the Dawn, I have drawn primarily on ethnographic, historical, and bibliographic research. The former is from my own fieldwork at the Valley's Mother Temple, supplemented by the literature that has been produced by Valley members as well as scholars, both Brazilian and non-Brazilian. Central to the Valley's canon of authoritative texts are the writings of Aunt Neiva. These consist largely of epistles concerning various topics and sporadic diary entries, as well her official autobiography, edited by veteran member Bálsamo Álvares do Brasil de Lucena (1992). Aunt Neiva's autobiography, as well as collections of her letters, doctrinal materials, and diverse historical accounts, were published by OSOEC and circulate widely among present-day members. Material drawn from these sources also is reproduced in countless internet sites, blogs, and social-media commentary.

Ranked alongside Aunt Neiva's letters in terms of its importance is the published work of her partner Mário Sassi, which includes several books about Aunt Neiva as well as numerous doctrinal texts. Like other OSOEC publications, these are sold at the community's official bookstore as well as other venues in town. Both Aunt Neiva and Mário Sassi gave regular explanatory lectures to the community, many of which were recorded by members, and so I also consulted these audio sources. Alongside such primary materials are myriad reference works, memoirs, doctrinal writings, and blog posts authored by past and present members as well as members of Aunt Neiva's own family. Those that most influenced my understanding of the Valley of the Dawn are cited in the bibliography. Beyond the robust literature produced within the community over the last fifty years, the Valley has been the subject of academic scholarship at various levels, including numerous masters' theses, dissertations, manuscripts, and journal articles, many of which also appear in the bibliography.

In the field, my methods included participant observation as well as interviews with over eighty different people who had some connection to the community: current and former members, clients, and residents of the town that has grown around the Mother Temple. In many cases, I interviewed people at length and on multiple occasions. After first visiting the Valley in 2010, I returned in 2012 for a six-month-long stay. Following that, I spent six weeks at the Valley in the summer of 2015 and another six weeks in 2017, for a cumulative total of nine months in the field. Throughout my fieldwork, I lived in the community with Valley members who rent rooms to visitors. This provided me opportunities to get to know adherents in a more domestic setting and to interview people I might not have met otherwise. All interviews were conducted in Portuguese, and all translations from the Portuguese, unless otherwise noted, are my own. Because I am writing for an English-speaking audience, however, I opted to use English terms wherever possible and to use the Portuguese when there was not an appropriate corresponding English term or where the English term would be misleading or confusing. Within the community, Valley members who joined before Aunt Neiva's death are referred to as veterans (*veteranos*) as a sign of respect, and so I have retained that usage.

Chapter Summaries

Because the genesis and development of the Valley of the Dawn is so inextricably linked to the person of Aunt Neiva, Chapter 2 offers a narrative portrait of her life history. In writing this chapter, I drew on several different biographies about Neiva (Lucena 1992; Sassi n.d.; Sassi 1985b), her daughter Carmem Lúcia Zelaya's memoir about the years leading up to the creation of the Valley of the Dawn (2014), and my own interviews with veteran members. In choosing to write this chapter primarily in the form of a biographical narrative, I have three goals. First, I hope to give the reader a fuller sense of who Aunt Neiva was and how the events and experiences of her life contributed to what would become the Valley of the Dawn. Second, because most present-day members of the Valley of the Dawn first encounter Aunt Neiva through narrative—written materials produced by the community as well as personal recollections shared by veteran members—this chapter offers the reader a similar experience.

Lastly, Aunt Neiva lived through an especially significant time in modern Brazilian history, one that saw seismic changes on the political, economic, and social levels. These impacted Neiva's life and shaped the movement she founded in specific ways. As Neiva came of age in the late 1940s and early 1950s, a series of state-sponsored development projects under President Getúlio Vargas, and later Juscelino Kubitsheck, had begun to modernize the economy, redirecting it away from traditional agricultural production and freeing labor relations from the control of the extended, patriarchal family. This meant new opportunities not only for women like Neiva, but for also for farm laborers whose lives otherwise would have been tied to the land. The landscape itself was changing as the government built at the monumental scale of the country: transportation networks linking the vast interior with the coast, energy and communication infrastructures, and domestic industries like steel production and automobiles. Such large-scale public investment promised a bright future, demonstrating Brazil's progress to itself as well as the larger world. And the population's optimism was palpable: historians cite as one of this period's major characteristics a widespread sense of enthusiasm for a future of continued progress and abundance (Ioris 2013; Lafer 2002; Oliveira 1991; Rodrigues 1994). Few at the time needed convincing that Brazil really *was* the country of the future.

Perhaps no development project epitomized the great hopes and paradoxes of Brazil's modernization more dramatically than the construction of Brasília. Neiva's experiences as a *candango*, as migrant workers to Brasília were called, were shared by thousands of other Brazilians who left their places of origin to participate in the materialization of the new capital city. At the same time, as one of very few women in an overwhelmingly male-centered and frontier-like environment, Neiva's biography offers an exceptional window into this tumultuous period. One of the arguments that I pursue later in the book builds on James Holston's claim that the Valley of the Dawn engages in a kind of mimetic dialogue with the vision of modernity embodied in Brasília (1999) and appeals particularly to those who found themselves excluded from the state's promise.

Employing a similar life-history framework as Chapter 2, Chapter 3 recounts the biography of Mário Sassi, arguably Aunt Neiva's most important collaborator. As Neiva's romantic partner and "twin soul" (*alma gêmea*) during the last two decades of her life, Sassi systematized, codified, and interpreted the founder's visionary inspiration, giving it a metaphysical framework that enabled the movement to be reproduced and expanded without her physical presence. Sassi's partnership with Aunt Neiva catalyzed an especially fertile period of creative efflorescence as well as institutionalization. His role as the Doctrine's "Intellectual" and first theologian was the culmination of his life experiences and interests, as I detail in this chapter.

Chapter 4 continues the focus on Mário Sassi's contributions but shifts from the man himself to examine the "Journey of the Jaguars," the master narrative that he devised from Aunt Neiva's visions and paranormal experiences. This mythological story charts Valley members' collective journey through time and space from their extraterrestrial origins to the present, establishing the group's collective identity and inspiring its ritual corpus and material culture. Some parts of this chapter first appeared in two earlier publications (Hayes 2013 and 2020a).

Chapter 5 examines how this master narrative gave rise to a vividly detailed imagined world into which Valley members enter fully via their physical senses and imagination. As T. M. Luhrmann contends, making an invisible, yet intersubjectively shared, world feel real and relevant to people's lives requires constant effort. It requires training and practice. But before all of this, it requires a good narrative (Luhrmann 2020a, 25). Drawing on Luhrmann's work, I argue that the Valley's imagined world comes to feel real to adherents through a two-pronged process of inner-sense cultivation in mediumistic training and multisensory immersion within the Valley's material culture of vestments, architecture, images, symbols, songs, and so forth. Some of this chapter's descriptions of mediumistic development and initiation were first published elsewhere (Hayes 2022).

Chapter 6 analyzes the Valley's gender ideology as a constitutive element of the Doctrine's understanding of human nature as well as its division of labor, organizational hierarchies, and ritual life. Valley members assert that masculinity and femininity are complementary energetic polarities that together form a dynamic whole, as exemplified in the (idealized) relationship between Aunt Neiva and Mário Sassi. Despite the language of complementarity, however, my analysis shows that the Valley's gender ideology systematically privileges masculinity over femininity when it comes to positions of greatest authority and public leadership within the community. An earlier version of this chapter was published in Hayes 2018.

Chapter 7 addresses the Valley's public mission as a "universal emergency room" and describes the Valley's healing rituals, which are the primary way that the community interacts with the public and gains new members. Patients bring a wide range of ailments to the Valley, from physical and psychological problems to more diffuse experiences of suffering. While outsiders and the media tend to define healing as the elimination of physical (or psychological) symptoms of illness, this chapter takes a broader approach to the topic. What unites the diverse conditions patients bring to the Valley for healing is that they are experienced as "unwanted conditions of the self," as Robert Hahn famously put it (Hahn 1995). Drawing on the work of Hahn, Arthur Kleinman, and Richard Shweder, I analyze the Valley's work of healing as a transformation in the *meaning* of suffering—not necessarily as the *elimination* of suffering. Healing is successful when the patient's unwanted condition is redressed or resignified in such a way that it no longer threatens the self.

Chapter 8 considers how the Valley's material culture hypostatizes the community's "transcendental heritage": a trajectory of past lives that Valley members believe they have shared in different historical times and places. Materialized through the sensuous presence of the Valley's imagined world, this collective vision of the past reinforces a felt sense of connection to the group and provides meaning, agency, and identity for members. Lastly, Chapter 9 draws some of the book's big-picture themes together and offers some final thoughts.

Spirits of the Space Age can be read in several ways: as an ethnographic description of an exemplary group situated at the nexus of popular religions, esotericism, modernism, and UFO philosophies; as an historical account of a new religious movement as seen through the stories of its founders and contemporary members; and as an analysis of material culture and narrative in the sense-making function of the Valley's imagined world.[15]

Read in the first way, the book adds to our knowledge of a globally burgeoning, yet understudied, trend. The Valley is one of a number of new religious movements to emerge in the second half of the twentieth century that feature extraterrestrials, parallel universes, and superior alien technologies as common themes, among them Scientology, Raelianism, Unarius, and other so-called New Age groups. The Space Age and the technological marvels associated with it have transformed the religious imagination, offering new ways to think about age-old problems and inspiring new mythologies. The celestial gods are still with us, these religions propose, but they are extraterrestrials now, their chariots replaced by UFOs.

Unlike other so-called UFO religions, however, the extraterrestrial component is not the most prominent storyline at the Valley of the Dawn (see Hayes 2021). Rather it is one narrative strand within a complex, multilayered epic centered on key episodes in the group's shared mythological past. For most adherents, the Doctrine's pragmatic focus on healing and personal transformation is the main draw. As reports by the Pew Foundation and others indicate, alternative religions that center on self-realization and cosmic transformation are growing worldwide as membership in mainstream religions decline (Pew Research Center 2013; 2015). The Valley of the Dawn provides an ethnographic window into this phenomenon from Latin America, a region that is not well represented in the literature on so-called New Age movements, but which rivals the United States in terms of its multicultural heritage and religious pluralism. Given the prominence of esoteric themes within Valley doctrine, *Spirits of the Space Age* also contributes to the scholarly field called Western esotericism, which focuses on the myriad ways that esoteric ideas and practices have influenced the Western world.

Read in the second way as a historical account of a new religious movement, the book offers an ethnographically rich contribution to the literature on NRMs that foregrounds how religion is firmly embedded in the everyday lives of individuals, an approach that has been called "lived religion." Robert Orsi, one of the foremost advocates of this way of studying religion, wrote:

> The study of lived religion situates all religious creativity within culture and approaches all religion as lived experience, theology no less than lighting a candle for a troubled loved one, spirituality as well as other, less culturally sanctioned forms of religious expression. Rethinking religion as a form of cultural work, the study of lived religion directs attention to institutions *and* persons, texts *and* rituals, practice *and* theology, things *and* ideas—all as media of making and unmaking worlds. (2003, 172)

As one of comparatively few religions founded by a woman, the Valley of the Dawn enriches our knowledge about the religious worlds made by women and whether—or how—these are different from religions founded by men.

Finally, read as an analysis of material culture and meaning, the book highlights the role of narrative, ritual, imagery, vestments, and other sensory-based phenomena in the production and reproduction of imagined worlds. By triggering certain kinds of phenomenological experiences, processes of materialization ground an imagined order's reality status in the individual's inner world of feelings, emotions, and sensations as well as in an external world of things. This focus on how religions operate through material and embodied practices counters presumed oppositions between spiritual and material or belief and practice (Houtman and Meyer 2012). As Luhrmann noted, if we start not with the question of why people believe the things that they do, but rather focus our attention on the effort that people invest in these beliefs and whether that effort changes them, then we will better understand religion's appeal and how it functions in people's lives (2020a). That is the task of the pages ahead

* * *

2
The Clairvoyant

Now she knew that she had always been a Clairvoyant, also in her previous incarnations she was involved with aspects considered mystical: she had the transcendent heritage of the prophetesses: Nefertiti, Pythia . . . She also was committed to a large group of spirits (of the same Spiritual Origin) who, between "comings and goings," now returned, at the Threshold of the Third Millennium, with the commitment to implement a technical-doctrinal system, based on the basic principles of the Doctrine of Jesus the Great Master, for the unified concentration of spiritual forces, in favor of lives on the physical and the etheric planes, through Disobsessive Healing.
—Autobiography of Aunt Neiva (Lucena 1992, 10)

Capella

Almost imperceptibly, in the spaces between the tentacles of the headache that had wrapped itself around her brain, Neiva Chaves Zelaya began to perceive that she was no longer lying on the sofa. Instead, she seemed to be inside the cockpit of some kind of vehicle surrounded by a dashboard full of strange instruments. As her brain adapted to this information, something in her peripheral vision drew her attention to a large window framing an enormous ball of colored fire that was pulsating in the sky, rising and falling before resettling in its initial position. "Look carefully!" said a voice, which seemed to be coming from inside her head. "This is the planet of those who are preparing for God's great work on Earth. You will soon get to know it better." There was more explanation from the voice, but when Neiva asked where she was, it fell silent and she felt herself gently sucked, as if through an impossibly long straw, back into her body (Sassi 1974, 26).

Neiva often saw and heard things that other people did not, but this felt like something qualitatively different. She sensed that she had disengaged from her physical body and, in spirit form, travelled through interstellar space on some kind of spacecraft. Later, she would visit this planet, called Capella, with regularity and would get to know some of its inhabitants. She would learn of the Capellans' great mission safeguarding the earth's evolutionary progression and their more immediate desire to help humanity negotiate the impending transition between civilizational cycles. The Capellans would explain to her that humanity evolves through cycles of approximately two thousand years as civilizations are born, reach their peak, and die out. The period in-between, as one civilizational era is dying and the next is taking form, is especially unstable and prone to social upheaval.

But all that would come later. Opening her eyes and seeing familiar surroundings, Neiva felt that she should not mention this brief but altogether strange experience to her companions at the Spiritualist Union of Father White Arrow. How could she explain it to them when she did not really understand it herself? It all seemed preposterous. Better to keep it to herself.

Early Life

Even as a young girl, Neiva Chaves had an odd way about her. Typically a curious and lively child, she often accompanied her father, Senhor Antônio de Medeiros Chaves, as he travelled from town to dusty town across the arid scrublands of central Brazil conducting topographical surveys for large landowners and other professional businesses. Every so often though, Neiva's normally animated brown eyes flickered into a strange, far-away look and she would detail snippets of events or report conversations as if she were witnessing them unspool before her on an invisible movie screen. Family members later would recall these preternatural episodes as the first signs of Neiva's "mediumship," or powers of clairvoyance, but Senhor Chaves had no patience for his first-born daughter's tendency toward what he regarded as fabulations. It was a trait he found particularly detestable in a young woman and, he felt, his solemn duty to correct.

Senhor Chaves took pride in his identity as family patriarch and was sensitive to any challenge to his authority or the family's honor, no matter how slight. He expected proper comportment on the part of his wife and children and did not hesitate to use corporal punishment to ensure their compliance. The most frequent recipients of his blows were Neiva and her brother Nivaldo, although their mother Dona Sinharinha and two younger siblings were not exempt from his ire. The older Neiva got, the more she resented her father's strictures and overbearing manner. As she would later tell her own children, Senhor Chaves's authoritarianism and demand for compliant obedience eventually drove her from his house and produced a long-standing rift between them that would be repaired only toward the end of the old man's life.

Like most men of his class and generation, Senhor Chaves believed that a woman's most important duty was to be a wife and mother, and he saw little need to educate his daughters beyond what was necessary for household management. So, Neiva, although quick to learn, received little formal education beyond the basics of reading, writing, and arithmetic. Eager to escape her father's household, she married Raul Alonso Zelaya just a day after her eighteenth birthday, on October 31, 1942.

The couple had met the previous year when Raul came to town to help administer the National Agricultural Colony of Goiás (CANG), an experimental program created by the federal government in the 1940s to resettle poor farming families in Brazil's vast interior and train them in modern farming techniques (Castilho 2012; Freitas and Mello 2014). Their relationship, at least initially, was a matter of mutual convenience: Neiva had fallen for a police lieutenant whom her father had forbidden her to see, and Raul was pining for a girl whose cancer diagnosis all but assured her premature death. Their common experience of frustration in love formed the basis of a friendship and one evening, after taking Neiva to the town's newly opened cinema, Raul made an unorthodox proposal. "Chaves won't let you marry the man you love," he told Neiva, "and I can't marry the woman I love." Before Neiva could reply he hurried on, "why don't we get married? I like you very much. Do you want to marry me?" (C. L. Zelaya 2014, 13).

Despite its unconventional beginning, the marriage was a happy one by all accounts, and less than a year later Neiva was pregnant with the first of the couple's four children. But Raul's precipitous death in 1949 set her life on a different course. Suddenly widowed at age twenty-three with four young children under six, Neiva was forced to discover capacities that might have remained latent had circumstances been different. Determined to support her family on her own, she found work as a photographer and opened her own studio in the small town of Ceres, Goiás. But the close contact with photographic chemicals left her with respiratory problems that would contribute eventually to her early death. So, she sold the studio and tried her hand at farming. That too did not work out. Ever pragmatic and entrepreneurial, Neiva would work as a seamstress, ambulatory vender, server of coffee, bus driver, and several other professions over the years.

To Neiva's great surprise, it was Dona Sinharinha, her very traditional mother, who first suggested that she learn to drive a truck and go into business for herself. The idea spoke to the young widow's intrepid spirit and desire for self-sufficiency and, in 1952, Neiva Chaves Zelaya became one of the first women in Brazil with a professional truck-driving license. Driving a truck enabled her to earn a living hauling and selling freight while keeping her children with her. And while Brazil of the 1950s was not an especially hospitable place for a young working woman on her own, Neiva was determined to make a go of it. "To deal with the drivers, she had to be a driver too," Neiva's youngest son Raul reminisced.

> She was very easy going, but she was very tough too. She always carried a gun, a 32-caliber pistol. And she did not tolerate any cheekiness or disrespect either at home or at work. But she had a charisma, an ability to make friends and bring people close to her. (R. Zelaya interview 2015)

"My mother was a woman of great courage," Neiva's eldest daughter Carmem Lúcia later wrote in her own memoir. "She transmitted to us a strength that, today I know, was not commonly expected of a woman, especially at that time. Her love for us gave her an inexplicable force to overcome difficulties and surmount obstacles that she encountered on her path" (C. L. Zelaya 2014, 20; see Image 2.1).

The work proved lucrative, and Neiva soon acquired a second truck. But her freedom and contact with male truck drivers had attracted the attention of local scandalmongers and it was not long before their poisoned whisperings reached Senhor Chaves's ear. "Sell everything and come home," he ordered

Image 2.1 Neiva and her truck. Courtesy of Arquivo do Vale do Amanhecer

Neiva, "I will buy you a rooming house so that you can earn a living and you will stay here under my watchful eye ... My daughter will not be the talk of the town!" When Neiva protested, he reiterated, "No daughter of mine is going to go riding around in a truck and staying at motels with male drivers!" Neiva, loath to trade her freedom for the sake of her father's pride, refused to comply. As she would later tell her own children, she could not subject them to the tyrannical rule of her father, whose demand for compliant obedience often left her feeling humiliated and mistreated (C. L. Zelaya 2014, 27).

So Senhor Chaves did the only thing he could: he disowned his eldest daughter and forbade her contact with the rest of the family. Although the two would eventually reconcile, her father's punitive behavior and the loss of her parents' support at a critical period affected Neiva deeply (C. L. Zelaya 2014, 27). It also made her more independent. Forbidden from seeing her beloved mother and siblings except on brief visits kept secret from Senhor Chaves, Neiva created her own network of family and friends. She was especially close with her children's nanny, an adolescent girl named Gertrudes who would remain with the family until her own death in 2006.[1] Neiva would rescue and foster many other young people over the years, later establishing an orphanage that housed several hundred abandoned and orphaned children.

Neiva's warmth and charisma were like a magnetic charge that drew people to her. "She forever was helping someone," her daughter Carmem Lúcia remembered, "whether it was a neighbor, one of the men who washed cars, or the mechanic ... Mama transmitted optimism to them, recounting stories and sharing her faith. In this way she inspired in them the hope of overcoming their troubles (C. L. Zelaya 2014, 81). "Neiva was a special creature," a longtime Valley of the Dawn member told me. "She had this energy that just made you want to be around her. She loved to sing and play guitar. She was extremely generous, but she was also funny and down to earth. She had a way of making you feel like whatever was troubling you, you could overcome it" (L. Pimentel interview 2015).

Gypsy

Freed from her father's yoke, Neiva and her children led a nomadic existence over the next few years, never settling for long in any one place: from the state of Goiás they went to Minas Gerais, then São Paulo, then Paraná and finally back to Goiás. "She was a gypsy, always traveling, she never stopped for long in any one place," explained Raul.

> And it was very difficult for us to finish school, we never completed a full year of classes because she had to go to another state, another city, wherever there was a harvest of rice, corn, beans, she would take the truck there to pick up the harvest and deliver it. We would go to sleep in a bed and wake up in the cab of the truck. And this was our life, practically gypsies. (R. Zelaya interview 2015)

Later, Neiva would say that one of her most significant past lives was as Natachan, a gypsy from the Katshimoshy tribe. This was one of several names by which she was known in the spirit world.

In 1957, at the invitation of Dr. Bernardo Sayão, an agronomist who had employed her late husband Raul, Neiva migrated to Brasília, children in tow. Dr. Sayão had been appointed as one of three principal directors of Novacap, the national development company responsible for planning, constructing, and administrating the new capital city then being built.[2] With his help, Neiva registered her truck with Novacap and began work immediately transporting workers, engineers, and surveyors to construction sites and hauling materials from place to place.

It was a time of great optimism for Brazil's future, symbolized most potently in the state's plan for its new, modern capital. Intended to mirror the "power and boldness that would transform the country," Brasília was the centerpiece of President Juscelino Kubitschek's promise to produce a modern Brazil and a modern Brazilian citizen.[3] The goal, as Kubitschek's campaign slogan put it, was to advance the country "Fifty Years in Five."[4] Aunt Neiva was one of thousands of Brazilians who heeded Kubitschek's call to "construct the Brazil of tomorrow" by participating in the materialization of its new capital city (Holston 1989; 1999).[5] Thanks to a massive labor force working round the clock, Brasília rose from the central Brazilian high plains in an astonishing forty-one months (See Image 2.2).

Pioneer

For the first month after their arrival, Neiva, the children, and their nanny Gertrudes lived in an improvised tent on the edge of a river before Neiva

Image 2.2 Brasília work force. Marcel Gautherot / Instituto Moreira Salles Collection. Used with permission.

secured a lot in the Free City, officially called Núcleo Bandeirante (Pioneer Nucleus), just outside the footprint of the planned capital (C. L. Zelaya 2014, 92–93). With the help of some colleagues, she built a simple house from bamboo, and the family settled in. Within no time the little house became a social center for the friends Neiva swiftly made among the other *candangos*,[6] or migrant workers, whom government recruitment campaigns and media of the time referred to as the "pioneers" of the new Brazil (Epstein 1973; Holston 1989). Like Neiva, these first migrants primarily came from the agricultural states of the country's northeast and central west.[7] Unlike Neiva, the vast majority were men.

Among them was Getúlio, a former colleague from Goiás with whom Neiva developed an intimate relationship. Carmem Lúcia later recalled the family's first few months in their new home as filled with friendship and animation, centered on the weekly Sunday dinners that Neiva and Getúlio hosted. Stretching over hours, these gatherings often concluded with impromptu rounds of the *sertanejo* songs of the rural interior, whose plaintive melodies helped soothe those heartsick for the homes and loved ones they had left behind. Accompanied by Neiva's guitar, the group would sing and dance away the chill that settled over the high plains once the fierce rays of the sun began to fade over the horizon.

Camaraderie and a sense of adventure tinged with loss pervaded the frontier community that was developing among the candangos in the Free City. One of three types of settlements sheltering the nearly 40,000 people involved in building the new capital, it was known as the Cidade Livre or Free City because anyone could take up residence or establish a business there tax free as part of Novacap's plan to attract commercial enterprises to sustain the thousands of workers building the capital (Fonseca 2007, 227).[8] It mostly housed entrepreneurs and contract laborers who, like Neiva, constituted a large segment of the emerging city's workforce, and who had constructed their dwellings themselves (Solomon 2019).[9]

Enlivened by the culture of its working-class residents, the Free City quickly developed its own social life. Neiva's four children and their playmates were especially delighted by the local circus and other amusements that organically sprung up there (C. L. Zelaya 2014, 95, 100). But it was not just workers who socialized in Núcleo Bandeirante. Prominent men like Brasilia's architect Oscar Niemeyer and President Kubitschek himself regularly toured the construction sites and frequented the workers camps and other areas where workers lived. "At that time, it was very common to see the president of the Republic, Dr. Juscelino Kubitschek, passing by in his car and waving to all with a warm and friendly smile," Carmem Lúcia recalled in her memoir. "We felt honored and responded by waving in the same way. There was a certain air of familiarity in Brasília. In truth, it was this: we were all adventurers, living the construction of a great dream" (101).

Visions, Voices, and Images

Although Novacap was overextended and not always prompt in paying its contract workers, Neiva was making more money than she ever had. Soon, she invested in a second truck and then a third. But less than a year after arriving in Brasília, Neiva's enthusiasm and good humor seemed to evaporate before her children's eyes. Carmem Lúcia described her mother arriving home from work nervous and irritable, a far-off look in her gaze. Neiva's customary good humor was replaced by an impatience that could explode into fury at unexpected moments. The children began to shoo visitors away lest they witness one of their mother's attacks (101–102). The merry evenings when friends would gather to play the guitar and sing country songs of love lost or stolen or unrequited became a distant memory, and the family's once lively house became drained and empty.

Neiva herself later described this period as one in which she was tormented routinely by "visions of enlightened beings, visions of deformed beings . . . voices and images, some beautiful, others seemed to want to explain, others ugly" (1992, 10). "It was," her autobiography explained, "as if she was dreaming while awake" (12). The verisimilitude of these waking dreams left Neiva terrified and confused. Driving down the road one afternoon in such a state, she felt her truck run over a pedestrian. Catapulted by an anguish-laden jolt of adrenaline, she ran to aid the victim. To her shock there was no mangled body beneath the truck's massive tires. She questioned a man standing nearby who had seen the whole thing. He looked at her quizzically before advising her to seek spiritual assistance (44; C. L. Zelaya 2014, 102).

As time went on, these auditory and visual hallucinations grew more disruptive. Caught up in their intensity and unable to differentiate the contents of her mind's eye from external reality, Neiva raged and broke things, or collapsed into a state of vacant-eyed muteness. "Each day things got worse," Carmem Lúcia reported, "and she did not want to hear anything about stopping work to find a doctor and get treatment. She became agitated and would leave the house disoriented" (2014, 102). More than once the older children had to tie Neiva to the bed to prevent her from going outside in such an altered state (101).

Eventually the situation became too much for the children to bear, and they sought help from a sympathetic neighbor who diagnosed Neiva's condition as *obsessão*, or the influence of perturbing spirits. Neiva, the neighbor gently explained to the family, had become spiritually vulnerable due to overwork and exhaustion. As a result, she was susceptible to the influence of low-level spirits who overwhelmed the boundaries of her ego-self and provoked the kinds of problems that she was experiencing. He urged the family to find a *centro espírita* or Spiritist center where Neiva could develop her abilities as a medium, strengthen her relationship with her own spirit guides, and thereby restore her spiritual equilibrium.

Spiritism

Spiritism is the name for an international movement that consolidated around the writings of Allan Kardec (1804–1869), a French schoolteacher, amateur scientist, and the author of several books about the invisible realities beyond the material dimension. Kardec claimed to have discovered an "empirical science of the spirit world" that provided a moral code for living based on the idea that life extends across a great continuum, alternating between material and immaterial forms as the spirit seeks its advancement and eventual reunion with God (Hess 1987, 16). By combining a modern discourse of science and progress with deeply rooted convictions about the human being as a union of body and spirit, Kardec's ideas resonated with many people in the late nineteenth century and continue to do so today.

Kardec taught that after death or "disincarnation," humans live on as disembodied spirits in an invisible spiritual dimension. From there they can communicate with incarnate humans through the phenomenon of spirit mediumship. Kardec identified numerous types of mediums, including hearing mediums, seeing mediums, talking mediums, and healing mediums. For Kardec and his followers, the phenomenon of spirit mediumship offered empirical evidence of the relationship between incorporeal intelligences and incarnate human beings and thus qualified Spiritism as a science.[10] In order to distinguish his doctrine from the "occultist and religious overtones of 'Spiritualism,'" the wider movement then underway in the United States and Europe, Kardec called it Spiritism (Hess 1987, 16).[11]

According to Kardec, just as in the material world, the spiritual realm is a place where spirits can continue to learn and evolve while they prepare for subsequent incarnations. Driven by karma, which he referred to as the "law of cause and effect," reincarnation on Earth is an opportunity for the spirit to redeem karmic debts and "learn lessons" that foster moral evolution. After the spirit reaches a certain level of moral development, terrestrial reincarnation is no longer necessary, and the evolutionary process continues in the spiritual dimension until the spirit finally reunites with God.[12] Both incarnate and disincarnate spirits also can evolve through the practice of "charity," or selflessly assisting others. Some truly advanced spirits like Jesus may voluntarily choose to reincarnate to show others the way forward.[13]

In certain cases, spirits of low moral development can "obsess" or influence the living through resonances between our psychological weaknesses and theirs, provoking all manner of emotional, mental, and even physical afflictions. Kardec's followers developed different therapeutic techniques of healing including disobsession, a method of removing the obsessing spirit by using reason to re-orient and educate it (sometimes translated as "spirit-release therapy").[14] They also adopted a version of Franz Mesmer's "magnetic pass," a means of rebalancing spiritual and physical energies by moving one's hands over the affected person's body.[15]

Kardec's teachings proved more influential in Brazil than in the country of his birth, and by the mid-twentieth century, Spiritism (or Kardecism, as it is sometimes called) had become "a constitutive part of Brazilian religiosity," as José Jorge de Carvalho observed (Carvalho 1999, 4).[16] Among other factors, Spiritism offered a way of thinking about the relationship between human beings and the supernatural that was framed in the language of science. Its doctrine of progressive evolution offered an optimistic view of the human condition that resonated with modern ideas about social and individual advancement. At a moment when physicians were professionalizing the knowledge and practice of healing, Spiritists were insisting that it be available freely to all as a form of charity (Sharp 2005, 319). Spiritist groups founded many orphanages and hospitals in Brazil, which helped disseminate the movement's teachings among the less favored classes (Brown and Bick 1987, 79).

Because Spiritist cosmology reflected many traditional Christian beliefs, it was compatible with Brazilian Catholicism while addressing some of its more puzzling doctrinal contradictions. To those who questioned how a good God could permit evil to flourish, the idea that human suffering was a product of one's actions in a past life and an opportunity for spiritual evolution made sense. Kardec's ideas also interacted with other esoteric currents in Brazil, as well as religions of African provenance, to produce Umbanda, sometimes heralded as Brazil's first truly Indigenous religion for its pantheon of spirits representing the country's mix of Indigenous, African, and European peoples (Engler 2012; 2020).

Within Spiritism's explanatory framework, Neiva's symptoms did not indicate incipient mental illness or demonic possession but rather a highly unusual spiritual sensitivity or clairvoyant mediumship. Neiva, however, resisted this diagnosis. As she would later say, her strict Roman Catholic upbringing had instilled in her a persistent fear of anything to do with spirits. But the children were hopeful and at their insistence Neiva began to attend development (*desinvolvimento*) sessions during which novice mediums learned how to identify and work with the spirits. "We children were the ones that encouraged her to follow Spiritism more than she wanted," Carmem Lúcia told me in a 2017 interview.

> Because at that time, Spiritism was disreputable, it was associated with poor people, marginalized people, and she did not want to bring her children to something like that. But we did not share that prejudice, for us, what was important was that it helped her. She would get better when she went to a Spiritist session. (C. L. Zelaya interview 2017)

Following her neighbor's suggestion, Neiva and her children visited several different Spiritist and Umbanda centers over the next few months, absorbing their lessons about the invisible realms beyond matter. These teachings exposed the family to a new worldview, Carmem Lúcia recalled in her memoir,

> revealing the face of a more just and benevolent God. They made us aware of the continuity of life after death in a dimension where love and forgiveness prevailed, principles that give us a new opportunity for growth. We began to comprehend that our suffering and illness was part of a plan of redemption. In short, the possibility of learning and evolving gave a new meaning to what we were living through. (2014, 112)

Despite the hope that Spiritist doctrine offered the family, Neiva continued to suffer occasional episodes of the volatile behavior that, within Umbanda and Spiritist circles, indicated the presence of *obsessores*, or obsessing spirits. In their ignorance or malice, these spirits are believed to attach themselves to human beings to deleterious effects. Often, they are identified as the spirits of the recently deceased, who do not realize that they have departed the physical plane and now inhabit the spiritual dimension. The family came to believe that one of Neiva's *obsessores* was the spirit of Raul Alonzo Zelaya, Neiva's dead husband and the children's father. Because Raul had died before his appointed time, Carmem Lúcia wrote, his spirit remained linked to Earth and "was wandering around Mother, trying to help, but not helping. On the contrary, it was hurting her" (2014, 109).

Eclectic City

Hoping to free Neiva from the deleterious effects of obsessing spirits, the family visited Cidade Ecléctica or Eclectic City, the spiritual community established by the charismatic former pilot Master Yokaanam (1911–1985) and his followers in 1956 (C. L. Zelaya 2014, 101). Born Oceano de Sá, Mestre Yokaanam had enjoyed a successful career as an airplane pilot, working for the national postal service and as a private pilot for former President Getúlio Vargas (1934–1945, 1951–1954). After narrowly surviving a devastating plane crash, however, he forsook the skies above Earth for more celestial realms and reinvented himself as a religious visionary, adopting the name Yokaanam after the Hebrew name of John the Baptist. The movement he founded, the Eclectic Spiritualist Universal Brotherhood (Fraternidade Eclética Espiritualista Universal), taught a doctrine that drew on many of the same Christian, Spiritist, and esoteric ideas that would later inform the Valley of the Dawn (Mello 2004, 27).

On the day Neiva and her children arrived, the mediums of the Eclectic Spiritualist Universal Brotherhood were performing a Spiritist ritual called the *linha de passe*, in which trained mediums transmit healing energies by "giving passes," moving their hands back and forth over the body of the afflicted without physically touching them. The ritual seemed to have a palliative effect on Neiva and the family returned for a second visit.

This time, according to Carmem Lúcia, Neiva was brought before Mestre Yokaanam himself, who solemnly informed her,

> You are a medium ready to realize a great mission. You should abandon everything and come live here. If you abandon everything and obey this call, all your troubles will disappear like a miracle, because you will be fulfilling your mediumship's mission. (2014, 114)

Mestre Yokaanam's message deeply unsettled Neiva. She ordered the children back into the truck, and they left Eclectic City, never to return.

A Culture of Spirits

There was no shortage of spirit mediums, clairvoyants, prayer-givers, and folk healers like Mestre Yokaanam offering their services to the suffering inhabitants of the Brazilian *planalto central* (central high plains). While the Catholic Church played a prominent role in the social life of major towns and cities, and most people, like Neiva, counted themselves good Catholics, beneath this surface burbled a deep current of popular traditions fed by the diverse cultural heritages that met, mingled, and metamorphosed in

Brazil. Despite originating in different cultural and historical contexts, these traditions shared a common focus on fortifying the relationships between human beings and otherworldly entities as a means of ensuring wellbeing. Scholars have referred to this effervescent stream as a shared "culture of spirits" (Aubree and Laplantine 1990) or "mediumistic continuum" (Camargo 1961).

In the late 1950s, however, the subject of spirit mediumship was not a topic of polite conversation. Those experimenting with alternative spiritual practices faced social prejudice, and the communities dedicated to them tended to be small-scale affairs with little public visibility. Only through an individual's own affliction might she discover that friends and neighbors, heretofore unbeknownst to her, were mediums who "worked" with the spirits and were alert to the telltale signs of undeveloped mediumship in others.

And so, it was not long after the family's final trip to Eclectic City that one of their neighbors, Dona Júlia, intuited Neiva's troubles and invited her to an Umbanda center. The truth was that no matter how hard Neiva tried to free herself of the visions and voices that echoed in her head or the premonitions that came unbidden, she could not stop them. And so, with her children's encouragement, Neiva began to attend Umbanda sessions that were organized and led by Dona Júlia herself (C. L. Zelaya 2014, 117). Carmem Lúcia observed that these evenings had a positive influence on Neiva, whose behavior began to normalize as she "developed her mediumship," that is, learned to recognize and work with the spirit entities identified as responsible for the perturbing voices and visions. Little by little, Neiva and her children became more adept at recognizing different entities by their energetic effects on Neiva. Some provoked feelings of confusion and a heaviness that could erupt unpredictably into anger or sorrow. Others brought a clarifying lightness that dissipated negative emotions, leaving Neiva with a sense of serenity and peace (110–120).

One entity was a source of special comfort to Neiva. The Lady of Space, as Neiva first referred to her, appeared in Neiva's visions as a beautiful woman confined to a wheelchair and emanating the radiant aura of a saint, according to Carmem Lúcia (2014, 108, 110). This figure would talk to Neiva about the universal laws of karma and reincarnation and recount her own past lives, stories that Neiva would tell her own children as they got ready for bed. Neiva was being prepared for a very special mission, the Lady of Space informed her, although Neiva herself could not understand why the spirits would bother with a humble truck driver possessing scarcely a grade-school education. Years later, this entity would reveal her name as Mother Yara (Mãe Yara). For the rest of Neiva's life, she would cite Mother Yara's beneficent presence as the source of much of her own saintly wisdom.

As a medium, Neiva did not just see and hear spirits in her mind's eye, however. According to her testimony and that of others, she also was subject to extraordinary states of consciousness in which the personality Neiva receded and evolved spirits of light, like Mother Yara, communicated through her (Cavalcante 2000). Among them were entities recognized within Umbanda as *pretos velhos* and *caboclos*, the spirits of elderly black slaves and unacculturated Indians, respectively. One of Neiva's most important spirit guides was Chief Tupinambá (Cacique Tupinambá), a caboclo who later revealed himself to be Father White Arrow. Others were the preto velho spirits Father John of Enoch (Pai João de Enoque), Granny Marilu (Vovó Marilu), and Mother Tildes (Mãe Tildes).

Where Umbanda caboclos tend to embody the trope of the noble savage—in tune with nature and possessing deep wisdom excluded from the civilized self—Chief Tupinambá was different (Hale 2009, 102, 105). His erudite manner and formal way of speaking suggested a philosopher of the Western tradition more than the undomesticated Indian. Neiva's preto velhos spirits, however, were truer to type. Personifying a complex, collective memory of Brazil's slave past transformed into a source of spiritual power, pretos velhos are beloved for their wisdom, humility, and grandparently mien. They are credited with deep knowledge of the foibles of human nature—the human capacity for unfathomable cruelty as well as deep compassion—gained from their lives of forced servitude.

As Neiva developed her mediumship, her children cultivated their own relationships with the spirit entities whom they believed communicated through the person of their mother. They were particularly attached to Father John, Granny Marilu, and Mother Tildes. "Not a day went by when we did not speak with one or another of those dear entities," Carmem Lúcia noted. "A question or unexpected necessity was enough to bring one of them to our rescue" (2014, 152). For the children, Neiva's ability to manifest different spiritual personas, each with their own personality and manner of speaking, came to be the most natural thing.

Yet Neiva herself continued to be ambivalent about her abilities to see, interact with, and incorporate spirits. It seemed to Carmem Lúcia that every step her mother took toward embracing her mediumship was accompanied, eventually, by a vociferous rejection. "I want my life back!" Neiva would cry.

"Ever since this nuisance of the spirits started, my life is not the same! I am so sick of all of this!" (2014, 115). During these moments of despair, Neiva sought out other remedies for her troubles—attending mass at the local church, undergoing counseling with a priest, praying nightly for liberation. She even visited a psychiatrist, convinced that the spirits were figments of her overactive and under-rested mind.

In her autobiographical account of that visit to the psychiatrist, Neiva described how she had been seated across from the doctor answering his questions when she perceived a spirit entity emerge from behind a standing screen in the corner of the room. The entity, who identified himself as the doctor's recently deceased father, began talking to her. Hoping that the psychiatrist would witness for himself the source of her torment, Neiva began gesturing, but the doctor lacked her preternatural vision. Finally, she blurted out, "there is a dead man who says he is your father!" Despite his initial disbelief, the psychiatrist was convinced of Neiva's sincerity when she conveyed a message to him from the spirit. In her narrative recollection of that moment, Neiva wrote that the doctor, an expression of joy spreading across his face, jumped up from his chair and exclaimed, "it really is my father, my dearly adored father, tell me more, tell me how he is!" (Lucena 1992, 42).[17] Notwithstanding the doctor's joy in reuniting with his dead father, Neiva herself felt only bitter disappointment. Far from helping her, the psychiatrist had only confirmed her ability to see and converse with spirits.

Becoming a Medium

As historian of religion Ann Taves observed, anomalous or ambiguous experiences such as Aunt Neiva's always invite multiple interpretative possibilities. The interpretation likely to make most sense to the individual is one that preserves their dignity and agency while offering them new possibilities for being in the world and narrating the self (Taves 2016, 2–3). The story of Aunt Neiva's journey into the world of the spirits—which progresses from outright rejection to ambivalence to eventual acceptance of her mediumship—is also one in which professional medicine failed her. Among those who find themselves involved with religions on the mediumistic continuum, as either patients or mediums, this is a common theme. Its ubiquity illustrates major differences between the worldviews of conventional medical and Spiritism in terms of their respective epistemological systems, or ways of knowing: not only what knowledge is considered valid but what methods of knowing are seen as legitimate.

Grounded in a materialistic framework that privileges scientific empiricism and reason as the only legitimate sources of knowledge, psychiatric medicine could not recognize as real symptoms that to Neiva were irrefutable. Neither could it offer a meaningful interpretative framework for her suffering. Existing only as figments of a troubled mind, spirits have no empirical validity within this epistemological system. The only interpretative frame is mental illness. By narrowing the focus to the individual's mental capacity and presuming dysfunction, this diagnosis stigmatizes the afflicted person. Moreover, it offers few opportunities for channeling disruptive symptoms in ways that are socially valued and that foster self-transformation, creative elaboration, or materialization.

At the same time, within the logic of Neiva's autobiographical account of visiting the psychiatrist, the doctor himself corroborated the legitimacy of her paranormal powers: he recognized Aunt Neiva's ability to see and converse with spirits, although he himself could not see them. Thus, the story marshals the social legitimacy granted to medical practitioners and their scientific epistemology in support of Aunt Neiva's parascientific claim.[18]

In contrast with professional medicine, Spiritism and Umbanda privilege the individual's phenomenological experience, seeing it as a legitimate source of knowledge. Within the sensory repertoire and epistemological framework shared by these religions, the visions and voices that Aunt Neiva reported were the manifestations of spirits who had breached the ramparts of her psyche, weakened by stress and overwork. The source of her troubles was external, not internal. To restore her psycho-spiritual equilibrium, Aunt Neiva needed to develop her mediumship faculties. This interpretation offered a framework of meaning that helped Neiva to assimilate these otherwise troubling experiences while both acknowledging the vivid sense of reality that accompanied them and preserving her sense of self. She had to go from being at the mercy of the spirits to working with them. In the process, she also had to persuade others of the reality of her visions as a source of paranormal abilities.

Learning Spiritist doctrine and undergoing training as a medium enabled Neiva and her children to begin the process of socializing Neiva's experiences by acquiring the vocabulary to talk about and understand them and learning specific practices that helped to contain their more disruptive aspects. In turn, the family's exposure to this body of knowledge and practices further molded and shaped Neiva's experiences within the conventions of spirit mediumship. Anthropologist Emily Pierini aptly described this multilayered form of learning as simultaneously "embodied, intuitive, performative, conceptual, and intersubjective." "Spirits become real for people," she wrote, "as they learn to experience them through their bodies and in their everyday lives" (Pierini 2020, 13). Or, as Neiva's autobiography explained it,

> There was no other way out. It was imperative to hear the spirits . . . gradually, little by little. And thus, amidst situations simple and complicated, happy and sad . . . Neiva Chaves Zelaya was enlightened by her natural condition of mediumship —biological, transcendent; therefore, imperative. (1992, 10)

As Neiva herself became more practiced at using this interpretive framework, she was able to assess her non-ordinary experiences and discriminate between what she came to understand as the clarifying energy of beneficent spirits and the darker, heavier energy of lower-level spirits. And as her subjective reality changed to accommodate and give meaning to these heretofore disruptive and troubling sensory experiences, her visions slowly coalesced into sensible forms. She began to cultivate ever-more-sensitive states of awareness and intuition, to tune into somatic, perceptual, and cognitive experiences as important sources of knowledge. This was an "education of perception," in Pierini's terms, that "draws upon discernment and may lead to the transformation of one's sense of self" (Pierini 2020, 7). By recasting Neiva's suffering as existentially meaningful, spirit mediumship offered expansive possibilities for narration and action that, eventually, allowed Neiva to remake herself as a charismatic healer and spiritual leader.

While the clairvoyant powers to which Neiva laid claim were unusual, the narrative framing she gave to the process of becoming a spirit medium followed the conventions of the genre: an initial period of denial and rejection followed by a struggle to assimilate and master the disruptive experiences, and then final acceptance as others recognize her skill and talent. In a pattern common among spirit healing religions, what begins as affliction is transformed into a power used to help others as well as a source of spiritual authority for the individual herself.

Central to this transformation was the encouragement and support of significant people around Neiva who validated and encouraged these interpretations. As Carmem Lúcia vividly captured in her memoir, Neiva and her children regularly talked about the spirits, discussing the new ideas they were learning both among themselves and with other mediums. These conversations gave a recognizable pattern to sensory experiences previously perceived as problematic, which helped them internalize the precepts of this new interpretative system.

In a now-classic work entitled *The Social Construction of Reality*, sociologists Thomas Luckmann and Peter Berger set out to understand the mechanisms through which human beings create shared social worlds or, like Neiva and her family, come to adopt new ones. They referred to the conceptual infrastructure that determines what a given group considers to be credible or plausible beliefs as its "plausibility structure." Plausibility structures shape a group's worldview, or conception of the cosmos and the nature of reality. They are internalized by individuals in the course of socialization, thereby becoming part of their taken-for-granted assumptions about what is real (Berger and Luckmann 1967, 174).

The support of a community thus is critical: the maintenance of any social reality depends upon an ongoing plausibility structure that is continually reinforced for the individual through social relationships. No radical transformation of an individual's inner or subjective reality is possible, according to Berger and Luckmann, without the support of significant others with whom the person has an emotional investment and who mediate the new plausibility structure to that individual. "These significant others are the guides into the new reality," Berger and Luckmann wrote. "They mediate the new world to the individual" by socializing her into the new plausibility structure (177). In the story of Neiva's journey from widowed truck driver to clairvoyant spirit healer, one of the most significant people to play this role was Maria de Oliveira, a Kardecist medium affectionately known as Mother Neném (Mãe Neném).

Mother Neném and the Spiritualist Union of Father White Arrow (UESB)

Like Neiva, Mother Neném was a single woman struggling to raise her five children at a time when such a thing was neither common nor well regarded. According to Carmem Lúcia, the rapport between the two women was instant. Mother Neném "was passionate about Kardec's teachings and did not hide her enthusiasm for Spiritist doctrine from anyone," Carmem Lúcia noted. "Mama told her about her mediumistic experiences and soon a great friendship was sealed between them" (2014, 144).

At Mother Neném's invitation, Neiva and her children began attending evening sessions in which Mother Neném would read a passage from Kardec's book *The Gospel According to Spiritism* and lead the group in prayer. Afterward Neiva would incorporate her various spirit mentors like Chief Tupinambá or Mother Yara, or the pretos velhos Father John, Granny Marilu, or Mother Tildes. Carmem Lúcia remembered these evenings as times of great learning when evolved intelligences speaking through her mother would instruct the group about the world beyond material existence: the astral planes where the spirit, freed of its corporeal form, passes after death; and the various dimensions, each corresponding to a different level of evolution, where disembodied spirits go to prepare for their next incarnation. In her memoir, Carmem Lúcia described how she and her siblings were especially intrigued by the lowest spiritual plane, a zone described as so thick with negative energy that all warmth and light were obliterated. Only the highly evolved spirits known as the Great Legions could penetrate this darkness and illuminate a path for the lost souls imprisoned there, spirits whose hatred had twisted them into grotesque, animal-like forms (Lucena 1992, 11). Such accounts echoed the detailed descriptions of the spiritual realms found in the works of Francisco (Chico) Xavier (1910–2002) and other popular Spiritist authors, which circulated widely within Spiritist communities at that time and continue to be well known.

Drawing on her knowledge of Spiritist doctrine, Mother Neném determined that Neiva possessed an extraordinary ability that Allen Kardec referred to as "conscious transport." This enabled her to leave her body and, in the form of a conscious spirit, travel through space and time. According to Kardec, all humans have the capacity to leave their physical bodies during sleep and travel in spirit form, but the vast majority retain no conscious awareness or control over this faculty—a phenomenon that accounts for dreams. Like dreams, any lingering memories of these nocturnal travels quickly dissolve as consciousness returns. However, Neiva seemed able to consciously control this process, which allowed her to transport herself at will to other dimensions as well as backward and forward in time. Although she had not known it at the time, Neiva later wrote, one of her earliest experiences with conscious transport occurred in 1959 when she awoke to find herself aboard an alien spaceship and glimpsed for the first time the planet Capella, pulsating in the sky like an enormous ball of colored fire.

With Mother Neném's learned explanations and support, Neiva began to feel more secure in her psychic abilities. As word of her mediumistic talent spread among neighbors and friends, people began to seek out Neiva for spiritual help and a small community formed around the two women. Central to Spiritist practice is Kardec's insistence that the wisdom of evolved spirits be put into practice by charitably assisting others. Neiva was being prepared, she later wrote, to avoid perpetuating "the same errors of the 'Old Way,' to speak and not do, to teach and not practice." Instead, she was to practice "the Law of Assistance," always putting "the pain of the other before your own pain" (Lucena 1992, 11). Using the wisdom and guidance of her spirit mentors to help others, Neiva realized, was the larger mission of which Mother Yara had foretold her.

So, when her spirit guides, speaking through Neiva herself, announced that they needed to establish a spiritual city in which Neiva could realize her mission, neither she nor Mother Neném hesitated. Following instructions, they set out to find a piece of land and in 1959 founded the Spiritist Union of Father White Arrow (União Espiritualista Seta Branca), or UESB. The name honored Neiva's primary spirit guide Father White Arrow, whom she had first known as Chief Tupinambá (See Image 2.3).

According to Neiva, in his final incarnation on Earth, Chief Tupinambá had been an Indigenous chieftain during the era of Spanish colonization. He had

Image 2.3 UESB (Spiritualist Union Father White Arrow), 1959–1964. Courtesy of Arquivo do Vale do Amanhecer

earned the name Father White Arrow after saving his tribe from slaughter at the hands of the Spanish conquistadors by the power of his Christ-like words, symbolized by a white arrow. Neiva, Mother Neném, and their followers came to believe that this highly evolved spirit had chosen Neiva to continue his mission of spreading Jesus's message of humility, love, and tolerance on Earth through the practice of spiritual healing (see Image 2.4).

Image 2.4 Statue of Father White Arrow. Credit Márcia Alves

At UESB, the community—comprising about twenty people including the children—began to offer spiritual healing sessions to the public in which Neiva and other mediums incorporated various spirit mentors. They also took in "orphans with living mothers and fathers," as Neiva called them— that is, children whose parents could no longer care for them (C. L. Zelaya interview 2017). Reminding her charges that "in life we only have one mother," Neiva insisted that the children call her Aunt Neiva (Pinto 2005, 35). Although she was known as Sister Neiva among the adult members of UESB, eventually the name Aunt Neiva stuck. To support themselves the group planted potatoes and peanuts and produced tapioca flour and terra cotta roofing tiles (Lucena 1992, 12). Over the years, Neiva and her followers would engage in many such small-scale enterprises as economic support.

Word of UESB soon spread throughout the federal district. "When we started, Brasília was still under construction and there was almost no hospital assistance," Neiva later recalled.

> The poor and misfits, who came [to Brasília] in large numbers, attracted by the mirage of a better future, ended up looking for help at UESB.... Every day a huge crowd gathered. They came on foot, by cart, on horseback, or got off the buses that made the Brasília route ... We improvised a kind of hospital, in our own way, and we treated all kinds of illnesses. Mental problems predominated. We worked day and night without stopping. (Sassi n.d., 35)

"They were lost travelers," Carmem Lúcia explained in her memoir,

> people who were not accepted because of their mediumship, young women who had lost their virginity and fled the wrath of their families, and so many others who we did not know how they had arrived. Mother welcomed all of them with love. With these brothers and sisters, we learned to exercise our faith. (2014, 204)

Faced daily with such unrelenting need, Neiva despaired at times. In an unusually candid 1959 diary entry, she expressed her anguish:

Charity took the better part of our material gain. Visitors, I could count 20 or 30 people, came on Sundays for lunch and dinner that I was obliged to offer, as they were staying in my house. My God! I thought a lot. Is it possible that you chose misers and accusers? May God forgive me for my moments of pain when I lacked understanding for those exploiters. . . . Everything triggered me. In fact, in addition to all the tortures felt by the poor and misunderstood who want to serve God, I felt as well for the rebelliousness of not liking to live in the bush. The lack of material comfort, the change of profession, seeing my children pulled from their studies—it was all torture for me and my partner. (Souza n.d., "União Espiritualista Seta Branca," November 3, 1959)

Bit by bit, internal fault lines within the community began to emerge. Neiva's habit of working with caboclo and preto velho spirits particularly discomfited Mother Neném, who, following Allan Kardec's teachings, thought that these spirits lacked the light of moral and intellectual evolution and were, therefore, unsuitable as spirit guides. In her autobiography, Neiva described how Mother Neném

disagreed with the pretos velhos and with Umbanda, which made me insecure again. One time they called a "great medium" to remove my mediumship, or rather, to examine my mediumship. Cisenando was his name. He did not like certain entities and condemned my brusque ways, always saying "Neiva, it is for your own good! God forbid! Let us fix this so you do not end up in a crazy ward." (1992, 47)

Privately, Cisenando advised Neném to flee to Goiânia, warning her that Neiva's spirits, due to their low level of spiritual development, would only cause trouble and divert the community from its mission (Lucena 1992, 47–48).

These and other differences between the two women, exacerbated by the stress of their difficult living conditions, increasingly tested their alliance, and in February 1964 Neiva and Mother Neném parted ways. Neiva, along with a small group of followers, family members, and the dozens of children for whom she was caring, moved to Taguatinga, one of the satellite cities outlying Brasília that had sprung up to house the candangos denied residential rights within the capital city itself (Holston 1989; Rodrigues and Muel-Dreyfus 2005, 239).[19]

Once liberated from the strictures of Kardecist Spiritism as enforced by Mother Neném, Neiva was free to fully embrace her voices and visions and follow them wherever they led. Looking back on that period many years later, she described her divergence from Mother Neném as a necessary step toward developing her own doctrine, one more suitable to the realities of the modern world: an "acceleration in the evolution of concepts by offering a 'new view' of the immutable truths proffered by established religions" (Lucena 1992, 47 fn18). Through the medium of her clairvoyance, a new world was being revealed to Neiva in enigmatic pieces. This was a world that had not existed, at least on the material plane, until she created it. And yet, for many of Neiva's followers, it seemed familiar.

Social Works of the Spiritualist Christian Order (OSOEC)

In Taguatinga, the group immediately set to work rebuilding and on June 30, 1964, Neiva registered her new spiritual community under the name Social Works of the Spiritualist Christian Order (Obras Sociais da Ordem Espiritualista Cristã) or OSOEC. Carmem Lúcia reported that the community grew rapidly and soon counted eighty full-time residents as well as those who arrived daily seeking a cure for various maladies or to assuage their curiosity about the widowed former truck driver rumored to see both past and future (2014, 229).

The break between Aunt Neiva and Mother Neném, and the former's move to Taguatinga, occurred against a backdrop of heightened economic, social, and political instability in Brazil, culminating in the 1964 coup-d'état that brought a repressive, right-wing military regime to power. The new regime immediately mounted a concerted effort to suppress resistance, targeting student organizations, labor unions, and communists as dangerous leftists and unleashing a wave of politically motivated persecutions that drove many dissidents underground or into exile. With the climate of suspicion and uncertainty intensifying daily, some at OSOEC feared that left-wing elements might seek refuge among them and attract the attention of the military police. "We are rural people," Aunt Neiva reassured her followers. "We are unknown and without malice. We owe nothing." Nevertheless, she advised, "be careful in your conduct" (C. L. Zelaya 2014, 274).

Instead of a flood of political dissidents, the new alignments of power in the capital brought increasing numbers of politicians, businessmen, government officials, and other elites to OSOEC in search of Aunt Neiva's spiritual counsel. These contacts with the well connected proved beneficial to Neiva at key moments over the years. As in the case of Dr. Bernardo Sayão, whose assistance had enabled her to start a new life in Brasília, Neiva sometimes turned to more powerful allies when she needed help negotiating the state's arcane legal structures or connecting family members and followers with employment opportunities.[20]

When it came to spiritual work, however, Aunt Neiva adhered to the ironclad rule that "what we receive freely from the spirits must be given freely" (C. L. Zelaya 2014, 277). No payment could ever be accepted, lest the spirits take offense and refuse to help. OSOEC's mission, Aunt Neiva repeatedly reminded her followers, could only be sustained by members who donated their time, energy, and whatever other resources they could commit of their own free will. Patients were never to be asked for money or any other form of recompense, a rule that continues to operate today.

This meant that much of the responsibility for financially maintaining the community and its operations, as well as the growing orphanage, fell on Aunt Neiva's shoulders. As the group's first year in Taguatinga ended, the stress and exhausting workload began to affect her health. Eventually she grew so debilitated that she agreed to medical care, much to her children's relief. But the diagnosis only alarmed them further: tests showed that Aunt Neiva had an advanced state of tuberculosis that required specialized treatment. In May 1965, she was hospitalized in a private sanatorium in the neighboring state of Minas Gerais for treatment that her doctor estimated would take three years (C. L. Zelaya 2014, 287). At Aunt Neiva's insistence, however, and against medical advice, she was released after only three months.

The Tibetan Master, the Mestrado, and Mário Sassi

Although the medical doctors linked Neiva's tuberculosis with the fragile state of her lungs, damaged by contact with photographic chemicals and a heavy smoking habit, Neiva herself maintained that the root cause lay elsewhere. Her illness was triggered not by physical factors, she insisted, but by the rigors of a spiritual initiation that she had undergone under the tutelage of a contemporary Buddhist monk named Umahã.[21] Despite the fact that Umahã resided in a monastery in the mountains of Tibet, Aunt Neiva reported that every day for five years between 1959 and 1964 she had left her body in the physical dimension and, as a conscious spirit, met with Umahã on the astral plane. There, he instructed her in advanced esoteric teachings that had been forgotten in the West, including a technique of returning to past times and places to redeem karma associated with previous lives. The stress of this daily astral travel had weakened her body, she maintained, leaving her susceptible to disease.

According to Neiva, Father White Arrow had arranged this course of study with a living Master of Wisdom as the final element of her spiritual training: the completion of her *mestrado* or master's degree. In recognition of this accomplishment, Aunt Neiva was granted the esoteric title Koatay 108. As she wrote in her autobiography, Koatay means "originality, original, or singular," and 108 references the "108 Mantras that power the complete mestrado" (N. C. Zelaya 1992, 12). Today, Koatay 108 is the name that Valley members use to refer to the highly evolved spirit whose last incarnation on Earth was in the person of Aunt Neiva.

In the narrative of the Valley's origins that Mário Sassi later would help stitch together, this esoteric training and initiation capacitated Aunt Neiva to implant the system known as the "initiatory gospel" and to create the *doutrinador* or indoctrinator, the "rational medium" whom she saw as her successor and greatest contribution to the world. Beginning in the 1970s, Aunt Neiva would bring the mestrado to her followers by creating a structure for training mediums based on an ascending hierarchy of initiatory levels, each accompanied by a series of training courses.

When Neiva left the hospital in August of 1965, however, the elaboration of the mestrado was still a decade into the future. Despite her weakened state, Aunt Neiva immediately resumed her spiritual duties at OSOEC and life quickly returned to normal. As Carmem Lúcia noted, however, normal

> meant an intense circulation of children and constant comings and goings of people in search of [Neiva's] spiritual orientation. It did not even seem like she had an illness so feared for being contagious. The faith and hope in her clairvoyance were so strong that the search for her mediumistic gifts only increased. (2014, 308–309)

Among the ceaseless flow of people seeking Neiva's spiritual orientation was Mário Sassi, the man who would become Neiva's partner in both work and life. Their first meeting impacted both parties deeply. In 1968, after three years of comings and goings, Sassi left his family and former life for good to become the official interpreter of Aunt Neiva's visions, spokesperson for the movement that had consolidated around her, and embodiment of the figure of the doutrinador. I narrate the story of their partnership in more detail in Chapter 3.

The Valley of the Dawn

Not long after Sassi's arrival, Aunt Neiva lost possession of the land in Taguatinga. OSOEC was forced to relocate for the final time to a rural area near the town of Planaltina, some forty-five kilometers from Brasília. With the permission of her spirit mentors, Neiva called their new home Valley of the Dawn (C. L. Zelaya 2009, 143). There was only one problem: the land occupied an area that the federal government had designated for flooding. The Valley of the Dawn now lay directly in the path of a giant hydroelectric plant that had been planned to ensure the capital's water supply (Grigori 2017). Despite Aunt Neiva's assurances that this dire fate would not happen, the community lived under the threat of forced removal for the next decade. Finally, in 1988, three years after Aunt Neiva's death, the government abandoned its original plan, saving the Valley of the Dawn and its environs from flooding.[22]

Despite uncertainties about the future and the absence of basic infrastructure (municipal water arrived in 1970 and electricity in 1973), OSOEC grew steadily over the 1970s from several dozen to several thousand resident mediums.[23] As it did, the Temple was enlarged multiple times to accommodate the growing number of patients and mediums. In response to the need, Aunt Neiva had begun distributing small plots of land to trusted followers and a rudimentary town emerged around the Temple. "People would arrive at all hours of day and night," veteran member Nymph Rosita told me.

> There was always work and Neiva needed mediums to be here. If a patient arrived in the middle of the night, they would ring a siren and everyone would get dressed and come to the Temple to help, just like they do today. (Rosita interview 2012)

Not everyone was granted residential rights within the community, however. "Aunt Neiva decided if you could live here or not," Nymph Ione confirmed.

> Because living here is difficult, the spiritual life is hard. With her clairvoyance, Aunt Neiva knew who would be able to make the necessary sacrifices

to attend patients at all hours of the day and night. So, she was selective. (Ione interview 2012)

In the mid-1970s, a Catholic priest named Father José Vicente César visited the Valley while conducting an ethnographic study of the region's popular religions for a publication aimed at Catholic theologians. He observed long lines of people waiting to be seen by Aunt Neiva and her fellow mediums. It was not unusual for patients to stand all day in the hot sun amid great physical discomfort and privation, he reported. In the absence of public transportation, many had arrived on foot or by horse-drawn cart. But poverty alone did not account for the crowds—scattered among them Father César also noted an "appreciable number of luxurious cars, ladies of society, official cars, etc." (César 1977b, 492).

Despite his reservations about the Valley's theology, Father César came to respect and admire Aunt Neiva and Mário Sassi, with whom he had a lively intellectual interchange. In his published report on the community, Father César represented the two leaders as leading

> a very poor life, rich in unselfishness, full of sacrifices and even financial anguish because it is not easy to maintain free services of social and spiritual assistance without stable financial resources, depending on occasional official subsidies and the goodwill of the mediums. (César 1978, 63)

The "poverty and simplicity" in which the couple lived was equally true of their followers, he explained, who "inhabit rustic buildings with miserable hygienic facilities, lack of sewage, in a word, an existence of slum dwellers" (César 1978, 103). For the committed, however, the grandeur of their mission more than recompensed for the daily privations it entailed.

As the decade of the 1970s wore on, the community continued to grow. Following the ongoing revelations of her spiritual mentors, Aunt Neiva, assisted by Mário Sassi and a cohort of veteran members, worked to institutionalize doctrines, authority structures, and rituals while also serving a growing clientele in search of healing for diverse ailments. With each new revelation the religion grew more complex, both conceptually and in terms of its material culture. Newly revealed rituals necessitated the creation of appropriate structures in which they could be performed as well as accompanying symbols, songs, vestments, and other objects. Veteran members recall this as a period of both incessant work and great trial and error as they attempted to re-create on the terrestrial plane the things Aunt Neiva experienced and learned in her visions, which were described as voyages to different temporal and spatial dimensions, or messages received from spirit mentors. "All of this that you see here now, all of these structures, all of the rituals, the vestments, all of these things, came to her bit by bit," Master Manoel informed me one day as we walked along the grounds. "The information was arriving so that these things could be structured to become what they are today. But the whole thing was not quick or all at once. Everything had its own time" (Manoel interview 2015).

Family members and followers skilled in construction, masonry, painting, tile laying, sewing, and embroidery contributed their expertise. Aunt Neiva tasked her eldest daughter Carmem Lúcia with making the prototypes of what would become one of the Valley's most distinguishing features: the elaborate vestments worn by members during collective rituals and meant to mimic spiritual realities. Like Aunt Neiva herself, Carmem Lúcia had been sewing clothing informally since she was a child, first for her dolls and later for herself. In an interview, she described the struggle to reproduce the luminous colors and forms of her mother's visions in the fabrics available in Brazil in the early 1970s: "At that time purple did not exist, strong colors could not be found, no black, no purple, even red we had difficulty finding. So, we painted, we started out in this way, painting. And then when it rained, everyone ran like crazy for cover [because the colors bled]" (D. Oliveira 2007, 88).[24]

Thanks to word of mouth and positive media coverage, by the time that American anthropologist James Holston first visited in 1981, the Valley of the Dawn "had become renowned for its cure and had attracted an enormous following. It had become a famous attraction, a place of spectacular ritual, and as such part of Brasília's fame as itself a spectacular place" (Holston 1999, 610). Celebrities and politicians visited and reporters for local media outlets appeared regularly to interview Aunt Neiva and ask her predictions for the coming year.[25] Under the guiding impetus of Neiva's eldest son Gilberto Zelaya, numerous "external temples" in other Brazilian cities were being established and over the next decade the Valley of the Dawn's membership expanded exponentially while the resident population around the Mother Temple grew to about 8,000.

But years of arduous work, combined with a lifetime of cigarette smoking, were taking their toll on Aunt Neiva's weakened lungs, and her health was declining rapidly. After a series of respiratory crises that left her dependent on an oxygen tank to breathe, she died on November 15, 1985, at the age of sixty. Her body lay in state in the Mother Temple before being buried in the municipal cemetery in Planaltina. Among the thousands of people who paid their respects were Valley of the Dawn members from across Brazil as well as politicians, including the governor of the federal district José Aparecido de Oliveira. In death as in life, Aunt Neiva's appeal transcended social divisions of class, race, and region.

For the followers she left behind, Aunt Neiva's mission on Earth had been realized: the Valley of the Dawn's imagined world was complete. In a little over twenty years, she had brought together into one system "the transcendental inheritances of the richest civilizations of the past, and the most beautiful doctrines," her grandson Jairo wrote, "uniting magic and spiritual science in one place" (Leite 2005, 4). What had begun as a small community offering works of spirit healing to the suffering public had become "the Doctrine of the Dawn: a precise, technical-ritualistic system conceived by our Spiritual Mentors for the spiritual evolution of humanity," as one adherent told me. The Mother Temple outside Brasília had become the center of a burgeoning new religion with affiliated temples throughout Brazil—and later, in the United States, England, Portugal, and other international locales. It had featured in countless news stories, been visited by celebrities, inspired a famous pop song, and appeared in a nationally televised telenovela.[26] "The work itself is ready," Aunt Neiva reassured her followers just before her death. It would now be up to them, her spiritual tribe of Jaguars, to carry it forward (N. Zelaya 1999, 29).[27]

* * *

3

The Intellectual

God, illuminating me, brought Mário Sassi, my ideal companion who translates on earth what I do and what I am.

—Aunt Neiva

After seven years of living by her side, I understood that this being represents the Spirit of Truth and whose fundamental mission is to prepare us for the future. However, this preparation is not made by a specific prophecy, but by her own prophetic life. The prophecy is Neiva herself, living the lessons that she transmits.

—Mário Sassi (1974, 19)

A Very Restless Sagittarian

Mário Sassi was a spiritual seeker with a restless mind. Born in the city of São Paulo on November 29, 1921, to a poor family of Italian immigrants, he described his childhood as marked by scarcity and "immense suffering for not having opportunities to develop his intellectual skills" (César 1977a, 375). His early schooling was interrupted by stops and starts and he was twenty-four years old when he completed the Brazilian equivalent of high school through a *curso de madureza*, a secondary-school program geared toward working adults.[1] Despite his own frustrated experiences with formal schooling, Sassi had a deep appreciation for education and became an autodidact who was drawn especially to spiritual and esoteric literature as well as philosophy. Although he often emphasized his intellectual credentials to Valley visitors, mentioning numerous college-level courses he had taken, it is unclear whether he completed a course of study or earned a degree.[2]

One constant in Sassi's life was his interest in spirituality: as a youth he was a leader in the Juventude Operária Católica, a Catholic lay movement focused on working-class youth, and he later experimented with various other religions, including Umbanda, Rosicrucianism, and Kardecist Spiritism, before joining the Valley of the Dawn (César 1977a, 375–376). Sassi's curiosity was seldom satisfied with established orthodoxies for long, and he was drawn to unconventional ways of thinking and alternative spiritual systems whose precepts he would later bring to Valley doctrine.

In 1946 Sassi married Moema Quadros von Atzingen (1921–2002) in the Immaculate Conception Church of the Capuchin Friars in São Paulo, and a year later the couple had the first of their four natural-born children, later adopting a fifth. As time went on, differences in the couple's individual temperaments and desires began to surface. Sassi's intellectual restlessness, along with a lifelong preoccupation with deeper questions of human origins and meaning, made him ill suited for the conventional life of father and household head, which he experienced as stifling and futile. Moema's desire for stability and the trappings of middle-class status clashed with Sassi's idealism, contributing to an atmosphere of tension in the marriage.

Remarking on her father's fitful nature and constant quest for something more from life, Sassi's daughter Cací explained: "he was a Sagittarian. Sagittarians are very restless and like novelties, and they go searching, searching, they are very free, very independent" (C. Sassi interview 2017). "My father lived in the clouds," Sassi's son Iraê confirmed in a separate interview, "he was very idealistic, very dreamy."

> Mário was a restless man. He was not happy with the prospects that life was giving him. He worked for one of the pioneers in the automotive industry here in Brazil. Later he worked for one of the leading aviation groups in Brazil, one of the first major companies. He had opportunities for professional growth. But he was always changing jobs. He was never satisfied . . . he was not the enterprising man who goes to work and makes a career in a company. (I. Sassi interview 2017)

Encouraged by Moema, who graduated from college with a degree in sociology but had foregone a career in order to raise their children, Sassi eventually enrolled at the University of São Paulo to study public relations. "And this changed his life because he learned to speak English," Cací recalled. "Then, from there, he began to read everything in English. He was fascinated with those science fiction collections and things like that—esoteric subjects." She continued, "He always had an unorthodox side. . . . He always was reading books about Buddhism, about spirituality, he had this curiosity" (C. Sassi interview 2017). Iraê also remembered Sassi's fascination with unconventional forms of spirituality and paranormal experiences as a constant in his life. "And ours, too," he added; "we also were readers of esoteric books and things of that nature. We children were quite enchanted with his ideas about extraterrestrials." He went on,

> My father had a passion for the subject of the paranormal. I remember an experiment that he did with levitation. It's something that I always wonder about, because the memory of a child can fantasize. But I have it as a fact engraved in my mind. We levitated our father, after a strange ceremony. I remember that he was sitting in a chair and we levitated him with our fingers in a moment of concentration. (I. Sassi interview 2017)

An aeronautics enthusiast and builder of model airplanes, Sassi was fascinated with aircraft and dreamed of being a pilot as a boy. "He liked aviation, my father lived literally in the air, he was passionate about aviation," Iraê remembered.

> He would take us to Campo de Marte airport to look at the planes, he'd take us to Congonhas airport to watch the planes taking off and landing. And he even paid what at that time would have been a lot of money for us children to take a ride in one of those small planes, *teco-tecos*, they were called. He was besotted. And I remember that excursion until today—he paid by the hour for us to fly over Sao Paulo by plane. . . . We would spend hours making model airplanes with him. So, in that sense he was an affectionate father. (I. Sassi interview 2017)

Sassi's interest in the technology of flight eventually led to a job in São Paulo's booming transportation industry (see Image 3.1). But after a few years, Sassi, ever restive, moved his family from the country's dynamic economic center to its provincial periphery in Brazil's sparsely populated planalto central (central high plains). The family rented a house in Anápolis, and Goiás and Sassi briefly worked as the manager of a department store before taking a position at Simca do Brasil, a subsidiary of the French automotive company lured to Brazil by President Juscelino Kubitscheck's efforts to establish a domestic auto manufacturing industry. Sassi's business experience and contacts among the Brazilian elite soon opened other doors and in 1962, and with the help of Darcy Ribeiro, he became a public relations advisor at the newly established University of Brasília. Ribeiro, one of Brazil's most famous intellectual figures

Image 3.1 Mário Sassi 1955. Courtesy of Cací Sassi

at the time, had been appointed by President Kubitschek to set up the new University as an innovative model of public higher education that would advance the nation's modernizing project.

The family moved to Brasília, where the strains in the Sassis' marriage became more evident to their children. "They were a profoundly unhappy couple who spent hours shut up in the bedroom arguing and discussing," Iraê remarked (I. Sassi interview 2017). "There were these little domestic crises that they tried to solve in their bedroom behind closed doors," Cací confirmed. "And according to Mário, these crises contributed to his unhappiness with the life he was leading and everything" (C. Sassi interview 2017).

Frustrated with his material life and wanting a sense of greater purpose, Sassi sought guidance in different spiritual pursuits, experimenting with alternative groups that focused on psychic realities outside the limits of the physical world. Iraê explained,

> My father joined a Spiritist group, a Kardecist group somewhere around 1964–1966, when he was still Mr. Mário Sassi married to Mrs. Moema Sassi, and he started to invite people who were members of this Spiritist group to the house and they would have sessions where people would incorporate spirits. These were educated members of the community, important people.

I remember a surgeon from the Base Hospital in Brasília, Dr. So-and-So. They were important people that my father would bring to the house. (I. Sassi interview 2017)

Cací also recalled ceremonies "where we children had to stay more or less quiet while this entity gave some blessings and cleansed the environment." She went on, "These weren't experiments—they were things that he was pursuing in his life because he had this quest, this curiosity" (C. Sassi interview 2017).

Moema

Although Moema herself was "profoundly Catholic," she seems to have tolerated her husband's forays into the world of esoteric spiritual practices to keep the family together. "She did everything to be at his side, even joining his [spiritual] quests," Iraê recalled.

> I know that they got involved with a Rosicrucian group for a time, my father went through various phases. . . .. He sincerely believed in that religious process and in the reality of existence beyond our terrestrial life, our materiality. (I. Sassi interview 2017)

"My mother tolerated everything from Mário Sassi. She suffered a lot," Cací affirmed. "All she wanted was to keep her family, that structure—that was her dream" (C. Sassi interview 2017).

As Moema's desperation increased, she herself turned to occult pursuits, trying "every kind of superstitious practice to bring her husband back," Iraê recalled (I. Sassi interview 2017). After briefly experimenting with Afro-Brazilian religions, Moema consulted a card reader (*cartomante*) who, in turn, recommended Aunt Neiva, whose reputation for helping people had spread throughout the working-class towns ringing Brasília. "My mother was the one who first went to Aunt Neiva," Cací told me. "And Neiva told her that she couldn't give her an opinion without meeting her husband. What happened next was totally unexpected: Aunt Neiva fell in love with my father."

According to Cací, Aunt Neiva invited the couple to take part in the spiritual healing works that she held at OSOEC, but Moema refused:

No way, that was not my mother's profile. She went there to help resolve the family problem, which was the most important thing for her, she only wanted an opinion—she didn't want to participate in esoteric works. She only went to Aunt Neiva because Neiva had been recommended as a person who had vision, who had the power to see things and help people. And from that point on my father continued to frequent Aunt Neiva's temple and my mother disassociated herself from it. (C. Sassi interview 2017)

A New World Opened Up to Me

Sassi never mentioned his first wife in his descriptions of his introduction to Neiva. By his account, he first met Aunt Neiva in 1965 when he gave an unnamed person a ride to her house in Taguatinga. His narration of that fateful meeting opens the first chapter of his 1974 book *2000: The Conjunction of Two Planes* (*2000: A Conjuncão de Dois Planos*), hereafter *Conjunction*. It is worth reproducing at length:

> The door of the house opened and the person whom I had driven indicated that I should approach. I got out of the car grudgingly and entered the modest house. In the small room sat a modestly dressed woman of about forty, whose long hair and piercing black eyes stood out. She was introduced to me as "Dona Neiva" and I, much against my will, accepted a cup of coffee. But I couldn't take my eyes off her. There was silence for a few minutes, and she looked at me with a pensive air. My passenger talked endlessly, praising the hostess's abilities, but I barely heard her. A rapport had been established between the woman and me, and the world had momentarily ceased to exist. After the usual pleasantries, she surprised me with her words:
> - You are suffering a lot, she said, couldn't you come back so we can talk?
> - How do you know? I said. What are you seeing?
> - Come back here later and I will tell you. See if you can come back tonight, she replied. Come, I want to see your spiritual profile (*quadra*).
>
> I took my leave hurriedly, somewhat confused, and spent the rest of the day in a more disconnected state than usual. That scene and the figure of Dona Neiva persisted in my mind, and my heart raced as I remembered the visit. As soon as it got dark, I headed for Taguatinga.
>
> I was admitted to the same room, and it displeased me that there were other people in it. I entered their banal conversation reluctantly. At that

time, I barely had the ability to be civil. Dona Neiva talked to everyone, and I already was discouraged about the possibility of talking to her alone. Although prepared for yet another disappointment, my curiosity persisted. It was almost eleven at night when we were relatively alone. I say relatively, because the people most intimate [with Neiva] had retired to the kitchen with family members.

She, sitting simply, crossed her arms over her bust and asked my name and age. She remained silent for a few minutes and then began to speak.

"Mário," she said, "you are a dissatisfied person, but you have a great mission to accomplish. Your life will change completely, and you will find the realization you have been looking for. Life has been very hard on you, but now is your time. Get this idea of suicide out of your mind. You have a lot to do."

That said, she fell silent and stared at me as if she didn't see me.

A little embarrassed by her silence and disbelieving what I had heard, I unleashed a torrent of bitter complaints laden with ironies to which she listened patiently. From time to time, she would make an observation, and I, more unburdened, came to realize that I was not in front of an ordinary creature. After the first moment of surprise, I noticed that she had referred to some episodes of my intimate life, drawing a very accurate picture of my reality. And that, without saying anything, or almost nothing, besides my name and age! (Sassi 1974, 13–15)

The conversation continued into the wee hours. As the dawn broke, Sassi finally took his leave feeling, he wrote, "as if my whole being had been invaded by unknown forces as a new world opened up to me" (15).

The sensation of enchantment that pervaded his initial encounter with Aunt Neiva was so strong that at the very end of his life Sassi remembered the conversation as being "so seductive, so charming, that I wanted to continue.... I stayed until dawn, had dinner with her in the kitchen of the temple... and only returned to my house at daybreak" (Santos 1994).

A Sophisticated Suicide

It was a difficult time in Sassi's life both personally and professionally. In addition to his marital unhappiness, Sassi had become disillusioned with his job at the University of Brasília, which required him to circulate in elite social circles that left him feeling ill at ease. Much of his work time was spent wooing the wealthy and well connected in the stately environs of the Hotel Nacional, the grandiose five-star hotel that served as the principal meeting grounds for the city's power brokers. Business frequently was conducted at the hotel's American bar, where politicians, ambassadors, and celebrities mingled with the city's incipient high society over imported liquor, or in the grand salon with its sleek, modernist aesthetic. This sophisticated world of cocktails and social events, where success depended on personal relationships, increasingly alienated Sassi for it demanded a persona for which his own social background had not prepared him (C. Sassi interview 2017; I. Sassi interview 2017).[3] As Cací recalled,

> That was when he got involved with a more bohemian kind of life, drinking whiskey, and so on, which was not common at the time here in Brazil. He even had the habit of saying that he was becoming an alcoholic when he decided to take that leap towards spirituality. But in fact, he already had this interest [in spiritual subjects]. (C. Sassi interview 2017)

Sassi's personal and professional malaise deepened as the country's political life grew more tumultuous. In late March of 1964, after a series of escalating tensions, a military coup overthrew the reformist government of President João Goulart. On April 11, the military, supported by a loose coalition of civil, religious, and business groups, established an authoritarian system of rule by generals that would last for the next twenty-one years.

The authoritarian regime began interfering with the University of Brasília almost immediately as part of their campaign against communists, leftists, and other "subversive elements." Nine days after the coup, military troops invaded the campus and seized books and materials. Not long afterward, they demanded the firing or house arrest of fifteen teachers, which prompted two-thirds of the university's faculty to resign en masse. The rector and other key members of the administrative leadership were replaced, innovative programs were eliminated, professors and students were imprisoned, and a climate of repression settled in.[4] Sassi survived the purges but the campus was riven by fear and suspicion. "The dictatorship began persecuting people," Iraê recalled. "My father was frowned upon because he kept his job despite the defection of the teachers and the staff. They even accused him of being a secret spy because he did not denounce the dictatorship" (I. Sassi interview 2017).

The University of Brasília represented an important ideological arena for the new regime to prove its legitimacy and stifle dissent. As a progressive institution modeled on a vision of higher education that, like Brasília itself, was intended to promote greater social inclusion and transform Brazilian society, it was a key center of resistance to the military regime and the social order it sought to preserve. Over the next two decades the campus was the site of multiple strikes, marches, sit-ins, riots, and successive occupations by military troops. Prominent student leaders were harassed and, in some cases, kidnapped, tortured, and clandestinely executed by the regime (Motta 2014; Salmeron 2007; Comissão Anísio Teixeira de Memória e Verdade 2015).

Like many young people at the time, two of Sassi's sons, Abaetê and Iraê, became actively involved in the student resistance movement, which was a particular target of violence by agents of the state.[5] As a result of their activism, the regime expelled the Sassi children from public school. Later Abaetê became a leader of the Federation of University Students of Brasília and was captured, interrogated, beaten, and briefly imprisoned.[6] Iraê, who had passed the University of Brasília's entrance exam in engineering in 1969, was labeled a "subversive element" and a "threat to disciplinary order" and prevented from matriculating (Comissão Anísio Teixeira de Memória e Verdade 2015, 168). He eventually left Brazil for Italy, where he lived for two decades before returning to Brazil in 2000.

Partly because of the political crisis, Moema left Brasília with the younger children, Cací and Inaê, the couple's adopted daughter, to pursue a course of study in São Paulo. Unbeknownst to them, Sassi moved to a separate apartment in the town of Sobradinho just outside of Brasília. "We spent a year in São Paulo," Cací told me, "and when we returned to Brasília, my father was gone." In Cací's recollection this turn of events was even more shocking because her parents had "exchanged many letters during this period," none of which indicated that Sassi had left the family home. "According to my mother's account," she explained,

> these letters did not suggest any possibility of a breakup. But the concrete fact is that when we returned, he had dismantled our house and had rented a house for himself in Sobradinho. He left some money on the television and was gone. (C. Sassi interview 2017)

With Moema in São Paulo and the university in crisis, Sassi had begun spending more and more time in Taguatinga learning the intricacies of the otherworldly realities to which, he believed, Aunt Neiva had access. The hours they spent together blossomed into a romantic partnership, and in 1968, three years after their first encounter, Sassi left the trappings of conventional life behind to join OSOEC full time. He was convinced, he later wrote, that Aunt Neiva was a "superbeing" who "represents the Spirit of Truth and whose fundamental mission is to prepare us for the future." His own mission would be to "bear witness to the Spirit of the Truth" by synthesizing Aunt Neiva's visionary experiences and forging a comprehensive doctrinal system from the revelations that she claimed to receive from highly evolved entities inhabiting other dimensions (Sassi 1974, 19).[7] To do so he drew on his lifelong interest in alternative metaphysics and esoteric literature (Hayes 2020a). By developing a theological framework grounded in esoteric metaphysics, Sassi's theological work established the intellectual foundations of the movement and helped facilitate its expansion.[8]

In a 1984 interview with the social psychologists Arakcy Martins Rodrigues and Francine Muel-Dreyfus, Sassi described the deep spiritual malaise he felt before joining the Valley:

> I followed the trajectory common to typical members of the middle class . . . who seek an outlet, who are anguished, who enter one religion, then another, first this one, then that one, seeking to relieve the anguish and cannot . . . I prepared myself to be a pastor and I tried esotericism. I didn't achieve anything exceptional, but in compensation I felt the classic anguish, I kept searching, searching, searching, and finding nothing. Until the day when I suddenly discovered Columbus's egg, it is the simplest thing in the world to find yourself religiously. It is our civilization that complicates everything. (Rodrigues and Muel-Dreyfus 2005, 243)

While the decision to leave his family and career was a dramatic one, Sassi confessed that he had been contemplating it secretly for some time. "I had already prepared my own suicide," he told Rodrigues and Muel-Dreyfus,

> But it was not the suicide of someone who puts a bullet in the head, I thought that was not very elegant! I wanted a sophisticated suicide—to leave my identity. I had already prepared everything: one day, I would disappear from circulation and reappear there in Europe. I dreamed of experiencing Europe because I was raised by European immigrants. At that time, I was

disgusted with people, I was irascible, I made many enemies. And so, I imagined that I would abandon everything; in fact, I left it all in a different way. It was not a romantic renunciation, no, it was a practical change. In one fell swoop I got rid of everything. (244)

From Mário Sassi to Master Tumuchy

The contrast between Sassi's former middle-class lifestyle and his new, far more rustic surroundings was acute. Neiva and her followers lived simply in roughly hewn constructions cobbled together from scavenged wood, and the community lacked paved roads and other basic infrastructure. Despite the material poverty of his circumstances, Sassi wrote, his "spirit was already awakened to its mission," and he dedicated himself to the task of absorbing everything that he could about the new world he had embraced.

> Little by little, in a patient and arduous work of listening and observation, I collected facts. In that environment, despite the modesty of its physical exterior, the most incredible variety of mediumistic phenomena happened. The most visible were the incorporations, almost always made in intimate moments, away from profane eyes. The people who lived around Neiva were simple, without schooling, and averse to rationalization. They were so accustomed to the phenomena that nothing frightened them. The presences of the spirit world and the invisible ethereal world were commonplace.... What struck me most was the human unconsciousness that surrounded Neiva. And thus, with displeasure, in the midst of a meal or a mundane act, I collected answers to millennial questions, from inquiries that philosophers and scientists had long ago made. My curious questions soon earned me the nickname "the intellectual." But my curiosity was satisfied only with difficulty. (Sassi 1974, 16–17)

As time went on Sassi began to take on a leadership position within the community, "not so much for my qualities," he admitted,

> but for my availability. I had been able, at a great price, to detach myself from common obligations, and so gradually I became adapted to my mission. As I experienced more, I understood better the depth of Neiva's mission. (Sassi 1974, 4)

In his book *Conjunction*, Sassi described the struggle of his first three years with Aunt Neiva, which he came to understand as a kind of novitiate that continually challenged his understanding and endurance:

> The mediumistic work was a daily test. Although I still devoted myself to the normal activities of life, all my free time was spent in or near the Temple, waiting for teachings. This life was full of unforeseen events. During this time, I witnessed the most striking personal cases in the Doctrine. I then began to feel prepared and in a better position to assimilate spiritual forces, in the contacts with other dimensions. (4)

Near the end of this period, Sassi wrote, Father White Arrow incorporated in the body of Aunt Neiva and solemnly informed him:

> You are a missionary of God, and, in the name of our Lord Jesus Christ, you will announce the foundations of the civilization of the Third Millennium, received through this clairvoyant medium. You will bear witness to the Spirit of Truth, whose mission is to mark the millennial transition. (4)

This spiritual rite of passage was complemented by a temporal one in 1978, when Aunt Neiva consecrated Sassi to a formal leadership position as one of three (later four) "Trinos Triada Presidentes," a level of authority just below Neiva herself. Known as Trino Tumuchy or the Great Master Tumuchy, Sassi was declared the official interpreter of the Doctrine and "scientist of the spiritual worlds," responsible for the Order's doctrinal production and its archive (see Image 3.2).

As Cací attested, Sassi's break with his old life was total. "Mário never returned to the family, he never visited, he never sought us out. Never. From the moment he left to join the Valley of the Dawn, he isolated himself there. If we wanted to see him, we had to go there."[9] In the alternative world created by Aunt Neiva, Sassi had freed himself of the mundane identity assigned to him by society. He was now First Master Jaguar Sun Tumuchy, amanuensis to Aunt Neiva and interpreter of her prophetic revelations. "Mário was inserted into the context of the Valley of the Dawn in something of a fantastical way," Cací recalled.

> They built a small hut for him to sleep in, a real straw hut. . . . And there he was, the First Master Tumuchy, while Aunt Neiva orbited around with her

Image 3.2 Mário Sassi and Aunt Neiva. Courtesy of Vale do Amanhecer

four children and the orphanage and all that. They did not acknowledge their relationship publicly, so it was kind of strange. Later he moved in with her and lived at what they call the Casa Grande [Big House]. (C. Sassi interview 2017)[10]

In 1974, after obtaining a divorce from Moema, Sassi and Aunt Neiva married following the Order's matrimonial ritual (César 1977b, 488). Although the marriage was never officially registered with the state, Sassi and Aunt Neiva considered themselves *almas gêmeas* or soul mates reunited on Earth to advance a divinely inspired mission.[11] In the book *My Life, My Loves (Minha Vida, Meus Amores)*, Neiva described how Father White Arrow had assured her that one day her perfect companion would arrive:

And then one day a traveler arrived at my door with his spiritual missionary baggage, but the baggage of this traveler did not confuse me! Right away I saw that it was my companion. As a Jaguar, he carried with him a bag of disappointments and frustrations. Arriving, he entered into the Doctrine and took his place beside the doutrinador and to this day, together in the mission, with one heart and one thought, we live the doutrinador. We are kindred souls, we love each other very much and today, 1985, we have 20 years together and embrace our married life with much love. Together we have our unconditional love, within the Doctrine, my achievement for having by my side the Master Jaguar Tumuchy Mário Sassi. (1985, 96)[12]

By all accounts, their relationship was a genuine partnership in life and in the leadership of the Valley of the Dawn. "I never saw my father love anyone like he loved Neiva," Iraê observed. "The love he had for her was total" (I. Sassi interview 2017). Each recognized in the other a complementary nature that together generated something more than the sum of its parts: Neiva, the Clairvoyant, whose preternatural vision provided the inspiration; Sassi, the Intellectual, putting into language the visionary landscapes she traversed, left brain to her right, reason to her intuition. "To me they were like an orange," Nymph Lúcia, a veteran member told me,

> She was one half and he was the other half. Aunt Neiva had not studied, she did not even finish primary school, and Mr. Mário was a very cultured person. So, what she wrote, he corrected. She brought the knowledge, and he wrote the books. . . . Aunt Neiva only got where she got because of him, of that I have no doubt. (L. Pimentel interview 2015)

Gender and Authority

But there was another, less poetic, truth to their relationship. As a woman, Neiva needed a man by her side not just to interpret her visions but to legitimate her status in the eyes of society. While the Brazilian counterculture of the late 1960s and 1970s had begun to nibble away at prevailing social norms, respectable women still were expected to stay at home and devote their energies to their husbands and families. Public leadership was the prerogative of men. Women who dared to exercise it troubled the gendered logic of the social order and confronted various kinds of social sanction, from corrosive gossip to legal discrimination.

Like many women who transgress the boundaries of domesticated femininity, Aunt Neiva was suspected of sexual immorality (César 1977a, 380). "We had heard that she had all these young ladies around her and was running a brothel," a Valley member who joined in the late 1970s told me, expressing a rumor that circulated widely among residents of the federal district at that time (J. Vilela interview 2017). By his mere presence, Sassi deflected some of that stigma, neutralizing the threat that Aunt Neiva's authority and influence posed to a profoundly male-dominated society. Neiva's own nurturing personality and genuine embrace of her maternal role of mother or aunt—both socially acceptable forms of female authority—also helped soften resistance.

While the details of their private life doubtless were more complicated, in public Aunt Neiva and Mário Sassi represented the ideal couple. Their personal and working relationship established a model for followers and exemplified the movement's gender ideology, or systematic understanding of the appropriate roles and fundamental natures of men and women.

An Esoteric Evolution

Notwithstanding his convictions about Aunt Neiva's prophetic status, Sassi's relationship with her also seems to have provided an outlet for his intellectual ambitions and a means of reconciling his interests in alternative spiritualities and science.[13] From the moment he joined the community, Sassi labored to develop an intellectually coherent explanatory framework for Aunt Neiva's visions and for the movement that had formed around her. In addition to clarifying the group's beliefs in official publications, he authored several narrative reconstructions of Neiva's spiritual journey, created lectures and training materials, and helped coordinate and lead the community's evolving corpus of rituals. As OSOEC's official spokesperson, he also received important visitors and gave interviews to the press.

Above all, Sassi sought to explain Neiva's clairvoyant abilities and visions as natural phenomena explicable by science, not supernatural phenomena belonging to the world of religion. The spiritual dimensions of reality to which Neiva had access were real, Sassi maintained, although they lay beyond the limits of the physical world. These dimensions had not been confirmed by scientific methods only because scientists had yet to develop instruments sophisticated enough to detect them. Similarly, he argued, while Neiva's particular faculty of clairvoyance was rare, spirit mediumship itself was a biological process that all human beings were capable of mastering with training and discipline. In his writings and lectures, Sassi worked hard to present Neiva's complex and sometimes baffling accounts of out-of-body travel or contact with alien life forms on other planets as logically consistent and compatible with science.

Sassi's understanding of science diverged from that of trained scientists, but his appeal to science as a legitimating discourse is not unusual. In fact, it is a common rhetorical strategy found among many of the new religious movements (NRMs) founded in the nineteenth and twentieth centuries, whose adherents justify their convictions using pseudoscientific arguments (Lewis 2003; Hammer and Lewis 2010). As scholar of religion J. Gordon Melton observed, those who claim contact with otherworldly beings typically articulate their experiences in terms of the scientific discourse of the day (1995). Often, as in the case of the Valley of the Dawn, these alternative worldviews offer a corrective to what the founder perceives to be science's moral and metaphysical shortcomings (1995).

Sassi was concerned with the destructive potential of science when unrestrained by morality, a prime example of which he found in the terrible loss of human life unleashed by the atomic bomb. Rather than bringing greater prosperity and peace to ever more people, modern science had been used for exploitative and even inhumane purposes. "This phenomenon," Sassi observed, was "particularly evident in this second half of the twentieth century, in which scientific achievements, for example, coexist with the progressive devaluation of human beings" (Silva 2004, 3). To address this, science must be leavened by faith because "the faith that negates science is as useless as the science that negates faith," as a doctrinal saying has it. Unlike the immorality of conventional science, Valley doctrine offered its adherents a "complete spiritual science," based on faith in the progressive evolution of human beings back to their divine source.[14]

But Sassi alone scarcely could keep up with the pace of Neiva's revelations. "The instructions from the spiritual planes did not stop coming," recalled veteran Master Adevaldo Sampaio Froes in an interview, "and we were always at Aunt Neiva's side to take notes about the laws and rituals and receive guidance" (A. Froes interview 2015). This continual innovation gave the Valley a dynamism that characterized the movement until Aunt Neiva's death in 1985. "Not a year passed without Neiva introducing two or three different [ritual] works," Sassi's daughter Cací explained to me. "That vitality was part of the whole thing" (C. Sassi interview 2017).

During this fifteen-year period, the esoteric elements of the Valley's doctrine and practices became more pronounced.[15] Prior to Sassi's arrival, OSOEC had functioned much like any other Spiritist center with Neiva and a growing cadre of mediums performing the Spiritist version of charity by freely offering works of disobsessive healing to the public. Photographs from the early years of OSOEC show adherents dressed in the white uniforms common among Spiritist groups.

Beginning in the mid-1970s, however, photos and veteran members attest to a series of transformations that culminated in the "third, initiatory phase in the evolution of the Doctrine of the Dawn" (Betinho 2005, 4). While the Spiritist practice of disobsessive healing remained central, at some point Neiva introduced a distinction in mediumship between the *doutrinador*, who stays fully conscious during mediumship to indoctrinate spirits, and the *apará* or semi-conscious medium who incorporates spirit entities. Around this division Aunt Neiva and Mário Sassi began to institute, piece by piece, a complicated organizational hierarchy of initiatory ranks and titles based on a "descending forcefield" (*força decrescente*) of spiritual powers.[16]

Valley members themselves attribute this esoteric evolution not to Sassi's influence, but rather to Aunt Neiva's progressive spiritual maturation. To the degree that she gained mastery of her psychic powers, they maintain, Aunt Neiva gained greater access to esoteric knowledge, which she gradually implemented on the terrestrial plane (Pierini 2020). According to veterans' testimonies, a key moment in this esoteric evolution occurred sometime between 1973 and 1975, when Aunt Neiva began to "bring the mestrado" to followers by creating a hierarchical system for initiating mediums.[17] This system was modeled on her own initiation into the "high magic of Jesus Christ" under the tutelage of her Tibetan master Umahã. Later, she expanded the mestrado by adding other initiatory levels and "consecrations."

The implementation of the mestrado was necessary, Aunt Neiva told her followers, for the group to perform *trabalhos iniciáticos* or "initiatory works." These precise and powerful rituals, she explained, would enable the Jaguars to access potent spiritual forces linked to the Great Initiates, highly evolved spirits who had mastered the secrets of the universe. As a result, participants needed to have the requisite level of spiritual mastery achieved through a graded system of initiation. In other words, they needed to be masters.

"She began to bring the initiatory forces around 1975," Master Froes told me.

> And for this she had to prepare the mediums, including me. It was a struggle to form the rituals and the laws, to make the *indumentárias* [ritual vestments], the capes, to prepare everything. But we were always by her side, helping elaborate the laws for the rituals, because each ritual has a procedure. Before we did the ritual, she would do a rehearsal and we all would have to be there to participate, to document everything, to write everything down and get everything ready for the ritual. In this way she brought the mestrado and we became masters. (A. Froes interview 2015)

With the mestrado in place, the Valley became something more than a Spiritist-Christian amalgam. It was now an initiatory-evangelical system: "a Doctrine offering a path to self-knowledge and spiritual development based on the initiatory wisdom of Jesus Christ, updated for the modern human" (Sassi 1977, 26). As another long-term medium, Master Paulo, explained to me one day, Aunt Neiva's "initiatory knowledge" enabled her to

> implant here on Earth the Doctrine of the Dawn: a precise, technical-ritualistic system conceived by our Spiritual Mentors for the spiritual evolution of humanity. This doctrine revives the true magic of our Lord Jesus Christ and by living out this Gospel, we are able to manipulate powerful energies for spiritual healing and karmic redemption. Formerly the focal point for this esoteric work was the Himalayas, but now it is here at the Valley of the Dawn. This is where the great energies are concentrated and where the great changes will start in the transition to the New Age. (Hayes 2022, 243)

Night Owls

Veteran members with whom I spoke recalled this period fondly as a time of great social camaraderie and a heightened feeling of mission as they worked collectively to reproduce on the terrestrial plane the complex spiritual hierarchies that were revealed bit by bit though Aunt Neiva's clairvoyance. Because most daylight hours were spent attending patients at the Temple, this creative work mostly happened in late-night sessions dubbed Corujões, or Night Owls, for their tendency to last until dawn. Once the workday was finished, Aunt Neiva would gather her closest associates around her in the relative privacy of her residence, affectionately known as the Casa Grande or Big House. There, fortified by rounds of *cafezinho*, the strong, well-sugared coffee central to Brazilian hospitality, they discussed the vast amount of information that seemed to flow through Neiva from the spirit world.

"She'd leave the Temple and say, 'oh my child, let's go have a cup of coffee at home,'" Master Froes recalled,

> And then we would sit at a long table, on benches around the table, and she would start talking with us and telling us things and talking about the entities. Sometimes she even incorporated entities, Father John sometimes incorporated, sometimes even Father White Arrow incorporated in order to give some instruction. So, we would stay up to four o'clock in the morning. Someone would say, "oh Aunt I am leaving," and she would reply "No my child, wait a little." So, I would leave the Corujão at three, four o'clock in the morning and I had time only to shower and get back to work. And sometimes I would sneak in a nap at noon and spend the next day recovering. (A. Froes interview 2012)

"That was when I spent a lot of time with Aunt Neiva up close because we were doing the Laws and a series of other things," Master José Carlos do Nascimento Silva told historian Marcelo Reis:

> I would stay for the Corujão. I would leave at one, one thirty in the morning. For practically two years: every day I was here with her.... Mr. Mário would get irritated and go to bed and I would stay with her. And then she would tell jokes, she would discuss cases. She liked it because it was a moment where no one was pressuring her: "Aunt Neiva, should I do it this way? Should I do it that way?" She relaxed. It was really good, very convivial. We had very important moments, explanations of transcendental things, things that are reflected to this day—aspects of the Doctrine, aspects about many masters. So, I got to know a side of the Doctrine very much through her eyes. (Reis 2008, 239)

The feeling of shared mission that pervaded these sessions was enhanced by the fact that Neiva herself did not always know the whys and wherefores of the spiritual plans she felt called upon to execute. Again, Master Froes:

We were always asking her lots of things—what does this mean and what does that mean and what is the purpose of this? And she would say, "Son, I will write it down." There were things that we asked her, and she would say, "it is like that, my child, it has to be that way, but I do not know why." And so, it was like that. But she brought what she had to bring: the basics, the essentials for us to conduct and be conducted within the Doctrine, the forces, the works, the energies, the invocations of forces, the emissions. She did not have time to write down all the details for every single thing, she gave some details to those responsible for the garments or the initiations, or whatever it was. (A. Froes interview 2012)

The energy necessary to fuel and sustain such creative efflorescence eventually proved too much for Aunt Neiva's fragile constitution. By the late-1970s, the respiratory problems that had plagued her for most of her life were flaring up more frequently and acutely, making speaking for longer than a few minutes at a time difficult. Conscious of her limited time on Earth, Neiva began to meet daily with her future successors to ensure that everything was in place for Father White Arrow's great work to carry on without her (Fonseca 2007, 248).

Already in 1978, she had begun the process of transferring spiritual and administrative power over the community from herself into a bureaucratic structure of authority. At the apex was the office of Trinos Triada Presidentes, formed of three co-equal positions, each occupied by a high-ranking male doutrinador or indoctrination medium. Alongside Mário Sassi, whom she consecrated Trino Tumuchy and assigned responsibility over the doctrine, Aunt Neiva appointed two other men. Michel Hanna, aka Trino Sumanã, was given charge of healing, and Nestor Sabatoviks, Trino Arakém, was made responsible for executive and administrative functions. A few years later, Neiva gave her oldest son Gilberto Zelaya the title of Trino Ajarã and charged him with coordinating and supervising the external temples that had begun to be established under his impetus.

After Aunt Neiva's death in 1985, Sassi's influence began to wane. His remarriage the following year discomfited many in the community, as did his work with a category of spirit entities, the "Great Initiates," whose implantation at the Valley of the Dawn, he claimed, had been foreseen by Aunt Neiva but interrupted by her death.[18] Among these highly evolved entities was Koatay 108—the spirit who had last appeared on Earth in the form of Aunt Neiva herself. Facing resistance from the other Trinos as well as members of the Zelaya family, Sassi left the Valley of the Dawn in early 1992 with his third wife Lêda Franco de Oliveira and a small group of followers. The group, believing themselves to be guided by Koatay 108, bought land in a rural area of the federal district called West Lake (Lago Oeste) and began the process of creating a new community, the Universal Order of the Great Initiates.[19] Sassi died there in December of 1994 after several years of declining health following a 1991 stroke.[20]

Today, despite the acrimonious disputes that had led to his departure, Mário Sassi continues to be held in great esteem by Valley of the Dawn members. He is revered as a great intellectual and "spiritual scientist" responsible for interpreting Aunt Neiva's visions and codifying Valley doctrine.[21] Without the theological and metaphysical framework that he developed, it is doubtful that the movement would have been able to function without Neiva's charismatic presence, let alone expand outside of Brazil.

However, it is not enough to have a charismatic founder and a coherent theology, as I discuss in the next chapter. Equally important is a compelling story that helps people make sense of their lives and experiences; provides a sense of mission, collective identity, and community; and offers strategies for overcoming personal obstacles, dealing with adversities, and imagining new futures or new ways of being in the world.

* * *

4
The Journey of the Jaguars

We are the exiles of Capella. We were put here on Earth, in a primitive place. Man, at that time, lived only within the animal phase, which was a very rudimentary phase. And we were sent here to see what we could make of this people. And, in truth, we also became more brute-like, we degenerated, we devolved a few levels. And today, we are on the path again to see if we can succeed in returning to Capella . . . we are here to redeem ourselves.

—Valley adherent (Reis 2008, 240)

Father White Arrow and the Journey of the Jaguars

To really understand the Valley of the Dawn, Mário Sassi wrote in a 1979 pamphlet aimed at visitors to the community, it is important to look beyond the immediate historical circumstances of its emergence (which I narrate in Chapters 2 and 3) to its "remote origins" in time and space. The "veteran spirits" presently gathered at the Valley of the Dawn, Sassi explained, belong to an ancient spiritual tribe, the Jaguars, whose members "specialize in the work of succor, in periods of confusion and insecurity" (Sassi 2004, 3). These situations always arise, Sassi continued, "at the end of civilization cycles, when Humanity moves from one planetary phase to the next."

According to Sassi, the origins of the Jaguars' special mission go back through the mists of time to their spiritual ancestors: a vanguard of highly evolved beings sent from the planet Capella to accelerate the evolution of Earth and its inhabitants.[1] Under the direction of a "planetary master" who would later be known as Father White Arrow, these extraterrestrial missionaries were responsible for the evolutionary progression of modern Homo sapiens from earlier species. Their sophisticated celestial and technological knowledge, for example, was the impetus for the extraordinary accomplishments of various ancient peoples, from the astronomically aligned constructions of Machu Picchu and Easter Island to the Egyptian pyramids. Over millennia, their descendants passed through multiple lifetimes, inspiring diverse civilizations in different times and places under the guiding impetus of Father White Arrow.[2]

With the passage of time, however, the Jaguars slowly began to succumb to the inexorable pull of materiality, eventually straying from their civilizing mission. As members of the tribe descended into internecine rivalries, power struggles, war, and chaos, their contacts with Capella dwindled. This history has generated a karmic legacy that fuels the cycle of reincarnation, ensuring the Jaguars' continual rebirth in the terrestrial world until the karmic load of the past can be fully discharged. The advent of Jesus marked a turning point in the tribe's collective history, making possible a universal form of karmic redemption known as the "Christic System" or "School of the Way." By emulating Jesus's teachings of love, humility, and forgiveness, all human beings can liquidate the karmic debts they have accrued over multiple lifetimes. According to Valley doctrine, those who adopted the Christic System as a way to redeem themselves and return to their original mission became known as Jaguars, an identity symbolized by a stylized feline face modeled on that found on the Incan Gate of the Sun in Bolivia (see Image 4.1). The name honors the group's collective incarnation as an Indigenous tribe living in the mountainous Andes during the period of Spanish colonization,

Image 4.1 Jaguar symbol. Credit Márcia Alves

led by Father White Arrow in his final terrestrial incarnation as the caboclo Chief Jaguar.

When Father White Arrow's evolutionary trajectory on Earth came to an end, he commissioned Aunt Neiva to carry on his mission of fostering humanity's spiritual evolution. Valley members consider themselves present-day Jaguars who have been reunited by Aunt Neiva at a critical cosmic juncture: the transition to the Third Millennium. By working to alleviate the spiritual suffering caused by this tumultuous event, contemporary Jaguars believe that they can redeem their karmic heritage before the crossover period draws to a close. At that time, the Earth will be convulsed by great social and geological catastrophes as it passes into a new metaphysical state and the era of karmic redemption ends. Those Jaguars who have liberated themselves will continue their evolution in the astral world before finally being reunited in their true spiritual birthplace: the "Mother Planet" of Capella.

This chapter examines the mythological story of the Jaguars from their extraterrestrial origins to the present day as documented in the writings of Mário Sassi. The "Journey of the Jaguars," as Valley members refer to it, establishes the narrative framework for the community's shared social reality, offering what scholars term a cosmology and a macrohistory—in other words, a grand narrative of the origins of the universe and the unfolding of human history as well as a story about the people who ultimately came together to form the Valley of the Dawn.[3] This sprawling, unruly epic is organized around key episodes in the Jaguars' collective mythic past, each set in a different time and place.

Like everything else about the Valley, the Journey of the Jaguars did not emerge at once fully formed but evolved over time through a constant process of interpretation, elaboration, borrowing, synthesis, and invention. Its generative impetus was Aunt Neiva's tales of former lives, extraterrestrial encounters, voyages to other dimensions, premonitions, and messages from highly evolved beings. As the official interpreter of the Doctrine, Mário Sassi played a critical role in transforming this constant stream of spiritual inspiration into narrative form.

Using Neiva's accounts of her visions as his raw material, along with the intermittent diary entries, letters, and other writings that she had produced over the years, Sassi endeavored to explain both the transcendent realities to which he believed Neiva had privileged access and the mediumistic phenomena he witnessed daily. This was his special mission, he felt, and it occupied him until the very end of his life. "I grew up hearing that Master Mário Sassi was the 'intellectual' of our Doctrine," Aunt Neiva's grandson Jairo Zelaya Leite told me.

> His work was to translate knowledge that our Clairvoyant Mother herself had difficulty assimilating and transmitting. Mr. Mário was the interpreter of her visions, the one who systematized them and put them in order. He wrote the first texts, the first books about the Doctrine of the Dawn, he also received journalists, researchers, students, religious and scientific authorities. He was responsible for the knowledge production at the Valley of the Dawn. (J. Leite interview, 2012)

Over nearly two decades, Sassi produced dozens of pamphlets and lecture materials, as well as four books, including a biography about Neiva. He also edited Neiva's writings, which consist mostly of short epistles recounting stories, outlining principles of doctrine, or exhorting her followers to embody them. Along with Sassi's written work, these *cartas* or letters hold canonical status among contemporary Valley members.[4]

Genealogy of a Bricoleur

The task of building a coherent narrative foundation for an emerging religion whose beliefs and practices were still being revealed was a challenging one. Aunt Neiva's visions occurred with an astonishing frequency and often were fragmented or disjointed in time and space. Some were indelibly vivid. Others were frustratingly nebulous, like the wisps of a dream that dissolve in the first rays of dawn leaving only vague sensory impressions. All were pieces of an obscure puzzle. To make sense out of gaps and contradictions and forge an explanatory structure capable of integrating the various pieces into a unified conceptual system, Sassi drew freely from his studies of esoteric and popular spiritual literature. His favorite works spoke in the language of science about experiences that, by Sassi's time, mainstream science firmly discounted as objectively real. "Mario was sincerely convinced of the reality of 'life beyond matter' as he called it," his son Iraê told me. "He was fascinated by the question of alternate universes and intelligences. He believed that, when properly understood, science confirms the existence of unseen realms" (I. Sassi interview, 2017).

Although Sassi's personal library has not survived, it is clear that he had access to a diverse body of esoteric, Spiritist, and New Age texts from around the globe as well as the works of popular Brazilian writers like Chico Xavier (1910–2002) and Edgard Armond (1894–1982), which circulated widely in Brazil. Sassi's own writing is dense with references to vibrational fields, astral planes, reincarnation, karma, chakras, auras, subtle energies, and other concepts common in this literature. His style can best be described as professorial: filled with complex, pseudo-scientific explanations for non-empirically verifiable phenomena such as the laws governing invisible dimensions or the "scientific" basis for communication with superhuman entities.[5]

The work of Allan Kardec was a special touchstone for Sassi. He frequently used terms like *perispirit*, Kardec's notion of an ethereal, nearly massless substance that links the incarnated spirit to a physical body, and *ectoplasm*, a kind of spiritual energy produced in mediumship. Sassi also referred to *animal magnetism* and *magnetic fluids*, two concepts derived from the theories of Franz Anton Mesmer (1734–1815), that Kardec adopted to describe an invisible natural force or vital energy possessed by all living things.

While Kardecist Spiritism was a major contributor to the Valley of the Dawn's doctrine and practices, the basic metaphysical structure that Sassi developed in his writings suggests the influence of other Western esoteric traditions, particularly the movement known as Theosophy.[6] Founded in the late nineteenth century by Helena P. Blavatsky (1831–1891), an aristocratic Russian woman who had immersed herself in Eastern religions and esoteric doctrine, and Henry Steel Olcott (1832–1907), a well-connected lawyer, Theosophy posits an emanationist universe in a constant state of evolution through different planes of existence.

As Theosophists described it, the universe is the dynamic, evolutive expression of pure spirit gradually descending into matter over eons until finally the process reverses on itself. At that point, matter slowly evolves back into spirit in a kind of vast, "cosmic U-curve."[7] Likewise, all living beings progress through an identical evolutionary process, with humanity passing through a series of stages or "root races" characterized by differing admixtures of spirit and matter (Santucci 2008, 38).

Countering the impersonal theory of evolution posited by Darwinian scientists, Blavatsky argued that an "intelligent consciousness" drives evolution. This intelligence is embodied in "a hierarchy of spiritually, morally, and technologically superior beings" known as the Masters of Wisdom or simply Masters (Partridge 2015, 397). Blavatsky claimed to have received insight into the true nature of the cosmos from members of this mysterious brotherhood of enlightened Masters, whom she referred to as the Mahatmas. Although Blavatsky described the Masters as human beings who were especially advanced in their own evolutionary journey, later Theosophists would describe them as purely spiritual beings, celestial deities, or even highly evolved extraterrestrials.

Because of its emphasis on the study of complex, philosophical doctrine, Theosophy as a formal movement was never very large in Brazil (or anywhere else it spread). Nevertheless, it has had a profound impact on the landscape of modern religions.[8] Among other things, Theosophy was a major route through which the ideas of karma and reincarnation, as well as other concepts originating in ancient texts of Indian philosophy, entered the West. Blavatsky's contention that a lineage of highly evolved Masters guides humanity's spiritual progress from afar proved particularly fertile as a source of charismatic authority for new religions. In the first half of the twentieth century alone, dozens of new religious movements were established based on a founder's claim to spiritual wisdom received directly from a member of this illustrious brotherhood.[9] From a history of religions perspective, Aunt Neiva's assertion that she had been initiated into esoteric wisdom by her own Master of Wisdom, the Tibetan Umahã, is not particularly unusual or idiosyncratic, but part of a broader historical pattern.[10]

Theosophical ideas had circulated in Brazil since the first decades of the twentieth century when members of a Spiritist community called Love Towards God (Amor a Deus) established the first Brazilian lodge affiliated with the Theosophical Society.[11] Shortly thereafter, works by prominent Theosophists like Charles W. Leadbeater (1854–1934) and others were translated into Portuguese and disseminated in Brazil.[12] However, Theosophical ideas reached their largest audiences in Brazil indirectly through Spiritist newspapers, conferences, radio programs, and other media.[13] It is likely that both Aunt Neiva and Mário Sassi were exposed to Theosophical ideas through Spiritism, or, in Sassi's case, other esoteric literature, rather than by direct involvement in Theosophy.[14]

Sassi's longstanding interest in alternate universes and intelligences also was fed by the tales of extraterrestrial life that, by the late 1950s and 1960s, were beginning to move from the fringes of Brazilian popular culture to its center. Space adventure stories like Buck Rogers and Flash Gordon had been circulating in Portuguese-language comic books since the 1930s, but the

Cold War–era space race and the wave of "flying saucers" (*discos voadores*) sightings that followed in its wake propelled debates about extraterrestrials into the Brazilian mainstream. Brazil even had its own nationally famous alien abductee, António Vilas-Boas, who claimed that he had been taken aboard an alien spacecraft in October 1957 and sexually assaulted by a female alien (Santos 2016b).[15] As is clear from his writings, Sassi followed these public conversations closely. Almost certainly he was familiar with popular authors like George Adamski and Erich von Däniken, who claimed that extraterrestrial visitors had long maintained contact with humanity.[16]

An Occultural Cosmology

These diverse sources furnished Sassi with terminology and a conceptual structure that helped him to synthesize Aunt Neiva's visionary experiences with a larger, metaphysical framework that is universal in scope. Bit by bit in writings and lectures to the community, he constructed a grand narrative of cosmic evolution grounded in Spiritism, Theosophical metaphysics, and extraterrestrial philosophies—the kind of esoteric blend that Christopher Partridge termed Western occulture (Partridge 2004; 2005).[17]

Partridge described occulture as a "spectrum of beliefs and practices sourced by Eastern spirituality, Paganism, Spiritualism, Theosophy, alternative science and medicine, popular psychology, and a range of beliefs emanating out of a general interest in the paranormal" that typically is rejected by the guardians of religious and scientific orthodoxies and constantly is feeding and being fed by popular culture (Partridge 2005, 2; 2004, 65). Like an underground spring from whose waters diverse alternative religions bubble up, occulture is continuously flowing and changing. It is not primarily a secret or esoteric phenomenon itself, Partridge pointed out, but is public and sometimes even mainstream (2014, 121).

A common occultural theme is what Partridge called the "sacralization of the extraterrestrial" or the systematic interpretation of aliens as cosmic Masters: technologically and spiritually advanced beings who intervene in human life out of a compassionate concern for our progress (Partridge 2005, 167, 174). This theme is the central premise of Sassi's 1974 book *2000: The Conjunction of Two Planes* (hereafter, *Conjunction*). Along with details of his first encounter with Aunt Neiva and early years in the community, the book reveals Sassi's efforts to integrate the Brazilian elements of Neiva's visionary experiences, like her caboclo spirit guide Father White Arrow, with an occultural metaphysics centered on the periodic intercessions of cosmic Masters working to foster human evolution.

Published more than a decade after the events it purports to relate, *Conjunction* combines descriptions of Aunt Neiva's alleged encounters with various extraterrestrial beings, along with a general account of the mission that they have entrusted to her, buttressed by Sassi's explanatory commentary. During these encounters, Aunt Neiva learns the protohistory of the Jaguars and their lengthy journey through time and space. As she discovers, Father White Arrow and the members of his tribe are actually the descendants of an extraterrestrial vanguard that, over the millennia, played a vital role in humanity's cultural and spiritual development.

An Interplanetary Education

Aunt Neiva's visionary experiences usually involved the disincarnate spirits of caboclos, pretos velhos, and other entities familiar within popular Brazilian religions. But in 1959, according to Sassi, she began to have contact with entities of a very different kind: inhabitants of the planet Capella. This distant star, located on the other side of the Sun, Sassi explained, "has presided over the destiny of the Earth from the beginning," and its inhabitants have maintained contact with Earthlings in many ways (Sassi 1974, 32).[18]

In notable contrast to the spirit entities with whom Aunt Neiva had habitual contact and whom she considered personal mentors and guides, the Capellans "are people like us, spirits occupying physical bodies," Sassi affirmed, and they inhabit a physical world similar to Earth (Sassi 1974, 31).[19] They are "molecular," Sassi continued, but with a different "composition" than humans, and as a result "their appearance did not have the diaphanous quality of the spirits, and their emanation produced an uncomfortable effect on [Neiva's] body" (Sassi 1974, 31, 53).

While not perfect, the Capellans are proto-Christians who are guided by "the principle of the Law of Forgiveness, the Christic Law," Sassi affirmed (1974, 80). As divine emissaries and Masters responsible for guiding human evolution, the Capellans have accompanied human beings throughout the centuries, "suffering with us, inventing new teaching methods, refining their contacts and continually searching for ways of guiding us" (Sassi 1974, 79).[20] They cannot tolerate the density of the Earth's atmosphere, however, and so they mostly communicate by projection "in a way similar to the transmission of television images" (Sassi 1974, 61).[21] According to Sassi, they do occasionally come in special vehicles, giving rise to the numerous tales of flying saucers that have become popular lore around the world. In another book, Sassi offers a more fanciful take, describing the Capellans as having "all the charm of the traditional blond and beautiful figures, belts full of mysterious buttons, typical of science fiction literature" (Sassi n.d., 131).

Their advocacy intensifies during periods of transition: in the current planetary cycle of the last 2,000 years, Sassi noted, they have expended tremendous resources trying to reorient humanity as we rush on blindly, with little sense of where we will end up (Sassi 1974, 17). Now, on the cusp of the Third Millennium and fearful that the tumult produced by the incipient transition between planetary phases will compromise the fragile progress that they have achieved on Earth, the Capellans have initiated contact with Aunt Neiva.

According to Sassi, this was because Aunt Neiva's superior and extraordinarily rare faculty of mediumship made her the perfect instrument to facilitate the Capellans' mission of shepherding humanity "through the difficult and catastrophic passage" into the Third Millennium (Sassi 1974, 32). Aunt Neiva, he explained, possessed the faculty of "simultaneous consciousness," or "conscious transport," which allowed her to be present within, while being fully conscious of, different dimensions. This enabled her to act independently in each dimension—physical, spiritual, and etheric or astral—traveling backward in time or forward into the future, or moving within and between dimensions, all while maintaining her normal existence in the terrestrial world. Thus, while her physical self continued to operate in the material dimension, Aunt Neiva's "etheric body" could travel to Capella, where she was schooled in the details of her mission and its prehistory (Sassi 1974, 41).[22]

Although Neiva did not understand its significance at the time, her first encounter with the Capellans occurred at the very beginning of her career as a medium. As Sassi described the scene in *Conjunction*, Neiva, Mother Neném, and the other mediums of the Spiritualist Union of Father White Arrow had gathered for their regular spiritual retreat one evening in 1959. Normally on these occasions Neiva would experience conscious transport and, in this state, would travel to other "vibratory planes" and describe to the gathered group everything she witnessed. On this evening, however, Neiva found the process of leaving her body more difficult than usual. "All at once," Sassi reported her saying,

I felt a strong headache and perceived that I was inside a machine, a kind of a large cockpit full of instruments. I noticed someone next to me and heard him call my gypsy name, Natachan, as I am known in the spirit world. I paid attention and saw that he was pointing me to a kind of huge window.

"Natachan,"—he said—"look at that ball!"

In fact, I saw a huge ball of colored fire, which seemed to rise and fall in the sky, always resuming its initial position. I heard, again, the voice of my guide, who seemed to speak inside my head:

"Natachan, look closely! I will move this lever and you will see better."

The ball became clearer then, and my guide continued:

"There, Natachan, is the world of those who are preparing for the great work of God on Earth. You will soon get to know it better. This world, this planet that you are seeing, is divided into four parts, four different worlds. One of these parts is called Umbanda, whose meaning is 'band of God' or 'side of God.' It is the pure part of the planet. The other part is called Capella, which also means 'last stop' or 'command post of the niche of God.' In Capella live the beings that you, on Earth, call the Knights of Oxossi. These beings play an important role in God's plans for the earth. They are physical beings, but, both on Earth and in the place where you are now, they appear in dematerialized form."

And I asked him: "Where am I?" But I no answer came, and I returned, gently, to my body. (Sassi 1974, 26–27)

This experience marked the beginning of Neiva's "interplanetary course of study," Sassi declared, an education that ran parallel to the practical mission of disobsessive healing that she was then pursuing alongside Mother Neném and the other mediums of the Spiritualist Union of Father White Arrow (Sassi 1974, 39).

Over the course of her interplanetary education, Neiva learned the cosmic extent of her mission and its roots in the Capellans' own longstanding efforts to guide human evolution over millennia. As narrated by Sassi, this information is presented in bits and pieces in the form of extended dialogues between Neiva and her Capellan interlocutors. While Sassi always presented himself as the mere instrument for the evolved intelligences who worked through Aunt Neiva, *Conjunction* also reveals his efforts to reconcile the local, Brazilian elements of Aunt Neiva's paranormal experiences with a more expansive metaphysics derived from his reading of various occultural sources.

Sassi took special pains to describe Neiva's chief spiritual guide, Father White Arrow, as the earthly avatar of a highly evolved planetary master responsible for executing God's civilizing plans for the earth. Notwithstanding the fact that Aunt Neiva consistently described Father White Arrow as a classic caboclo figure, Sassi inserted him into a narrative quite different from the fierce, unacculturated Indian of Umbanda and Candomblé mythology.

The Vanguard from the Mother Planet: Equitumans and Tumuchy

In one of *Conjunction*'s most pivotal anecdotes, Aunt Neiva learns that Earth was first colonized some 32,000 years ago by a vanguard from the "Mother Planet" of Capella (Sassi 1974, 167–178). Much of what she discovers in this and subsequent encounters with the Capellans echoes the mythological history described by Brazilian Spiritists Edgard Armond and Chico Xavier. The notion that technologically advanced extraterrestrials from the planet Capella were responsible for advancing terrestrial evolution, for example, was the central premise of Armond's 1949 work, *The Exiles of Capella*, and appeared in Xavier's *On the Way to the Light* (1939).[23]

Adapting the Theosophical figure of the Master of Wisdom, Xavier and Armond both claimed that highly evolved beings from the planet Capella were responsible for humanity's development, over the course of successive evolutionary cycles, from a primitive to a more advanced state.[24] From colonies scattered across the globe, these cosmic Masters established technologically sophisticated civilizations in ancient Egypt, Mesoamerica, and the mythical Atlantis, among other locales. Over time, however, their descendants succumbed to the lower forces of the material world and became corrupted by their love of hedonistic pleasures and the quest for power, necessitating the dispatch of new missionaries or other interventions to reorient humanity on the path toward spiritual and scientific advancement. As described by Xavier and Armond, human history unfolds in a classic gnostic trajectory, alternating between periods of advancement and decline, as Earth itself transitions through successive planetary phases.[25]

Appropriating this narrative frame in *Conjunction*, Sassi referred to the first wave of alien missionaries as Equitumans and described them as a highly evolved race of giant beings more spiritual than physical in nature.[26] In fulfillment of God's plan, they were sent some 32,000 years ago to make

Earth more suitable for civilization and to accelerate humanity's cultural and spiritual advancement. For this purpose, they established themselves in seven centers spread over the globe. With the passage of time, however, the Equitumans became increasingly entrapped in the material world. As they succumbed to "animal-like physicality" and the thirst for power, they "began to distance themselves from their Masters and the original plans," Sassi wrote (Sassi 1974, 173). Finally, they were eliminated from Earth when a Master who would later be known as Father White Arrow was dispatched to crash his spacecraft into the main Equituman settlement. "How this happened will be difficult for you to understand," a Capellan named Amanto advises Aunt Neiva in Conjunction.[27] "It was a huge ship called the Incandescent Star (Estrela Candente), which traversed the earth's skies, performing the divine sentence" (Sassi 1974, 173).

Neiva subsequently learns that the crater left by the impact formed Lake Titicaca, the mythical birthplace of the Incan civilization (Sassi 1974, 173). Referencing this mythological connection to the Andes, the Valley's Mother Temple complex features an artificial lake known as "the teardrop of Lake Titicaca," which Aunt Neiva inaugurated in 1978. Likewise, the symbol representing the Jaguars, which appears in various formats throughout the Valley of the Dawn, is modeled on the iconography of Viracocha, the creator god of the Incans and their predecessors (see Image 4.2).

Continuing the story, Sassi, via the character Amanto, explains to Neiva that in order to complete the civilizing process that had been interrupted,

> A great missionary, who is known to us today as Father White Arrow and who was responsible for the Estrela Candente, collected the most pure remnants of the Equitumans and divided them into seven tribes which were distributed among the old focal points of the Equitumans. (Sassi 1974, 174)[28]

Each of the seven tribes was composed of a thousand spirits and was led by an evolved Master or Orixá, the term for a pantheon of West and Central African–derived deities venerated in Afro-Brazilian religions like Candomblé. In the case of the Americas, Amanto tells Neiva, the Orixá in charge was the Great Tumuchy, the same spirit who later would be called Father White Arrow (218).

This second wave of missionaries, known as Tumuchy after their leader, appeared approximately 30,000 years ago. *Conjunction* describes them as

Image 4.2 Virachocha, Sun Gate in Bolivia. Wikipedia

great scientists and technicians, skilled in astronomy and the use of metallurgy and psychic communication. Their main objective was to attract and concentrate cosmic energies in different spots on Earth, for which purpose they constructed great pyramids around the world. Using their advanced scientific knowledge, the Tumuchy built spaceships, known as *chalanas*, which enabled them to travel to Capella, and other celestial bodies and to transport themselves between any of their seven centers.

Due to the primitive and dangerous conditions of Earth, however, the Tumuchy encountered difficulties in their civilizing task. They eventually retreated to Easter Island, which they transformed into the "scientific headquarters of the planet and the center of interplanetary communication" where "great spaceships coming from Capella arrived and departed" (Sassi 1974, 190).[29] They also maintained "points of irradiation" in seven centers around the globe where they "constructed fabulous monuments" that were "intended for the reception of forces from the Mother Planet and other bodies of the Solar System" (Sassi 1974, 190).

Finally, the Great Tumuchy (Father White Arrow), exhausted by the physical demands of the terrestrial environment and having completed his mission, disappeared from Earth. His people "continued on for some time, but without the impetus of their leader, they eventually left the island and dissolved." Later, in successive incarnations, they "carried notable civilizing traits, which served to prepare the great cradle of the Third Millennium" (Sassi 1974, 190).

Although humans do not recall the Equitumans and Tumuchy today, Sassi noted, the memory of them was transformed over time into the various myths of celestial gods who brought civilization to humans (Sassi 1974, 174). Yet the physical evidence of their legacy, "the knowledge and documentation of the planetary plans, the basic instruments and means of communication," remains buried deep within the ancient pyramids and other monuments built by the Tumuchy (Sassi 1974, 195). Scientists have yet to properly understand this legacy, Sassi maintained, because of their refusal to recognize spiritual realities. But thanks to Aunt Neiva, present-day Valley members believe that they are able to access the powerful cosmic energies that remain concentrated in the seven centers established by the Equitumans and Tumuchy—referred to as rays (*raios*) or roots (*raizes*)—in special rituals revealed to Aunt Neiva in her astral travels.

The Jaguars

With the disappearance of the Tumuchy, a third civilizing vanguard emerged to carry on the great work some 25,000–15,000 years ago. Later they would be known as Jaguars in honor of their leader the Great Jaguar, aka Father White Arrow in his final terrestrial incarnation as an Indigenous chieftain. *Conjunction* describes the Jaguars as "great manipulators of social forces" who left their mark on various ancient peoples. Spreading out from the seven colonies founded by their predecessors, they inspired the advanced civilizations of the ancient Mayans, Egyptians, Incans, Assyrians, and so forth (Sassi 1974, 190). Elsewhere Sassi explained,

> Within these races and peoples, over thousands of years, these experienced spirits always ended up in command positions and distinguished themselves as kings, nobles, dictators, scientists, artists, and politicians. In this gigantic movement, over time and space, we can trace the proximate origins of the spirits that today are part of the mission called Valley of the Dawn, from the Hittites, then the Ionians and the Dorians. Later, we will find them

in Sparta, Athens, Egypt, and Rome. Especially in Sparta and Macedonia, began the path that we might call the "Modern Era" of the Jaguars. (Sassi, 2004 [1979], 19)

But the struggle between the lower forces of materiality and the more refined spirit element that had plagued the Jaguars' predecessors had not been overcome. Inevitably, the age-old pattern of decline took hold. In the 5,000 years before Christ was born, civilizations organized solely around the pursuit of material power self-destructed in a terrible cycle. For the Jaguars, a particularly low point was their incarnation in ancient Sparta—a culture so preoccupied with military conquest that "neither love, nor mercy nor charity existed" (Silva 1998).

Finally, Sassi wrote, "the Master of Masters, decided to come to Earth personally," and Jesus was born (Sassi 1974, 225). And thus "Spirit once again began to reclaim the planet," albeit in "continuous struggle," with the more primitive forces of the material world (Sassi 1974, 226). This marked the dawn of the "Christic System" or "School of the Way," a mechanism for karmic redemption based on Jesus Christ's moral teachings of unconditional love, humility, forgiveness, and the practice of charitably helping others. Now, by emulating Jesus and using their mediumship to help others, the Jaguars could redeem their negative karma and thereby reclaim their original mission, returning "to the path towards God" (Sassi 2004, 21).

Since "giving their oath to Master Jesus and initiating their new phase," Sassi explained, the Jaguars have been striving to repay the karmic debts that they have accrued over their long sojourn on Earth, first as Equitumans and Tumuchy, then as Jaguars, and later in different incarnations across time and space (Sassi 2004, 19). According to Aunt Neiva, most Jaguars had experienced at least nineteen different incarnations on Earth. The sum of the Jaguars' collective experiences over time is known as its "transcendental heritage" (*herança transcendental*)—a legacy of collective deeds and misdeeds, and their karmic consequences (Sassi 2004, 19).

As part of her mission, Aunt Neiva reunited the Jaguars at the Valley of the Dawn for what may be a final chance to redress their troubled karmic legacy before the transition to the Third Millennium ends and a new era dawns. As a Valley member told me during my first visit in 2010, "because of the ascendancy of the planet, passing on to another dimension, a higher dimension . . . we Jaguars have the opportunity to repay our karmic debts faster." Some say that once this transition is complete, Father White Arrow will return from his astral abode to usher the most evolved spirits, some incarnate in human form, home to their true spiritual birthplace: Capella.

Through the Occultural Looking Glass

One of the striking things about the story of the Jaguars that Sassi laid out in *Conjunction* is how he inserted Father White Arrow into a grand narrative whose basic themes are shared among many occultural groups: an imminent New Age that will metaphysically transform the earth, the cyclical progression of both cosmic and human development, a gnostic struggle between the spiritual and the material, the alien inspiration behind ancient civilizations, the idealization of science and the identification of advanced technology with spiritual advancement, the reinterpretation of ancient pyramids and other monuments as part of a vast extraterrestrial communication system, the common origins of the world's religions, and the beneficent concern of enlightened Masters who intervene periodically from afar. Re-imagined through an occultural framework, Father White Arrow was transformed from the classic caboclo of Brazilian folk tradition into a scientifically and spiritually advanced cosmic Master guiding human evolution. In one of the story's more memorable details, he pilots a spaceship charged with executing "the divine sentence."[30]

Also of note in *Conjunction* is Sassi's identification of Father White Arrow as an orixá, even though he appeared to Aunt Neiva as a caboclo and is depicted as such in Valley of the Dawn iconography. This "Afro-Brazilian word is very apt," Sassi observed, "because it means exactly intermediate divinity between the believers and the supreme divinity" (174). The tendency to conceptualize the orixás as a class of evolved entities of light who inhabit the highest echelons of the spirit world is present in Umbanda, especially its more esoteric forms. But Sassi, re-reading these African-derived deities through an occultural framework, took it a step further. Transformed into rarefied planetary Masters, the orixás are purified of any connection to Afro-Brazilian religions or Africa itself and positioned as powerful intermediaries who are even "more evolved than the Masters of Capella." In the great spiritual hierarchy envisioned by Mário Sassi and Aunt Neiva, the only cosmic entity above the orixás (e.g., Father White Arrow) is God.

Even Jesus Christ is reconfigured in *Conjunction* as a cosmic Master who established a universal system of karmic redemption. While Valley members acknowledge the image of Jesus presented in the Gospels and Catholic tradition, theirs is an esoteric Jesus. According to the Doctrine, Jesus is not God, but a highly evolved spirit whose major contribution to humanity was his wisdom and moral teachings rather than his suffering and death.[31] The "cult of the bloody Jesus hanging on a cross," as Aunt Neiva learns in one of her many interchanges with the Capellans, is merely a reflection of humanity's "unconscious masochism, your unaccepted pain and frustration" (29). The real Jesus, she is told, is found in his example of unconditional love, and his humility and forgiveness: the virtues enshrined in the Christic System.

Rather than the sacrificial Jesus of Catholic tradition, awash in blood and thorns, the Valley's Jesus is the *Caminheiro*, or Wayfarer. "Aunt Neiva always told us to remember Jesus the Wayfarer," Alexandre explained to me. "Not that Jesus nailed to the cross, but the Jesus who spoke words of love, who brought those lost brothers with him. Jesus the Caminheiro is always present with us, helping us and protecting us along our journey."

Some observers have suggested that the Valley's vision of Jesus is derived from the "hippy Jesus" prominent in pop-culture products of the 1970s like the musical *Jesus Christ Superstar* (Cavalcante 2011, 80). But an alternate translation of Caminheiro is "Pilgrim," which suggests a Theosophical connection more in line with the Valley of the Dawn's conception of Jesus as a cosmic Master sent to Earth to course-correct the divine plan for human evolution. In Blavatsky's thought, Pilgrims are highly evolved "individual centers of consciousness" who have completed a full course of evolution, progressing from Source through each of the seven worlds and back. As scholars Robert Ellwood and Catherine Wessinger wrote, Masters were those Pilgrims "well in advance of the norm in collective evolution" who were ranked in an Occult Hierarchy and "directed the divine plan of collective evolution back to the Source"—an apt description of Jesus the Caminheiro (Ellwood and Wessinger 1993, 70–71).

Tiãozinho/Stuart

Jesus and Father White Arrow were not the only supernatural figures transformed into cosmic Masters in Sassi's writings. One of Neiva's oldest and most beloved mentors, Tiãozinho, underwent a similar metamorphosis. The spirit of a man named Sebastião Quirino de Vasconcelos, "a simple Brazilian citizen from Mato Grosso, the son of a prosperous cattle rancher," Tiãozinho died tragically sometime around 1916, according to Aunt Neiva. As the story goes, he perished alongside his young wife Justininha when the *chalana* or ferry that they were riding wrecked and they drowned (Sassi 1974, 112; Sassi 1986).

One of Aunt Neiva's most steadfast spirit guides, Tiãozinho accompanied her from the early days and was known for his "versatility and ability to solve intricate situations" (Sassi 1974, 113). His unpretentious manner and folksy way of speaking "puts everyone at ease," according to Sassi, and gives Tiãozinho an important role in the Valley's mission of preparing humanity for the Third Millennium (Sassi 1974, 113). A scene in *Conjunction* describes the moment when Neiva discovered that the familiar "happy spirit from Mato Grosso" that she recognized as Tiãozinho was, at the same time, the highly evolved Capellan she had come to know as Stuart:

> Neiva's surprise could not have been more pleasant. Tião, the friendly and constant spirit, who had rescued her in many difficult hours, the simple and always cheerful Brazilian, was there with his imposing stature, his affable smile and his devoted friendship. Tiãozinho, a Capellan! She cried with joy. (Sassi 1974, 112)

In Sassi's telling, Aunt Neiva immediately felt much more at home in her meetings with the extraterrestrial Capellans knowing that her familiar guide Tiãozinho was present with her, albeit in a form different from that he usually took. Sassi explained that this kind of multiplicity is due to the spirits' capacity to exist simultaneously on different planes: "As Stuart, he is a citizen of Capella, performs technical duties in one of his worlds, and, probably, must be very busy. As Tiãozinho, he serves as a Spiritual Guide of the Valley of the Dawn," where he is in "great demand" (Sassi 1974, 128).

Tiãozinho/Stuart's multiplicity is captured brilliantly in a large painting that currently hangs in the Mother Temple. Rendered in the style of a classical portrait, the painting depicts a mustachioed cowboy in a dark green shirt, hat in hand, facing the viewer in a frontal pose. He is encircled by a bright aura of yellow flames that flicker around him, seeming to burst forth from the painting's dark background. Around his waist is a wide, studded leather belt. As scholar Altierez dos Santos pointed out, on closer examination, the studs on the belt form dials reminiscent of the instrument panel of a vehicle, a subtle reference to the spaceship that Stuart piloted in several of Aunt Neiva's visits to Capella described in *Conjunction* (Santos 2016a; 2016b; 2018) (see Image 4.3).

96 SPIRITS OF THE SPACE AGE

Image 4.3 Painting of Tiãozinho from the Mother Temple. Credit Márcia Alves

According to the Doctrine, while Aunt Neiva was establishing her mission at the Valley of the Dawn, Stuart was pursuing his own advancement in the astral world. "In the first seven years that he worked with us," Sassi wrote, "he graduated as a 'Sidereal Engineer,'" becoming a "specialist in the spiritual world dealing with planetary problems. He possesses a *chalana*, the name our group gives to certain spacecraft, and he is the commander of a mother ship, which we call *estufa*" (Sassi 1974, 113). Beyond these details, Sassi continued,

> We know little of his functions. We are only told that Sidereal Engineering is concerned with problems of astronomical calculations and activities related to the physical aspects [of celestial bodies], which makes us wonder if he does not have "other personalities" besides these. (Sassi 1974, 128)

Worthy of note here is the detail that even as Sebastião Quirino de Vasconcelos's life on Earth ended prematurely and tragically, the spirit known as Tiãozinho/Stuart continued to live on in another dimension, studying, working, graduating, and becoming part of an elite hierarchy of cosmic masters. Meanwhile the chalana whose shipwreck ends Tiãozinho's earthly life becomes, in the astral world, the spaceship that Stuart pilots between dimensions.

Tiãozinho/Stuart's dual personality points to more than just the capacity of the spirits to exist simultaneously in different multiverses, as Sassi would have it. It also suggests how Aunt Neiva's spirit mentors speak to and about Brazil and its people. As Santos pointed out, unlike an entity like Father White Arrow, Tiãozinho is said to be the spirit of a man who lived in the twentieth century and the details of his life as a rural rancher resonate with many members of the Valley of the Dawn. Santos argued that Tiãozinho's status as a "simple Brazilian citizen" and his folksy ways make him a stand-in for the candangos, the generation of migrants who, like Aunt Neiva herself, came to work in the construction of Brasília, only to be excluded from the realization of its utopian promise (Santos 2016b).

Return of the Repressed

A recurrent theme in the oral histories collected from the candangos who arrived in Brasília in the late 1950s and early 1960s is the difficult living conditions: long workdays, poor food, precarious living conditions, a lack of medical assistance coupled with the prevalence of accidents and disease, and the violence and general lawlessness of the male-centered frontier culture. The work was frequently dangerous and always physically demanding—the kind of manual labor that, during the colonial period, was reserved for slaves. And the frenetic "rhythm of Brasília," during which work continued around the clock throughout the three years of the city's construction, fostered an environment of lax oversight and exploitation.

Counterbalancing these privations, however, was a spirit of adventure, enthusiasm, and solidarity. Although most migrants came to the federal district in pursuit of a better life, they also were genuinely excited to be participating in the realization of a great national dream (Pires 2013, 180; Epstein 1973, 62–63). Incentivized by government promotional materials and mainstream media to see themselves as heroic nation-builders whose herculean efforts would bring modernity, industry, and progress to Brazil, candangos felt a sense of inclusion and citizenship—many for the first time (Holston 1989; von Hartenthal 2019).

But the hopes they might have nurtured for inclusion in the future made possible by their labor collapsed in the aftermath of the city's 1960 inauguration. That event, James Holston wrote in his monumental study of Brasília, marked the end of employment and financial security for many workers, who now found themselves living in areas distant from job opportunities in the city (Holston 1989, 215). The new capital was intended to be an administrative center inhabited by civil servants and functionaries of the federal bureaucracy transplanted from the former capital of Rio de Janeiro. No provisions were made to permanently house the massive force of workers whose manual labor built the city. Brasília's planners had assumed that those laborers, once their work was complete, would simply return to their far-off homelands (Holston 1989; Pires 2013). In the state's idealized vision, Holston argued, the inauguration would reveal a "gleaming new city, empty and ready to receive its intended occupants" (1989, 199). But this required the denial of the population it had already acquired: the candangos.

To help assure their desired outcome, government officials had instituted a number of strategies, including the planned demolition of all temporary housing settlements after Brasília's inauguration. This applied not only to the construction camps but also to the Free City, where workers who had arrived in the initial stages of the capital's construction, like Aunt Neiva, had created a sizable town. The resulting disputes over who was authorized to live and work in the new capital created a situation that characterizes the federal district today: a class-based social order that is reflected in, and reinforced by, the physical layout of Brasília and its outlying districts with a central core occupied by an elite and a periphery inhabited largely by the poor and working classes.[32]

With little desire to return to the even more difficult circumstances they had left behind, many candangos moved—or were forcibly relocated by the government—to peripheral areas outside of Brasília's planned footprint like Taguatinga. Located twenty-five kilometers (about 15.53 miles) from the new capital, Taguatinga was part of an ad hoc government plan to remove and resettle thousands of migrant workers who had built a squatter encampment on land near the main entrance to the Free City (Holston 1989, 260; Epstein 1973, 66–71). Other so-called satellite cities quickly sprung up in the shadow of the capital, some created by the government and others by the initiative of those who had no legal claim to live in Brasília itself.[33]

This "zone of exclusion" on Brasília's periphery was not part of the original design for the federal district. It was, rather, the inevitable outcome of what Holston called Brasília's "paradoxical development" (Holston 1989). In a bitter irony, the city designed by its modernist planners to liberate residents from the urban forms of the nation's colonial past—characterized by chaotic growth, unregulated development, widespread inequality, and overcrowded *favelas*— ended up reproducing these dystopic elements. As Holston observed, where the state's "populist rhetoric of recruitment" had emphasized the vital role of the working classes in building the hopeful future symbolized by the new capital, the real world of "plan, policy, and practice" systematically excluded them (Holston 1989, 217). Once his labor was no longer needed, the "anonymous titan," in President Juscelino Kubitschek's famous phrase, whose sweat and toil had built the city, was relegated to its distant hinterland (Holston 1989, 210).[34]

Distilling this mordant history into metaphor, acclaimed Brazilian author Clarice Lispector wrote that Brasília had been constructed "without a place for rats." "An entire part of us, the worst, exactly the part who are terrified of rats, that part has no place in Brasília. They wished to deny that we are worthless.... But the rats, all of them huge, are invading" (Lispector 1992, 136).

In Lispector's evocation, the utopian aspirations of Brasília's planners required them to deny something fundamental about human nature in pursuit of an austere, symbolic ideal. But social problems cannot be resolved by consigning them to other locales. Those prevented from living in the new capital did not simply disappear when it became clear that there was no place for them. The inauguration laid bare the fact that, despite the idealistic blueprints of its master plan, Brasília did not engender a new *civitas*. The past could not be abolished by rearranging the built environment; justice and equality could not be magically produced by the performative enactments of architecture and urban planning. The bureaucracy of the state continued to function on behalf of a coalition of elite interests, as it always had. And those who were excluded continued to be relegated to the nation's periphery: a population of rats continually gnawing the boundary between the imagined city and its real-world counterpart.[35]

This was the population that Aunt Neiva served. Like the Clairvoyant herself, her followers were mostly migrants to the federal district who, through choice or circumstances, had linked their futures to the new capital only to find most of the same problems that they had left behind: lack of opportunity, difficult living conditions, frustration, despair. A small number, like Mário Sassi, were part of an educated middle class. But the majority were illiterate or semi-illiterate rural laborers who had fled the poverty and drought of the northeast, bringing only the strengths of their backs and hope for a better life.[36] All had come to a new world where the social ties that had previously sustained them—family, church, neighbors, employers, and patrons—were no longer there.

"My story is the story of many people who came to Brasília," veteran Valley member Master João Nunez told me.

> I'm from a very poor family, an agricultural family. I came from the state of Piauí, one of the poorest states in the Northeast. We lived in the interior, in the bush. There was no electricity and no running water. We spent every hour of daylight working in the fields. We children broke coconuts and gathered cashews to sell. My father used to say studying does not fill the belly of anyone. What fills the belly of a person is work.
>
> When I arrived in Brasília I had very little education and no skills, so I went to work in the simplest service possible. I was a servant; I worked as a cleaner in a building in the South Wing (Asa Sul). But I saw that there was no future in that, and I began to despair. Because I had no family here, no friends, nobody, and I could not go back. But then I met some mediums, and they invited me to visit the Valley. And forty years later I am still here.

The people who found their way to Aunt Neiva, like the people who come to the Valley of the Dawn today, were motivated by suffering of one kind or another. For some it was a physical or mental illness, either their own or that of a child or loved one. For others it was difficulties finding or keeping a job, lover, marriage, or a home. Still others had been abandoned by families unable to care for them or, like Master João, had left families behind. Always they came after exhausting other options within their reach and suspecting some deeper, unseen origin to their troubles. "The folks who came to Neiva were really in anguish," veteran Nymph Lúcia Pimentel told me.

> Families who were experiencing difficulties—the father of a family who was unemployed, the mother of a family whose spouse had left her, the family whose daughter or son had run away or gotten into drugs or crime, they would come out of nowhere and pour out all their troubles to Aunt Neiva. And she would listen with the greatest patience. She would take them, mold them, and return them to society as a different person. (L. Pimentel interview, 2016)

Slowly, through the force of her own great empathy and capacity for love, Aunt Neiva transformed people. "Only work lifts us up and makes us understand that while we work with our brothers, we are in contact with God," she advised followers, while putting them to work staffing the Temple's spiritual works and building her visionary city (Message from August 14, 1984; reproduced in Silva 2001, 79). Mobilizing her network of well-placed friends and acquaintances, Aunt Neiva connected people with jobs and opportunities throughout the federal district. She offered shelter to those in need, hope to those in despair, and food to the hungry. By the 1970s, the number of orphaned and abandoned children she had taken in reached the hundreds, and a large dormitory had to be built to house them all.

For those who joined the community as mediums, Aunt Neiva offered more than a welcoming community, a sympathetic ear, and the promise of assistance—although undoubtedly this was part of her appeal. She offered a new way of understanding life and imagining the self that reconciled the frustrating present with a desired future. As Mário Sassi remembered of his first meeting with Aunt Neiva,

> When I left the house, with dawn already breaking, I had entered a new world. My life now presented itself clearly, with an explanation for each fact. Suddenly, everything started to make sense, to have a logical perfection.

I felt invaded by unknown forces, and I saw a welcoming world in which there was a place for me! (Sassi 1974, 15)

This was a different kind of utopian vision, one that did not negate the past in the quest for an idealized future or deny the worst parts of human nature. Rather it asserted that everyone had a place in a great cosmic journey. By discovering their true nature as spirits in evolution and working to make amends for past errors, Neiva's followers could transform the adversities of the present and create a better future. Her great genius was to model these teachings within the context of her own life and in ways that spoke to the lives of her disciples.

"She worked the Law of Assistance twenty-four hours a day," veteran Master Cunha recalled. "She never failed to attend those who sought her . . . just when we thought that she was ready to go to bed, she was wide awake and ready to help whoever needed her." What Aunt Neiva "always wanted us to learn is this: Humility, Tolerance, and Love for others" (Cunha 2008, 30–31). "She had this intelligence, this way of communicating, that was special," veteran member Master Carlan told me.

> You could be yourself with her, rich, poor, beautiful, ugly, whatever you were, she treated everyone with love, with an amazing force of love. She was always teaching, there were always twenty, thirty mediums around her. She would attend patients and in between patients she talked and talked, teaching us about the spiritual planes. And one day I was there, and I looked at her and I had the vivid sense that God was speaking through her, because everything she said was so beautiful and perfect. I had the impression that it was God manifesting through her to teach us. She would never tell people what they should not do, she would speak in metaphors. Instead of saying "my son, do not beat your wife," she would say "yes, my son, the body is young, but the spirit is ancient." In other words, she would let that person know that they have a karmic inheritance and a responsibility and that their actions have consequences beyond this life. (Master Carlan interview, 2015)

Neiva's followers "were simple folk really, everyday people, workers," another veteran, Master Manoel, told me in 2015. "They were humble people, many were drivers, bricklayers, street sweepers, none of them were doctors [i.e., from the educated elite]. But Aunt Neiva believed in them."[37] In Neiva's eyes, these humble workers shared more than just the adverse circumstances that brought them initially to OSOEC. They were Jaguars, she told them, fellow members of Father White Arrow's spiritual tribe. Their present suffering was simply a karmic reckoning for errors committed over many lifetimes, part of the transcendental baggage that had brought them to her. As Master João Nunez informed me:

> When I came to the Valley I had a real spiritual encounter, I found myself. I learned that I am a Jaguar. The Doctrine helped me to become what I am today, to have what I have today. As a Jaguar I have spiritual baggage—disappointments and frustrations—but that heritage is also a strength. The past is never entirely past, it determines the present. You must look inside yourself. Everything in this system is for you to look inside of yourself and discover who you really are.

A Modern Religion for the Space Age

The Valley of the Dawn was built by and for a generation of Brazilians who experienced the great social transformations of the mid-twentieth century: the candangos who had left Brazil's agrarian past behind to share in the dream of the modern future promoted by the state's nationalist project. That project's lynchpin, the construction of Brasília, created new centers of power and economic opportunity, drawing populations and materials to the interior. But it also promised something more intangible: a utopian dream of progress that would deliver the nation from the sins of the past while advancing it "fifty years in five." Whereas Kubitshek and his mythmakers articulated this vision in the language of nationalism, Aunt Neiva and Mário Sassi expressed it in the language of religion.

Charged with interpreting Aunt Neiva's visionary experiences, Mário Sassi created a doctrinal foundation for the movement that was important for its internal organization and expansion. At its center was a sweeping, multilayered epic of progress, decline, and redemption centered on the Jaguars and their spiritual ancestors. Like all great epics, the Journey of the Jaguars contains numerous storylines and mythic themes, some internally generated, some borrowed from elite, literate culture, and some tapping into a rich vein of folklore stored in the bedrock of the country's collective imagination. Anthropologist Claude Lévi-Strauss famously called this synthetic process of creation "bricolage," and identified it as a characteristic pattern of mythological thought and a primary means through which humans give meaning and order to the world we live in (1966).

Outsiders often point to the kaleidoscopic character of the Journey of the Jaguars as evidence of its falseness, but for Valley members that is precisely what makes it so compelling. Within the narrative's capacious frame, novel ideas about space travel, the alien origins of human civilization, and progressive evolution coexist with traditionally religious figures like Jesus Christ and the spirits of Umbanda. This capaciousness allows Valley mediums to integrate past experiences with different religions while preserving a commitment to Christianity and to reconcile modern values with a deep sense that the world is suffused with spiritual forces.

Sassi utilized ideas from a globalized occultural milieu to present Neiva's spiritual revelations as belonging to an ancient wisdom tradition passed down through the ages through a hierarchy of Great Masters but updated for modern times. This spoke to Brazilians for whom science was the foundation of modern life but who "looked to religion for guidance as well" (Zeller 2010, 38).[38] Occultural metaphysics enabled Sassi to reinterpret entities from the world of popular Brazilian religions, like Aunt Neiva's chief spirit mentor Father White Arrow, as local avatars of highly evolved "planetary masters" working for spiritual progress and guiding humanity through the dawn of a New Age.

However, something more than the translation of an older conceptual system into the terms of newer one is at work here. The Capellans symbolize modernity and technological progress, but they also embody a deep uncertainty about the social effects of such progress and the need for a "spiritualized science" that measures advancement not solely in terms of technology but also in terms of the welfare of human beings and their access to the resources necessary for lives of dignity.

In offering its followers a cosmology more congruent with the Space Age—conversant with science and technology, couched in the language of empirical rationality, and promising self-knowledge, personal transformation, and evolution—the Valley of the Dawn also offers a different way of being modern.[39] Unlike the Brazilian state's vision of modernity, a project symbolized most concisely in its master plan for its capital city, the Valley of the Dawn affirms that human progress is not measured solely by advancements in technology and the rationalized forms of bureaucracy or in utopian ideals of egalitarianism via social engineering but also, more importantly, by moral evolution and "doctrinal conduct." The irony of Brasília is that the past had no place in its planners' vision of the New Era and in this refusal to recognize the weight of history, they ended up reproducing the very same inequities of the past (Holston 1999). Instead, the Valley of the Dawn proposes that by confronting the past and transforming it through moral and ritual action, the Jaguars can liberate themselves from its continued grip in the present and achieve the future they desire.

To be sure, the Valley's version of history is not that of historians. It is a mythological narrative—that is, a story that is not about events per se but about their meaning. In fantastical tales about times before our times, dimensions beyond the physical, and the cosmic beings that inhabit them, Aunt Neiva spoke to her followers about who they were, where they came from, and where they could go. She taught them that the past, with its karmic debts, could be transformed into a more evolved future and that the simple, rural folk of the land, like Tiãozinho, could become space engineers and live among the stars (Santos 2016b).

* * *

5
A Total Synesthetic Experience

At the heart of the religious impulse lies the capacity to imagine a world beyond the one we have before us. To do so requires a narrative, but it also requires the capacity to hold in abeyance the matter-of-fact expectation that the world of the senses is all there is.
— T. M. Luhrmann (2020a, 76)

Paracosms, Imagined Worlds, and the Process of Enchantment

Religious myths, like the Journey of the Jaguars, do not just exist in discursive form as oral or written narratives. They also are communicated in images, colors, sounds, symbols, hymns, prayers, and even smells, forming a total sensory environment through which the stories seep into the deepest parts of one's being. In this way, myths begin to shape people's perceptions and their dreams, becoming part of a common language and structure of thought that gives imaginative ballast to the otherwise unseen and transcendent. Bit by bit, people begin to inhabit the stories that shape their common life, organizing their ideas of the self and its possibilities within the universe revealed in the stories. That transformation is the subject of this chapter.

For Valley members, the Journey of the Jaguars is the narrative heart of a vividly detailed imagined world: an intersubjectively shared, holistic reality that they enter into and experience through their physical senses and imagination, rather than a set of beliefs that they accept on a cognitive level (Pierini 2020). In other words, it is primarily through an accumulation of sensory experiences that the Valley's imagined world comes to *feel* real to adherents: they begin to sense the presence of spiritual energies that are invoked and released in Valley rituals and to perceive the determinative role of karma in their lives. They start to understand difficult interpersonal relationships as the working out of past-life debts and everyday triumphs as evidence of spiritual merit. The pretos velhos, caboclos, and otherwise invisible denizens of the Valley's imagined world become as familiar as adherents' own heartbeat. And this process transforms people.

This transformation does not happen all at once, however, and it does not happen for everyone to the same degree. The felt reality of the Valley's imagined world is continually produced by and for members through a combination of multisensory immersion, inner sense cultivation, embodied action, and, most of all, practice. It takes constant effort to make an invisible otherworld feel real, as the work of anthropologist T. M. Luhrmann demonstrates. In her book *How God Becomes Real: Kindling the Presence of Invisible Others* (2020a), Luhrmann refers to these vividly imagined otherworlds as paracosms and explains how they become intimate realities for many religious practitioners.

The term "paracosm" was first used in the literature on developmental psychology to describe elaborately detailed and highly developed fantasy worlds created by children, often with their own languages, histories, geographies, and cultures.[1] Typically, paracosms are private universes that fade away as the child grows older and becomes more engaged in the outside world. If sustained over a long period of time, however, a childhood paracosm can become the foundation for creative works of art, such as writer J. R. R. Tolkien's tales of Middle Earth, filmmaker George Lucas's Star Wars series, or the epic saga of the Vivian girls depicted in outsider artist Henry Darger's drawings.

More recently, the concept of paracosm has been expanded beyond the childhood imagination and applied to shared forms of imaginative world-building among adults, such as the alternative universes created within role-playing games (Laycock 2015), fan fiction (Barnes 2015), or, in Luhrmann's case, the ways that evangelical Christians enter into vividly imagined relationships with God (Luhrmann 2018; 2020a). Like the invisible worlds conjured by children or artists, these paracosms are built around a master narrative that incorporates both real-world and imaginary elements, and this mixture, along with an abundance of vivid detail, gives them an immersive, all-absorbing quality. Unlike the childhood form, however, these paracosms are collective and intersubjectively shared. The number of people involved and the high level of organization necessary to sustain a collective paracosm further enhances its felt realness for participants. For Luhrmann, what defines a paracosm is the specificity of detail, the emotionally charged nature of the individual's relationship with the paracosmic world, and how that world is internalized in ways that become personally meaningful and transformative. The paradox of the paracosm, she writes, is that it is both collective and private, shared and deeply personal.

While all religions propose imagined worlds—universes we inhabit before birth or after death, realms outside the dimensions of space and time, or heavens and underworlds peopled by gods, deities, spirits, saints, ancestors, or other kinds of special beings—not all religions become paracosms for their followers. When they do, Luhrmann argues, practitioners begin to live imaginatively within the stories told within that tradition. Whether they are conveyed in written scriptures or through prayers, hymns, and ritual reenactments; in the form of suggestive fragments or exact details, these stories become personally vivid and emotionally engaging for their audiences in ways that spark a perceptual shift. The narrated world becomes elided with the ordinary in such a way that otherworld of the stories begins to feel viscerally real to people. Its sacred beings are experienced not as abstract figures to be worshipped or obeyed but as agentive beings who respond to, interact with, and enter into reciprocative relationships with their followers. This intimate and deeply felt interaction—this level of imaginative and affective engagement on the part of the follower with the story—is what transforms a religion's imagined world into a paracosm. It also is what differentiates a religious paracosm from a fictional one (Luhrmann 2020a, 48).

How does the paracosmic world come to feel real? Luhrmann discusses the mechanics of this process in detail, but two factors are key: narrative specificity and imaginative absorption. The former is important because expressive, detailed stories capture people's imagination and center their attention, enabling them to enter into and interact with the paracosmic world in ways that, with practice, make it feel real (2020a, 32). "The more richly detailed the shared imaginative landscape," Luhrmann explains, "the more vividly individuals can rework it as their own" (2020a, 32).

While narrative provides the template, imaginative absorption is what transforms story into lived reality. This term describes a cognitive and emotional state in which the individual becomes so engrossed in the paracosmic world of the narrative that it begins to feel like a reality that can be apprehended through the senses. This involves a state of heightened awareness, developed through training and practice, whereby the boundaries between the individual's inner, subjective world and the outer, objective world become progressively blurred.

In such a state of imaginative absorption, gods, spirits, and invisible others may be experienced as palpably present and responsive—as something simultaneously inside and outside of subjective consciousness, both imagined and actual. Luhrmann calls these moments "kindlings." Over time, such kindlings "change the way in which the person envisions the boundary between the everyday and spiritual worlds, making it seem increasingly permeable. This, in turn, enhances the chances that the person will experience further kindlings" (Johnston 2021). Moments in which the invisible other is experienced as present and responsive are important to people because they provide phenomenological evidence, outside of the testimony of others, that reinforces their commitment to the paracosmic world (Luhrmann 2020a, xiv).

Like a fire that burns steadily if given sufficient kindling, thereby transforming its fuel from one state of matter to another, the accumulation of these moments changes people's experience of the everyday, material world. The ordinary becomes enchanted: suffused with deep meanings connected to the transcendent realities detailed in the paracosmic narrative. Otherwise prosaic moments may be experienced as hierophanies, that is, occasions when the invisible other is felt to be immediately and physically present. These experiences can cause people to reassess their lives in ways that have physical, psychological, and emotional benefits for them, a subject I address in Chapter 7.

The scholarship on paracosms by Luhrmann and others indicates that individuals deeply involved with religious paracosms begin to perceive events in their lives as evidence of a larger pattern. Reassured by this pattern, they discover a sense of order and meaning in which experiences of loss, suffering, hopelessness, fear, and chaos are converted into purpose. In essence, the paracosmic storyline offers people an alternative cognitive model for understanding the self and its relationship to the world and others. And because the kindling process occurs in the context of a larger community, the cognitive and affective transformations it sparks are further fueled by a group of supportive others engaged in their own parallel journeys.

At the Valley of the Dawn, kindlings happen in two major ways. The first is through a lengthy, multi-level process of training referred to as "mediumistic development," during which participants learn to cultivate certain habits of mental and somatic perception. Luhrmann terms this kind of training "inner sense cultivation." The second is through participants' immersion in the Valley's material environment, with its richly detailed vestments and insignia, colorful architectural spaces, elaborate iconography, and choreographed rituals that stimulate all of the senses at once. These two processes, mediumistic training and immersion in a multisensory environment, operate in tandem to create a felt presence: an accumulation of sensory, perceptual, and embodied experiences that imbues the Valley's imagined world with a palpable realness or verisimilitude for adherents.

Language and Metaphor

As newcomers to the Valley deepen their involvement with its imagined world, they learn a shared elementary language—words, concepts, themes, and metaphors—through which they begin to remake themselves and their understanding of reality. Some of the structuring metaphors that organize the Valley's imagined world derive from the world of science and technology: references to vibrations, electromagnetic fields, frequencies, polarities, currents, and forces fill the Valley's vernacular.[2] Thus, the Mother Temple and its grounds are "a cosmic power plant," the Doctrine is a "current," mediums become "ionized" and "tune into" their spirit mentors, and mediumship is a process of receiving, transmitting, and transforming "energies." This vocabulary helps mediums develop a sense that the world is permeated by invisible and subtle substances that have an intentionality and propulsive force, that can be directed and accumulated, and whose residues can impregnate material objects like uniforms. It also simultaneously evokes and sustains participants' sense that the Doctrine is a "spiritual science."

Another set of metaphors derives from esoteric traditions. In its most simplified form, esoteric thought posits a hidden truth about the universe that can be apprehended only through direct experience, intuition, contact with non-human entities, or some other extraordinary state of consciousness (Melton 2020).[3] To borrow Kocku von Stuckrad's formulation, at the heart of esoteric movements is a claim to "real" or absolute knowledge and the *means* of making this knowledge available (Von Stuckrad 2005, 10). Often this involves some sort of initiatory structure or practical training. At the Valley, hidden knowledge is associated particularly with the ancient wisdom tradition of the "Great East," that is, India and Tibet. It is embodied and transmitted by a lineage of enlightened masters or "Great Initiates," among them Aunt Neiva's Tibetan master Umahã as well as the Dalai Lama and Jesus himself.

Valley members attest that through her own initiation by Umahã, Aunt Neiva brought this transformative knowledge to the Valley, institutionalizing it in the mestrado. References to "the Great East" (*o Grande Oriente*) and the "enchanted worlds of the Himalayas" regularly feature in the community's corpus of prayers and ritual formulae. Members describe the Doctrine as an "initiatory-evangelical system" that works with forces from the Indian Space Current (*a Corrente Indiana do Espaço*) and the White Current of the Greater East (*a Corrente Branca do Oriente Maior*).

The term "current" signifies on both metaphoric levels. In its more restricted sense, it refers to an energetic force field like an electrical current, but it also designates a particular spiritual tradition through which adepts access spiritual energies. Thus, Valley members refer to their own and other religious traditions as currents. Learning to feel and "manipulate" these energies is the first step and the goal of mediumistic training, which culminates in a series of "initiatory steps" through which the initiate is transformed from a novice into a master. This learning process happens formally in courses but also informally in conversations with other mediums and through being immersed in the Valley's imagined world.

Master Alexandre explained the process of energy manipulation to me in this way:

> The simplest way to talk about these energies is that all living beings on Earth have energies in them. Humans are the maximum condensation of universal energies on the physical plane. Our thoughts generate energy, destructive thoughts generate destructive energies. One bad word begets other bad words. And the positive energy that we talk about is simply having positive thoughts: thoughts of hope, believing that everything can be transformed, that a patient can get better, that a person who made a mistake can get it right, this generates another energy. If you suffer intensely for something, you generate a certain energy, and if you can deal with that suffering in a more conscious way, you change that energy. The initiate is the person who has the ability to consciously transform these energies, to modify them, to transmute negative into positive, this is what we call manipulation. Through our rituals we Jaguars are able to transmute and transform the energies of everyone, the entire planet. From people who are suffering in other states, on other continents, to people who have no hope of living anymore, we are able to manipulate those energies.

Just as humans represent the "maximum condensation of universal energies on the physical plane," so do spirits on the astral plane. And because energy can be neither created nor destroyed, Valley members reason, the energies condensed in the form of a human being persist in spirit form upon death. Having passed through the portal of death and shed its material envelope, the spirit proceeds to the level in the spiritual planes that corresponds to its state of moral evolution.

Lower-level spirits are said to inhabit the denser vibrational planes closest to the earth. When a medium "lowers" their vibration by engaging in negative thoughts or behaviors, they can become vulnerable to these spirits. Spirits of light, by contrast, occupy a much higher vibrational plane and radiate positive energies. To be recognized by human beings on the physical plane, these highly evolved spirits may take on different *roupagens* or forms, manifesting in their mediums as pretos velhos, caboclos, healing doctors (*médicos de cura*), knights (*cavaleiros*), gypsies (*ciganos*), and other spirit entities cultivated in Kardecist Spiritism, Umbanda, and other Afro-Brazilian religions and familiar to many Brazilians.

Conceptualizing Mediumship

All of the work of the Valley is based on the technique of manipulating energies. The force that allows one to control different types of energies is mediumship. (Sassi 2004, 13)

Valley doctrine teaches that all human beings possess the faculty of mediumship, which it defines as the ability to connect to spiritual planes and to receive, transmit, and transform different types of energies. This is understood to be a biological capacity linked to the circulation of a "subtle energy" known as ectoplasm or animal magnetism. As Sassi explained it, ectoplasm is produced by all "organisms on Earth," but in humans it "achieves a different quality and an elevated quantity." Its "fundamental property is to put into contact two different vibrational planes, two dimensions" (Sassi 2004, 13). When ectoplasm concentrates in certain regions of the human body, the person becomes more receptive to energies, or "vibrations," from dimensions otherwise imperceptible to the ordinary senses (See Pierini 2020, 137). "The medium," Sassi wrote, "is a person who admits and knows this energy through experience and seeks to be able to consciously control it" (Sassi 2004, 14).

Like other Spiritist groups, the Valley of the Dawn holds that an excess of ectoplasm can lead to a state of psychic imbalance or "spiritual disequilibrium" if the person does not know how to properly assimilate or distribute that energy. Spiritual disequilibrium is considered a sign of undeveloped mediumship and, if untreated, can lead to physical, psychological, or social problems, such as chronic illness or persistent troubles with relationships or financial matters. By "manipulating" this excess ectoplasm, an instruction manual for mediums explains, the medium "transforms that vital energy for his benefit and, later, for the benefit of other people. Little by little he begins to encounter his equilibrium, his intimate fulfillment and, above all, begins to evolve spiritually through his mediumistic work" (*Manual de Instruções*, 13). Undeveloped mediumship is only one of the diagnostic etiologies employed at the Valley. Other kinds of disturbances, such as depression, obsessive thoughts, or addictive behaviors, may be diagnosed as the influence of low-level spirits who have attached themselves to their victim for different reasons, a subject that I address in more detail in Chapter 7.

As established by Aunt Neiva, an integral part of the Valley's mission is to provide spiritual assistance to the public through rituals of disobsessive, healing which are said to release the victim from the influence of low-level spirits and guide the latter to their proper place in the spiritual world. This happens through the coordinated efforts of a pair of mediums: an *apará* or incorporation medium who incorporates the obsessing spirit and a *doutrinador* or indoctrination medium who "indoctrinates" the spirit, educating it about the reality of the spiritual planes and the process of evolution.

By becoming aware of and learning to use their mediumship to help incarnate and disincarnate spirits, Valley members believe that they are working within the Law of Assistance, established by Jesus Christ, thereby assuaging some of their own karmic debts. As Mário Sassi explained in his pamphlet aimed at visitors, "medium is the denomination of the former patient who, due to his transcendental obligations, felt the necessity to develop his mediumship and participate in the Current, that is, to work mediumistically" (2004, 9).

Developing one's mediumship, therefore, is the first step toward becoming a recognized member of the community. It also is the first step in a multistage, multi-sensory, and crossmodal training process whereby participants learn the kind of inner sense cultivation that helps them to experience the Valley's imagined otherworld as vividly phenomenal, that is, as an objective reality with which they interact. In other words, mediumistic development is vital to the real-making process as Luhrmann describes it.

Apará and Doutrinador

The Valley teaches that the faculty of unconscious or semi-conscious mediumship embodied in the apará has existed since the time of King Solomon, but Aunt Neiva created a new kind of medium: the doutrinador or conscious medium able to control mediumistic phenomena and indoctrinate lower-level spirits (Siqueira et al. 2010, 154).[4] Doutrinadores are said to transmit the superior force of their mentor spirits while remaining conscious and in total control of their cognitive faculties. Aparás, by contrast, enter a semi-conscious state in order to become instruments for spiritual entities at various stages of evolution, not only low-level spirits who remain connected to the material plane, but also highly evolved spirits of light who have committed themselves to helping humanity by working in the Indian Space Current.[5] By working together, the two mediums are said to unite spiritual intuition with reason, the force of the moon with the force of the sun, forming a perfect pair.

In practice, this means that the apará cedes her body and voice to the spirits, while the doutrinador uses reason to persuade low-level spirits of the truth of their condition and an initiatory key (*chave iniciática*) or ritual formula to elevate them to the spiritual plane where they can continue their evolutionary path. "The duty of the doutrinador is to indoctrinate," Aunt Neiva explained in a 1974 letter to her followers, "talking amicably with the spirit, seeking to clarify it, to continue being its friend while delivering it [to its proper place in the spiritual world], thereby upholding his or her responsibility before the Mentors" (Aunt Neiva May 7, 1974).[6] Elaborating on this idea, veteran member Master Itamir informed me, "the doutrinador is that person who has the gift of speaking well, the art of being able to converse with the spirit, to teach the spirit."

Because doutrinadores bring the superior faculty of the intellect to bear on "the mediumistic intuition," they also are able to correctly interpret the spiritual knowledge transmitted from the ethereal planes through aparás in accordance with Valley doctrine. Mário Sassi explained,

> Who will then be able to interpret a spiritual orientation with authenticity?—The answer is unique: the Doutrinador. Only this Medium has the conditions to correctly interpret a message, simply because his normal reasoning is illuminated by his mediumship. The Doutrinador listens, reads, compares and synthesizes with a much greater possibility of immunity [from personal bias]." (Sassi 1974, 87–88; cited in César 1977b, 462)

Hence Doutrinadores "are responsible for lecturing, teaching spiritual development courses to aspiring mediums, and exercising command of [the Order's] spiritual works" (Sassi 1974, 87–88). A Valley member interviewed by Brazilian scholar Joice Meire Rodrigues echoed this sentiment, which I also heard frequently during my time at the Mother Temple:

> The doutrinador is more intellectually inclined and more knowledgeable and he is the one that orients the apará when they are incorporating. He controls the negative energies of disincarnate spirits who are trapped in the material world. His presence is necessary to maintain equilibrium and order during the rituals of incorporation. (Rodrigues 2011, 159)

This division of spiritual labor between the apará and the doutrinador is reinforced and communicated through a complex system of symbolic associations analyzed in more detail in Chapter 6. For now, I will note that the two mediums are differentiated visually through overlapping sets of symbols that appear on their garments and accessories. Doutrinadores, who represent conscious rationality, are associated with the sun and the element gold. In addition to a stylized image of the sun and golden trim, their distinguishing emblem is a black cross draped with a white mantle. Aparás, associated with intuition and the force of the moon, are represented by a crescent moon and the element silver as well as the symbol of a red triangle enclosing an open book (representing the Gospels) (see Image 5.1 and 5.2).

Mediumistic Development

In the first phase, the novice—or aspirant—develops his mediumship to obtain his own personal equilibrium, to put himself in a position of harmony with the world around him. Once this is achieved, he is credentialed to assist others, which, in fact, is just the continuation of his own development. The more the medium works, the more he learns and gets to know better how to use his energies. Constant progress grants him consecrations that bring him personal fulfillment. (Sassi 2004, 14)

While mediumship is a biological capacity that everyone is believed to possess, not everyone shares in the mission of Father White Arrow's tribe of Jaguars. In order to develop one's mediumship at the Valley, an individual

Image 5.1 Symbol of the doutrinador (cross with draped mantle). Credit Márcia Alves

Image 5.2 Symbol of the apará (triangle with open book). Credit Márcia Alves

must be invited to do so by the spiritual entities of the Indian Space Current. Typically, such invitations are extended during the ritual of the Thrones (*Tronos*), where preto velho spirits, communicating through an apará, consult with patients who have come to the Valley seeking healing. The majority of Valley members thus were once patients themselves. By developing their mediumship, they transform what previously was experienced as an affliction into a capacity to heal others similarly afflicted.[7]

Once an individual has received an invitation and decided to pursue a path of spiritual development at the Valley of the Dawn, she or he completes a series of "development classes" taught by trained instructors.[8] These are arranged in a hierarchy of levels and initiatory steps (*passos iniciáticos*), each of which is said to permanently transform the participant at a psycho-energetic level, capacitating them to work with ever more powerful *forças* or spiritual energies. As the individual completes each stage of development, he or she is "consecrated" in a special ceremony and earns the right to wear specific clothing and insignia, participate in certain rituals, and take on specific duties in accordance with their position within the Valley's complex, multileveled bureaucracy.[9] "It is a chain, it is a sequence," Master Froes told me. "Each consecration is a step, a magnetic pulse that we search for, each is part of a transcendental heritage."

Along the way, participants are immersed in a multi-sensory or plurimedial environment that works in and through the senses, focusing on the phenomenological body as the instrument for perceiving, transforming, and emitting energies. Valley members often describe each stage as a step along a path of spiritual and intellectual development through which they are transformed, acquiring greater knowledge of themselves—their capacities and karmic trajectory—in an encounter with their higher self, referred to in Valley parlance as the "individuality."

In the development classes, which combine theory with hands-on training, participants are taught different techniques of quieting and focusing the mind so that they can "harmonize with the spiritual planes," a process called "mediumization" (*mediunização*).[10] They learn to perceive the energetic processes associated with mediumship in their bodies and to discern and differentiate the various spirit entities recognized at the Valley. They practice "manipulating energy" and the bodily postures, gestures, and techniques involved in the group's major rituals. In lectures they receive details of their shared history as Jaguars and their mission of advancing humanity's spiritual evolution. These lectures also expose mediums-in-training to the finer points of the movement's metaphysics and doctrine. Throughout, participants are encouraged to reflect on how Valley teachings are confirmed by reason as well as their own experiences and life histories and to meet regularly with their cohorts or more advanced masters for further discussion.

Given the intricacy of the Jaguars' transcendental history and the large number of rituals, each with its own choreography and script, there is much to learn. "It takes a long time to digest the Doctrine," Nymph Geny warned me early on in my research, "a lot of study, a lot of meditation, and no one person knows all of it." "The Doctrine is learning," another member said simply. "We are always attending new lectures, we are always meeting to talk about the doctrine," Nymph Valda, a medium-in-training, told me. "It seems like every day, every hour, you learn a little more."

As Nymph Valda's comments suggest, the desire for knowledge is not limited to a theologically inclined minority. Valley members at all levels share a commitment to learning. This is evident in the many informal study groups organized by mediums as well as the sheer quantity of didactic information about the Doctrine available in venues that range from official publications to unauthorized blogs and internet sites. Some veteran members have taken it upon themselves to continue Sassi's work of systematization by creating encyclopedias and dictionaries, and it is common for people to pass around among themselves these and other ancillary study materials.

Guiding this knowledge production is the principle of "master teaching master" (*mestre ensinando mestre*): the notion that all Jaguars have the right to, and responsibility for, doctrinal knowledge according to their abilities but that everyone has something to share because of their own lived experience of the Doctrine. This ethos was well captured by anthropologist James Holston, who wrote:

> What has never failed to impress me is that most mediums discuss their "scientific study" with remarkable intensity. People who otherwise appear quite humble become even physically transformed—faces animated, gestures assured, bodies confident—with the new vocabulary and sense of discourse they learn. Although Doctrinators in particular consider themselves intellectuals, I have also met many Aparás who are passionate interlocutors of the doctrine. . . . As the Valley's public spaces are devoted to rituals, curing, classes, and study groups, the whole place always seems abuzz with the activities of learning. (1999, 620)

Indeed, with its many courses, lectures, instructors, diplomas and certificates, insignia of rank, and various degrees and titles, the Valley presents itself as a university dedicated to fostering the spiritual advancement of both incarnate and disincarnate spirits. This contrasts markedly with the reality of the educational system in Brazil, where higher education is the province of a small elite and poverty prevents many from completing their schooling. Unlike the Brazilian state, the Valley of the Dawn offers an education that is premised on merit, not wealth or privilege, and is available to all regardless of their intellectual capacities.[11] In a society in which few have access to higher education, the ability to use the language of education and its symbols is a powerful mark of social distinction, carrying prestige and conferring social dignity.

It is worth recalling that Aunt Neiva scarcely had a primary-school education, while Mário Sassi had a frustrated relationship with public education in Brazil and largely was self-taught. Many of their followers shared (and continue to share) a longing for what education promises in terms of knowledge, self-improvement, and dignity, as well as its social capital in the form of status and social advancement. Numerous veteran members whom I got to know shared with me stories of growing up in rural poverty and leaving school early in order to work and support their families. A few were able to finish their schooling as adults only after a protracted period of study at one of Brasília's night schools while also working full time. Others were not. But all spoke with great pride about the various "consecrations" (*consagrações*) and "classifications" (*classificações*) they had achieved at the Valley. Everyone can become a master at the Valley of the Dawn because everyone has access to the mestrado.

As a handbook for developing mediums puts it,

> The Master is not the teacher who teaches the lesson and applies the paddle to the student. He is the medium who has evolved within the Doctrine of the Dawn and lives his mediumistic life with love and assiduity. He is not the most cultured or the one who knows the most, but rather is the wisest. Generally, he is the humblest, most simple, most compassionate, most tolerant medium who has assimilated the profound meaning of [the dictum] "the pain of others is always greater than your own . . . " The Master is the one who follows the precepts of Christ Jesus. (Sassi 1977, 12)

First Stage: Aspirant

The path that leads to the mestrado begins with a series of seven classes held on consecutive Sundays. These classes offer a basic introduction to the concepts necessary for understanding the Doctrine, but the main focus is teaching "the science of mediumship" to participants, who are known as aspirants (*aspirantes*). Attendance is taken seriously and if a student misses more than one class in the series they are removed from the group and must repeat the course at a later time. Individuals are free to stop attending at any time in accordance with the Valley's emphasis on free will.

Determining which type of mediumship an individual demonstrates is one of the first tasks. This happens via a "mediumship test" (*teste de mediunidade*) taken at the end of the first class whose results determine whether the individual will be trained as an apará or a doutrinador. From this point on, aspirants are divided into two groups and at the end of each subsequent lesson will attend a specialized training session according to their particular faculty of mediumship. These determinations are not set in stone, however. There are some people who train and work as a doutrinador for a time and then discover that they are an apará or vice versa. In such cases, the individual simply completes the practical training portion for their current form of mediumship.

Throughout this first stage of mediumistic development, aspirants wear a special uniform, known colloquially as the *branquinha* or "little white": a white shirt and black pants for men and a long white dress for women (see Image 5.3). They also use a sash known as a *fita*, which loops over the right shoulder and descends diagonally across the chest to the left hip. The fita is described as a "portal of disintegration" that protects the wearer from negative energies. On a practical level, it bears the corresponding symbol marking the medium as either a doutrinador or apará, enabling Valley members to quickly identify potential partners for ritual works.

As mediums develop and ascend through the hierarchy, they will wear different types of clothing and accessories, but the fita will become a permanent part of their uniform. Each item of clothing, each color and symbol, is believed to have its own purpose within a greater force field of energies. White, for example, is said to be "totally impervious to many vibrations and forms of energy" and therefore is appropriate for beginners to use as well as in rituals dealing with "heavy charges" (C. L. Zelaya 2009, 76). Black acts as "a true magnetic magnet for negative forces" and thus is used for rituals of disobsessive healing. Brown is a neutral color with no specific energetic attributes, but rather symbolizes Saint Francis of Assisi, said to be one of Father White Arrow's many terrestrial incarnations.

Guided by their instructors, aspirants learn to attend to a complex inner landscape of bodily sensations, feelings, and intuitions associated with mediumship. In practice sessions they are taught to feel the energetic presence of spirits in their own bodies (aparás) or environment (doutrinadores) and to discern the different categories of spirit entities recognized at the Valley. Aparás in particular must learn to recognize and differentiate among the highly evolved spirits of light who serve them as personalized mentors and whom they will incorporate in different healing rituals. These mentors are believed to manifest themselves in three specific "*roupagens*," literally garments or guises: pretos velhos, caboclos, and healing doctors (*médicos de cura*). Valley members describe the latter as the spirits of former physicians. These entities also are found within other Spiritist groups, where, embodied in a medium, they perform spiritual or "psychic" surgeries—and sometimes minor physical ones as well.[12] At the Valley, the medicos de cura transmit healing energy to patients in specific rituals.

Image 5.3 Branquinha uniform or "little whites." Credit Márcia Alves

For some mediums-in-training, a spirit's presence may feel like a localized change in the body's temperature or a sensation of pressure, constriction, or tingling. For others, it may manifest as a thinning of conscious awareness, a feeling of disassociation, or a sudden intuition or emotion. Some describe feeling their pulse quicken or their body shaking or moving as if controlled by some other force. These sensations may be subtle or intense, soothing or agitating, joyful or distressing. "It is not easy to explain in words," Nymph Flaviane, an apará with seven years of experience, told me of the changes that she felt during this period.

> It is an inexplicable thing, it is something you feel, something you experience, something you know in the depths of your being. When you start developing [your mediumship] you feel your body shiver, you feel something different inside you, your heart races as if something inside you has changed.

Zack, an apará from Australia who was completing the first set of development classes when I spoke with him in 2015, said:

> For me it feels like someone is literally standing behind me grabbing my arms and moving them, like a marionette. Imagine a person six feet tall standing behind you and grabbing you from under the arms and lifting you up and just moving you. I feel a lot of energy, my hands shake, my hands sometimes stop and move.

Aspirants are encouraged to understand these various phenomenological sensations as external forces that, with practice, can be manipulated and transformed through ritual. Pierini aptly characterized this as an "ongoing education of perception" through which newcomers learn how to *feel* the presence of spirits as a psychosomatic phenomenon rather than absorbing a belief (2020, 166).[13]

Mediums in development often describe what Luhrmann and Julia Cassaniti termed "bodily affordances." These are events of the body that happen in many social settings but are identified as religious only in those settings in which they afford, or make available, an interpretation that makes sense within a given religion (2014, S334). For example, all humans experience strong emotions, but these will be seen as religiously significant only in settings where they make sense as an indicator of the supernatural.

At the Valley, the most common bodily affordances associated with mediumistic development are headaches and other bodily pains. These are interpreted as physical evidence of the inner transformations taking place within the bodies of participants that prepare them for initiation. When Givanildo, an apará in his early thirties, began the development process, he told me that he suffered terrible headaches, which he attributed to his "chakras being cleansed and opened." Similarly, Pierini reported that for the first month of her development she was affected by strong headaches of a kind she had not previously experienced, which diminished after her Sunday development class (2020, 164). Other mediums with whom I spoke experienced back pain or fevers that they attributed to their development. These bodily events reinforce the idea of mediumship as a biological capacity whose actualization changes people on a psychosomatic level. As Pierini concluded, the process of developing mediumship is " 'felt' as acting simultaneously upon the different dimensions of the medium, producing a transformation, a sense of becoming" (2020, 165).

At the same time that they are cultivating a finely attuned awareness of their psychosomatic state, aspirants also are learning the social codes that govern mediumship at the Valley of the Dawn and the repertoire of bodily postures, gestures, and ritual techniques through which it is expressed corporally. For example, unlike the spirit-based traditions of Candomblé and Umbanda where incorporating spirits dance and sing or exhibit uncontrolled movements, the Doctrine teaches that aparás should work with eyes closed and a minimum of movement. Doutrinadors are expected to work with eyes open and with an elegance of bearing, performing the various ritual techniques expected of them exactly as taught without personal flourishes of any sort.

Even as it defines the spirits in abstract terms as energies or vibrational frequencies, the Doctrine also draws on a rich tradition of endowing otherwise incorporeal spirits with distinctive character traits, storylines, moral valences, and mannerisms of speech, posture, and gesture. For the most part, these are well known, since the spiritual beings cultivated at the Valley are archetypal in nature: symbolically vivid characters present in popular religions and folklore and deeply embedded in the Brazilian imagination. Thus, each of the different lines (*linhas*) of "spirits of light" who collectively comprise the Indian Space Current embodies a cluster of character traits and resonant themes, or what Claude Levi-Strauss (1955) referred to as mythemes: the elderly slave whose great suffering gave him insight into the human condition, the noble Indian at one with the forces of nature, the valiant knight who rescues those in distress, the skilled doctor, the beautiful princess.

These traits are communicated through an expressive poetry of the body in which a gesture or posture, even a word, evokes the whole. Just as a skilled actor can convey a character's entire personality with a well-chosen detail, allowing the audience to fill in the backstory, the spirits become real in the imaginative space between a set of stylized cues and the shared subtext evoked by those cues. Thus, the preto velho's backbreaking life of toil is signaled in the hunched posture of his medium, his humble wisdom expressed in old-fashioned turns of speech and an unpretentious manner. The torment of the *sofredor* or suffering spirit is evident in tightly clenched fists, the vital force of the caboclo in a vigorous chest-thumping and upright bearing. Mediums-in-training are given some guidance as they master these expressive codes, but for most this is knowledge they already possess from earlier experiences with spirit-based religions or through popular culture.[14]

"With each incorporation you feel a different sensation," a young medium named Edu told me.

> Sometimes you feel like you are swimming, other times you feel like you are floating, each one brings a different sensation. I like to incorporate pretos velhos because you feel love, calm, patience, like you don't have any problems in life. And with caboclos, it is pure happiness, the energy of the virgin forests, a strong energy.

Here is how Master Anderson, an apará who had been a member for eleven years at the time we spoke, described the respective "energetic profiles" of different entities:

> With a preto velho, the energy is more folksy, familial, like a wise grandparent. And you feel calm, a feeling of security and love. With a caboclo you feel the energy of the forests, a strong energy, like an Indian running, fishing, pounding on his chest, receiving the energies of the forest. It is a refreshing, invigorating energy that feels purifying. The energy of a sofredor is heavy, the energy of hatred. It is like a twisted feeling in the center of your being, an anguish. There are some aparás who even see the sofredor as a deformed spirit, like a monkey. Sometimes it is tearing at its head or clawing its throat, so you might feel an intense headache or like your throat is blocked.

Zack, the Australian medium-in-training, described to me the first time that he had incorporated a low-level obsessor spirit:

> There came a point where I started feeling angry. And then like, all of a sudden, it was just like, bam. And apparently, I clenched my hands, I did not even do it by choice, my hands just sort of went together and you know, when you have so much rage you just feel like you are going to explode? That is exactly what happened to me. It was happening and I was like, holy shit, what is going on? Oh, wait it is an obsessor, a lost brother. And then it was like I was looking down from a bird's eye view and I saw rocks and crystals, and I do not know why, but I just knew it was the bottom of a well and this dude who was coming through had been killed and left down there and completely forgotten. It just came to me in a flash: that is it, that is who this obsessor is! And man, was he frustrated. Like it was rage, but it was more so anguish and injustice.

Although they can seem like retrograde stereotypes—the wise slave who offers comforting counsel, or the proud, vigorous Indian at one with the forest—these archetypal characters afford imaginative entrance into the stories of people whose lives have been excluded from dominant narratives of Brazilian history. They enable mediums to tap into reservoirs of folk knowledge and channel otherwise inchoate feelings into expressive form. These entities also represent a valued form of knowledge, subverting the prevailing order that associates knowledge and power with white people. Over time, Valley mediums develop rich, layered relationships with the spirit mentors incorporated by themselves and others.

The first level of mediumistic training concludes with the *Emplacamento*, when participants receive a badge (*placa*) listing the name of their main spirit mentor. The placa is pinned to the front of the white uniforms that all aspirants wear. Those who have received their badges are referred to as *emplacado* mediums and are permitted to work in certain "sectors of spiritual work" in the Temple. Thus, mediumistic training also is a process of "enskillment" in that initiates actively practice what they are learning by participating in various rituals of disobsessive healing performed at the Valley alongside more experienced mediums (Pierini 2020).

In order to be considered fully developed, *emplacado* mediums must complete three additional "initiatory steps," each comprising a series of lectures and a culminating ritual. As the levels advance, the content of the lectures becomes more theoretical. Participants receive more detailed explanations of mediumship, the operation of karma, the distinction between individuality and the personality, the structure of the spiritual planes, what happens at death, and other points of Valley doctrine and metaphysics. They also learn about particularly resonant episodes in the Jaguars' shared mythological past.

Each initiatory step is said to endow the participant with specific "mantras of force" that permanently transform her at a psycho-energetic level and mediate her contact with the higher spiritual planes (Pierini 2020, 155–159). These transformations are manifested externally through an astonishing array of titles, insignia, articles of ritual clothing, and privileges that announce the wearer's rank and position within the Valley's overlapping spiritual and bureaucratic power structure. In this way, hidden capacities are made visible, materializing what is otherwise an interior process linked with the acquisition of esoteric knowledge and forces believed to transform the self. Both the gradual nature of the process and its performative display heighten the sense among participants that they are being transformed spiritually. At the same time, the garments, insignia, and other forms of material expression further immerse people in the Valley's imagined world, reinforcing its status as a sensually evident reality.

The Initiatory Steps

The levels of the hierarchy of the mestrado are established according to what our spiritual mentors project onto our plane. At the top of the hierarchy was Aunt Neiva, as if she were the "apex of a pyramid," generating a descending force following the Official Call, where the aspirants are at the base of the pyramid. (Santos 2012)

The first initiatory step is called the Dharman Oxinto initiation (*iniciação Dharman Oxinto*), and it requires three preparatory classes.[15] Aunt Neiva told her followers that Dharman Oxinto means "on the path to God" in the language of the spirit worlds. Instructors explain that to embark on this initiatory step signals the individual's commitment before God that they are consciously assuming a journey of self-transformation and spiritual development. Unlike the other initiation ceremonies that the community performs, the Dharman Oxinto initiation is not open to the public. Only those involved in the ceremony as participants or officiants are permitted to attend and all are expected to refrain from discussing it even among themselves (Pierini 2020, 156). Despite these injunctions, descriptions of the ceremony circulate widely.

This first initiatory step is laden with multiple allusions to the transformative power of esoteric wisdom associated with ancient Egypt and the Himalayas, two civilizations that are important within the Jaguars' transcendental heritage as sites of past incarnations and as repositories of spiritual forces summoned in certain rituals. The ceremony itself is held to derive from an ancient Egyptian rite, the initiation of Osiris, which was "carried out in the Royal Chamber of the Great Pyramid" by priestesses with whom Aunt Neiva was associated in one of her previous lifetimes (Acioly 2018).

The figure of Osiris recurs in various esoteric traditions, usually as a representation of spiritual transformation or the death of the lower self and its regeneration in higher form through initiation into esoteric mysteries (McLaren 2016). As Carmem Lúcia explained in a book written for Valley members, the medium who undergoes the Dharman Oxinto initiation is setting out on the path to encounter his or her higher self by "dedicating herself to the Law of Assistance and becoming conscious of the Christic System" (2009, 49).

According to Aunt Neiva, Jesus established the Christic System after his own initiation into esoteric wisdom in Tibet. Just as Jesus did, Dharman Oxinto participants are initiated into the "Enchanted World of the Himalayas" and receive "seven mantras of light," or spiritual forces from the Masters or Great Initiates. Explains Pierini, these are "initiatic forces that open all of the chakras and that especially mark the solar plexus, transforming its nature" and thereby distinguishing that individual as "initiated in the spirit worlds and in future incarnations" (2020, 156).

To mark these inward transformations, those who have completed the Dharman Oxinto initiation are permitted to wear a short white vest, called a *colete*, over the white garments worn by aspirants. On the back of the colete is either the doutrinador's black cross or the apará's red triangle (see Image 5.4 and Image 5.5). As the individual continues to develop their mediumship and progress through the hierarchy, they will acquire additional badges, symbols, and insignia collectively referred to as mediumistic weapons (*armas mediúnicas*) that are displayed on the colete. The vests of fully initiated mediums are almost totally covered by these armas, so called because they are believed to protect the wearer from the adverse effects of powerful spiritual forces (see Image 5.6).

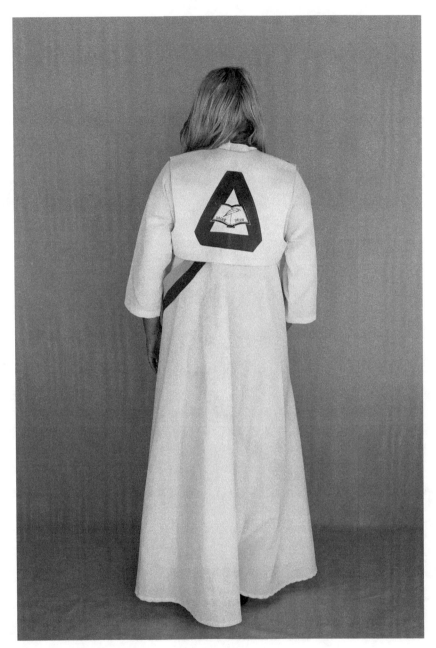

Image 5.4 Colete back (apará). Credit Márcia Alves

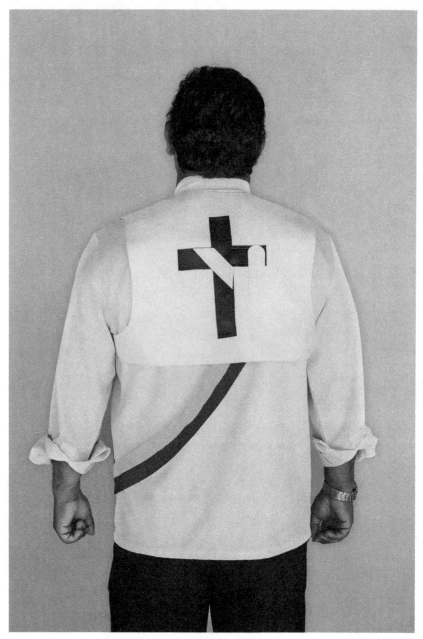

Image 5.5 Colete back (doutrinador). Credit Márcia Alves

A TOTAL SYNESTHETIC EXPERIENCE 131

Image 5.6 Colete badges. Credit Márcia Alves

Elevation of Swords

After completing another "development course" or series of four lessons taught by trained instructors, the "initiated medium" is considered ready for the second initiatory step. This is called the Elevation of Swords (*Elevação de Espadas*) in reference to the swords that symbolize the initiate's oath (Pierini 2020, 156–157). In the course of the ceremony, individuals are said to receive another seven mantras of force from the Great Initiates, adding to the forces previously received in the Dharman Oxinto initiation (Pierini 2016, 36). According to the Doctrine, this further transforms the solar plexus, a psychic-anatomical nexus point of body, soul, and spirit that is associated with mediumship.

Following the Elevation of Swords ceremony, the individual is considered an official member of the mestrado, the master's degree or corps of masters. Henceforth men are referred to by the title Master (*Mestre*), as in Master So-and-So. Women, who as part of the mestrado also are considered Masters, are addressed as Nymph (*Ninfa*). At this point, the "elevated medium" is considered to have the necessary knowledge and preparation of their solar plexus to evoke the *corrente mestra*, or master current, the spiritual force that powers the Valley's *trabalhos iniciáticos*, or initiatory works. These are elaborate, collective rituals involving dozens of mediums that occur in specific built environments, follow a specific script and a set schedule, and require a certain number of participants representing different positions and spiritual forces within the Valley's hierarchy.

Elevated mediums receive a certificate attesting to their status as well as additional armas as an outward sign of their inward spiritual capacities. They are permitted to wear the work uniform, known colloquially as the "Jaguar." This consists of brown pants or skirt and black shirt, over which is worn the white colete or vest (see Image 5.7). Because they are now capacitated to work with a greater complement of spiritual forces, elevated mediums also wear specific items of clothing when participating in initiatory works that are intended to protect them from the intense spiritual energies said to be manipulated in these rituals. For men this consists of a *capa* or cape with a high, vampire-like collar. Women wear a special dress and matching cape called *indumentária de ninfa*, or nymph vestment, adorned either with a golden sun or a silver moon embroidered in sequins, depending on their faculty of mediumship, and finished with matching trim (see Image 5.8).

A TOTAL SYNESTHETIC EXPERIENCE 133

Image 5.7 Jaguar uniform. Credit Márcia Alves

Image 5.8 Indumentária male and female. Credit Márcia Alves

Consecration of the Centúria

After the Elevation of Swords comes the third initiatory step, called the Consecration of the Centúria (*Consagração de Centúria*). The name alludes to the Jaguars' past in ancient Rome, where a *centuria* was a unit in the ancient Roman legion consisting of about a hundred men commanded by a military officer called a centurion. Mediums who have completed this initiatory step are referred to as centurions. Valley members like to say that "a well-prepared centurion is worth 100," referencing a quote attributed to Father John of Enoch, one of Aunt Neiva's spirit mentors (C. L. Zelaya 2009, 54).

While there are higher ranks that an individual may pursue afterward, the Consecration of the Centúria is understood to produce a fully initiated medium. Those preparing for it attend a series of seven lectures and receive further "mantras of force" that qualify them to participate in the full quota of the Valley's numerous rituals.[16] They also acquire a number of other spiritual identifications as well as personal spirit guides who assist and protect them spiritually. The centurion medium's newly acquired spiritual status is represented externally through additional insignia and symbols worn on her or his ritual vestments (see Image 5.9). As centurions, men achieve the title Deputy (*Adjunto*) plus the name of their personal *ministro*, an illuminated

A TOTAL SYNESTHETIC EXPERIENCE 135

Image 5.9 Radar de Centúria. Credit Márcia Alves

spirit mentor of high rank, such as Master Froes, Deputy Adejã. There is no comparable process for women (see Image 5.10).

Finally, each centurion medium officially is issued an "emission" (*emissão*), a ritual formula specific to that individual, which they must memorize and recite in certain rituals. These formulas, which are quite lengthy, specify the medium's initiatory level, spirit guides, spiritual lineage, titles, and numerous other identifications acquired in the course of initiation that I have not discussed. The emission also indicates the medium's relationship to more senior members of the hierarchy, stipulating her exact spiritual and social identity within the community. When Valley members ascend in the hierarchy, affiliate with a particular subgroup within the community, or take on specific ritual positions their emission changes to reflect this new status.

Master Eder, a high-ranking member of the Devas, a group responsible for keeping track of all the data related to the development process and the Valley's hierarchy, explained the emission to me in this way:

> When the individual receives his emission, all the work he has been doing from the Emplacamento to the Centúria is incorporated into his emission.

Image 5.10 Centurion Medium. Credit Márcia Alves

So, each classification that he has received, each spiritual designation, is incorporated into the emission. Because the emission is a key which the medium receives in order to be able to perform his spiritual works. Through the emission he will be able to identify himself to the spiritual planes so that he can do his work.

When recited without error, an emission is said to open a direct channel through different spiritual planes, permitting the circulation of energies across the chasm that separates the dense, terrestrial dimension from the upper reaches of the *Astral Superior* or superior astral plane, home of the Great Initiates. Doctrinal literature describes the emission as an extension of the medium's higher self, or individuality, into the spiritual planes as well as a means by which forces associated with the Great Initiates descend into the terrestrial plane through the hierarchy of the mestrado. For this reason, emissions feature prominently in certain initiatory works, where each participant gives his or her emission following the hierarchical order of the *chamada oficial* or official call. Higher-ranking members are believed to be better prepared to handle more potent spiritual forces than those at lower levels.

As a vocal performance, the emission serves two functions. On the social level it functions as a "hierarchical code" that communicates each member's exact place within the "hierarchy of the mestrado." During her lifetime Aunt Neiva occupied the apex of this pyramid as the community's ultimate spiritual and temporal authority. Since her death, and following a bureaucratic structure that she herself established, the topmost ranks of the pyramid are open only to men. These ranks correlate to positions of greatest authority and decision-making power over the community, as I discuss in more detail in Chapter 6. According to Aunt Neiva, this male-dominated pyramid reflects on the physical plane the regnant hierarchy of forces on the spiritual plane. Thus, for those who can understand their coded language, emissions offer a symbolic diagram of social power, bureaucratic authority, and status within the community.

Within the group's collective imagination, the emission also signals that the medium has reached a certain level of spiritual development, possesses an "initiated plexus," and therefore is able to mobilize corresponding spiritual energies as part of the group's ritualizing. When they are performed as part of a collective ritual, emissions are held to catalyze a *força decrescente* (decreasing or descending force): a spiritual force field that descends into and is distributed through all the levels of the Valley's hierarchy.

Absorbed into the initiated medium's solar plexus, this force field is then redirected outward to power the community's projects of spiritual healing and karmic redemption. As Master Eder informed me, "When a medium gives his emission, it travels to the spiritual planes and then returns in the form of a spiral of energy that is distributed for disobsessive healing." For this reason, Valley mediums describe themselves as veritable "power plants receiving and emitting forces" (Sassi 1977, 39). Emissions, then, to keep with the metaphor, serve as a switch that activates the Valley of the Dawn's psychic voltage system at the highest levels, enabling its most potent spiritual current to flow into the physical world.

Kindlings

At the Valley of the Dawn, developing one's mediumship is a progressive process of inner sense cultivation and embodied learning that trains participants to attend closely to an interior world of sensations, feelings, thoughts, and intuitions. This takes place within a structured environment that gives meaning to certain psychosomatic events as evidence of spiritual energies and amid a community of like-minded others. At the same time that they are learning how mediumship feels in their own bodies, participants also are learning its function at the Valley of the Dawn as a means of disobsessive healing and karmic redemption. They are mastering the repertoire of expressive codes through which it is performed: the behaviors and gestures that differentiate a lower-level spirit from a spirit of light or a caboclo from a preto velho, for example. They are rehearsing the ritual techniques of indoctrinating a spirit or disintegrating negative energies. They are interpreting their everyday experiences through their newfound knowledge of the Doctrine. Finally, they are learning to see themselves not only as mediums but as Jaguars whose personal and collective past shapes their present mission.

These processes of attention, embodied learning, and personalization alter people's perceptual experiences. In other words, they produce kindlings or moments in which the Valley's imagined world is experienced as vividly real. Kindlings, in turn, change the experience of the body, which over time becomes more habituated to these moments, and thus more subject to them. "Evidence begets evidence," Luhrmann writes. When religious practitioners put in the work to make the otherworld real, she explains, it begins to feel real more easily: the medium who has felt the spirit as a quickening pulse is more likely to hear the spirit speak, feel it move their limbs, be overwhelmed by its power (2020a, 135). "Faith," Luhrmann explained elsewhere, "is the process of creating an inner world and making it real through constant effort" (Luhrmann 2018). Through this effort, the boundary between the medium's ordinary reality and the spiritual reality they are trying to perceive becomes increasingly porous in ways that are felt to be transformative. As a Valley medium told Emily Pierini, "Imagine what it feels like to be touched and then embraced by an angel. Your life is never going to be the same afterwards" (2020, 167).

Simultaneously, as mediums-in-training move from aspirant to master to centurion and beyond, they gain access to symbolically significant vestments, insignia, consecrations, titles, and emissions that materialize their level of knowledge and embodied expertise. This aesthetic display externalizes otherwise internal transformations, multiplying them across different sensory registers in ways that make the Valley's imagined world feel ever-more palpable and irrefutable. "From the moment you first put on the branquinha you feel different," Nymph Tatiane, a young medium visiting the Mother Temple in 2012, told me. "With each consecration you feel the forces of your guides and mentors around you increasing and you feel empowered." Nymph Madalena, whom I spoke to in 2015, characterized the effect that the Valley's *indumentária* or attire had on her as "an electrical charge":

> The energy that arrives when you put on this indumentária gives you goose bumps. Sometimes you are walking down the street, but you feel like you are floating on air. It's fantastic. It is like that with my emission, too. When I am giving my emission, I feel a force that makes me shiver all over and my hair stands on end.

Like Madalena, Valley members frequently describe the experience of wearing ritual attire or giving their emissions as triggering embodied sensations akin to an electrical current. According to the Doctrine, this is because each item of clothing, each accessory like the fita and colete, each color and symbol, operates within a greater psychic force field in specific ways: capturing energies from the spiritual planes, protecting the wearer from powerful forces, disintegrating negative charges. "The colors and forms of the clothing are related to the energies to be manipulated," Carmem Lúcia wrote in a book about the Valley's symbols. This "results in the correct utilization of each item of dress in the Works that need to be performed. The vestments provide protection, that is, they ionize the medium against negative charges" (C. L. Zelaya 2009, 75). The very act of donning ritual clothing thus reinforces Valley members' sense of inhabiting a larger force field of energies that can be harnessed, directed, and transformed to produce tangible effects in the material world.

Like uniforms more generally, wearing this ritual attire also enhances members' sense of mission and communal belonging. Longtime veteran Master Francisco expressed a sentiment that I often heard from Valley members: "Because of our uniforms, no one knows who is who, who is rich and who is poor, who is a lawyer and who is a street sweeper. We are all masters, and we are all here with the same goal: helping people." Another veteran, Master Jorge, put it slightly differently. "When I put on my uniform, I remember who I really am," he told me. "The uniforms remind us that we are Jaguars with a great mission on this planet." Similarly, Joice Meire Rodrigues records the testimony of Camila, who told her,

> Ever since I came here and was invited to develop my mediumship, I began to feel part of this place. After I was *emplacada* and started to wear the white garments, which represent simplicity and humility, I felt a sense of self-recognition, that I could help people. (2011, 183)

Running through these testimonies is the notion that the embodied experience of wearing ritual clothing triggers powerful feelings associated with the garments' symbolic meanings in a Pavlovian cycle of positive reinforcement. Cognitive psychologists term this process "enclothed cognition." To put it simply, wearing a particular garment activates the abstract concepts linked to its symbolic associations, such as simplicity and humility. With repetition, these mental abstractions elicit associated feelings and behavioral responses. Thus, the person not only starts to feel humble but behaves with humility (Hojo and Galinksy 2012, 918). In turn, these psychological and behavioral shifts fortify the symbolic meanings attached to specific items of clothing, enhancing their ability to transform people's subjective states.

A Total Synesthetic Experience

The saints, gods, demons, ancestors, and so on are real in experience and practice, in relationships between heaven and earth, in the circumstances of people's lives and histories, and in the stories people tell about them. Realness imagined this way may seem too little for some and too much for others. But it has always seemed real enough to me. (Orsi 2005, 18)

By definition, the imagined worlds to which religions orient their followers—the celestial kingdom of God, the spiritual colonies detailed in Chico Xavier's Nosso Lar, the fiery torments of hell, and so on—exist in a realm apart from, and inaccessible to, our ordinary senses. The work of T. M. Luhrmann indicates that when these worlds are structured around a compelling storyline; abound with color, detail, and emotional resonance; and facilitate transforming experiences—then they can feel as palpably real and relevant in the lives of followers as the everyday world. They can, in a word, become paracosms: incredibly detailed, richly imagined worlds in which the extraordinary becomes credible.

Making the extraordinary credible, however, requires sustained effort on both a personal and collective level. Participants must master what Luhrmann called "rules of engagement": community-defined ways of talking and acting that affirm the reality of the invisible world and its denizens. They must develop habits of imaginative absorption that blur the boundaries between the outer world of the senses and the inner world, making it easier to experience the invisible Other as not only perceptibly present, but responsive. And they must practice these habits. Habitual practice, in turn, transforms the practitioner, making it easier for her to emotionally engage with the invisible world and for this emotional engagement to feel deeply fulfilling. Regardless of whether gods, spirits, or supernatural beings exist independently of these practices, they become part of the practitioner's inner landscape as agentive beings with whom she enters into a relationship. And just like other social relationships, this relationship transforms people (Luhrmann 2020a, xiv).

At the Valley of the Dawn, the process of real making begins with a protracted period of training referred to as mediumistic development. Through courses that combine lecture and practice sessions, mediums-in-development acquire a shared vocabulary and body of knowledge and gain practical experience alongside other trainees. Among other things, mediumistic training teaches the individual to attend to an internal landscape of bodily sensations, thoughts, emotions, and events that are understood as phenomenological proof of spiritual realities revealed to Aunt Neiva. This close attention to our mental and perceptual experiences, Luhrmann observed, changes those experiences in ways that further reinforce the imagined world's reality-status (2020a, 134–135).

As Valley mediums ascend through the ranks of initiation, this inward-focused process is externalized in a profusion of garments, symbols, images, emissions, and other sensory media. The cumulative effect is one of tangible presence, consolidating the felt reality of the Valley's imagined world as something that is both objective and subjective, internal and external. The number of people involved, and the community's high level of organization, further solidifies the aura of realness.

Where the Valley of the Dawn differs from other religions is the exuberantly sensuous, multilayered, and immersive qualities of its imagined world. The Mother Temple complex is a self-contained "affective atmosphere" (Anderson 2009), a fully realized environment of colorful spaces, artwork, garments, music, classes, and ritual pageantry.[17] This offers adherents a "total synesthetic experience," that is, something that is at once sensual (felt through the senses), cognitive (mentally apprehended), psychological (partly unconscious), and intersubjective (shared with others). Such an environment is exceptionally propitious for kindling moments in which the invisible otherworld is felt to be vividly and incontestably real. Through the accumulative flow of such moments, adherents enter fully into the Valley's imagined world, experiencing themselves as, and thereby becoming, Jaguars.

Regardless of whether one believes in their objective existence, imagined worlds have powerful real-world effects. As Yuval Noah Harari observed in his book *Homo Deus*, humans rule the world because we can weave an intersubjective web of meaning: a web of laws, forces, entities, and places that exist purely in our common imagination (2016, 150). Although these imagined orders do not have the same ontological reality as objects in the everyday physical world—rocks, trees, animals—they nevertheless have real power. They motivate people to action or quiescence, to create economies, reshape the environment, make art, wage war against an enemy, or "forgive them their trespasses," as a well-known Christian prayer has it.

The question, then, is not whether the Valley's imagined world is "real" in the minds of members. The question is how their continual efforts to experientially inhabit that world changes them. How do the intimate, dynamic relationships that Valley mediums kindle with their spiritual mentors affect them? How do these kindled relationships alter mediums' interactions with family, community, and the larger social environment? What behaviors and virtues are tacitly sanctioned or encouraged and what are discouraged? What kind of people do they become, and what kind of community is produced? How do Valley members seek to align the everyday world that they simultaneously inhabit with the cosmic order of the movement's imagined world? Such questions inform the remaining chapters of this book.

* * *

6
Knights and Princesses

There can be no magnetic force with only one pole and for this reason, the presence of Woman—who is denominated Nymph—is necessary at all times and in all areas of ritual work.
 —Valley of the Dawn adherent (Siqueira, Reis, et al. 2010, 268)

Aunt Neiva and the Valley's Gender Ideology

Insiders like to say that each element of the Valley's imagined world is an exact reflection of the regnant spiritual order brought to the terrestrial world by Aunt Neiva. As detailed in Chapter 2, however, the Doctrine of the Dawn also bears the strong imprint of its charismatic founder's personality and the difficulties she faced as young widow and mother in mid-twentieth-century Brazil. Forced to choose between a sheltered life of dependence and material comfort within her father's household or the insecurity and freedom of life on the road, Aunt Neiva opted for the latter. For the rest of her life, she considered herself a *cigana* or gypsy—an identification that later would find imaginative expression as an especially resonant incarnation within the Jaguars' transcendental journey (Betinho 2006, 6).

Beyond rejecting the patriarchal restrictions that impinged on her own autonomy, however, Aunt Neiva showed little interest in questioning or abolishing patriarchal social norms themselves. Like many pioneering women, she became a truck driver for practical reasons: because it provided a way for her to earn a living independently while keeping her children with her. And while she believed that women could do many of the same jobs that men could do—even better than men in some cases—she also felt that men and women possessed very different natures that inclined each toward specific social and religious roles.

Throughout her life Aunt Neiva took great care to emphasize her feminine appearance. Photographs of her posing with her truck reveal a stylish woman dressed in dungarees tightly belted at the waist, black hair cascading over her shoulders, and the dark lipstick, heavily shadowed eyes, and plucked eyebrows of a Hollywood starlet of the 1940s and 1950s. So rigorous was Aunt Neiva's commitment to self-presentation that she refused to be seen even by close family members without full makeup and carefully styled hair, a standard that she maintained until her death. "She didn't let us see her when she woke up, without makeup, her hair in disarray," Master Raul, Aunt Neiva's son, confided to me. "We had to wait for her to put on her face before we could get close" (R. Zelaya interview 2015). "My mother was always vain," daughter Carmem Lúcia affirmed,

> not in the pejorative sense, [rather] she was vain with herself, she was always a very feminine woman, this was one of her traits, and of course she ended up passing this down to her children. . . . She taught us to be very feminine, she was a truck driver but she [cared about her appearance], she always was dressed well, she always was pretty. (Oliveira 2007, 33)

Even as her health declined and she became dependent on an oxygen tank to breathe, Aunt Neiva retained her signature look. Photos at the end of her life show the same pencil-thin eyebrows, dark lips, and jet-black hair sprayed into a high bouffant. Having worked as a photographer herself, Aunt Neiva knew how to pose, and photos of her appear throughout the temple and its grounds. In a lengthy profile published in 2007, journalist Isabel Fonseca described Neiva as looking "like a gypsy of Spanish origin."

> She is brunette, robust, pretty. She uses various accessories, large earrings like the type you find at hippie fairs, necklaces with pendants that symbolize various religions, and bracelets. Her thick black hair reflects the light and falls to her shoulders in waves that break at the back. Her black eyebrows, thin and imposing, are done like a tattoo and give her the impression of being a strong, severe woman. . . . Her brown eyes are wide and entranced, lined with pencil and black mascara, and seem to be looking far, far beyond what we imagine. (Fonseca 2007, 225; see Image 6.1)

Above all, Aunt Neiva wanted women to be valued for their distinctively feminine attributes and abilities, which she believed made them inherently different from men. Women are "Father White Arrow's roses," she liked to say, and therefore should take the utmost care not only with their appearance

Image 6.1 Aunt Neiva. Courtesy of Arquivo do Vale do Amanhecer

but also in their demeanor and interactions with others. "A woman should be exuberant," she advised her female followers,

> exuberant in every way, in love or in life. When fate made me the first professional woman truck driver in Brazil, my safeguard was the exuberant spirit that resonated in me. To be exuberant and loving, with the sensual tenderness of your womanly nature, whether at home or at work—both [places] should have the same spirit of this Light![1]

The "sensual tenderness" of a woman's nature is expressed especially in her capacity for unconditional love and nurture according to Aunt Neiva. But while it is a source of great power, this sensitivity also makes women vulnerable, requiring the protection of men who possess greater physical force and will. For their part, men are more aggressive, selfish, and violent—even brutish—qualities tempered by women's loving and spiritualizing influence.

As I detail in this chapter, Aunt Neiva's convictions formed the basis for a gendered ideology in which men and women possess opposing natures that complement each other, like the two poles of a magnet. When brought into productive alignment, men and women form a dynamic circuit that generates an energetic current that can be directed toward the community's spiritual work. This principle of gender complementarity, putatively anchored in physiological differences between men and women, is linked with a series of binary oppositions, such as reason/emotion, strength/sensitivity, positive/negative, and terrestrial/spiritual, forming a gendered dialectics that runs throughout the Valley of the Dawn. Elaborated through symbolic correspondences, enacted in ritual pageantry, and internalized through rules of etiquette and behavior, this gender ideology anchors an imagined world in which men are envisioned as masters and chivalrous knights while women are nymphs and fairytale princesses.

The fact that the Valley espouses a system of gender complementarity is not unusual: many religions define masculinity and femininity as opposing yet interdependent principles. However, the Valley adds a special twist by dividing human beings not only by gender but according to a second classificatory distinction: conscious or semi-conscious mediumship. Together these two axes of distinction, gender and mediumship, serve to differentiate bodies, divide labor, allocate ritual roles and responsibilities, and structure relationships within the community. Through the continuous application and materialization of this dual classification schema, the Valley works to create an orderly world. In this chapter, I analyze this system, paying special attention to its internal logic as well as the points at which it ceases to be logical. The latter moments in particular reveal how the Valley's classificatory apparatus recodes conventional meanings assigned to male and female bodies, sanctioning these meanings by projecting them onto a transcendent spiritual dimension. In doing so, it recasts gender not as a social artifact—a product of human social arrangements, preferences, and prejudices—but as an immutable cosmic law.

Masters and Nymphs: Gender as a Binary System

There is nothing pejorative when, in our Doctrine, we learn that Man is the positive pole while Woman is the negative pole ... because with this we understand that the Master has more animal magnetism and the Nymph has less, with a plexus that is softer and more tender, more harmonized with the superior spiritual worlds, with love and sensibility, while the Man is more rational and violent, more subject to the forces of the Earth. (Souza 2000, "Polaridade")

In the initiatic language of the Valley, women are known as nymphs. Like the nature spirits of Greco-Roman mythology from which the term derives, the figure of the nymph embodies the community's ideals of feminine beauty and supernatural power. According to the Doctrine, nymphs represent love, tenderness, self-sacrifice, and spiritual sensitivity, and thus they naturally embody a kind of energy or "magnetic force" that is described in various theological texts as being closer to the spiritual world (e.g., Siqueira, Reis, et al. 2010, 268). As Aunt Neiva's grandson Jairo explained to me, "the woman represents the spiritual being, sensibility, and spiritual light and women have that particular energetic force" (J. Zelaya Leite interview 2012).

These qualities distinguish the "feminine plexus," which is "subtler and subject to the emotions" but also "more harmonized with the superior spiritual planes" (Silva n.d., "Ninfas"). One result of women's proximity to the spiritual planes is that they have less "animal magnetism" or "ectoplasm"[2] than men and thus are understood to be less subject to the lower forces of the physical world that manifest as violence, carnality, and instinctual cravings of various kinds. By contrast, men or Masters are believed to have more animal magnetism and thus are more subject to "the forces of the Earth" than women. In practice, this means that men are more physically forceful but also, in a contradiction that is never explicitly addressed, more rational than women, qualities that contribute to a distinct "masculine plexus." According to Valley teachings, this makes men more capable of handling strong spiritual forces that could overwhelm the more sensitive feminine plexus. As Jairo put it to me, because men represent "brute force, physicality, and the earth, they are responsible for commanding ritual works—the part that requires more force."

As discussed in Chapter 4, the term "master" associates Valley mediums with the Masters of Wisdom recognized in Theosophy and its offshoots: enlightened sages who no longer are subject to reincarnation but choose to remain on Earth in order to guide human beings. While most Valley members are unaware of the term's connection to Theosophy, its conventional semantic load includes expertise and the accumulation of wisdom. Although these are qualities that ostensibly all Valley members develop, the fact that only men are referred to as masters associates these qualities more with men than women. Indeed, several researchers have observed that women adherents tend to be reticent to answer questions about doctrinal matters and in mixed company often will defer to men when asked to speak about the group or its beliefs (Galinkin 2008; Rodrigues and Muel-Dreyfus 2005, 248).[3]

For Valley members, such gendered behavioral patterns corroborate the differences between the feminine plexus and its masculine counterpart. According to the Doctrine's conceptualization, these psychic organs exist in a state of dynamic opposition. Each possesses its own distinct magnetic polarity: negative (feminine) or positive (masculine), reflecting their respective proximity to the spiritual or terrestrial planes. This basic dyad of masculine and feminine is correlated with a series of binary oppositions that range from macrocosmic level to microcosmic (See Table 6.1).

This binary system has consequences for the Valley's ritual and organizational structures. Because men and women are conceived as generating opposing magnetic fields, "a master is incomplete without a nymph at his side," as Valley members like to say. "There can be no magnetic force with only pole," another oft-repeated maxim puts it, "and for this reason, the presence of Woman, who is referred to as Nymph, is necessary in all moments and in all spiritual works" (Souza 2000, "Ninfa"). By bringing their respective psychic polarities and psychological tendencies into productive alignment, men and women together form a dynamic whole through which spiritual energy can be generated and directed to specific purposes. Consequently, each of the Valley's numerous rituals requires the participation of a certain number of masters and nymphs and great attention is given to the balance of men and women in various settings. Aunt Neiva explained,

TABLE 6.1 Master and Nymph

MASTER	NYMPH
Masculine plexus	Feminine plexus
Closer to terrestrial plane	Closer to spiritual plane
More animal magnetism	Less animal magnetism
Positive polarity	Negative polarity
Strength	Sensitivity
Reason	Emotion
Violence and force	Love and tenderness

Each master, each nymph brings their energy, which alone can accomplish little. However, when united, each building on the energy of the others, we form an energetic crown; we are a power—forces united for a common objective. These are forces in a state of convergence. They are men and women who, in union, channel their energies with the same intention. Accordingly, this provokes a transformation. (Patricio 2012, "Poder Evangélico, Iniciático Decrescente")

Not surprisingly, men and women are seen as naturally suited for different tasks within the community, with women's greater emotional sensitivity and capacity for nurture placing them in auxiliary roles while positions of decision-making authority and community leadership are thought to require men's greater physical strength and rationality (Pierini 2013, 99–100). For this reason, only men serve as *comandantes*, or commanders, charged with supervising the dozens of complex group rituals that are regularly performed.[4] And while Aunt Neiva occupied the apex of the Valley's spiritual and bureaucratic command structure during her lifetime, since her death in 1985, all positions of executive leadership over the community at large have been restricted to men.

As this suggests, the Valley's gender ideology is hardly neutral or value free, notwithstanding the language of complementarity in which it is couched. Consider the fact that all of the qualities associated with femininity are positively valued (+), while most of the qualities associated with masculinity are negatively valued (-) (see Table 6.2). And yet greater proximity to the superior spiritual plane, for example, does not translate into greater terrestrial power for women nor do other positively valued feminine attributes grant women access to positions of decision-making authority over the community.

Correlatively, the negative attributes associated with masculinity have no effect on men's access to leadership positions or standing within the community. Thus, at the level of practice, even as it recognizes femininity as important and valuable, the Valley's gender ideology underwrites men's terrestrial authority and status while awarding women what historian of religion Bruce Lincoln once called "compensatorily enhanced religious meaning": the deliberately vague and mystificatory idea of spiritual power that, while spoken of reverentially, in practice does not give women actual decision-making power (2013, 212).

Clearly, these ideas reproduce conventional notions of gender that assign qualities associated with leadership and communal authority to masculinity

TABLE 6.2 Implicit Valuations of Masculinity and Femininity

MASCULINITY	FEMININITY
Closer to Terrestrial plane (−)	Closer to Spiritual Plane (+)
More animal magnetism (−)	Less animal magnetism (+)
Positive polarity	Negative polarity
Physical Strength (+ when protective; − when aggressive)	Spiritual Sensitivity (+ when influenced by higher-level spirits; − when influenced by lower-level spirits)
Reason (+)	Emotion (+)
Violence (−)	Love (+)

and qualities linked with dependence and vulnerability—however highly valued and positively appraised—to femininity. And yet Valley doctrine does not explicitly ground gender in physiological differences between the sexes. Like other spirit-oriented religions, the Valley maintains that individuals are transcendent spirits temporarily incarnated in physical form. What endures is the spirit, reincarnating over and over in various material forms in order to recuperate the negative karma it has accumulated in past lives and return to its immaterial source: God.

Central to the Doctrine's understanding of the human being is the distinction between the individuality and the personality. According to the Valley, the spirit (individuality), in accordance with its karmic path, produces the material form (personality) in which it will incarnate on Earth. Various writings suggest that the spirit possesses certain intrinsic qualities, and gender is one of them. In one of her written communications to the community, for example, Aunt Neiva remarked:

> In the spiritual worlds or worlds outside of the material realm, life is composed of positive and negative, that is, man and woman. A man's spirit continues as a man and a woman's spirit continues as a woman. Despite the affirmation of some initiates that the spirit does not have a sex, my eyes say otherwise. (Aunt Neiva June 26, 1965)[5]

Like mainstream Brazilian society, the Valley's discourse and practice collapse biological sex, gender, and gender roles such that biological females are understood to be naturally feminine and predisposed toward traditionally feminine roles, while biological males are naturally masculine and predisposed toward traditionally masculine roles. Unlike the mainstream view, though, the Valley speaks of gender not as the product of sexual differences and their associated physiologies but as the visible expression of an indwelling "magnetic force" or "plexus" that inclines the individual toward certain behavioral and psychological traits.

This metaphysical plexus is an aspect of the spirit's individuality and therefore is both prior to and determinative of the physical body. In the Valley's understanding it is gender (i.e., characteristics socially assigned to femininity and masculinity) that determines the sex of the physical body into which the transcendent spirit will be incarnated. As I explain in the next section, the physical body is responsible for the second major classificatory distinction by which the Valley orders its world: faculty of mediumship.

Suns and Moons: Mediumship as a Binary System

According to Valley doctrine, once a spirit has incarnated in a physical body, that body produces a magnetic fluid that allows it to maintain a connection to the spiritual plane. This fluid or ectoplasm is what makes communication between the spiritual and material planes possible, and variations in its distribution are believed to be responsible for mediumship. According to Sassi, for doutrinadores, ectoplasm accumulates in the superior part of the body, principally the head or crown chakra, resulting in greater blood flow to that region and enhanced intellectual capabilities. This type of mediumship "functions with a base in the active central nervous system, where will and consciousness predominate," explained another Valley intellectual.[6]

Among aparás, ectoplasm is said to accumulate in the region of the solar plexus, resulting in greater blood flow to that region and a corresponding loss of "cerebral irrigation." This produces a semi-conscious, trancelike state during which the apará can receive the projection of a spirit entity. In principle, anyone can be an apará or a doutrinador, but in practice aparás, who are associated with receptivity, intuition, and the energetic force of the moon, tend to be women, while doutrinadores, who represent rationality, intellect, and the force of the sun, tend to be men. As Mário Sassi explained, "because of its emotional tenor, incorporation is more frequent among female mediums. The indoctrination medium is more inclined towards rationality and so one finds the greatest number of *doutrinadores* among men" (Sassi

1972, 38–39).[7] In a 2012 interview with me, Master André Luiz explained further:

> The doutrinador works with the energy of the sun, the apará works with the energy of the moon. So, for this reason we always work in pairs. Why? Because we transmit energy from the sun and the moon and we form a conjunction of magnetic forces and through these magnetic forces, we work in the Law of Assistance.

As diagrammed in Table 6.3, the distinction between doutrinadores and aparás is conceptualized and related to other dyadic pairs that structure the Valley's imagined world such that each member of a pair stands in an oppositional relationship with its dyadic partner while corresponding with a series of diverse homologues (See Table 6.3).

These extend from the microcosmic level of the body to the macrocosm of the universe, forming a set of symbolic correspondences by which the two types of mediums are identified in ritual clothing and symbols (See Images 6.2 and 6.3). Thus, the apará "represents the unconscious, the occult, and the mystical and is symbolized by the moon, which is the symbol of those things," Aunt Neiva's grandson Jairo explained to me, while the doutrinador "represents consciousness and reason and is symbolized by the sun, which is the symbol of reason, consciousness, the faculty of logic, and scientific thinking" (J. Zelaya Leite interview 2012). In a further set of symbolic correspondences, a red triangle with an open book (representing the Gospel) identifies aparás, and a cross adorned with a white mantle represents doutrinadores.

TABLE 6.3 Mediumship

Mediumship:	Doutrinador	Apara
Magnetic Pole:	Positive polarity	Negative polarity
Celestial Body:	Sun	Moon
Metal:	Gold	Silver
Quality:	Rationality	Receptivity
Faculty:	Intellect	Intuition
Consciousness:	Conscious	Semiconscious
Body region:	Superior (Crown chakra)	Inferior (Solar Plexus chakra)
Symbol:	Cross with mantle	Triangle with an open book

Image 6.2 Doutrinador: Positive Polarity/Sun/Gold. Credit Márcia Alves

Image 6.3 Apará: Negative Polarity/Moon/Silver. Credit Márcia Alves

TABLE 6.4 The Intersection of Gender and Mediumship

	Doutrinador (+)	Apara (−)
Gender M (+)	Sun Master + +	Moon Master + −
Gender F (−)	Sun Nymph − +	Moon Nymph − −

The binary system of mediumship overlaps with the binary system of gender to form a quadripartite system according to which all Valley members are classified into one of four named categories: Sun Masters (*Mestres Sol*) or male indoctrination mediums, Moon Masters (*Mestres Lua*) or male incorporation mediums, Sun Nymphs (*Ninfas Sol*) or female indoctrination mediums, and Moon Nymphs (*Ninfas Lua*) or female incorporation mediums (see Table 6.4).

Not only is this quadripartite classification the means through which Valley members are organized into mutually exclusive categories, but the categories themselves determine the ritual duties for which individuals are responsible, the kinds of working relationships that they have with others, their access to positions of authority or status, the kinds of clothing and symbols they wear, their ability to influence others or rise in the hierarchy, and even details of their private lives. Thus, a Sun Nymph wears a distinctive uniform (see Image 6.4) that distinguishes her from a Moon Nymph (see Image 6.5), and each is responsible for certain ritual tasks specific to her category. Other differences will become apparent as we progress.

For Valley members, this system reflects a cosmic order that was revealed and brought to the terrestrial world by Aunt Neiva. Nevertheless, such classificatory operations are never neutral, as Bruce Lincoln observed in *Discourse and the Construction of Society* (Lincoln 1989). Rather, they recode socially salient stratifications as taxonomic categories, thereby helping to establish and authorize social hierarchies. In the case of the Valley, this becomes clearer when we consider the differences between Sun Masters and Sun Nymphs, on the one hand, and Moon Masters and Moon Nymphs, on the other. Despite the Valley's rhetorical insistence on gender complementarity and balance, masculinity is linked with autonomy and femininity with dependence in ways that reinforce women's subordination to men's authority.

Image 6.4 Sun Nymph. Credit Márcia Alves

Image 6.5 Moon Nymph. Credit Márcia Alves

Recall that positions of greatest rank and decision-making power in the community are reserved for men—and more specifically, for Sun Masters, who alone combine the physical strength associated with masculinity with the enhanced rational capacity attributed to the doutrinador. For the same reason, only Sun Masters are permitted to command rituals and instruct classes of aspiring mediums. Even though as doutrinadoras Sun Nymphs share the same rational capacity and intellectual ability of their male counterparts, their "feminine plexus" makes them unsuited for positions of public authority and teaching according to Valley doctrine.

This does not mean that women are exempt from all leadership roles within the community. As I discuss in the next section, women head the female-only missionary phalanxes, special groups charged with the performance of specific ritual duties and linked with particular episodes in the community's shared mythic past. And during her lifetime Aunt Neiva held ultimate authority as First Mistress Sun Jaguar (*Primeira Mestra Sol Jaguar*), a title unique to her. However, since Aunt Neiva's death and following a system of bureaucratic and spiritual authority that she herself implemented, men in their role as Sun Masters exercise authority over the community at large, while women have authority only over other women. In this the Valley exhibits a pattern common among many new religions where, once a founder's initial charisma becomes institutionalized in a bureaucratic structure, women's opportunities for public leadership are restricted or eliminated (Wessinger 1993; 2020).

A similar logic of masculine autonomy and feminine dependence differentiates Moon Masters and Moon Nymphs. Because aparás and doutrinadores always work in pairs and there is a concern to balance feminine and masculine energies following the principle of complementarity, Valley members exhibit a strong preference for man-woman pairs: either a Sun Master working with a Moon Nymph or a Sun Nymph working with a Moon Master. Under certain circumstances (usually when there are fewer women than men available) two masters can form a Sun-Moon pair. However, Valley members believe that it is inadvisable for two women to work together as a Sun-Moon pair. "A nymph does not work with another nymph," a high-ranking Sun Master explained,

> because technically her plexus has a special preparation. Different from the masculine plexus (which has a ruder character), the feminine plexus is subtler and more subject to the emotions. We can observe this clearly

in the greater facility that women have to express their sentiments naturally. To protect nymphs from the strong emotional charge that *sofredores* [low-level spirits] carry, Father White Arrow, who considers all nymphs to be roses of his garden, determined that they should not be subject to the risk . . . of being emotionally overwhelmed by the negative emotions of these spirits. . . . To translate, this offers [nymphs] true protection from the emotional disequilibrium caused by the most unbalanced spirits. (Kazagrande 2011, 210)[8]

Two masters, however, can work together as Moon and Sun since both possess a masculine plexus and thus "constitute a pair of positive polarities which is stronger and more resistant to the impact of powerful forces which can act during a ritual and which would be disastrous for two nymphs, who have more sensitive plexuses" (Chiarotto 2013, "Polaridade").

In the Valley's logic, the sensitive feminine plexus always requires the protective strength of the masculine plexus, although the reverse is not true. As Brazilian scholar Erich Gomes Marques observed, "the feminine gender does not have autonomy—she should be accompanied always by a representative of masculinity, even when that representative has their consciousness impaired (i.e., as an incorporation medium or Moon Master)" (Marques 2008, 2–3). In terms of their relative autonomy and authority, then, the four categories within the Valley's quadripartite classification system exhibit the following hierarchy:

1. Sun Master
2. Moon Master
3. Sun Nymph
4. Moon Nymph

Ajanãs and Escravas

Moon Masters also are known as *ajanãs*, a special designation that, according to a doctrinal tract, recognizes the

> different conditions between the masculine plexus [which is] positive, strong, and capable of receiving projections and powerful incorporations from evolved spirits as well as those without light, and the feminine plexus

[which is] negative, sensitive, suited to manipulating powerful and intense, yet soft, energies. (Souza 2000, "Ajanã")

This might lead us to believe that Moon Masters or ajanãs are able to handle any kind of spirit. Yet with some exceptions, in practice they incorporate only male spirits, a rule that Marques attributed to Aunt Neiva herself, who felt that it would be "inelegant" for an ajanã to physically incorporate a female spirit (2008, 2–3).[9]

The discomfort with ajanãs incorporating female spirits makes more sense when we recall that the Moon Master's particular faculty of mediumship already assigns him the feminine characteristics of receptivity and sensitivity. The rule that ajanãs do not incorporate female spirits may help preserve the masculinity of the ajanã by protecting him from what would otherwise be an overwhelming association with femininity and the stigma of the effeminate man. Moon Nymphs, on the other hand, incorporate both male and female spirits since association with masculinity does not compromise a Moon Nymph's status.

Signaling their position at the bottom of the hierarchy, certain Moon Nymphs are referred to as *escravas* or slaves of the high-ranking Sun Masters with whom they regularly pair off. Valley members are careful to emphasize that the designation "slave" denotes a "spiritual classification," not a physical status. As a doctrinal tract explains, the term refers to

> a condition of the Moon Nymph, which, in reality, only exists on the spiritual plane during the realization of a ritual work, where she has to act as if she really is a slave of her master, obeying and serving him for the perfect realization of that ritual work. (Silva n.d., "Escrava")

A Moon Nymph does not function as a slave to all Sun Masters but only a specific Sun Master, usually someone she is married to or with whom she has some other longstanding, often romantic, relationship. The Sun Master in question must have reached a certain level in the Valley's hierarchy, after which time he may ask a Moon Nymph to be his slave, a prerogative that many Sun Masters seek since it is seen as intensifying their spiritual power. It is considered especially important that a Sun Master be paired with his slave when he is scheduled to command a particular ritual, since a Moon Nymph's "activities as slave are vital for [her master's] performance in the realization of his work or, especially, his command" (Souza 2000, "Ninfas").

This condition of (spiritual) slavery becomes part of the Moon Nymph's *emissão* or emission, a verbal formula specific to each person. By specifying the individual's exact rank within the spiritual and terrestrial worlds, the emission becomes part of her or his identity. It is said to enable the spiritual world to recognize that person, but it also alerts other Valley members to her place within the community. The emission of a Moon Nymph who is a slave to a particular master contains the line "slave to Master So-and-So," a relationship that then becomes part of the Moon Nymph's identity. Here again, the reverse is not true for the Sun Master, whose identity is never defined in relationship to a woman.

Other examples could be added but the overall pattern is clear: masculinity, which is linked with intellectual capacity, autonomy, and physical force, is systematically privileged over femininity when it comes to positions of status and public leadership within the community. And while femininity is assigned great spiritual significance, this does not actually translate into independent power or autonomy—a fact that is particularly clear in the case of the Moon Nymph, who becomes the slave to a particular Sun Master.

Because this gendered schema reproduces conventional meanings assigned to masculinity and femininity, few question it. However, there are a number of ways that the Valley works to produce the gendered selves it asserts are utterly natural. In the next section I examine how idealized feminine qualities both are modeled in and engendered by the *falanges missionárias* or missionary phalanxes, specialized, sex-specific subgroups within the Valley that simultaneously represent highly evolved spiritual entities on the astral plane and their present-day compatriots on the terrestrial. In 1975, with the increasing number of ritual works being performed, Aunt Neiva began to bring the missionary phalanxes "from the spirit world to the physical world," a process that continued until her death. Each phalanx was assigned specific organizational and ritual tasks within the community and distinguished by special garments or *indumentárias*. Wearing the distinguishing *indumentária* and participating in the activities of a missionary phalanx gives women opportunities to practice appropriately gendered virtues and attitudes while inviting them to see themselves as members of a powerful and distinctively feminine collective that transcends barriers of time and space.

Knights and Princesses

Aunt Neiva taught that after death, disincarnated spirits with similar karmic profiles become associated with one another in the astral world before being reincarnated on the terrestrial world in different times and places. Based on these transcendental affinities, they form a missionary phalanx: a collective of like-minded spirits who share a common past and spiritual profile. On the terrestrial plane, each phalanx has its own area of actuation in the ritual and organizational life of the Valley, from consecrating and serving the "wine" (grape juice) used in certain rituals to summoning specific spiritual forces with their chants. After passing through the Consecration of the Centúria, Valley members can join any one of the twenty-one missionary phalanxes; nineteen are reserved for women and two for men.[10] Their choice is understood to be a result of something in their past lives that links them to that phalanx; in other words, that person's higher self or individuality shares an affinity with that particular phalanx's transcendental heritage. By using its special vestments and symbols, Valley members believe they can channel that phalanx's spiritual energy toward their mission of karmic redemption and healing.

According to longtime members, Aunt Neiva would recount the stories of some of the missionary phalanxes in her classes. "For example, Yuricys were women who lived together with Pythia [the priestess of the Oracle of Delphi], which was one of Mama's incarnations," Carmem Lúcia advised me in an interview. "They were women whose husbands left for war, and they joined together. When a wounded soldier returned, they helped treat his wounds and so on. And these women became highly evolved spirits who are there in the spirit realms now watching us here" (C. L. Zelaya interview 2017). Nymph Olivia, whom I interviewed in 2010, explained the Dharman Oxinto phalanx. The name Dharman Oxinto, she told me, "Means the path of God. We originated in Egypt during the era of the Pharaoh, the Ramses." Valley teaching materials describe the Dharman Oxinto as the original "priestesses of Horus with great gifts of healing. They were guardians of powerful secrets and in their rituals manipulated powerful, curative forces." In other incarnations, Dharman Oxinto helped wounded soldiers in the Peloponnesian wars, lived as cloistered Catholic nuns in France, and, as gypsies in Andalusia, "enchanted noblemen and kings with their magic and beauty" (*Manual das Dharman Oxinto* n.d., 9).

Notwithstanding some differences of detail, the transcendental biographies of the women's missionary phalanxes are remarkably similar. Although quite schematic, they offer a cluster of resonant details and a loose narrative organized around a recurrent set of themes that associate women with spiritual strength, great powers of healing, esoteric knowledge, purity, high moral conduct, and magical abilities. Like the Dharman Oxinto, each phalanx is comprised of a group of spirits who shared multiple incarnations across time and space. In some lifetimes they were cult priestesses, prophetesses, or nuns; in others they were nurses and healers or women whose husbands were sent off to battle leaving them to fend for themselves. Some worked alongside Aunt Neiva in her previous incarnations as the gypsy Natachan or in ancient Greece and Egypt. Occasionally they were queens and princesses or alluring beauties who used their seductive power over men to benefit their communities. Always they were exemplary figures notable for selfless dedication to others and paranormal powers—like Aunt Neiva herself.

Taken as a whole, the missionary phalanxes model strength and spiritual mastery in a feminine key: motivated by the heart more than the head and by the communal good rather than individual benefit. They present Valley members with allegories of feminine virtue distilled into archetype. And where men can continue to acquire "classifications" or ranks not available to women that enable them to ascend in the Valley's hierarchy and attain positions of authority within the wider community, the missionary phalanxes offer women one of the few routes to formal positions of leadership as heads of phalanxes or *Primeiras* (literally "firsts").

Significant elements of a given phalanx's transcendental heritage are referenced in multiple ways: in symbols adorning the phalanx's unique vestments, in specific songs and chants associated with each phalanx, and in the ritual duties performed by phalanx members. This multiplicity helps to create a kind of material presence: an accumulation of various sensory media that imbues each phalanx with a sense of palpable realness or verisimilitude. By wearing their phalanx's indumentária, reciting details of its transcendental heritage in songs and chants, fulfilling its ritual duties, and performing its unique gestures or postures, Valley members come to experience that phalanx as tangible—they embody and vocalize its history, they perceive and feel the weight of its karmic legacy, and they come to see themselves as products of its mythic past. Nymph Sisenanda, a member of the Samaritana missionary phalanx, explained it to me in this way:

> I identify a lot with the story of the Samaritanas. We go back to that Gospel story of the woman of Samaria who gave Jesus a drink of water from the well when no one else would. But also, the woman who defied the Roman soldiers to serve water to Jesus when he was carrying the cross on his Calvary. That is why we have this amphora on the front of our indumentária and we serve the wine in many ritual works, which symbolizes the blood

of Jesus. I relate to the story because I am like that—I feel fulfilled taking care of others, making sure that people have what they need. That is rooted in my transcendental heritage. The Doctrine helped me see that serving others is the greatest blessing. As Samaritanas we are representing Jesus, serving his masters in a mission to serve him.

Like Sisenanda, Valley nymphs affirm their connection to a particular phalanx by perceiving affinities between personality traits or patterns in their own lives and details of their phalanx's mythical past, focusing on the aspects that most resonate with them. Nymph Vera Lúcia, a widowed housewife in her sixties who was serving as the Primeira of the Rochana phalanx when I met her in 2012, told me that her no-nonsense nature and forceful personality confirmed her sense of connection to the Rochana phalanx.

According to Aunt Neiva, the Rochanas were a group of women in ancient Greece whose husbands had been sent off to war. The king, seeking to take advantage of the situation, had attempted to have his way with the women, angering his queen, who persecuted the women mercilessly. In despair, the women fled their homes for an isolated, rocky island (whence the name Rochana derives), where they subsisted on the fish they caught and adorned themselves with seashells. In reference to this history, the indumentária of the Rochanas is adorned with pearls. "I feel very connected to the Rochanas," Nymph Vera Lúcia affirmed, "they were strong women, and they did what they needed to do to take care of themselves and their children." Similarly, she went on, "the women who are members [of the phalanx] are very strong women, women who are fighters and women who, regardless of their social position, are strong women, warriors and fighters who battle for what they want and move forward, breaking through any obstacles in their path and following their goals."

Of course, scholars can never really know the inner lives of other people,: all we have access to are their descriptions and the ways they live out their commitments in word and deed. Time and again, however, I have been struck by how much evident pleasure and self-worth Valley women derive from participating in their phalanx and the intensity of their identification with it. The transcendental biographies associated with the missionary phalanxes are simultaneously so laconic and varied that whatever the realities of a woman's present life, she is sure to find aspects of herself reflected in them. As a homemaker and mother happily married until her husband's death some years previously, Dona Vera Lúcia strongly identified with the Rochanas' self-sufficiency and ability to overcome the impediments in their path. And while she made no overt reference to the part of the story involving the king's unwanted advances and the queen's harassment, these details might be very significant for other women.

An important mechanism by which both women and men come to identify themselves as heirs to a powerful spiritual heritage while simultaneously assimilating the community's gendered ideals is by wearing the indumentárias particular to each phalanx. Not only do these garments function as part of a larger system of signs that reflects and reinforces the Valley's imagined world, but the embodied experience of wearing them helps shape the wearer's gendered identity.

With their flowing gowns encrusted with sequined embroidery and metallic trim, multilayered capes, elbow-length lace gloves, and beaded headpieces with multicolored veils, women's indumentárias play into fairytale notions of women as beautiful princesses. These gowns are custom sewn in a variety of bright colors and follow a standard silhouette with a long, loose skirt and a form-fitting bodice, which makes them flatter a wide variety of body types. Valley members, both men and women alike, often comment on the transformative power of these garments to make even the most plain of women comely and the wearers report feeling graceful and radiant.

In the Valley's understanding, this is because when she is wearing her phalanx's indumentária a woman aligns herself with and becomes a channel for that phalanx's spiritual mentor or *guia missionária* (missionary guide). Irradiated by that highly evolved entity's vibratory force, the nymph who is properly uniformed temporarily steps out of her everyday identity or personality to align with her higher self or individuality. For this reason, Valley members assert that the indumentária spiritually enhances and protects its wearers, "isolating a nymph in such a way that she is rendered immune to negative forces and scattered energies" (José n.d., "Indumentárias"). In a letter to her "missionary daughters," Aunt Neiva wrote:

> You have no rival, there is no one more beautiful than you because each woman has her own grace. In a thousand missionaries, each one vibrates her harmony, her beauty, because in her is the divine touch of the Great Initiates and their Missionary Guides . (Zelaya, N. 1999, 238)

In addition to the phalanx's missionary guide, each member also has her own personal missionary guide who is associated with, yet distinct from, the phalanx's guardian spirit. Phalanx members are encouraged to line their capes with the color associated with their individualized missionary guide and to wear matching jewelry as a means of harmonizing with that entity's energetic vibration, further consolidating their identification with her. Images of both kinds of missionary guides circulate widely, and adherents usually have these in their homes or carry them in their purses like Catholic prayer cards. Without fail whenever a woman showed me one of these images, she emphasized the physical beauty of her missionary guide.

In 2015, I accompanied a friend when she picked up an image of her spirit guide, an entity named Arana Amarela, which had been created for her by the Doctrine's official illustrator, Joaquim Vilela. Nymph Neide was overcome with emotion when she saw the portrait. Arana Amarela was even more radiantly beautiful than she had imagined, Neide told me, gazing at the entity's likeness (see Image 6.6). She intended to place the image on her *aledá*, the private altar that Valley members maintain in their homes, "so that in my prayers I always have her close to me."

When I asked Neide why she wanted a picture of Arana Amarela, she answered:

So that I can visualize her more easily, imagining her by my side. It is not required by the Doctrine, but it really helps us mediums get to know our

Image 6.6 Missionary Guide Arana Amarela. Courtesy of Neide Coelho de Assis

spiritual guides ... it's like they are our guardian angels, you know? It helps us to recognize them so that then we can mentally visualize them when we are working in the Law of Assistance. Now when I ask for her protection, I can see her alongside me. (Neide interview 2015)

In a similar fashion, the garments worn by men—pants in somber tones of black or brown and dark-colored capes with stiff, high-necked collars—are believed to help connect a master with his guardian *cavaleiro* or knight (see Image 6.7). Envisioned as spiritual warriors of the ethereal realms, knights are said to project their magnetic force onto the individual masters whom they serve. Master Kazagrande, author of a highly regarded blog on doctrinal matters, compared the knight to an agent of the federal police (responsible for border security in Brazil):

Your knight is the federal police! Your guard and security. Blessed force of the spiritual planes, [the knight] is assigned to accompany you, to be at your side whenever you invoke him. Ensuring your safety, your [spiritual] equilibrium. Not allowing anything that does not belong to your karma, or that is not permitted by your own vibratory pattern, to affect you. (Kazagrande 2011, 51)

Like the federal police, knights are paramilitary figures who serve at the border between the terrestrial and spiritual worlds, acting to protect and defend Valley masters. They also are said to perform heroic missions in the ethereal planes rescuing spirits who have been captured by lower-level entities in the *Mundos Negros* (Dark Worlds). And where female missionary guides are described as beautiful princesses radiating tenderness, compassion, and love, knights embody the idealized qualities of masculinity: strength, courage, honor, justice, and a readiness to defend and rescue those in need (see Image 6.8).

When gathered to perform a ritual or simply waiting for one to begin, Valley members are a spectacular sight, evoking a kind of courtly spectacle or what one observer aptly characterized as a "sacralized aristocracy" populated by proud knights and regal ladies. Commenting on the garments, Master Kazagrande asserted:

We are beautiful! Our indumentárias are ball gowns, our capes add a touch of elegance and sophistication that normally is lacking in our profane

KNIGHTS AND PRINCESSES 169

Image 6.7 Master. Credit Márcia Alves

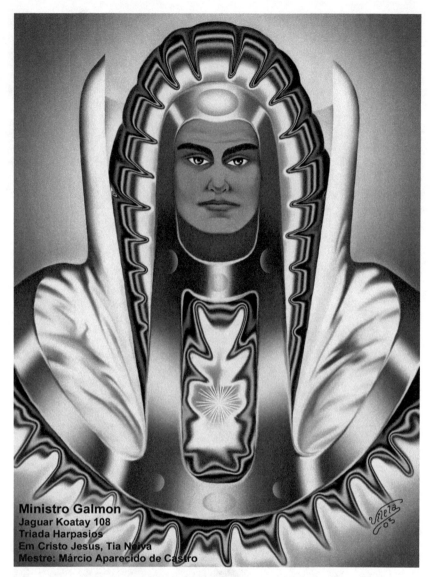

Image 6.8 Knight. Courtesy of Joaquim Vilela

lives. What nymph is not beautiful in her indumentária? What master is not transformed into a prince with his proud cape? Beyond this, when we wear our indumentárias, we reflect the light of our Mentors! We are the projected Knight and the Missionary Guide in all of their splendor! (Kazagrande 2012)

As Master Kazagrande's remarks suggest, in addition to contributing to the Valley's visual pageantry, the garments are key elements in a larger process by which participants come to identify with their mentor spirits and internalize the community's ideals of masculinity and femininity (Carvalho 2000, 281). When garbed in their indumentárias, mediums are expected to adopt specific bodily postures, gestures, and comportment that communicate this level of refined splendor: standing upright, avoiding exaggerated movements, refraining from unnecessary conversations, sitting with legs uncrossed. This disciplining of the body further deepens adherents' sense of themselves as channels for the gender-specific energetic force of their mentor spirits.

Constantly encouraged to align themselves with their spirit guides, Valley members are expected to manifest the community's core values of love, tolerance, and humility in gender-specific ways. Aunt Neiva encouraged nymphs to radiate love, serenity, and sweetness, frequently reminding them of "the necessity of every woman to take care of herself, to be exuberant, to maintain an elevated vibration, in other words, to always be conscious of her mission as a true queen" (Souza 2000, "Mulher"). "Be perfect *cavalheiros* (gentlemen)," Aunt Neiva counseled masters, "and learn to give due respect to others."[11] Particularly in their relations with female members, Masters should behave as "true missionaries," avoiding flirtatious behavior and exhibiting the highest levels of self-control.[12] Proper behavior, known as doctrinal conduct, is absolutely central to the Valley's mission of karmic redemption because "outside of doctrinal conduct there is no individual evolution for the medium nor can we proceed along our evolutionary path within the Doctrine... Through our doctrinal conduct we can overcome our karma" (Moura et al. 2010, 9–10).

Since the Valley's gendered division of spiritual labor requires men and women to work together, an environment of mutual respect and professionalism is critical for the smooth functioning of the community's numerous rituals. This emphasis on doctrinal conduct makes the Valley an exceedingly pleasant place to be, especially for women. Many told me that they appreciated the atmosphere of chivalry that the Valley promotes, contrasting this with other public spaces in Brazil where they regularly experienced unwanted male attention ranging from comments on their appearance to various forms of sexual harassment. If a man violates the principles of doctrinal conduct, the spiritual significance given to ethical norms helps women feel empowered to call it out. "If I hear a master say something rude or inappropriate," a nymph told Brazilian scholar Gercilene de Oliveira Lima:

I do not hesitate to tell him that it is his own evil mind talking and if he really looked at [a nymph wearing her indumentária] he would not see sensuality, but rather a warrior with her weapons . . . I do not tolerate comments like that. The indumentária symbolizes armor . . . it will never be used to flirt or charm someone, because it is part of our essence, and we demonstrate all this with conduct and resolve in our actions. (2019, 225)

The Androcentrism of Gender Idealism

Aunt Neiva taught her followers that when men and women work together, harmonizing their corresponding masculine and feminine plexuses, they can transform human suffering and help humanity itself evolve to a higher state. The movement that she founded sanctions women's spiritual agency and male-female partnerships while working simultaneously to curb the worst excesses of male chauvinism. Through narratives, vestments, rituals, and practices of etiquette, men are encouraged to identify with and embody the chivalrous virtues associated with knights—valor, strength, honor, and protection—and women to see themselves as "true queens" worthy of respect and protection.

Contemporary proponents of chivalry argue that these norms, though relatively rigid, can promote certain forms of social justice (e.g., Smith 2012; Wollock 2011). For example, in a 2010 article on chivalry, Emily Esfahani Smith argued that women and men alike benefit from chivalry because it recognizes that men tend to be physically bigger and stronger than women and provides a code of behaviors and an ethic that tempers male aggression. "Masculinity with morality and civility is a very powerful force for good," one of her interviewees told her. "But masculinity without these virtues is dangerous—even lethal." Chivalry, Smith asserted,

> is about respect. It is about not harming or hurting others, especially those who are more vulnerable than you. It is about putting other people first and serving others often in a heroic or courageous manner. It is about being polite and courteous. In other words, chivalry in the age of post-feminism is another name we give to civility. (Smith 2012)

Smith goes on to argue that if both men and women adopt the principles of civil and chivalrous conduct, this would not only foster a kind of equality between the sexes but also help curb male boorishness. While I am not endorsing Smith's argument, it articulates what many women with whom I spoke find appealing about the Valley.

Aunt Neiva knew from her own life experiences how important what she referred to as doctrinal conduct was in a world in which gender roles and other social norms were in flux. As a single woman trying to support her family, she was forced to take on the traditionally masculine role of family provider, becoming both father and mother to her children in an era when few women worked outside the home (Vásquez and Alves 2013). Her decision to become a truck driver required her to transit in spaces of male sociality, which she navigated not by trying to be like a man but by emphasizing her femininity and identity as a mother.

Neiva instilled her commitment to conventional ideals of femininity not only in her daughters but also in her followers, hypostatizing these ideals in the figure of the nymph. Representing beauty, tenderness, sensitivity, nurturing love, and spiritual power, the nymph exists in a relationship of opposing complementarity with the idealized masculinity of the master, who represents physical force, will, reason, and terrestrial power. Echoing the romanticized chivalry portrayed in medieval courtly literature, this gender ideology is reinforced by a cosmic paradigm of paired masculine and feminine spirit mentors imaged as knights and princesses. It is materialized in special vestments, enacted in complex ritual pageantry, and continually reproduced through rules of etiquette and doctrinal conduct.

The Valley's emphasis on an idealized partnership between men and women makes it particularly attractive to heterosexual people uncomfortable with the sidelining of women as sacerdotal agents in more mainstream Christian traditions.[13] As my informants repeatedly stressed to me, women's active and visible participation is vital for the community's spiritual work. "The sacred feminine is very much in evidence here and is continually represented by nymphs and invoked within the rituals," Nymph Vanda declared.

> The Doctrine is based in a dynamic of partnership in which a master is incomplete without a nymph by his side and vice versa. As women we have fundamental roles in all of the rituals. We do not command the same ritual works as the men; however, our responsibilities as women are equal to, if not greater than, men's because we do a lot of work in the community organizing events, making food for parties, cleaning the work sectors,

setting up raffles and other means of raising money to help maintain the Temple. So, I do not think that women are treated as less than men.

Following the model established by Aunt Neiva and Mário Sassi, the ideal is for husbands and wives who possess complementary forms of mediumship to work together as mediums. Of course, not all adherents can reproduce this model in their own religious lives (if, for example, both partners possess the same faculty of mediumship), but most recognize its importance to the movement itself. "Even when they don't please you," a Valley nymph told scholar Joice Meire Rodrigues,

> these norms and postures, have to be followed because they go back to the ideal of the founding couple, Aunt Neiva and Mário Sassi, woman and man, with different functions and different energies, but together they raised the doctrine of the Valley of the Dawn. (Rodrigues 2011, 190)[14]

Although most women that I spoke to, such as Nymph Vanda, expressed a sense of satisfaction and fulfillment as nymphs, others like the woman quoted above are more ambivalent. This discontent is seldom, if ever, broached in public, but it is a topic of private conversations. Gercilene Oliveira de Lima recorded the testimony of several women such as this one, who told her:

> I would like to command all the rituals that men command, even with the issue of physical protection. For example, when a patient arrives who is unconsciously incorporated, he can hurt a woman if she is in command of the ritual. But, on the other hand, she will not be alone, she will have more women and men nearby, who together can help each other and help that patient in the best possible way. (2019, 206–207)

In addition to the rule that precludes nymphs from commanding rituals, the practice of referring to Moon nymphs as slaves is another source of discomfort.

> As a woman, an incorporation medium, I do not like the term slave used in the emission. In the twenty-first century it ends up generating embarrassment, although we have the explanation that the Clairvoyant left us, which means spiritual companion, because man does not work at the head of the woman, it is actually a partnership. When a master does not have a nymph,

he cannot do a lot alone, so the woman symbolizes openness in reaching the goals of the spiritual journey. (Lima 2019, 207)

Another nymph echoed these sentiments:

Despite the presence of women being central, I find the Doctrine somewhat sexist, as I do not agree with the term slave used in the [Moon nymphs'] emissions. I know that the Doctrine has an explanation for this spiritually, that is, the woman is not the slave of the man, she is the slave of an Adjunct [evolved spirit mentor], however, the people who are not from the Valley do not understand this, which contributes to prejudiced judgments. (Lima 219, 213)

Cognizant of these sensitivities, Valley leaders exhort members to be careful. "Never play around with this term," Master Kazagrande warned his readers in a blog post entitled "Slave???" Being referred to as a slave is a great test of a nymph's humility, he advised, while for masters "the proof of your humility is understanding that you can NEVER, under any circumstances, play around with this term."

The condition of "Slave" only exists for Moon Nymphs in the exercise of their mediumship within our ritual works. Apart from that, she absolutely is not and should not be a slave, but the companion, the encourager, the sweetness and love, the great support so that her master can walk and fight with confidence. It is really a great test for the proud spirit to carry the term "slave" throughout her life, within her spiritual work. (Kazagrande 2010)

As Master Kazagrade's remarks hint, despite the Valley's emphasis on male-female partnerships and gender complementarity, women's roles are construed in terms of the encouragement, love, and companionship that they give to men and their support of men's spiritual journeys. In these and other ways, the Valley of the Dawn exemplifies Rosemary Radford Ruether's description of androcentric gender symbolism, which

treats the female as the "other": inferior in relation to superior, weaker in relation to stronger, negative in relation to positive. Even when the qualities assigned to women are positive, such as love or altruism, these are defined in such a way as to be supplemental or auxiliary to a male-centered definition of the self. The female becomes the unconscious that completes the conscious, the affectivity that completes rationality. Thus, despite the appearance of balance in such gender complementarity, the female is always relative and complementary to the male, rather than herself the one who is complemented or completed in her own right. (Ruether 2005, 334)

Androcentrism is the structuring principle of the Valley's quadripartite classification system, which gives men access to positions of communal leadership and influence that are not available to women while systematically subordinating women to men's terrestrial authority. Hence, at the same time that Valley members valorize women's spiritual power and point to their equal participation with men, the differences between the Sun Master and the Sun Nymph, on the one hand, and the Moon Master and the Moon Nymph, on the other, reveal how the system tacitly defines femininity as subsidiary to masculinity. This is explicit in the case of the Moon Nymph, whose emission defines her as the slave of a Sun Master, a condition that does not apply to the Moon Master or ajanã.

Given how Aunt Neiva herself navigated the prevailing androcentrism of her surrounding culture, it is not surprising that the movement she founded reproduces a gender ideology that subtly privileges men. Like many religions founded by women, the Valley reinterprets the meanings assigned to masculinity and femininity in ways that sanction women's spiritual power while preserving a male-dominated leadership structure. No matter how reverentially women's superior spiritual sensitivity is spoken of in discourse, it does not actually grant women access to the communal authority and decision-making power that Aunt Neiva herself exercised during her lifetime. In this, the Valley also conforms to a familiar pattern in the history of religions: the decline of opportunities for women's public leadership after the death of the founder and the institutionalization of charisma in a bureaucratic structure. While Aunt Neiva held ultimate authority over the community during her lifetime, she herself instituted a system that today restricts positions of greatest decision-making power to men.

While there is much about the Valley's gender ideology that members find uplifting and meaningful, scholars also must examine the ways that religious discourse and practice embellish "some aspects of lived experience while occluding others," as Lincoln put it (2013, 212). The Valley's imagined world offers participants a narrative of idealized heterosexual partnership and gender complementarity that, like the fairytales to which it bears a striking resemblance, forecloses difficult questions about masculinity and femininity, autonomy and dependence, individuality and coupledom, in favor of a romanticized fantasy that defines women as beautiful princesses with great spiritual powers who need the protection of knights in shining armor. The issue is not that the Valley offers a certain vision of how society should be organized or how humans should behave toward one another. Rather, by presenting this vision as supernaturally sanctioned, it precludes participants from considering the question of why this arrangement is best and for whom.

* * *

7
The Work of Healing

The desire to make suffering intelligible and to turn it into some advantage is one of those dignifying peculiarities of our species . . .
—Richard Shweder (1997, 119)

My children, it does not interest me that people believe in me, in the mentors, in the current, but that upon leaving here, if possible, they feel more fortified, believing more in themselves. But, my children, if someone leaves here disbelieving in themselves by being here, then, yes, it will be our ruin!
—Aunt Neiva (Lucena 1992, 13)

The Spirits of Controversy

It was a hot Saturday, and the fierce highlands sun was irradiating the Valley in a phosphorescent shimmer. The cool, darkened interior of the Temple offered a respite from the sun's glare and heat, but it too was galvanized by an undercurrent of frenetic energy as the mediums staffing the Thrones (*Tronos*) attended a lengthy line of patients sitting shoulder-to shoulder and hip-to-hip on the hard tiled benches of the waiting area. Now and again the ambient thrum of the room was rent by the cry of a *sofredor*, or suffering spirit, whose rage and anguish were conveyed in the guttural moans of the apará incorporating it. "You can almost feel the pain people are in," Peter Owen-Jones announced, speaking directly to the lens of a video camera, before joining the apará and doutrinador pair that was awaiting him in the Thrones. A former adman-turned-Anglican vicar, Owen-Jones was filming an episode for his BBC documentary series "Around the World in 80 Faiths," originally broadcast in January of 2009 ("UFO Airport," 2009).

Highlighting the sensational, exotic, and unusual in briskly edited, eight-minute segments, "Around the World in 80 Faiths" was keyed to the prejudices and predilections of its mainstream audience. As its host, Owen-Jones played the role of genial everyman with whom viewers could identify—curious and open to new experiences, but skeptical. The premise, Owen-Jones told me in a 2020 interview,

> was for me to go in as a novice, consciously not knowing about the religion. So, whilst the director and the producer had researched it, the whole idea was that the presenter didn't know. Therefore, the presenter discovered, in the very limited time that the presenter had, what the religion was all about.[1]

According to the segment that ultimately aired, the Valley of the Dawn was all about flamboyant costumes, obscure pageantry, and beliefs worthy of the supermarket tabloids (aliens who colonized Earth! Space hospitals for the spirits of the dead!). Given the language barrier and the limited time that Owen-Jones spent there, it is not surprising that he had little sense of how the various pieces all fit together. "It's like being taken to another planet," he told me when we spoke about his time at the Valley.

> Walking into the complex, you're confronted with a whole lot of imagery and a whole lot of architecture, which you are not aware what it is rooted in. . . . I was not aware of what any of it meant. I was there to find out. And I do not think anyone ever really told me.

The resulting eight minutes on the Valley of the Dawn perpetuated the usual stereotypes about the movement as a low-budget, sci-fi spectacle. But it also hinted at something darker and more menacing. Its depiction of Valley rituals as summoning malevolent spirits seriously misrepresented the healing work central to OSOEC's mission.

After an opening bit centered on the Doctrine's beliefs about colonizing aliens and space hospitals, Owen-Jones is shown participating in the ritual of the Thrones. The first stop for most patients arriving at the Temple, the Thrones serve as a kind of triage unit where patients are evaluated, spiritually cleansed, and dispatched to other healing works for more specialized treatment. What Owen-Jones did not tell his audience—and later told me that he had not known—was the purpose of this ritual and its significance within the Valley's larger worldview and mission. By removing negative spiritual influences and restoring patients' psychic equilibrium, Valley members believe that they are facilitating the spiritual evolution of both patients and the disincarnate spirits responsible for their suffering. But since Owen-Jones did not know this, the viewers of "Around the World in 80 Faiths" had no way of understanding what they were seeing except as a kaleidoscopic amalgam of elements familiar and strange.

The Thrones gets its name from the specially designed seats, or Thrones, where patients consult with preto velho spirits. These are arranged in multiple rows of yellow or red seating units facing several long benches holding the waiting public. Each Throne is staffed by an apará-doutrinador pair who work as a unit attending patients one by one. The patient sits next to the apará, who acts as the channel for his or her preto velho mentor. Standing immediately behind the apará is the doutrinador, whose task is to indoctrinate any low-level spirits that show up, discharge negative energies, clarify any misunderstandings that arise, and keep the general proceedings on track.

Patients are encouraged to discuss whatever troubles or worries they are experiencing with the pretos velhos, who listen and offer words of comfort. Famously benevolent and loving presences, these aged spirits radiate empathy and offer hope in an atmosphere free of judgment. They "act with simplicity, tenderness, and affection," as a Valley publication puts it,

> disintegrating negative charges by the force of love. They are characterized by messages of optimism, guidance, and warning, giving the patient strength to face life-related problems, without, however, interfering with his free will. (Damião 2004, 31–32)

At the end of each individual consultation, the preto velho will recommend additional healing rituals for the patient to pass through before leaving the Temple, or advise drinking the water from the Temple's fountain, believed to be "fluidified" or magnetized with spiritual energies that help purify and restore harmony.

The BBC documentary's audience, however, was told none of this, and it is unclear from the episode what Owen-Jones himself had been told about the standard operating procedure of the Thrones. He explains to the camera before entering the Temple that he will be meeting with a medium who will give him a special message that he can reveal to no one. Although Valley members believe that the wise counsel of the pretos velhos is confidential, there is no rule that it must remain a secret. Nevertheless, the entire segment about the Thrones is edited to suggest that something ominous is about to happen and emphasizes Owen-Jones's apprehension.

The next scene consists of footage from inside the Temple that shows Owen-Jones sitting in the Thrones, eyes closed, next to an apará.[2] "I try to make the most of it and attempt some soul searching myself," he says in voice-over narration. As the camera cuts to a close up of the apará whose features are now twisted into a terrible rictus, the voice-over continues, "but the secret revelation discloses more than I had bargained for." The apará convulses with deep, gut-wrenching howls, her hands frozen in the distinctive claw-like shape characteristic of an obsessor spirit. "I find I have to leave to clear my head," Owen-Jones explains in another voice-over, and the camera shows him fleeing toward the Temple's entrance. The scene ends with Owen-Jones, his voice markedly more agitated, saying, "I can't do it anymore, that's it, that's it."

The next shot shows him sitting outside the Temple, head down, seemingly wearied. A woman approaches him. "What did they say?" Owen-Jones inquires of her, "I was in a bit of a state in there, what did they say? What were they saying?" The woman explains that the mediums who attended Owen-Jones want him to go back to the Thrones so they can "release your soul." "Into the jaws of the lion then," he tells her resignedly and strides back into the Temple. "Apparently my presence attracted a powerful spirit," the voice-over intones, "and they need me back to release it."

The scene now shifts to a doutrinador standing behind Owen-Jones and performing the ritual sequence meant to elevate the spirit and release the Englishman from its influence. The latter is now drenched in sweat, hair plastered to his skull. Another jump cut and the two men are standing outside the Temple talking. "I think I've come to a point," Owen-Jones informs Master João, the doutrinador who had attended him in the Temple, "where I need to sit back and reflect." "Yes, that will be very good for you," Master João exclaims cheerfully after this has been translated for him, clapping Owen-Jones on the back. But Owen-Jones himself seems perturbed. When the translator tells him that he is in good hands, he chortles and looks away before assenting with a kind of shrug. His body language suggests that he does not agree. "Exposing myself to that experience was nerve wracking," he states in the voice-over that ends the segment.

Valley members who had spent time with Owen-Jones and his crew were dismayed by the episode when it finally aired in Brazil, although not surprised. Its initial emphasis on the colorful and exotic aspects of the Doctrine combined with the absence of any explanation of how the pieces fit together made the group seem off-kilter if not quaintly ridiculous. But more disquieting to them was the scene from the Thrones, which left the strong impression that the group trafficked in dark and nefarious forces so disturbing that the usually unflappable BBC host had to leave the premises in a rush.

In 2012, a couple of years after the show was broadcast in Brazil, Master João shared with me his perspective on the events that had transpired during the BBC crew's visit. Peter Owen-Jones had come with his own preconceptions about the Valley of the Dawn, he explained,

> He spent a day here, he arrived on Saturday morning and left in the afternoon. And he had an idea about our doctrine, a malicious idea and as a result of his negative thinking he produced a negative current. If you lower your vibrational level, you will attract a lower type of spirit. That's what happened with Peter, he came in with a very low vibrational level, in search of controversy. And then he was besieged by the spirits of controversy. So, he attracted the energetic influence of those low-level spirits, and he was unable to control it.

As a result, Owen-Jones "became very upset."

> He was a little out of his mind. He ran out of the Temple, and we had to approach him outside and persuade him to come back. And he returned to finish the ritual, but he had a negative current so strong that he managed to irradiate all the Thrones in the vicinity, all the incorporated mediums. Everyone was irradiated by the negative energy that he was carrying—that he produced, in reality, he produced that negative energy.

Master Itamir, who also accompanied Owen-Jones that day, described to me how the BBC host had "lost control of himself."

> He didn't know where he was, and he became desperate. And so, we stayed with him, talking to him, orienting him, calling him back to reason. He really lost himself. Why? Because he was in that inferior level. We had to bring him back to reality, we had to reason with him, talk firmly with him until he could return to normal. He got scared, you see? Because he was messing around with spiritual realities. He came to play with something serious.

Master Itamir continued,

His profession is this: to seek out facts and to analyze them through a particular lens. Because television has to create a polemic, it has to create a controversy. The media makes a living from controversy. But we are here at the Valley of the Dawn to receive all people. Aunt Neiva said something very interesting: "My child, there are three lost causes in life: waiting for someone who isn't coming, crying for someone who died, and helping those who don't want help." We tried to help Peter, but he did not want help. At least I am certain that our positive intention was registered on the spiritual planes, and this is what is important. Here at the Valley of the Dawn, we are prepared for this.

I tracked Owen-Jones down in 2020 to ask him about the episode and his experience at the Valley of the Dawn. He told me that he had had no part in the editing process and had not watched the final series himself. He had left the Thrones that day not because he was disturbed by the "secret revelation" or felt personal discomfort with the ritual, he assured me, but rather because "I felt that, in terms of my interest and the interest of the show, we had gone as far as we could go."

> I was given a message that I couldn't tell anyone, there was a grimacing medium, and that was as far as we could go. It's an old trick: you've got something wrong with you and we're going to help you. Everywhere we went, they always uncovered some issue. So, after fourteen months of filming, I probably thought, oh my god, not again. Here we go again.

Although he found the ritual of the Thrones a predictable gambit, Owen-Jones reported that otherwise he had enjoyed a "wonderful experience" at the Valley of the Dawn and was concerned to learn that the final program had so discomfited his hosts, whom he described as "utterly delightful."

For Owen-Jones, the fact that the Valley had found "something wrong" with him and then proceeded to try to rid him of it was evidence of its insincerity—part of a common ruse used by religions to attract followers. Certainly, this is an opinion shared by many skeptics for whom the causes of human suffering are properly sought in the material world rather than a supernatural one. This perspective presumes that religious participants are either dupes who have been conned into participating or charlatans who knowingly deceive others with false promises. Undoubtedly religion has its share of dupes and charlatans, like any other human endeavor. However, this common fact does little to illuminate the complex sociological, emotional, and psychological reasons that people get involved with religion or why they continue to be involved even when their problems are not magically resolved.

On the other hand, Valley mediums' interpretation—that Owen-Jones had attracted an obsessor because he had "lowered his vibrational level" with negative thinking, necessitating their spiritual ministrations to free him of its baleful influence—requires that we accept claims about the agency of immaterial beings for which there is no universally agreed-upon, empirical evidence. Accepting such claims would depart from the standards of academic inquiry. Rather than dismiss the Valley's healing practice as a ruse or unquestioningly accept its view of healing as a product of spiritual operations, in this chapter I seek to understand healing as a dynamic social, cognitive, and psychological process. In essence, I argue, the Valley offers patients a narrative frame that assigns existential meaning to suffering as well as a set of rituals for overcoming it. Of course, not everyone who comes to the Valley finds its diagnosis of the human condition persuasive. But the many who do feel that the Valley has made their lives qualitatively better.

In order to establish the groundwork for this argument, I describe in the next section the daily operations at the Temple and the kinds of problems that patients typically bring. I then detail its understanding of healing as an energetic re-balancing, exploring how the community's concern with harmonizing energies is expressed in its elaborate material culture and forms of aesthetic expression. Turning to ritual, I examine one of the elaborate spiritual works through which Valley mediums seek to transform their transcendental heritage. This accumulation of karmic energies from the past is believed to account for an individual's present circumstances. By identifying and ritually redressing past wrongs, the Prisoner's ritual helps participants reframe present struggles as meaningful opportunities to evolve. Finally, I end by discussing the story of Zack. A young medium-in-training from Australia, Zack came to the Mother Temple after being introduced to the Doctrine in Sydney. Like so many of the mediums who shared their stories with me, Zack felt that the Doctrine had transformed his life by helping him "find the strength, mindset, and motivation to start living more intentionally and more powerfully."

A Universal Emergency Room

As a self-styled *pronto socorro universal*, or universal emergency room, the main business of the Valley of the Dawn is alleviating human suffering.[3]

"The mission of the Valley is not to indoctrinate, establish a religion, attract converts, or proselytize," Mário Sassi explained in a pamphlet directed at visitors. "The only mission has been to attend distressed human beings who seek relief" (1974, 88). Indeed, from her very first days as a Spiritist medium until she became reliant on an oxygen tank, Aunt Neiva spent long hours consulting with patients. Her efforts to assuage the never-ending suffering that surrounded her established a model for her followers. It also left a lasting impression on Father César, the Catholic priest who arrived a skeptic but came to respect and admire the community. "Serving people individually," he explained,

> each in turn, without haste or rush, nor time and space limitations, without the smallest financial requirement—that's the basic and unique purpose of the Valley of the Dawn, all carried out through a "modern spiritism," up to date, the "Mediumism or Doctrine of the Dawn." (1977a, 369)

Today as then, the Temple is open to the public seven days a week, staffed by trained mediums who have volunteered to be on duty for the day, either as part of a regular work shift or for their own spiritual development. Because Valley mediums regard this work as part of the Law of Assistance, patients are never asked for payment or recompense of any kind. "The patient who comes here to our service," Master Antônio Carlos explained to me,

> will go through several work sectors. At the end of all the work, the entire process, he leaves. He doesn't need to say thanks, he doesn't have to pay anything, he has no commitment to the mediums or to the Doctrine. If he wants to come back, the doors are open. There are many who received a healing, received a benefit, and they feel the need to help, and they stay. They begin their development and also become mediums. Being helped is important but helping is also important.

At 9:45 a.m., three blasts of a siren summon mediums to the Temple for the opening ritual that formally commences the workday. This is divided into two sessions: the first from 10:00 a.m. to 12:00 p.m., and the second from 3:00 p.m. until the last patient is attended, which sometimes runs late into the night. In general, mediums work both sessions, which can mean a twelve-hour day or more. The largest variety of healing rituals or "works" (*trabalhos*) is offered to the public on the community's "official workdays" of Wednesdays, Saturdays, and Sundays. On these days there may be several hundred patients and mediums circulating the grounds. Valley officials estimate that every month up to 12,000 people visit the Mother Temple alone to participate in healing services.[4]

Patients bring a wide range of ailments, from chronic illness and psychological distress to more diffuse experiences of suffering. "All types of people frequent the Valley of the Dawn," Carmem Lúcia assured me.

> People with material problems, financial, spiritual, health—all types of problems—come here. We do not differentiate people based on their social or financial condition, their color or belief. The only distinction is this: if they are wearing a uniform, they are to serve. If they are not wearing a uniform, they are to be served.

Most patients arrive at the Valley after unsuccessful experiences with conventional medicine or other forms of alternative healing. Given Brazilians' widespread belief in spiritual ailments and distrust of publicly funded institutions, it is not unusual for people to seek assistance for their troubles in religion. Indeed, some observers have compared Brazil's contemporary religious landscape to a marketplace in which healing is the main product on offer (Chesnut 2003; Greenfield 2008).[5] While this oversimplifies the complexity of Brazilian religiosity, it is true that most Valley mediums are themselves former patients who came in search of healing and subsequently developed their mediumship in order to work within the Indian Space Current.[6] When Master Antônio Carlos observed that being helped is important, but helping is also important, he articulated a core Valley principle. As I detail later in this chapter, my informants experienced the act of serving others as integral to their own healing journey.

A significant percentage of patients come from what Brazilians refer to as the *classes desfavorecidas* or "disadvantaged classes." The problems they bring often are a result of, or exacerbated by, the poverty and precarious living situations they face. Alcohol abuse, addictions, domestic violence, and mental illness are common complaints, as are cases of the various folk ailments through which Brazilians classify different types of somaticized distress such as fright (*susto*), nerves (*nervos*), evil eye (*mal olhado*), or spiritual influence (*encosto*) (Rebhun 1994). Those who lack the financial resources to stay in the Valley while undergoing treatment can avail themselves of temporary housing and three meals a day at a facility on the Temple grounds established by a veteran member for that purpose. Otherwise, the town hosts a number of guesthouses and rooms for rent of varying levels of sophistication.

Among the dozens of patients in the Mother Temple waiting to be attended on the afternoon of October 17, 2012, was a woman who feared she had lost her eldest child to drugs and another who had lost her spouse to drink. A weathered-looking man told me that he had not been able to find steady work. A young woman whose older brother kept a tight grip on her arm throughout our conversation was tormented by voices that invaded her head unbidden. Others with whom I spoke that day shared stories of chronic and otherwise inexplicable physical ailments, incapacitating sadness, fatigue, dizziness, insomnia, relationship problems, and financial woes. In the years that I have been frequenting the Valley and talking to patients, their complaints encompass the spectrum of human suffering: from physical and emotional ills to addictions, relationship problems, and economic hardships.

Unwanted Conditions of the Self

What unites the disparate conditions treated at the Valley is that they represent "an unwanted condition in one's person or self—one's mind, body, soul, or connection to the world," in Robert Hahn's influential formulation (1995, 5).[7] An epidemiologist and medical anthropologist, Hahn proposed this definition of sickness as a means of understanding and comparing systems of healing practiced in different cultures. Because it foregrounds the perception and experience of the individual who is suffering, Hahn's definition is useful for recognizing how the Valley can meaningfully address the broad range of maladies brought by patients.

Hahn built on the pioneering work of Arthur Kleinman, whose research into cross-cultural interpretations of illness established a number of key theories in medical anthropology (2020 [1988]). Like Kleinman, Hahn made a critical distinction between *sickness* (or illness in Kleinman's terms) and *disease*. Where the former designates the patient's lived experience and narrative of suffering, the latter constitutes the physician's diagnosis of that experience according to biomedical theories of illness. Long dominant in the Western world, biomedicine (sometimes called conventional or allopathic medicine) focuses on the biological determinants of illness and decides treatment based on material, proximal causes.

Biomedicine has many strengths and is effective for many kinds of illnesses. Having eliminated most of the infectious diseases that were a leading cause of death in the Western world until the mid-twentieth century, for example, it contributed to a marked increase in human life expectancy. But it also has blind spots. It pays little or no attention to the existential and metaphysical significance of illness for the sufferer, to whom chronic suffering may feel like a punishment and for whom questions about ultimate causes, responsibility, and blame arise (Shweder et al. 1997). Its narrow concern with pathology and dysfunction, and exclusion of symptoms that cannot be ascribed to biological factors, means that biomedicine is significantly less successful with mental and emotional disturbances, chronic disorders, and stress-related ailments like high blood pressure, heart disease, digestive problems, headaches, fatigue, anxiety, and depression.

Not surprisingly, these are the most common complaints addressed by Spiritist healers in Brazil (Lucchetti et al. 2016) and elsewhere in Latin America (Moreira-Almeida and Koss-Chioino 2009). Spiritist forms of healing like those practiced at the Valley of the Dawn offer what cultural anthropologist Richard Shweder termed an "alternative causal ontology" for suffering (Shweder et al. 1997). As Shweder and his colleagues observed, most people experience suffering—especially its chronic forms—as an existential dilemma that requires explanation beyond the physical, proximal causes on which biomedicine focuses. The afflicted speculate about the deeper meaning of suffering: why they suffer, how it will affect their future, and what they can do to make it better. They wonder about ultimate causes and consider questions of responsibility and fault.

A powerful way to render suffering meaningful, Shweder wrote, "is to trace its genesis to some 'order of reality' where one may point the finger at events and processes that can be held responsible as suffering's cause" (Shweder et al. 1997). Because alternative causal ontologies address these deeper, existential questions about suffering, they tend to persist alongside or in place of biomedicine, often labeled as "folk" medicine or religion. Alternative causal ontologies reassure people that their suffering has a deeper purpose while enabling them to assign accountability or blame, identify modes of treatment, and feel a sense of control over events.

At the Valley of the Dawn, most forms of human suffering are traced to a spiritual order of reality. Only by recognizing and attending to this spiritual dimension, Valley members insist, can the conditions for wellbeing be restored. "Our concern is the spirit, not the person, not the physical body,"

Master Itamir reminded me. "We do not negate medical doctors," he continued. "If someone would be helped by a medical doctor, the entities will say so, and we never tell people to stop taking their medicine or pursuing medical treatment." Neither does the group offer any physical remedies, aside from the fluidified water said to be imbued with healing energy that is freely available inside the Temple and elsewhere on the grounds.

During the process of initiation, Valley members are trained to use an interconnected set of diagnostic categories as well as prophylactic and curative treatments that are intended to free the afflicted individual of negative spiritual influences and restore a state of spiritual equilibrium. In general, Valley members recognize three major spiritual causes of suffering and illness: unenlightened spirits, past life karma, and undeveloped mediumship.

In cases such as Peter Owen-Jones, for example, an individual may inadvertently attract low-level spirits by engaging in negative thinking. Thoughts and feelings are considered forms of energy that vibrate at specific frequencies and resonate with universal energies that share those same frequencies. Because they resonate at a lower frequency, negative thought patterns lure low-level spirits who consume that energy in the form of ectoplasm. This creates a kind of feedback loop that manifests in the individual as obsessive or demeaning thoughts; feelings of depression, despondency, anxiety, or mania; and/or addictions, compulsions, and other adverse behaviors. When English speakers say that they are "in low spirits" or "haunted" by negative thoughts, they express a similar sense of being overtaken by unwanted emotions experienced as originating outside of the self.

Alternatively, illness may be linked to the individual's karmic debts from a past life. Most often this takes the form of a *cobrador* or debt-collector spirit. This is the spirit of someone whom the afflicted harmed in a past life, either directly or through an ethical lapse or failure. In an attempt at karmic recompense, the cobrador is said to perturb the living in order to collect the debt he feels he is owed. More rarely, the afflicted person is understood to have chosen a particular illness before reincarnating on Earth as an expiatory act or in order to learn lessons that facilitate his or her evolution.

Finally, certain physical and social problems may indicate a "mediumistic disorder" caused by an excess of ectoplasm. Treatment in these cases involves learning how to recognize and develop one's particular faculty of mediumship, equalizing excess ectoplasm through the practice of mediumship. Because the Doctrine considers ectoplasm to be a subtle substance produced by normal biological processes of the body, undeveloped mediumship as a diagnostic category has both spiritual and biological dimensions.

Regardless of the etiology of a given illness, Valley members assert that the single most important ingredient for healing is faith. As Mário Sassi explained, at the most fundamental level healing requires "rebalancing a person, not only in relation to the problems he has, but also helping him to find his Spiritual path which will be his source of support" (Sassi 1977, 38). Individuals are free to pursue whatever spiritual path best suits them, in accordance with the Valley's emphasis on free will, but some form of faith is seen as necessary support for successfully negotiating one's journey on Earth. "Your healing depends on your faith," Master Antônio Carlos told me.

> Why do people experience physical healing here? Because that person has faith. We humans are motivated by faith. And when you have faith that something positive will happen, you can be sure that it has a 100% chance of happening. Our faith overcomes everything.

Continuing, he assured me,

> We don't try to convert people. Everyone is welcome here, regardless of their religious or political convictions. In fact, we never discuss those topics. Our only mission is this: to help humanity in its evolutionary journey on this planet of atonement and suffering.

Healing, then, is envisioned not as the elimination of afflictions or suffering, but as a state of spiritual equilibrium that enables the afflicted to weather their problems with love, tolerance, and forgiveness—even to embrace them as the means of greater self-knowledge and spiritual growth.[8] To put it in Hahn's terms, healing is successful when the patient's unwanted condition is redressed or re-framed in such a way that it no longer is experienced as unwanted, but rather as an opportunity for self-transformation, empowerment, and spiritual and moral development. "We don't perform miracles here," Nymph Vanda told me.

> No one gets up from their wheelchair in the middle of a ritual and starts walking around. The blind don't miraculously see. Here we help people heal spiritually. We help alleviate suffering by giving people encouragement,

helping people better understand themselves and their mission here on Earth.

Overhearing this conversation, a passerby named Zuleica paused to intervene. "The Doctrine does not eliminate the problems from your life," she said.

> No. It teaches you to accept, keep going, and work to resolve your issues yourself, without being overwhelmed by frustrations and whys. The Doctrine did not cure me of my multiple sclerosis, which is a genetic disease. But it has helped me learn to deal with it better. Today I have fewer relapses. I am calmer, more serene. And when I feel nervous or stressed or out of control, I come here and work spiritually so that I can manipulate that energy.

Those who report themselves healed may have experienced the diminution or elimination of their unwanted condition. But as Zuleica's comments suggest, it is just as likely that their involvement with the Doctrine has successfully transformed the existential meaning of their unwanted condition from something overwhelming or out of the person's control to something manageable. Paraphrasing Master Antônio Carlos, when you have faith that something positive will happen, you are more likely to see your condition in a positive light. For Zuleica, the Doctrine not only helped her accept and manage her chronic illness, but also provided a set of rituals through which she could "manipulate" and thereby transmute the negative emotional states associated with it. Her illness was not cured, but it no longer threatened her sense of being a whole self.

The Work of Disobsession

The Valley's public healing mission centers on the practice of disobsession. Like other Spiritist groups, the Doctrine holds that obsessing spirits or obsessores can energetically attach themselves to people through psychic affinity and provoke all manner of problems, from compulsive behaviors, addictions, and negative thought patterns to more serious diseases like cancer. Obsessing spirits are not necessarily malicious, however. Some may be confused by sudden death and its accompanying shift from embodiment to disembodiment. Disobsessive rituals aim to free people from these troubled "spirits without light" while restoring the patient's spiritual equilibrium so that she is less vulnerable to their prejudicial influence. At the same time, the rituals are said to assist obsessores who themselves are trapped in a nether world, unable to continue their evolutionary journeys.

Valley doctrine identifies three main categories of obsessing spirits, although in practice there is overlap among them: *sofredores* (sufferers), *obsessores* (obsessors), and *cobradores* (debt-collectors). Sofredores are spirits who do not realize that they have disincarnated and now wander the lower "subworlds" that surround the material plane. Described as lacking sunlight and sound, this shadowy realm is a purgatory where recently disincarnate spirits remain until they have exhausted their karmic commitments or are rescued by mediums working in the Christic System. Bereft of other energy sources, sofredores feed off the ectoplasm of the living, provoking emotional or physical disturbances in their victims (Sassi 1977, 20). "Normally," Mário Sassi noted, their parasitic effect is "neutralized" by the body's natural "bio-psychical" defenses. However, when human beings lower their "vibrational standard" by indulging in negative thought patterns or behaviors, they become vulnerable to sofredores and other low-level spirits (1977, 20). According to Master João and Master Itamir, this was what happened to Peter Owen-Jones in the Thrones.

Obsessores are spirits who seek to absorb the ectoplasmic energy of incarnate humans by creating strong feelings of rage, desire, jealousy, and so on. "To obsess means to chase, harass, lay siege," instructed Sassi. Obsessors typically are attracted to their victims because of a past relationship in which the obsessor feels that he is owed something from the victim (1977, 22). Unlike a sofredor, who can be removed by a simple disobsessive ritual, permanently freeing someone from an obsessor may require settling the debt through ritual action (22).

Finally, cobradores are the spirits of those whom the victim cruelly mistreated in a previous incarnation and who seek their revenge over multiple lifetimes as a karmic debt owed to them (Pierini 2020, 120). A cobrador may manifest in disincarnate form as an obsessor spirit, but it also might incarnate as the victim's parent, spouse, child, sibling, in-law, or other close family member or associate. In this way, present-day family tensions, personality clashes, and interpersonal dramas are understood as the karmic legacy of past malfeasance. Bound by transcendental ties, victim and oppressor continually reincarnate over multiple lifetimes, now as husband and wife, now as mother and child, until the karmic debt that links them can be fully reconciled.[9] As I explain in a later section, reconciliation requires a long-term process of "readjustment" (*reajuste*) through ritual and ethical behavior.

Differentiating themselves from other Spiritist groups who perform disobsession rituals, Jaguars claim that the Valley's practice of disobsessive healing is exceptionally effective because it does more than simply remove negative spiritual influences. It also educates the spirit and its victim about their true natures and encourages both to rethink their conception of life, moral values, and habits, and to return to the path toward God (Holston 1999). This pedagogical function is the job of the indoctrination medium, the doutrinador. According to the Valley, indoctrination is more than a process of rational persuasion. Because it transforms the "dense molecular structure" of perturbing spirits, thereby making them "lighter," it also is metaphysically efficacious. Once sufficiently light, the spirit can then be "elevated" or "magnetically projected" by the doutrinador to the spiritual planes through a ritual "key" (*chave*), where it can resume its evolutionary progression. In the Valley's conception, then, indoctrination "enlightens" low-level spirits literally as well as figuratively.

This molecular transformation is said to occur through an ectoplasmic exchange whereby the spirit absorbs the ectoplasm emitted by the doutrinador, typically (but not exclusively) in the form of a spoken ritual formula. While there is some room for adaptation, the basic formula is something like this:

> *Salve Deus* (Hail God).[10] Welcome, my brother, to this universal emergency room! Take advantage of this happy opportunity to realize that you have disincarnated and that only through love and forgiveness will you encounter equilibrium in your mind and harmony in your heart. At this blessed moment, let us ask Jesus, divine and beloved master, to illuminate your path.

In cases for which the obsessing spirit is so full of rage or hatred as to be dangerously beyond rational suasion, indoctrination occurs through a nonverbal mode of ectoplasmic transfer. In these situations, the spirit is said to absorb the doutrinador's ectoplasm through contact or proximity, becoming indoctrinated in the process. Again, Sassi expounded,

> [The Doctrine] is not just a set of well-articulated words with a nice literary construction. Also, it is not simply well-elaborated thought representing

precise ideas. It is, essentially, the emission of positive energy, which can be manifested either through words or through the application of the hands, through the gaze, and even through simple directed thought. (1972, 34)

Doctrinal materials are full of dense, pseudo-scientific explanations of the molecular effects of indoctrination, and many mediums can discourse learnedly on the subject, but patients themselves receive little explanation about the Valley's treatment methods. Those visiting for the first time are welcomed and given some orienting instructions by medium-receptionists, but otherwise can come and go as they please free of any obligation. This fact, along with the Doctrine's aversion to proselytization, fosters a general atmosphere of informality that is at once hospitable and patient-centered yet undemanding. At the same time, it is clear from the mediums' professional, compassionate demeanor and attention that the work of healing is serious business. Like its counterparts in the medical world, the spiritual emergency room of the Temple is staffed by people who have dedicated their time and energy to the work of alleviating human suffering.

Energetic Currents

On official workdays when the community's full complement of healing rituals is in session, the Valley of the Dawn is a busy place, its ritual spaces thick with moving bodies, myriad colors and sounds, the smell of incense, and the constant play of light glinting off sequined garments. Within the stone walls of the Temple, the bright sunlight of the high plains diffuses into a luminous penumbra, creating an atmosphere that even the staunch Catholic Father César described as possessing "indescribable mystical tranquility" (1977a, 370). Adding to the overall sensory experience, ranks of women dressed in ritual finery periodically traverse the Temple's corridors in regal procession singing *mantras* or hymns. These are said to cleanse and harmonize the environment, helping both mediums and patients to "tune into" the energetic frequency of healing.

According to Valley lore, Aunt Neiva received the lyrics and music to these *hinos mântricos*, or mantric hymns, directly from the spiritual planes. This repertoire constitutes one of the Valley's most distinctive elements, with live or recorded hymns featuring in many rituals. Jaguars say that the soothing atmosphere created by the hymns begins to "work" on people as soon as they enter the Temple, disintegrating negative charges and "heavy emanations." And indeed, scientific studies have shown that music can positively affect people's moods, lift depression, lower stress, increase blood flow, and ease pain.

With their recurrent references to sacred figures like Jesus, Father White Arrow, and Mother Yara, as well as to the healing work performed by masters "elevating spirits to heaven," the hymns also convey the idea of supernaturally mediated healing. The lyrics and melody have a way of insinuating themselves deep into the unconscious. During my first visit to the Valley, I inadvertently found myself singing a line about "healing hands, divine hands" from the "Hymn of the Doutrinador" that had been broadcast repeatedly over the speakers during a lengthy outdoor ritual I had attended. Although the line's catchy appeal does not readily translate to the page, it is not hard to imagine the psychological effect that repeated references to mediums' hands as vectors for divine healing might have on patients desperate for help.

Like individual instruments in an orchestra tuned to the same key, each aural, aesthetic, and architectural element within the Temple and its grounds is believed to contribute its energetic resonance, creating a total environment propitious for healing. The concern with harmonizing energies and directing their flows is evident in the layout of the elliptical-shaped Temple itself. Patients and visitors are advised to follow a specific trajectory, proceeding clockwise from the entrance through various healing sectors arrayed around the Temple's central core, which is cordoned off by low walls and restricted to uniformed mediums. In order to exit, one must complete the circuit back to the entrance or go against the prevailing flow of people and energy.

At the center of the Temple, visible but physically inaccessible to visitors, is the *Pira* or Pyre, a raised platform containing the sacred symbols of moon, sun, and the "divine presence." The latter is a representation of the sevenfold nature of man, a reference to the complex of spiritual, psychic, and material components that is believed to constitute both the human being and the larger universe.[11] Enhancing the sense of mystery, the sacred symbols of the Pira are shielded from the viewer by a semi-transparent veil of sheer curtains, preventing them from being touched or seen directly (see Image 7.1).

Referred to by Valley members as the "control center" of the Temple, the Pira is considered a gateway through which spiritual and extra cosmic energies are captured and then distributed to the Temple's various healing sectors. This is where the rituals that open and close each work shift are performed, and uniformed mediums come to make their preparations. The

196   SPIRITS OF THE SPACE AGE

Image 7.1 Pira. Credit Márcia Alves

energy beamed into the Temple through the Pira is believed to be so potent that mediums are advised to open their arms and expose their solar plexus when entering the building or crossing its midway point at the far end, lest they absorb a "shock" by interrupting its flow.

This idea of energetic flow or *corrente* (current) also structures how mediums conceptualize the work of healing. As patients pass through the Temple's diverse healing rituals, their energetic profile is said to be assessed, cleansed, adjusted, and recalibrated in ways intended to restore spiritual equilibrium. "When you arrive at the Valley of the Dawn," Master Itamir explained to me,

> The entity will clean your aura, remove all the negative impregnations so that you can regain spiritual equilibrium, receive positive vibrations, and recover your normal balance, right? This is our work.

The effects of this treatment are believed to extend beyond the spiritual domain to include psychological, emotional, and even physical benefits. Depending on the nature and severity of the problem, multiple treatments over an extended time period may be required, providing steady business for the town's various guesthouses.

The Thrones

The first stop for all patients—and the heart of the Valley's healing endeavor—is the Thrones (see Image 7.2). This is where highly evolved spirits of light, who manifest in the form of pretos velhos, evaluate the individual's spiritual profile (*quadra espiritual*), remove negative energies, determine an appropriate course of treatment, and serve as counselors offering words of wisdom and personal advice. For their part, patients are free to say as much or as little as they choose. At the conclusion of the ritual, the preto velho recommends an itinerary of healing works suited to that particular patient's needs.[12]

Aside from its putative spiritual effects, the psychotherapeutic benefits of patients' contact with the pretos velhos should not be overlooked. As Master Raul Zelaya, Aunt Neiva's youngest son and the current president of OSOEC, told me:

> Often people have no one with whom they can talk and get things off their chest and receive guidance. And this is a serious illness. So here come the pretos velhos spirits and the person can vent everything and then receive guidance. Half of his healing is there. Then he goes through the healing rituals, all of the steps, and this balances him.

Image 7.2 Thrones. Credit Márcia Alves

"What is the point of talking to a preto velho spirit?" Master Itamir queried me rhetorically, before answering himself. "It is to receive a word of succor, of hope, of life, of strength. These dear entities are always lifting people up, encouraging them towards the positive." Like a cherished grandparent, the nurturing presence of these familiar and much beloved entities creates an immediate sense of comfort for many people. And as Master Raul noted, the mere experience of unburdening oneself to a sympathetic ear and receiving guidance in return can be transformative.

An experience related to me by Sergio is a case in point. A thirty-four-year-old, heavily tattooed resident of São Paulo, Sergio had been visiting the Mother Temple regularly in his struggle to overcome an addiction to street drugs. Because we often stayed in the same guesthouse, I accompanied his story over several years. One afternoon he related to me an experience with a preta velha (female preto velho spirit) that had affected him deeply. Their conversation illustrates the loving encouragement and positive affirmation for which these spirits are known.

> When I sat down, she started to tell me everything that I was going through in life at that time, things that I had never told anyone else about my life in São Paulo, things that no one at the Valley could possibly have known. And I started to cry. Then she asked me to remember that I am a son of Father White Arrow and that I carry his blessing with me regardless—even when I am messing up and even when I think I'm not worthy. She told me that everything that I have gone through in life has made me the person that I am today. It sounds trite but that touched me a lot. It was something that I needed to hear at that moment because I was beating myself up a lot.

Consulting with the pretos velhos and receiving their guidance is not the only purpose of the Thrones, however. As Peter Owen-Jones discovered to his chagrin, periodically during the consultation the preto velho will attract and then give way to any sofredores and obsessores who have attached themselves to the patient, both feeding on and feeding into their negative habits. The doutrinador's task is to indoctrinate and elevate these lost souls, thereby disobsessing the patient. Once the spirit has been elevated, the apará then incorporates his or her preto velho mentor again and the consultation continues. Usually, the disobsession process happens in the space of a few moments and is repeated more than once, with the apará alternating between her preto velho mentor and multiple obsessores. When Owen-Jones got up in the middle of the ritual and left the Temple, his obsessor had not yet been indoctrinated and elevated. Loath to leave him in a state of disequilibrium, the mediums had run after him and coaxed him back to complete the process. The disobsessive process is considered dangerously incomplete and potentially harmful to the patient until the perturbing spirit has been indoctrinated and elevated and the patient has been "discharged" of any residual negative energy.

Bonuses, Spiritual Debts, and Debt-Collectors: The Economy of Karma

Understood in its broadest sense, obsession is a widespread condition in which human beings find themselves in the present cycle of the planet. Most people suffer the influence of spirits, in one or another obsessive form. In the common sense of the word, it is only recognized when the patient has visible signs of abnormality, such as convulsions, attacks of aggression or sudden collapse. As a result, there are two applicable therapies: one of emergency, and another long term. (Sassi 1972, 70)

While Valley members affirm that the disobsessive rituals performed at the Temple are effective for diverse ailments, they are considered an emergency treatment for acute symptoms of spiritual imbalance. Long-term healing, according to Aunt Neiva, requires a transcendental reckoning that is possible only when the patient discovers her higher self, or "individuality," and begins to align with that transcendental self, recognizing her karmic debts from past lives and working to pay them by earning spiritual merit—either at the Valley of the Dawn or within another doctrine. "We don't like to admit it, but we ourselves are the problem," Master Itamir explained to me as he led me around the Temple during my first visit. "Only when we get to know our true selves can we begin to evolve spiritually."

This self-knowledge is considered the ultimate purpose of mediumship. As part of the development process, the novice learns to differentiate between her individuality, described as a transcendental repository of wisdom and experience accumulated over many lifetimes, and her ephemeral personality, that is, the contingent or material self that is limited to the present life. "Usually, you are so preoccupied with your personality," Sassi noted in a pamphlet for mediums-in-training, that you rarely notice your Individuality. However, your spirit has the experience of many incarnations, of experiences lived over thousands of years. It has the accumulated experience of approximately 19 to 21 different personalities you once were! It's just that you don't remember that, you don't have the habit of thinking about your own spirit. This is not very concerning until . . . things start to go wrong. It is at this point that you came to the Valley of the Dawn and ended up becoming a Valley Medium. And because the Valley exists precisely to revive your spiritual memory, the main thing it will teach you is to regain contact with your own spirit [individuality]. This will be done through the mechanism of Mediumization." (Sassi 1977, 9)

Sassi went on to explain that once the medium has regained contact with her spirit or individuality by developing her mediumship, her life path becomes clearer. She begins to understand herself simultaneously as a personality who has incarnated on Earth in order to rectify past karmic debts and as an individuality with a transcendent mission. Her life becomes more comprehensible and balanced, and she becomes "a person who radiates empathy and concern for others" (48). She begins to attract "the emanations of the Superior Spirits, of her Guides, her Mentors, and becomes the spokesman for these Spirits" (48). At this point, according to Sassi, it becomes possible for her to work in the Law of Assistance and earn the spiritual merit that brings long term healing.

At the Valley, spiritual merit is measured in something called "bonus hours" or, more simply, "bonus" (*bônus*). Envisioned as a credit received for spiritual work, the concept of bonus hours was portrayed in Chico Xavier's enduringly popular 1944 book *Our Home* (*Nosso Lar*), which purports to describe in detail the world that awaits us after death.[13] Since its publication, *Nosso Lar* has been translated into multiple languages and sold millions of copies worldwide, becoming part of an international canon of Spiritist literature.[14] As David Hess observed, the book's representation of the otherworld was thoroughly absorbed into, and became characteristic of, Brazilian Spiritism (1991b).

According to Chico Xavier, *Nosso Lar* was dictated to him by the spirit of a doctor named André Luiz, for whom Xavier served as medium. It recounts André Luiz's experiences and the lessons he learns after passing through the portal of death and eventually arriving in the spirit colony known as Nosso Lar. To André Luiz's surprise, his new environment is remarkably like the terrestrial world he left behind: the spirits of Nosso Lar reside in houses and have families, they study in universities, recuperate in hospitals, and spend their time working and pursuing projects of self-improvement.[15]

As André Luiz quickly learns, because each spirit's basic needs for shelter, clothing, and food are provided for by the colony's governing body, no one is obligated to work. However, those who do acquire "bonus hours," which can be used for certain privileges like nicer clothing, entertainment, special time with loved ones, or access to more advanced teachings. There is one condition though: the work must be performed freely for the collective good without attachment to its reward. Such work is understood to instill values important for the spirit's continued moral development and evolution. The book's depiction of a utopian-like afterlife built on progressive ideals captivated audiences in Brazil and elsewhere, and the concept of bonus hours became a central Spiritist tenet.

At the Valley of the Dawn, bonus hours are conceived as "vital energies that are transferred from one to the other," as Aunt Neiva told her followers in a letter (J. Souza n.d., 91). Mediums affirm that these spiritual energies "are given to us in return for the love with which we dedicate ourselves to our activities in the Law of Assistance" (Siqueira et al. 2010, 254–255). In other words, by participating in Valley rituals, working to help others, and living out the Christic virtues of unconditional love, humility, and tolerance in their daily lives, mediums earn a certain number of bonus hours. Master Raul explained it to me in this way:

> True healing is the product of your merit (*merecimento*). Our doctrine seeks the equilibrium of mankind. It is not working miracles or anything. There is no miracle, there is only healing based on your merits. It is God who determines everything. And if you are doing good for others, no matter if it is within this doctrine or another, you will receive bonus hours, you will receive spiritual merit.

Spiritual merit can be used to settle karmic debts, request the assistance of spirit mentors on one's own or others' behalf, or release cobrador spirits. Bonus hours, in other words, are the medium of exchange in a spiritual economy structured much like the capitalist workplace: in return for their spiritual work, mediums earn the means of paying off debts and acquiring certain privileges and benefits believed to improve their lives in the present and ensure a better future.

Imprisonment and Liberation

We cannot remain oblivious to our past, to what we did or neglected to do, because in the evolutionary cycle of life we cannot leave marks where we have passed. At times, through unconsciousness, vanity, or even self-affirmation, we hurt someone and continue on as if nothing happened. But one day the re-encounter will happen, there has to be a reckoning, and Prison is the most subtle means, because there is love and conscience. –Aunt Neiva

The process of earning bonuses and using them to redeem karmic debts is publicly dramatized in the *Prisão* or Prison ritual. During this weeklong endeavor, Valley members spend their free time accumulating bonuses. These will be used in negotiations with disincarnate cobradores in a culminating ritual modeled on a courtroom trial. According to Aunt Neiva, cobradores, or debt-collectors, are spirits imprisoned by the animus they bear toward those who mistreated them in the past. Instead of pursuing their own evolution, they create problems for their victims to recoup the "debt" they believe is owed them. Many of the personal challenges that Valley mediums face, from relational dynamics and emotional issues to physical illness and chronic misfortune, are attributed to cobradores. These spirits "invisibly approach the person and provoke discomfiting situations," Mário Sassi wrote. "With that, they cause pain, and this releases the energies that they feel they are owed. . . . Thus are our annoyances and daily disasters" (1972, 63). Because "we stole a specific energy from him," Sassi elaborated in a later publication, a cobrador "only feels 'avenged' when he sees his debtor 'punished' in the same way he was reviled" (1977, 69).

"We believe that we have cobradores who are both incarnate and disincarnate," Nymph Janaína clarified to me,

> Most of the time, the incarnate cobradores are our husbands, our wives, our mothers, our fathers, those whom you can't stand sometimes, but you have to live with. And within that relationship is where you work humility, love, tolerance. By treating that person with love, tolerance, and humility, you prove to your cobrador that you have changed, that you're no longer that person from other times. It's a *reajuste* (readjustment): you transform that karmic debt through your behavior with that person.

Operating according to the same principle of *reajuste* or readjustment, the Prison ritual targets disincarnate cobradores, offering contemporary Jaguars an opportunity to use their spiritual merit to redeem past transgressions of which they may be completely unaware. Master Itamir described the process to me in this way:

> We are Spiritists and we believe in reincarnation and that we have lived in other opportunities. And in those other opportunities, many times we contract debts, moral debts, where we have harmed someone and we haven't had enough time for forgiveness. Then what happens? I disincarnate and this other person disincarnates with a lot of hatred for me, charging me for all those things I did to him. There in the spiritual planes, there is no way for us to evolve with this debt pending. So, we are given the opportunity to reincarnate on Earth and repair our mistake. Generally, the debtor is the one who incarnates and the cobrador, he is waiting for an opportunity to collect. So, when I feel that cobrador start demanding recompense from me, then I assume a Prison, we call it a Spiritual Prison, where we have seven days to collect bonuses for my release. (Damião 2004)

The Prison ritual was inspired by a vision that Aunt Neiva had in 1981, a period when James Holston was conducting fieldwork at the Valley.[16] As Holston recounted it, Neiva's vision centered on the story of Aragana, a woman who had murdered her husband in a previous incarnation. The husband's hatred and rage toward Aragana at the moment of his death was so great that his spirit was imprisoned in the lower subworlds where it could not reincarnate. Trapped in endless darkness, the spirit sought vengeance as Aragana's cobrador, tormenting her so thoroughly that she referred to it as "her prison."

Eventually the spirits of light, seeing that Aragana was a good and hardworking woman, agreed to convene a spiritual tribunal. Attorneys for the prosecution and defense gave their arguments before the court, and Aragana, confronted by her victim, begged his forgiveness. Her love, sincerity, and sorrow were absorbed by her cobrador in the form of ectoplasm, dissolving his rage. Thus "indoctrinated," the cobrador declared the debt paid, and the tribunal pronounced both parties liberated. As a result, the husband's spirit was able to resume his evolutionary journey and move on, and Aragana was freed from prison (Holston 1999, 621).

Modeled on Aragana's tribunal, the Prison ritual purports to help contemporary Jaguars free themselves from disincarnate cobradores that otherwise would require four or five lifetimes to appease. At first Aunt Neiva decided who in the community needed to assume prison, and, using her powers of clairvoyance, she would describe the crimes that person had committed in previous lives (Holston 1999, 621). With Neiva's passing, however, participation became a matter of individual choice. Today, mediums who take on the status of prisoner usually do so in response to marked changes in their mood or life circumstances that suggest a cobrador's pernicious presence. This includes sudden or otherwise inexplicable feelings of anguish, rage, or depression, sudden behavioral changes, or bodily aches and fevers.

Jaguars who commit to becoming "prisoners of Greater Spirituality" for the week wear special uniforms signaling their state. For women the Prisoner's uniform consists of a colorfully striped dress, a special hair ornament worn on the left side of the head, and a silver or gold arm band, in accordance with her faculty of mediumship, which is worn on the left upper arm (see Image 7.3). Men dress plainly in brown pants and a black shirt topped by a special leather sash called an *ataca*. Without the protection afforded by their customary spiritual armaments, prisoners are said to be more vulnerable to their cobradores, who can more readily identify and approach them.

To be eligible to participate in the ritual of liberation that culminates the weeklong proceedings, prisoners must have accumulated at least 2,000 bonus hours. These are earned by participating in works of disobsessive healing and by gathering written signatures from fellow Jaguars in small notebooks, referred to as *"livros de bônus"* or bonus books. Each signature represents a bonus for the prisoner as well as the person named, so those signing typically write their own name as well as the names of others they judge to need healing. Likewise, each work of disobsessive healing in which the prisoner participates is worth a certain number of bonus hours. Because half of the 2,000 bonuses must be in the form of signatures, the Mother Temple's central square often is filled with prisoners collecting the autographs of passersby (see Image 7.4).

There are two different versions of the liberation ritual, which alternate weekly: the *Julgamento* or Trial, and the *Aramê*, a term unique to the Valley. Both envision the spiritual release of prisoner and cobrador. The most significant difference is that the Aramê is directed at anonymous cobradores linked to episodes within the Jaguars' mythological past, while the Julgamento targets specific victims known to mediums in their previous lives.

Both rituals proceed in the form of an elaborate courtroom trial, complete with various court officials as well as prosecuting and defense attorneys and other formal positions, all filled by designated Valley mediums. In general,

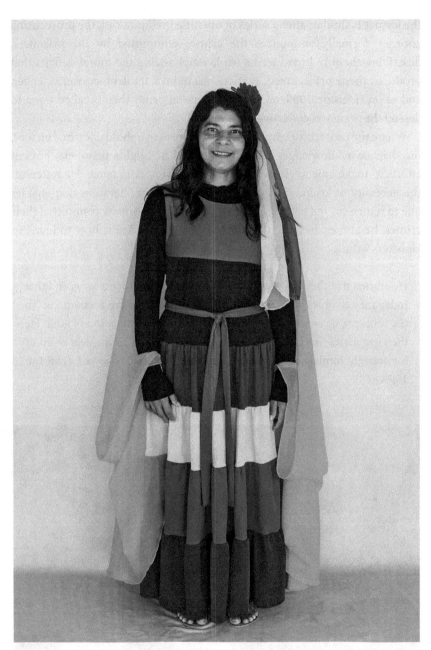

Image 7.3 Female prisoner. Credit Márcia Alves

the format is similar: after a series of opening preliminaries, the prosecuting attorney formally announces the crimes committed by the prisoners, describing them in broad terms while emphasizing the moral deficits that produced them: pride, greed, avarice, lack of love, intolerance, vanity, anger, and so on (Holston 1999, 623). The defense attorney then is called upon to defend the prisoners collectively.

Where the prosecutor emphasizes past failures to uphold doctrinal virtues, the defense acknowledges these failures and highlights prisoners' present efforts to make amends by working in the Law of Assistance. He reiterates the necessity of love and forgiveness as a means of liberation that enables one to return to "the path of Truth and Life." The prisoners committed their crimes, he argues, because ultimately "they did not know how to love." In Holston's words,

> He affirms that they have already paid dearly for their ignorance, and that today they have learned. He does not excuse or deny the accusations. To the contrary, he emphasizes the prisoners' heartfelt admission of guilt. He then negotiates for clemency, pleading for a reduction of the debt owed or for outright forgiveness on the basis of the time already served. (Holston 1999, 632)

Image 7.4 Gathering bonuses. Credit Márcia Alves

Following the attorneys' speeches, the pretos velhos are summoned, and, depending on which version of the ritual is being performed, the prisoners may be called up individually for a consultation with these elevated souls. On occasion, a preto velho may give way to a cobrador, and the prisoner will have an opportunity to talk with his tormentor and former victim directly. Finally, the court pronounces both prisoner and cobrador liberated. "He forgives me, I forgive him, he leaves, and I am released," a member pithily summarized the process to me. "This is a wonderful thing that we like very much, we feel relieved and fulfilled" (Hayes 2020b). Jaguars with whom I have spoken over the years are unanimous in considering the Prison an effective means of resolving present-day troubles.

As dramatized in the liberation ritual, past harms, conceived as karmic debts, are publicly aired and adjudicated. Throughout the proceedings, the transformative power of the community's doctrine and moral values is emphasized in various ways: via the words spoken by the attorneys, the conduct of the prisoners, and the final outcome itself. The entire ritual, as well as the prisoner's preparatory work of gathering bonuses, references the modern legal system and the paperwork and official signatures through which it operates. But unlike the Brazilian legal system, this ritual process seeks to achieve justice for both parties in the form of spiritual liberation, rather than punishment and retribution.

By conducting themselves with love, humility, and compassion during their week of prison, prisoners demonstrate to their cobradores that they have morally evolved—that they are "no longer that person from other times," as Janaína put it. "He will know this because of our harmony," a doctrinal resource explains,

> through our dedication to the Law of Charity, by the vibration of our love and, especially, by our reaction to those situations in which he puts us. We have to make him perceive and believe that we have changed. He has to have certainty that the hand that is today extended to him is the hand of a loving sibling who wants to bring him to the Light, and not any longer the hand of someone dominated by passion, by vanity, by ambition, the armed hand that took away his life and cut off his dreams, his hopes, the instrument of a heart without love! (Souza 2000, entry on Prisão)

Where the Prison ritual envisions suffering and healing through the transactional metaphor of debt and recompense, my last example illustrates how the

Valley helps people overcome suffering by transforming their understanding of the self.

Zack: With Great Power Comes Great Responsibility

Zack, an Australian national from Sydney, came to the Mother Temple in 2015 order to develop his mediumship. When we spoke, he was still an aspirant and was completing his first set of development classes.[17] Zack told me that he had been introduced to the Valley of the Dawn back in Sydney when he attended several "cleansing sessions" held by Australian mediums who had been initiated at the Mother Temple.[18] These cleansing sessions had had a profound effect on Zack, and he credited them with helping him find his purpose in life. "For me this is just the start," he said,

> I want to bring this to more people like me. I want to bring this doctrine around the world where it can start to change people's lives for the better because there are a lot of people who suffer. In the words of Spiderman, with great power comes great responsibility and I want to help people like I have been helped.

Zack had experienced a great deal in his twenty years, he confided to me in a series of interviews, his childhood inexorably marked by an absent father and constant strife with his mother. Both strong-willed people, the two clashed frequently. By his own account, Zack was the kind of kid who was allergic to rules and wanted to know the reason for everything: why did he have to come home and such and such an hour? Why did he have to make his bed every morning when he was just going to mess it up again that night? Nothing rankled him more than rules grounded in tradition or the mere exercise of authority. And Zack's mother, for her part, felt no compunction to explain herself to anyone, least of all a child. Mother and son "seemed to bring out the worst in one another," Zack recalled.

When Zack turned thirteen, their disagreements started to get physical. Feeling like she could not handle him anymore, Zack's mother sent him away to a residential camp for troubled youths. When he returned home, Zack reported, "it was okay for a while, then it all turned to shit again." Before long he was kicked out of his mother's house for smoking marijuana and stealing, and the next few years were marked by a cycle of reconciliations and rejections. Zack spent his last year of high school "sleeping on couches, sleeping in friends' garages, begging for food from pantries." He would talk with his mother from time to time, "but it wasn't good." Zack's drug use escalated, and soon he was going on weeklong benders fueled by cocaine and crystal meth. When he was not high, he felt depressed and despondent. "I was never fulfilled, and I did not know what I was chasing, but I was chasing something constantly," he told me.

> I was an absolute druggie, I was partying all the time and hating life. And I could not really get out of it, it is not like I could just stop. Some people can just quit but I could not physically stop. Injecting and shots, and ice [crystal meth] and other stuff that I thought was disgusting, who would ever do that? But I was doing it and I could not stop. I was working as a busboy in a sports bar-type place so I could be high all the time and not have to interact with too many people.

Eventually, Zack realized that he felt angry all the time. "I had so much rage inside of me, like it was always boiling right beneath the surface." So, when his friend Anton invited him to what was billed as a "cleansing ceremony," Zack readily agreed. "It is like the ones they have at the Thrones, where the pretos velhos incorporate," Zack explained to me.

> I did not know what to expect. I just needed something. I am an open guy, I like to try everything, and I am kind of spiritually inclined. But you gotta convince me pretty hard if you want me to believe something. So, I walk into the room where they were conducting [the ceremony] and I did not know what to expect. I just knew you had to sit down and say your name and you could ask a few questions. That is what we were told. And when I walked into the room, before I even sat down, the woman who was incorporated—did you ever see the movie *The Dark Knight*? You know the voice that Heath Ledger uses as the Joker, which is so sinister and evil and just freezes the blood in your veins? She says to me in that voice, "I know you; we have played together a long time." And this woman does not not know me from a bar of soap. I have never really expressed this to anyone before in my life, but that particular voice—I have spoken in that voice to myself. Not like schizophrenia or anything, it just sometimes happened. And sometimes when I would get angry with my mom I would speak in that voice. Just an evil, sadistic, scary voice. So, when she spoke to me in that voice, I freaked out.

> I was like, ok, whatever this is, that is the realest stuff I have ever heard in my whole life. Nobody knows that I spoke like that. It was crazy, I could not believe it. I was literally, absolutely gobsmacked. And then I had a number of obsessors, lost brothers, come through. At one point she literally started punching herself in the face and I just had to sit there and be like, what the hell is going on? But at the same time, I knew, because I have had a lot of demons for a long time. I honestly never really knew that it was demons per se, I just thought it was me, that I am just totally messed up.

At some point during the ceremony, Zack reported that his hands started to shake, and his eyes started to close, and he could not open them.

> And what is happening is that I am incorporating without even meaning to. That is when Anton starts whacking me on the back as hard as he can, saying, "open your eyes, open your eyes!" I did not really know what it all meant until later. But when the ceremony was over, I just felt light: extraordinary, indescribable lightness. Like, awareness, peace. It was unbelievable, it was so cool. It was a purification, I felt clean.

Zack started going to the cleansing sessions regularly. He found that the pretos velhos "gave me the advice I needed to hear."

> One time they said, "you need to learn to say no." That's what they said: "you need to learn to say no." So, I began to think about the practice of saying no, whether it was smoking weed or something else. I did not want to, but I just thought about the practice of saying no, and that totally altered my life.

The combination of the advice and the cleansing ritual in which obsessing spirits would manifest and be indoctrinated gave Zack a way to think about his life and a set of tools to take control over the behaviors that felt out of his control. In his words,

> It gave me the strength, mindset, and motivation to start living more intentionally and more powerfully. It gave me the impetus to start to change things. I had been to rehab camp, I had been to psychiatrists, I had done programs, I had had counseling. I had done all of that. I have had so much self-development, but nothing made the difference like this did.

Eventually, the pretos velhos informed him that he needed to go to Brazil to develop his mediumship because it was "way too over-developed." As Zack described it,

> They told me that I was supposed to come to Brazil a while ago and I needed to be here right now. And more and more as I started to open up, my natural, spiritual side was reawakened, and I started to see people's auras and be more intuitive with people in their intentions and it just became pretty clear, yeah, I gotta go do this. That is why my mom was so on board with getting me over here, because she had seen this change finally in me and she was like, ok, this kid is serious, and we have got to get him to Brazil.

With the financial help of his mother Zack flew to Brasília and went directly to the Mother Temple. He began the development classes the following day, training as an apará. The training was not quite what he had expected, as he explained to me.

> It is intense. The past few weeks I have been quite frustrated. Because I came here expecting—wham, straight back in it, like I cannot even control it. But I learned for starters that it is not a complete takeover, it is 50/50. So, you have to be aware. And because my mediumship is what they translated as "expired," it is not going to come strongly for me at first. That does not mean permanently, what it means is that I have all this energy built up on top, so I have to work it all down to actually be in the prime state to incorporate. If that makes any sense. So, expired, but not completely gone.

A few weeks later as the training continued, Zack felt that his mediumship was becoming stronger. "It has been easier to go into and get rid of the self and let this thing come through," he affirmed. "This sort of stuff cannot really be taught, it can only be practiced, because if it had to be taught, I would be a doctor." The trick, he felt, was learning to give way. "To me it is just about getting into the flow, letting go of the need to control or understand, just becoming a better vehicle to help that cosmic force come through," he said. "It is like I am a race car, and they are the driver."[19]

In one of our last conversations, Zack confided, "I think my purpose was to come here and to spread the Gospel, if you know what I mean. I want to help other people like I have been helped." The Valley of the Dawn, he explained, "taps into an inherent spirituality" with which people in the modern world have lost touch.

> It reawakens that part of you, it gives you motivation to succeed, because you are actually doing something you are meant to be doing in life. Not just going to work, having kids and a family and buying a television, filling up your life with material things. When people truly open themselves up spiritually, it is life changing. So many people think that just going to the psychiatrist or buying that new thing or going on a holiday is going to change everything. But it is not dealing with what is internally going on with them. Whether it is an obsessor spirit, whether it is just breaking down some mental shit and anguish they have not dealt with. And the Valley is, just like, straight bang into it. It gets to the core of you immediately, because it is not a human being talking, it is a superior, cosmic force that knows everything about you, knows exactly what you need and knows exactly what you need to be doing to get well.

Although Zack did not frame his desire to help others as a means of redeeming his own negative karma, as many Valley members do, it is clear that he was compelled by the Doctrine's interpretation of psychological distress as the influence of negative energies or spirits. Participating in the cleansing ceremonies in Australia had given him resources to reframe his life experiences as well as strategies for exerting self-control, such as learning to say no. By practicing these strategies, he had seen positive changes in his life that filled him with the desire to help others like him. Perhaps most dramatically, he had come face to face with his own "demons," which enabled him to see his rage and drug use as a product of external forces, rather than an inherent condition of being "totally messed up." The process of developing his mediumship had given Zack a set of techniques to objectify and release these demons and the passion to help others like him. Importantly, Zack saw the Valley as tapping into a transcendent dimension of human existence at odds with the materialist values of the modern world, which gave him a profound sense of higher purpose. He began to see a future for himself as a medium. No longer a problematic kid alienated from those around him, he was working to become a better vehicle for a superior, cosmic force in order to help others like him.

Zack's story demonstrates how the Valley's causal ontology imbues suffering with existential meaning while identifying it as amenable to transformation through ritual and ethical action. This causal ontology helped Zack reinterpret the troubled patterns in his life and recognize and channel their more disruptive energies. Training as a medium offered Zack a route to greater self-knowledge and moral development. It gave him a purpose that aligned with his values and what he felt were innate spiritual sensitivities. It immersed him in a community of like-minded people who had dedicated themselves to serving others. While its details reflect the particulars of Zack's life, his story's basic elements were echoed in my interviews with other Valley mediums: (1) an initial period of suffering experienced as an "unwanted condition of the self" (illness, depression, addiction, disruptive relationships, or some other chronic malady that impacts the person's body, mind, spirit, or connection to the world); (2) an inchoate longing for purpose beyond worldly measures of success and material consumption; (3) a self-described sensitivity to energies, emotional states, intuitions, and other non-ordinary states of consciousness that can be interpreted readily as mediumship; and, finally, (4) a shift from feeling like someone in need of help to feeling like someone who can help others.

The positive effects of helping others for one's own sense of wellbeing are well documented in the psychological and scientific literature (e.g., Hui et al. 2020). This includes enhanced feelings of social connection and empathy, as well as the release of mood enhancing neurochemicals that psychologists call "helper's high" (Inagaki et al. 2016). Among these are serotonin, oxytocin, and dopamine, some of the same neurochemicals activated by street drugs like crystal meth (Kish 2008). For people with chemical additions like Zack, this may help alleviate symptoms of withdrawal or cravings, although more research would need to be done to support this hypothesis.

The Ultimate Transformation

Every unwanted condition or experience of suffering has more than one potential cause and more than one path to resolution. Yet the biologically based paradigm of modern medicine tends to leave unaddressed the deeper, existential questions that suffering poses by restricting its scope to physiological—and, to a lesser extent, psychological—symptoms. But suffering, especially chronic suffering, fundamentally disrupts how people understand themselves and their connection to other people and the larger world. The uncertainty and chaos that attend suffering threaten the sufferer's sense of self-worth, agency, relationships, and expectations for a viable future. Bereft of a larger context of meaning, suffering can corrode the quality of life itself.

I have argued that the Valley of the Dawn offers its adherents a causal ontology that imbues suffering with transcendent meaning; a set of practices intended to mitigate its corrosive effects; a program of self-development centered on the cultivation of positive virtues, discipline, and service; and a community of like-minded others.[20] By linking suffering with the evolutionary journey of the self and offering a set of ritual and ethical practices intended to transform it, the Valley of the Dawn makes the afflicted an active protagonist within her own saga of progress and redemption. The narrative frame provided by the Doctrine helps participants reevaluate an unwanted condition as a positive opportunity for spiritual growth, self-development, and the acquisition of transformational knowledge and capacities. This empowers people to understand themselves in new ways and make changes in their lives that enhance their sense of wellbeing, agency, and alignment with a greater, cosmic purpose.

However, this is not the ego-driven project of self-enhancement that psychologist Scott Barry Kaufman dismissed as "spiritual narcissism" (2021). Rather, the Valley emphasizes the so-called Christic virtues of unconditional love, compassion, forgiveness, tolerance, and charity as primary to the work of self-transformation. These values are put into practice by using one's mediumship to serve others. Nymph Aparecida was particularly eloquent on this point:

> This is a doctrine that promises you nothing. Quite the opposite: it asks a lot of you. It asks you to have love, tolerance, humility, it asks you to help everyone without regard. It asks you to serve others, to love others. The Doctrine shows you that you must help others in order to be helped. And when you think you have nothing to do, there is someone who still needs you. The pain of others is always greater than your own, and this makes your problems seem very small.

The ultimate transformation, Nymph Janaína told me, was learning to embody the "living Gospel" of Christ:

> The main thing that I have learned in the Doctrine is this: I don't change anyone, I change myself. With humility, love, and tolerance I transform

myself, because we work with the manipulation of energy. And when I transform myself, I can live at peace with everything and everyone. This is the ultimate transformation: it is learning to be a serene person, to respect the limits of others, to respect the disability of others and also to help that person without interfering in her life, forcing her to do what I think she should do. To serve others unconditionally, without expectations and without attachments, that is the living Gospel of Jesus and that is what we practice here.

As Aparecida and Janaína's remarks make clear, this kind of self-transformation is a gradual, long-term process. Where the daily work of disobsessive healing performed at the Temple is considered an emergency treatment for acute suffering, true healing involves an "ultimate transformation" of the self through ethical and ritual conduct. This is predicated on the sufferer becoming immersed in—and transformed by—the Valley's imagined world.

* * *

8
Transcendental Heritages

The power of material culture resides in its ability to make physically present what is otherwise distant or absent or insensate, to embody the inchoate feelings, dim presentiments, the distant past, the deceased leader or saint, the religious community, the intangible or transcendent reality, and to discipline and enlist the body in acts of shared imagination. —David Morgan (2010, n.p.)

Transcendental Heritages

"According to Aunt Neiva," Master Antônio Carlos informed me in 2012 as we sat in a ritual space adjacent to the Temple, "the Jaguars have had between nineteen and twenty-one incarnations. The youngest member here is 12,000 years old. The oldest is 32,000 years old." Before I could interject with a question, he resumed:

> We passed through Egypt, through Rome, through Sparta, we were among the Greeks and Trojans. We were in imperial Brazil, colonial Brazil, Peru, we were gypsies in Russia. So, for each of these incarnations, we have transcendental inheritances that we carry. Each of us has a debt from the past. Aunt Neiva, through her spiritual powers, was able to bring to the present age the energies that are localized in various dimensions of the past. Today we are here to redeem ourselves from former mistakes, to transform that energy into something positive. That is the great essence of the Valley of the Dawn.

According to the Doctrine, Aunt Neiva's clairvoyance enabled her to see the complex web of karmic entanglements that ensnared the Jaguars across axes of time and space as individuals continually reincarnated, sometimes as family members or lovers, sometimes as bitter rivals. Veterans recall that the

Spirits of the Space Age. Kelly E. Hayes, Oxford University Press. © Oxford University Press 2024.
DOI: 10.1093/oso/9780197516393.003.0008

Clairvoyant periodically recounted events from her previous incarnations as well as details about the past lives of the people surrounding her. "She could see your spiritual quadrant (*quadra espiritual*) and tell you all about [the conflicts and interpersonal dynamics] that account for your present situation," Master Manoel assured me. Sometimes Aunt Neiva's stories about the past were relatively developed chronicles detailing the Jaguars' internecine rivalries in ancient Egypt, for example, or their adventures as a clan of gypsies in Russia, or when, as an Indigenous tribe in the Andean mountains, they faced off against Spanish conquistadors. Other times they took shape as laconic, but evocative, references to interpersonal dramas set in faraway times and places. No matter how fragmentary, Neiva assured her followers, each of these incarnations had contributed to the community's transcendental heritage.

Among Aunt Neiva's own roster of past lives were incarnations as the legendary Egyptian queens Nefertiti and Cleopatra; Pythia, priestess of the Oracle of Delphi; and the prophetess Veleda, who led her Germanic tribe in resistance against Roman invaders in the first century CE. But Aunt Neiva was not the only one with a lineage of notable incarnations as historic personalities. In one lifetime, Mário Sassi had been Mark Antony to Neiva's Cleopatra, while the veteran master, José Carlos Nascimento Silva, was Julius Caesar. "What most affected us was when [Neiva] was Cleopatra and I was Julius Cesar," the latter recalled in an interview with historian Marcelo Reis. "And Mário [Sassi] was Mark Anthony. And so, I understood why, at times, me and Mário had some squabbles, some friction. I also understood why [my wife] Dinah had a certain precaution with [Neiva]" (Reis 2008, 208, 240–241).

Likewise, other veteran members had played leading roles in diverse civilizations spread across time and space. These histories are understood to explain the personality dynamics or "transcendental ties" among individual community members, but they also have karmic consequences for the Jaguars as a collective that must be redressed. "We were slaves, slave masters, kings and queens, subjects, all kinds of people," Nymph Olivia explained to me in 2010.

> In ancient Rome, we were soldiers helping expand and consolidate the Empire. Among the ancient Mayans we developed advanced astronomical knowledge. Later, as gypsies in nineteenth century Russia, we practiced the arts of prophecy. We have been reunited in various incarnations on this

planet and we have reunited again here in Brazil. We are here to recover our transcendental heritage or what we were in the past. Because we believe—and I am absolutely sure—that we bring to this present life many things from other incarnations that must be rectified. I am sure of that, and I have had many proofs that this is exactly what happens.

For contemporary Jaguars like Olivia, the Valley of the Dawn offers a precious opportunity to learn from the lessons of the past and *"reajustar,"* or reconcile, their karmic debts by transforming that energy "into something positive," as Master Antônio Carlos put it. The ways that the Doctrine materializes the Jaguars' collective past—how the community envisions and invokes, represents, and reckons with its transcendental inheritance—is the subject of this chapter.

Valley members describe the ancient civilizations of Egypt, the Mediterranean, pre-Columbian Mesoamerica, and other imagined spacetimes, as highly resonant locus points for forces—cosmic, spiritual, and karmic energies—that are manipulated in ritual. "Aunt Neiva brought our transcendental inheritances from the richest civilizations of the past and unified them in one complete system," Master Antônio Carlos explained:

And these transcendental heritages are represented in the vestments, in the master's capes, in the symbols, in the missionary phalanxes, in every corner of this Temple, in each construction. For example, here where we are sitting presently is the Turigano and it has a strong connection with the Oracle of Delphi. Here on Sundays, we relive a part of our history that happened in Sparta with King Leonidas, so it is living our incarnations and bringing the energies from those times, from that ancient people, and transforming them.

Each detail of the movement's intricate material culture contributes to the mise-en-scène for this work of energetic transformation. "The Valley creates a certain fantasy, as if it were Alice in Wonderland," Sergio, the São Paulo native whose experience with a preta velha I recounted in Chapter 7, told me.

Trying to represent what other spiritual planes would be like, trying to communicate that life is not only here on the physical, terrestrial plane, it is something far more extensive. At the Valley, you can travel through various epochs. The Valley recalls different times and eras, which are suggestions to your mind of different worlds. There are lots of colors and garments that give you suggestions, so your mind is working with colors, images, symbols, songs, clothing, rituals—these are suggestions for you to travel in your mind. So, I see the Valley as a school of life, not a place where exceptional things happen. It teaches you about life and its possibilities, by messing with your fantasy, with your creativity, with your senses. And by messing with your imagination, you begin to see life in a different way.

Indeed, one of Aunt Neiva's greatest talents was her ability to holistically engage people's imaginations by immersing them in a paracosmic world expressed in "colors, images, symbols, songs, clothing, and rituals."[1] In Chapter 5 I discussed how this paracosmic world is made real for adherents—that is, becomes an intersubjectively shared and experientially grounded framework of reality—through mediumistic development and sensory absorption. This chapter builds on that argument, but my focus here narrows to the imagined space-times, or *chronotopes*, of the Jaguars' transcendental past. More precisely, I examine how the Valley's material culture evokes select chronotopes through different sensory media, thereby bringing them into the mind-space of the present. While Valley members understand these chronotopes as repositories of energies that are accessed and transformed in ritual, I will focus on how they function in a larger project of community formation and self-transformation.

Chronotopic Regimes

At its most basic level, a chronotope is a way of imagining past times and places and constructing a relationship to them. The concept was first proposed by literary theorist Mikhail Bakhtin (1981) to identify the ways that narrative genres invoke particular configurations of time and space to tell different kinds of stories. But it also offers a way of thinking about the Valley's notion of transcendental heritages as a means of conjuring distant places and forging relationships between past, present, and future. This alternative method of "imagining continuity" (Lambek 2002, 4) contrasts with how we customarily think about space and time as being either fixed (space) or flowing in a single direction (time). It opens other possibilities for understanding events, determining past relationships, and constructing memories, thereby making possible other configurations of community and other ways of being in the present. This has consequences for identity as well as people's sense of self-determination, agency, and action.[2]

Famously more evocative than precise, Bakhtin's concept of the chronotope has been adopted by scholars in many different fields outside of the study of literature. Anthropologists Stephan Palmié, Charles Stewart, and Kristina Wirtz have refined and extended it to think about how different groups of people conceptualize, represent, and derive knowledge about the past. These "spatiotemporal imaginaries," as Wirtz refers to them, often diverge from the conventional, Western notion of history as linear and progressive (Wirtz 2016). "Cultural notions as to what constitutes 'time,'" Palmié and Stewart wrote, "what is an 'event,' what kind of agent can bring about 'change,' how perceived 'change' is set apart from the regular flow of happenings—all of these vary from society to society and modulate the understanding of what we might call history" (2016, 211).

They go on to explain that conventional history, or what they label historicism, regards the past as past—that is, as temporally separate from the present. Likewise, the present is conceived as temporally distinct from the future. Time is understood to move in a forward direction, accumulating progressively and irreversibly (212). Causality also is linear: while a past event may give rise to a particular present, the reverse is not possible. Historicism also excludes the supernatural as a causal agent for events. Of course, this conventional view is consistent with natural science and has become the standard way of thinking about history throughout much of the world. It was not always so, however, and alternative "chronotopic regimes" persist. "The underlying principles of historicism are not fully espoused by everyone all the time," Palmié and Stewart observed. "People operate with multiple tenets of historical thought in the West, as, indeed, they do in other societies" (222).

These alternative chronotopes differ in their basic assumptions about causality and the flow of time. For example, quantum physicists speak of time as relative and posit that in certain corners of the universe it can flow backward (212). Within Hinduism time is conceived as cyclical and degenerative, with the universe eternally flowing through vast cycles of creation, decline, destruction, and rebirth. The ancient Gnostics held that time unfolds through various stages of evolution and devolution as creation gradually morphs from pure spirit to matter and back. Advocates of the multiverse argue that a plurality of different space-times exist, each following different laws.

As Palmié and Stewart explained, chronotopic regimes also involve assumptions and strictures about how knowledge of the past should be generated. For example, historicism prizes empirical evidence and reason as legitimate means of acquiring historical knowledge. It excludes as illegitimate revelation, prophecy, dreams, intuition, and other non-rational ways of knowing the past. These, of course, are fundamental to the Valley of the Dawn and many other religious traditions as valid sources of knowledge.

The concept of chronotopic regimes as distinct spatiotemporal imaginaries can help us think about the ways that social groups create and use different arrangements of space-time and with what effects. It directs our attention to the ways that people distinguish significant events within the flow of time and assign causal relationships to these events, how they situate themselves in relationship to specific places and times, and how these different understandings of history and locality shape participants' sense of themselves and others. For example, in the chronotopic regime Palmié and Stewart call historicism, past events are understood to be distinct from, and yet related to, the present. The converse, however, is not true. As a result, conventional historical time is linear and unidirectional: past leads to present leads to future in a one-way progression only. Events consigned to the past cannot exist simultaneously in the present, and present events cannot affect the past. If we were to put this sequential conception of time in graph form, it would look like this: Past—>Present—>Future.

Certain Valley of the Dawn rituals operate under a chronotopic regime quite different from that of conventional history. Aunt Neiva taught that by performing determined "kabbalistic rituals" (so-called because they are based in "initiatory knowledge") a group of initiated mediums working together can generate spiritual energy sufficient to open a space-time portal into their collective past in order to recuperate karmic energy left there.[3] Known as *charme*, this karmic energy is associated with specific space-times significant within the Jaguars' collective transcendental heritage. According to Aunt Neiva, by "manipulating" this energy in ritual and directing it to positive uses in healing others, the Jaguars can "soften" its hold over them and mitigate their present suffering while ensuring a better future.

As mediums described it to me, by using their emissions and *cantos*, or chants, during kabbalistic rituals, they are able to access potent spiritual channels through which energies linked to specific episodes in their transcendental heritage can be manipulated. "When we refer to rituals performed in the Doctrine of the Dawn as kabbalistic," a community newsletter instructed readers:

We are, among other things, recognizing the possibility of access to transcendental baggage. The kabbalistic power of the Dawn is that which authorizes and enables the transfer and the installation of transcendental inheritances. These are legacies of forces responsible for fortifying the corps of mediums, and consequently, providing support for mediumistic accomplishments. (Reis 2010b, 5)

Within the chronotopic regime governing kabbalistic rituals, then, the relationship between temporal events is altered such that ritual action in the present is believed to affect the past and changes in the past transform both the present and the future. In graph form, the temporal sequence held to operate within these rituals is: Present<—>Past—>Future. In other words, specific kabbalistic rituals require participants to temporarily switch chronotope from that of conventional time and space to an alternative configuration of time and space in order to be perceived as effective.

This chronotopic switching allows Valley members to engage a spatiotemporal imaginary in which relationships among past events are organized according to a different logic, producing new possibilities for understanding the present, interpreting experience, and creating the future. In his own way, Master Antônio Carlos had said something similar when he told me that every Sunday, Valley mediums ritually return to ancient Sparta to "relive" a part of their collective history, "bringing the energies from those times, from that ancient people and transforming it." This happens in a ritual called the Turigano, the subject of the next section. In this ritual various Valley members act as a collective to correct "errors" generated by an event that supposedly took place in ancient Greece. While much more could be said about this complex ritual, I analyze it as a specific "chronotopic regime" or spatiotemporal imaginary whereby the community works to reshape members' sense of themselves as products of a particular past and instills the importance of Christic virtues as a means of transforming that past and ensuring their continued spiritual evolution.

The Turigano: Creating the Space of Memory

My children, we are removing centuries, in search of the roots we left behind. We return! Yes, we return to evolve the world that we hurt when we turned away from God. –Aunt Neiva (Sassi 1977, 2:23)

The elaborate weekly ritual of the Turigano is one of several regularly performed rituals that purport to *resgatar*, rescue or recuperate, a significant episode in the Jaguars' transcendental heritage in order to lessen its karmic potency. The ritual returns participants to the era when Jaguars were incarnated as soldiers and citizens of ancient Sparta, a space-time regarded as one of the moral nadirs of the Jaguars' past. In this "militaristic and insensitive civilization, violent and without love," as a high-ranking veteran described it, "the Jaguars reached the final level of our spiritual decay" (Silva 1998, "Turigano").

The narrative associated with the Turigano centers on the legendary warrior-hero Leonidas, a Spartan king during the fifth century BCE. Conventional history remembers King Leonidas for leading an alliance of Greek forces against the invading Persians at the battle of Thermopylae. Outnumbered and outmaneuvered by the Persians, the king ordered his troops to retreat, keeping only a small guard of warriors with him to fight to the death. By detaining the enemy in this way, he bought the Greeks precious time at the cost of his own life and that of the men under his command. Legend has it that the king had been warned of his death by the oracle of Delphi, which declared that Sparta would be spared from destruction at the hands of the Persians only by the death of the king (Smith 1873).

Aunt Neiva's version of this ancient history retains the figures of King Leonidas and the Delphic oracle but elaborates considerably, adding a whole new character, an exiled queen around whom much of the drama revolves. According to Aunt Neiva, King Leonidas was an incarnation of First Master Jaguar Nestor Sabatoviks, whom she had consecrated as Trino Arakém and appointed to the male-dominated council that would steward the community after her death. Neiva herself was incarnated as the Pythia, high priestess of the Delphic oracle and voice of the god Apollo.

In Neiva's account, Leonidas was the younger son of the king of Sparta, to whom the king had chosen to pass his throne. Leonidas' elder brother, enraged by their father's actions and seeking to overthrow Leonidas, went to the king of Athens and asked him to raise an army to defeat his younger brother. However, Leonidas learned of the plot to overthrow him and took offensive action by kidnapping and imprisoning the Athenian king's daughter, referred to in the story as the exiled queen.

The king of Athens, in despair over his daughter's plight, sought counsel from the Oracle of Delphi. The Delphic priestess, seeking the liberation of the exiled queen, went to intercede with King Leonidas. As a veteran member told me the story, Leonidas

> did not believe in the gods, he believed in the strength of the sword. So, he challenged the Pythia because he did not believe in Apollo. He said that he would only believe in the God Apollo, according to the story that Aunt Neiva told us, if Pythia made the drums beat by themselves. And it happened that the drums beat by themselves, and King Leonidas was then in shock because he found that above him there was a greater power. So, he called on his troops to go in search of the exiled queen. But it was too late: the opposing forces were lying in wait, and no one knows what happened to the exiled queen.[4]

Valley members consider this version of events to be historically accurate and to have generated a legacy of karmic debt for the Jaguars, the Spartans' spiritual descendants, which ripples out to the present day. In the ritual of the Turigano, the Jaguars reenact this story in an "indoctrinated" form that reflects Jesus' law of love and forgiveness, thereby *suavizando* (softening or reducing) its karmic effects.

The Turigano ritual is a complex affair requiring a specific cast drawn from the corps of masters. Among the players are various highly evolved spirits of light, represented by specially trained mediums, as well as members of specific missionary phalanxes who have a connection to ancient Greece. The ritual follows a precise sequence that requires those playing lead roles to speak scripted parts, make their emissions and *cantos* or chants,[5] and move about the ritual space in a choreographed manner. It thus has a theatrical quality, not in the sense of play-acting, but rather as a performative staging of significant events in the Jaguars' transcendental journey intended to impress upon participants the importance of the past, the principle of karmic responsibility, and the moral virtues central to the Doctrine.

The ritual begins with a lengthy series of invocations meant to "open the current." Then participants are asked to:

> Bring your thoughts to the frontier of karmic destinies, because within a few minutes, we will be revisited by our Peloponnesian kings, guided by the great Apollo. Pythia will bring the transcendent law of Turigano, with the order of God all mighty father, to take all the bitterness from our hearts,

returning to us the cup of life, the achievement, power, and light which shall pulse throughout our being. (Silva 1998, "Turigano")

Following this comes the lengthiest section of the ritual, which centers on the introduction of various ritual participants who are called upon to perform their emissions and specific chants. The chants summon specific spiritual forces to the proceedings and call attention to the "lost heritage" the Jaguars left in ancient Greece. At the ceremony's dramatic apex, a female medium representing the Pythia engages in a ritualized exchange with King Leonidas (also represented by a medium), telling him that "only his goodwill can free [the exiled queen]." To this, the medium standing in for King Leonidas asks her to submit to a test: if Pythia can make the drums play by themselves, he will release the queen. After Pythia has satisfied his request, the king replies,

> From now on, everything that you say I will believe. I want to be one of the many Spartans to bring offerings to your oracle and lay them at your feet! Bring the queen, who will no longer be exiled. She will return, escorted by one of my troops, who will defend her from her feet to the last strand of the hairs on her head.

After more scripted exchanges between the two, a presiding medium announces:

> O god Apollo, unified in Christ Jesus! It is the day of liberation! Let us receive, in this instant, our queen, the message from Apollo, the benevolence of Leonidas, who converted to a supplicant of the oracle of Delphi, the oracle of the god Apollo, who unified Greeks and Spartans, the power of Pythia, today in the figure Aunt Neiva, our clairvoyant mother in Christ Jesus!

A medium representing the exiled queen then is escorted to center stage, where, after greeting the assembly, she speaks:

> Here you have me, by the grace of God and my grandmother Pythia, coming from beloved Delphi, reminding us of the sad paths we have taken, doing this out of great love for her people. Today, however, the biggest and most powerful light has risen, in the strength of the great god Apollo, unified in Christ Jesus, for my and our liberation, uniting us in strength and love. (Silva 1998, "Turigano")

By reenacting a different ending to the story of the exiled queen in which she is successfully liberated, contemporary Jaguars "rescue" a past event and recover its charme, transforming it into a source of positive, rather than negative, energy.[6] This not only mitigates the original event's karmic valence, but it also demonstrates that the principles of love and forgiveness represented by Aunt Neiva (in her incarnation as Pythia) prevail over the militarism and violence of ancient Sparta. In one of the few written explanations of the ritual that she gave, Aunt Neiva characterized the Turigano ritual as an especially potent energetic force field produced by uniting the physical force of the ancient Spartans with Pythia's spiritual force:

> The Turigano represents an accord of two different forces, symbolizing the impact of Sparta's physical strength and the spiritual strength of Pythia. Two magnetisms forming double energy, which intertwine like the Master Current; a braid, a canopy of light. (letter of October 1, 1980, reproduced in Souza n.d., 12)

For Valley members, the ritual's high point is when Pythia demonstrates her spiritual potency by making the drums beat by themselves, thereby galvanizing King Leonidas and his troops to accept "the transcendental force of the God of Apollo" (Souza n.d., 12). This event is understood as the beginning of the Spartans' "spiritualization": the moment when the Jaguars' spiritual ancestors turn away from the earthly pursuit of material power and return to their original mission of fostering human cultural and spiritual evolution.[7] "We are Spartan spirits," Master José Carlos do Nascimento Silva responded in answer to my question about the ritual's significance.

> In Sparta we reached the end of our long decline from our former positions as God-Men, when we arrived from Capella, into Beast-Men, motivated by the power of physical force alone. But the divine light flowing from Pythia transformed the darkness of our hearts. A new opportunity had been given: love, tolerance, humility, a new life, a new hope, a new meaning. A revolution took place in our hearts.

"It was Pythia (Aunt Neiva), in that distant era, who was responsible for spiritualizing that people," Master Kazagrande instructed readers of his blog. Because of Pythia, "fierce Sparta came to have the protection of the god Apollo. More than that: they came to have faith, something to believe in and respect! Discipline, the main characteristic of the Spartans, began to rely on the light of the sun god" (2011, 304).

As a solar deity, Apollo plays an important role in Valley mythology both as a symbol of the doutrinador (who is associated with the force of the sun) and a prefigurement of Christ.[8] Apollo's oracle at Delphi is understood to be a repository of the primordial spiritual energy initially established in seven centers around the globe by the Jaguars' ancient ancestors, the Equitumans. After lying dormant for millennia, Valley members assert that this powerful spiritual *raiz* or root was revivified by Aunt Neiva and united with other spiritually potent space-times important in the Jaguars' transcendental journey, forming a constellation of histories continually referenced in the Valley's material culture and ritual life.

Today, thanks to the Greek historian Herodotus (c. 484–c. 425 BCE), King Leonidas is considered a heroic figure in Western history, an embodiment of masculine honor legendary for his valor in the face of foreign domination. By contrast, in Aunt Neiva's version of the story the crucial event was not King Leonidas's self-sacrificial act, nor the values that his tale conventionally represents: fortitude, heroism, and bravery against overwhelming odds. Rather, as performed in the ritual of the Turigano, the crucial event is King Leonidas's acknowledgment of Pythia's spiritual power and the liberating virtues of love and forgiveness she represents. This is what motivates the king to free the exiled queen and prompts the Jaguars' Spartan forbears to accept "the divine light." In consequence, the famous discipline and courage of the Spartans becomes illuminated by Pythia's message and redirected toward the project of spiritual evolution: "returning to us the cup of life, the achievement, power, and light which shall pulse throughout our being," as the opening ritual script puts it.[9]

For Valley mediums with whom I spoke, the factual veracity of the events depicted in the ritual is less important than their sense that the ritual is an affirmation of the Jaguars' transcendental heritage and a collective act of reparation. A nymph named Bethânia told me:

> Unlike other doctrines, here at the Valley, we really find our transcendental [heritage], what, in one way or another, we left behind. When we speak of transcendental inheritances, we are referring to spiritual baggage from past lives. We were involved in many bad things; we committed many negative acts against others. And that is why we have to go back, to remember and redress, to repair our karma in order for us to return to God. We have to repair the mistakes that we made because we did not know how to love.

Bethânia's words highlight how karmic redemption is closely tied to remembering, redressing, and repairing past wrongs—a project that James Holston characterized as "historical accounting" (1999, 62). Through the chronotopic switching involved in ceremonies like the Turigano, present-day Jaguars revisit significant episodes in their collective history to remember and redress previous failures. By means of a carefully scripted ritual in which a past misdeed is relived in light of the Doctrine's moral virtues, the Jaguars believe that they transform some of the negative karma, or charme, left in that particular space-time into positive energy that can then be directed to healing.

At the same time, the ritual continually reminds participants of the necessity to live out the Doctrine's teachings in their everyday lives by exhibiting "doctrinal conduct." This instills new moral habits, fostering mediums' continued spiritual evolution. "The Doctrine is important for this: every day we learn," Nymph Ilza confided to me. Referring to her sometimes fractious relationship with Master Paulo, who was standing with us, she continued:

> The Doctrine is important because it helps you understand your life, understand the things that happen to you and the people you meet. So, I keep that in mind, because sometimes you clash with someone, like I did with Paulo. Sometimes someone just instantly irritates you or rubs you the wrong way and you do not know why. So first I observe, because it could be my cobrador from a previous life. Then I will have to prove to him that I have evolved, and I am no longer that person who hurt him in a past life. I do that in my relationship with Paulo. To get along with Paulo, I will have to watch myself, control my annoyance, treat him with love and compassion. In other words, practice doctrinal conduct. That is how I show my cobrador that I have evolved and that is how the Doctrine teaches us. And when my cobrador sees that I have evolved and changed, when I treat him with love and compassion, then he can begin to let go of that hurt from the past. It is a reajuste (readjustment). So, he too is changed by that.

Our conversation recalled a comment that Nymph Olivia had made to me a few years earlier. "Father White Arrow said that this doctrine is not for us, it is for the spirits that we have harmed in the past," she asserted.

> For me, in my opinion, the coolest thing is this. The Doctrine teaches you to know your true self, your individuality. When you know your true self, you

see the mistakes you made in the past and how you can correct them. And that not only transforms you, it transforms others.

Applying the Valley's lessons to their personal relationships and seeing the results reinforces mediums' sense of the Doctrine as an efficacious path toward self-knowledge, moral progress, and, ultimately, spiritual evolution. Throughout my fieldwork, Valley mediums told me that alongside the everyday practice of doctrinal conduct, the work of "recuperating the past"—redressing their collective and individual karma in rituals like the Turigano and the Prisoner's Ritual, respectively—connected them to their higher self. Nymph Aparecida's comments make explicit the link among ritual work, self-knowledge, and doctrinal conduct:

> In the Doctrine we encounter our truest self. Within the ritual works we learn that we owe, we have our *cobranças* or karmic debts, we have our transcendental inheritances, and we can work on those energies, manipulating them to help ourselves and others. You see, the past is never entirely past, we carry it with us. In Greece we Jaguars were barbarians, in Sparta we were known for our cruelty. We had many incarnations in the Roman Empire, in Egypt, in Russia, and later in colonial Brazil. And now we are here again, and we have the opportunity to repay our karmic debts, to evolve, to make up for all the times we made others suffer for our lack of empathy, our lack of tolerance, our lack of love. We have experienced all these incarnations to rediscover our true selves.

Imagined Places and Transcendental Personhood

So far, my discussion of the Valley of the Dawn's chronotopic imagination has focused mostly on *chrónos*, the first root term of Bakhtin's concept, derived from the Greek word for "time." In the previous section I analyzed the Turigano ritual as an example of a spatiotemporal imaginary that is non-linear and reparative rather than linear and progressive. This alternative chronotopic regime differs from conventional historical time in terms of: (1) the relationship among past, present, and future; (2) the nature of causality and causal agents; and (3) what constitutes an event. I have argued that the chronotopic switching triggered by rituals like the Turigano fosters new possibilities for interpreting everyday experience, creating meaning, and understanding the self. These new possibilities are grounded in a vision of the relationship among past, present, and future that is organized primarily around moral behavior and its consequences rather than linear chronology. Here I pursue that argument in greater detail by turning my attention to the second root term, *topos*, the ancient Greek word for place.[10]

More specifically, I examine how specific imagined places of the Jaguars' collective past figure in the development of what I call transcendental personhood. This transtemporal sense of self encompasses what the Doctrine refers to as the "individuality" or higher self and the present self or "personality." By continually directing mediums' embodied awareness to key chronotopes within their transcendental heritage, the Doctrine works to reconstruct mediums' subjective sense of themselves as beings in evolutionary transit, simultaneously finite and infinite, morally responsible for their actions in the present as well as in former incarnations. As Aunt Neiva told her followers, "We have to learn to reconstruct our life in terms of the knowledge of our transcendental heritage, our karmic journey."

This reconstruction project takes place through a full-bodied, aesthetic and kinesthetic immersion that engages the imagination through multiple sensory modalities. The cumulative effect is a kind of "narrative emplotment" (Pierini 2013) by which Valley mediums come to see their lives and selves as intertwined with the Jaguars' transcendental heritage. By affectively engaging with this history through ritual works and doctrinal conduct, mediums develop a sense of transcendental personhood that helps them make sense of their lives and experiences, overcome personal obstacles or adversities, and practice new ways of being in the world.

At the broadest level, the Valley works to engage Jaguars in their shared transcendental heritage through the built environment of the temple complex. Constructed over some twenty years, the temple complex includes the 2,400-square-meter Mother Temple as well as the Solar dos Médiuns, or Mediums' Estate, an "initiatic ensemble" of brightly colored ritual edifices located about 300 meters away from the temple square. This open-air ensemble includes an artificial waterfall, a star-shaped water mirror called the Estrela Candente (Incandescent Star), a large lake bordered by a ritual promenade, a pyramid, and a series of other structures meant to symbolize "the great journey of the civilizing forces from the period of History that preceded our Era, traversing the great historical events—Spartans, Macedonians, Egyptians and the Christic Era in its fullness of the life of Jesus—and reaching our times" (Patricio 2012, "1º de Maio dia do Doutrinador").

Image 8.1 Pyramid. Credit Márcia Alves

One of the largest and most striking of these structures is the great Pyramid (see Image 8.1). Symbolizing the Jaguars' passage through ancient Egypt, the Pyramid is said to function as a channel for the transcendental inheritance associated particularly with the Pharaoh Akhenaten (ruled 1353–1336 BCE) and Queen Nefertiti, known to history for advocating the worship of one god, Aten, god of the sun. Valley members understand this to be evidence that Akhenaten and Nefertiti were fellow Jaguars working to facilitate humanity's spiritual evolution by introducing an early form of monotheism. In fact, Nefertiti is considered one of Aunt Neiva's most notable previous incarnations and her image, along with that of other Pharaohs, is displayed prominently inside the building (see Image 8.2).

Explaining the significance of the pyramid, Master Solon described it to me as:

a transcendental heritage brought by Aunt Neiva through her spiritual powers, her ability to unify these forces so that she could bring to the present age the energies that are localized in various dimensions of that ancient epoch. . . . That is why we have the [images of] entities, Tutankhamon, Ramses, Amon-Ra, Nefertiti, all these grand pharaohs and queens of that era represented here, they bring energies for our doctrine. In essence, the

Image 8.2 Nefertiti and Tutankhamon in Pyramid. Credit Márcia Alves

pyramid is a great generator of energies, it integrates and disintegrates energies, bringing healing to all who come here.

Notwithstanding Master Solon's description of the Pyramid as a "great generator of energies," the atmosphere inside is one of serenity and quiet. "I come here to meditate," Nymph Sisenanda told me in a whisper one bright morning in 2015 as we sat on a tiled bench in the relatively dark coolness inside. Despite the floor-to-ceiling array of images lining almost every inch of the space around us, there was an abiding sense of stillness, the air lightly perfumed by a stick of incense burning in the corner.[11] A fountain burbled in the center of the room, and every so often the lilting sparkle of a wind chime joined it. "There is so much powerful energy here," Sisenanda continued after a moment.

> I like to come here and mediumize myself. I really feel the presence of the energies, the spiritual mentors, and the great transcendental heritage that is represented here in the Pyramid. I tune into that energy to connect to my individuality and everything that is great inside me. Aunt Neiva said that we need to be as great as our own transcendental greatness, our transcendental heritage, and I feel that here. I use that energy to think about my loved ones and the people I want to help, and I vibrate positivity to them.

For Sisenanda, the Pyramid is a place of concentrated energies that helps her tune into a deeper, more enduring part of herself. She and Master Solon articulated a sentiment that I heard often among Valley members: the Pyramid is important primarily as a locus of energies associated with an imagined space-time rather than as a symbol of specific events that took place in ancient Egypt. The "memories" that the Pyramid evokes are not about empirical facts as much as essential virtues and their emotional resonance. Just as Americans reference the founding fathers to symbolize sacred ideals and values that we purport to cherish and which shape our national identity, the Pyramid reminds Valley members "to be as great as our own transcendental greatness, our transcendental heritage," in Sisenanda's words. In other words, what the Pyramid evokes is a mythic past distilled into a powerful feeling-state. This feeling-state spurs people to locate those same ideals deep within themselves and project them outward in thought and action, "vibrating positivity," as Sisenanda put it.

Another way that Valley members forge a personal connection to the imagined space-times of the Jaguars' transcendental heritage is through chants, a formalized ritual discourse used in ritual settings. Like the emissions that mediums receive during initiation, chants are said to open a metaphysical channel to other dimensions. Particularly for veteran Valley members who received them directly from Aunt Neiva, chants describe in highly condensed form the transcendental trajectory of the spirit (individuality) presently incarnated in that member's personality, referencing previous incarnations he or she has passed through.

Consider this chant, which conjures the speaker's past in ancient Greece. Originally it was performed during the ritual of the Turigano by Trino Arakém, the veteran master who was incarnated as King Leonidas during the era when Aunt Neiva served as the Delphic priestess Pythia:

> Oh Jesus! I feel obliged to prove, here, my contribution to my nostalgic Spartan world, in which I lived the last moments of Leonidas, I appreciated Pythia's contacts and felt the purest science transform into light. I saw that everything is love and reparation, and the great need to recognize the god Apollo as the great force of the transcendental heritage that, even in that distant world, suffered the injuries of the Peloponnesian people.
>
> Today we know that you are the reason for this corporation. You are all the greatness . . . that touches everything, for this great advent of the Third Millennium. Today I am here, knight, God Apollo! I, who faced the Macedonian plains, and all the power of my beloved Sparta, Leonidas, the impetuous king, who it humbles me to think of![12]

Not all chants are as geographically precise in their evocation of the past. Nevertheless, Valley mediums with whom I spoke reported feeling a range of emotions when they performed their chants. Explaining to me their affective power, Master João Nunez used the example of the Chant of the Minister Japuacy. In his role as representative of this highly evolved spirit of light, Master João regularly performs this chant in rituals.[13]

> Chant of the Minister Japuacy
> Oh Jesus, I am the Minister Japuacy. I am a master who prays and knows what he wants, I am a master who comes from worlds beyond in search of my salvation.

> Jesus, I crossed sky and sea, I was a sailor and commanded many galleys, I destroyed people to please my King. Today I come back to find you. I want to teach the whole world your holy name. I want to live accompanied by your graces. I lived the life of a mercenary knight. I felt and heard the rumors of your arrival, but I did not have the courage to meet you.
>
> Today we are on this journey towards the new Amanhecer (dawn), and I know that the [energetic] currents will arrive because my Father White Arrow, Simiromba of God, says so.[14]

The chant "speaks of other lives, past lives, things that have been lived in other incarnations," Master João instructed me after reciting it in his stentorian voice.

> It is a past history, a lived history in a different world from this world. When I say, "Oh Jesus, I am that Minister Japuacy, I am a master who prays and knows what he wants, I am a master who comes from the worlds beyond in search of my salvation," I am telling Jesus who I am and that I am seeking redemption. Then I tell Jesus who I have been in past lives: a sailor who destroyed people, a mercenary whose terrible deeds made me afraid to meet him. Then I tell Jesus what I intend to do: I want to live accompanied by his graces and to teach people his holy name. What are his graces? Love, charity, fraternity.

Master João paused and looked at me solemnly. "So, this is a chant of repentance," he resumed.

> I am no longer the one who commanded galleys and fought against people. I have recognized the crimes of my past and I am now seeking amends. It is a spiritual story and when I say it, I need to be very focused on Jesus and on the spiritual mentors. I need to really feel it: I need to feel the regret for my past deeds, I need to feel my desire to make amends, I need to feel the love, charity, and fraternity of Jesus to continue this journey towards a new dawn.

Like the previous example, Minister Japuacy's chant is addressed to Jesus and describes a past rooted in a different place, "a lived history in a different world from this world," as Master João phrased it. Interwoven with the details of this lived history are references to the transformative virtues of love and the great force of Jesus/Apollo. These are chants of repentance, but they also tell of a moral shift in preparation for "a new dawn": the Third Millennium. Moreover, in a point articulated most clearly in the words of Master João, the chants invite speaker and audience to *feel* an emotional connection with the imagined past delineated in the chant as a moral debit that can be transmuted by faith in and adherence to the example set by Jesus.

A final example of how mediums cultivate an affective connection with the imagined places of the Jaguars' transcendental heritage is through the use of indumentárias. According to Aunt Neiva, these vestments originate in the Kingdom of Zana, "one of the most civilized kingdoms in the spiritual planes" and the astral home of evolved spirits who work with Valley mediums as mentors and guides (C. L. Zelaya, 2009, 77). Meant to replicate the spirits' radiant appearance, the indumentárias are said to establish an energetic connection between the medium and his or her missionary guide or knight, as I detailed in Chapter 6.[15]

One of the most popular missionary phalanxes, especially among younger women, is the Gregas or Greek Women.[16] According to Aunt Neiva, the Gregas were young women in ancient Delphi who served Pythia by collecting the weapons of soldiers slain on the battlefield and bringing them to the temple of Apollo to be consecrated, thereby liberating the soldiers' spirits to continue their evolutionary journey in the astral world. During the ceremony of consecration, the Gregas served as honor guards at the temple gates holding imposing lances (Silva n.d., "Grega"; see also Pierini 2013, 280; Queiroz 2015, 114–115).

Evoking this transcendental heritage, the indumentárias worn by members of the Grega phalanx feature a gown that bares the left shoulder, a style said to mimic that of ancient Greece, and a symbolic lance in the form of a tall zinc pole topped with an arrowhead. This is held in the left hand, and Gregas are expected to carry their lances on nearly all occasions in which they are representing the phalanx. Moon Gregas wear a mint green gown encrusted with silver trim while the gown of Sun Gregas is white with golden trim (see Image 8.3). The Gregas play an important role in the Turigano ritual where they serve as members of Pythia's court and invoke the forces of Apollo with a special chant.

In her doctoral research, Brazilian scholar Gersilene Oliveira de Lima interviewed a group of Gregas from a temple in the Brazilian state of Ceará. Without exception, the women expressed a strong sense of identification

Image 8.3 Moon Grega. Credit Márcia Alves

with their phalanx, something that I also observed throughout my fieldwork. What is of interest here is that the women linked this feeling of identification to embodied sensations provoked by some element of the phalanx's material culture. "The Grega's indumentária fit my life like a glove," one woman asserted.

> The Grega's lance has the function of piercing the veil of negativity and this really resonated deeply with me. I was always bossy, very forward, always pragmatic, I think action is sovereign. So, the warrior in me always existed, I just didn't understand where she came from. (Lima 2019, 223)

Other women described being overcome with emotion upon first hearing the Grega's chant: "I cried so much that it seemed that I had a faucet behind my eyes that wet my clothes," one confessed (2019, 223). "When I first came to the Valley, I joined the Mayas because my best friend is a Maya," Nymph Ariana told me.

> But every time I went to put on my indumentária, something would happen: it would not fit right, or I would rip a seam, or snag it, or trip on the hem. There was something that just was not right. And then one day I was passing by the Turigano and I heard the chant of the Gregas. I immediately was overcome with emotion. The hair on my arm stood on end and I felt a bolt of electricity go through my body and I knew that I was a Grega.

"The Grega chant represents my past, present, and future; that is, the lines of my life," another nymph told Gersilene Oliveira de Lima.

> I have a lot of affinity with all its symbology. So, when I perform the chant, it is like I am entering a very special place, I feel like I am going through a portal, receiving all these forces, and bringing my unified self to continue the missionary life. (Lima 2019, 202–203)

Noteworthy in this woman's testimony is her description of the chant as representing her past, present, and future, a transtemporal convergence she characterizes as a "unified self." This unified self is comprised of: (1) the self that has experienced multiple incarnations in past space-times (the individuality), (2) the self incarnated in the present space-time (the personality), and (3) the future, (presumably) perfected self.

This is the kind of self-knowledge that other mediums described as "encountering our truest self" and that I am calling transcendental personhood.[17] As the examples I have discussed suggest, this feeling can be powerfully triggered in the imagination by neural, chemical, and bodily responses to sensory stimuli. By insistently conjuring the chronotopes of the Jaguars' transcendental heritage, breaking down conventional barriers between past, present, and future, the Doctrine works to shape participants' sense of self, identity, and moral conscience on both the individual and collective level.

The Past Is as Much a Work of Imagination as the Future

Materialized in the built environment of the temple complex; vocalized in hymns, emissions, and chants; and visually compressed into symbolic elements, clothing, and adornments—the imagined space-times of the Jaguars' transcendental heritage surround contemporary Jaguars as a sensually perceptible presence. Because our senses form the basis for our knowledge and understanding of reality, engaging them via material culture—constructed environments, imagery, rituals, and other kinds of created objects—orients us within a particular horizon of meaning (Promey 2014, 11). It trains perception, engenders a particular consciousness, and shapes a person's sense of self and connection to the collective.

I have argued in this chapter that the Valley's material culture reflects an alternative chronotopic regime, or what Palmié and Stewart called "a particular form of awareness of human being and becoming in time" (223). In order to foster new forms of being and becoming—or new horizons of meaning—Aunt Neiva changed her followers' understanding of the past (Palmie and Stewart 2016, 217). This is a past that does not correspond to historical facts as they are widely understood. It is an affective past that reflects a moral vision: that humans must atone for negative actions and time is the theatre in which this atonement process is worked out. Rather than being temporally distinct from and unaffected by the present, this is a past that can be accessed imaginatively and experientially in ritual and thereby transformed.

As an immersive, sensory-rich environment of architectural forms, symbols, vestments, songs, chants, and rituals, the Mother Temple complex inspires Valley mediums to affectively "remember" their transcendental heritage, feeling both its lessons as well as its karmic weight. Rituals like the Turigano do more than simply recall significant episodes in the

Jaguars' past, however. They also are believed to grant Valley mediums direct access to the karmic residues or charmes left in this past so that these energies may be manipulated and transformed. Access to the transcendental past is an integral component of the Valley's notion of karmic redemption: by "recuperating" their transcendental heritages, Valley members can "correct the errors" of the past through a form of chronotopic switching made possible by certain rituals.

These chronotopes have a complex emotional register: simultaneously provoking sorrow for wrongs committed but also a kind of nostalgia. The distance between an idealized past of greatness (we were once royals and priests) and the reduced conditions of the present generates a poignancy or longing. The Jaguars must pay for their past errors by their reduced conditions in the present as well as by their missionary work. And so, week after week in the Turigano, Valley mediums redirect the warlike charme of the ancient Spartans to "the conquest of the spirit": the practice of love, tolerance, compassion, and humility among contemporary Jaguars, the heirs of the ancient Spartans' transcendental legacy. Participants in this ritual are not simply actors playing a role, Emily Pierini observed. Rather, given their understanding of reincarnation, "they *are* those characters, enacting aspects of their selves, of their past individual and collective identities of Jaguars." Reflecting upon themselves in this way, Pierini wrote, "they reaffirm the present principles and meanings of the doctrine" for their mission and their everyday lives (2020, 80). In other words, ritual becomes a means of mediums' self-knowledge in the present and facilitates their future spiritual evolution.

At a more general level, stories about significant episodes within the Jaguars' transcendental heritage are significant for Valley members for the same reasons that the Gospel stories of Jesus are significant for Christians: not primarily as accurate, empirically verifiable records of past events, but because of the ethical lessons that the stories offer for the here and now and the sentiments they stir in their audience. They are past-oriented narratives that are told for the purposes of molding moral subjects in the present. As past-oriented narratives, they can be considered a form of history—but this is not the history of professional historians. Rather, it is history as a chronicle of the significant events and figures that have shaped a community's identity and moral conscience—or as Valley members might say, their transcendental heritage.

The Mother Temple complex maps out the Jaguars' transcendental heritage as it unfolds through different civilizational epochs, immersing mediums in its tangible presence. Although the Valley's built environment strikes visitors as unusual, quirky, or simply bizarre, the community's effort to materialize its imagined past has always reminded me of an example closer to my own home: the architecture of the American state. The founders of the United States self-consciously modeled the great public buildings of the federal government on Greek and Roman structures[18] They did this for a reason: to conjure in the mind of the beholder the democratic ideals and accompanying moral virtues associated with the Greco-Roman world that they wished the new nation to embody, namely: freedom, order, liberty, and the rule of law. Hence, the columns and pediments of this neoclassical style can be found in a significant number of state capitals, courthouses, and post offices around the United States today[19] In founding her own capital, Aunt Neiva seems to have intuitively recognized how material culture can evoke an imagined past to remind a community who they are and continually impress upon them who they ought to be.

* * *

9
A Space Age Religion for Modern Brazil

> Aunt Neiva, in her clairvoyance, formed the entire structure that is today the Doctrine of the Dawn. Making use of her exceptional clairvoyant mediumship, she built in people's hearts a whole doctrinal philosophy, where each day lived was a lesson. These lessons joined together as in an immense encyclopedia where each architectural construction, each ritual, the garments with their different colors, and all the symbols would gradually find access in all who arrived here.
> — Conceito de Doctrina do Amanhecer, "Termologia Doutrinária," 19

A Great Work of Imagination and Synthesis

From the beginning, the Valley of the Dawn was deeply tied to Aunt Neiva's personal biography and the difficulties she encountered as a young widow and mother. Estranged from her family of origin and raising four children on her own, Neiva led a peripatetic life before migrating to Brasília in the late 1950s. There, she began to experience vivid, hallucinatory-like phenomena and mood swings that disrupted her household and affected her ability to work. Valley lore locates the inception of Aunt Neiva's spiritual calling to these troubling incidents.

Through her participation in several Spiritist and Umbanda groups, Neiva was introduced to practices that helped contain their most disruptive aspects. Just as importantly, Spiritism provided an interpretative framework that helped her transform her unwanted condition into something positive and meaningful while preserving a strong sense of her own mental capacity and independence. Neiva's writings and biographical materials reveal a protracted struggle to accept the reality of what she came to understand as encounters with highly evolved intelligences inhabiting other planes of existence.

This process of meaning-making led to a personal transformation. Rooted in her developing sense that she could communicate with unseen presences and travel in dimensions beyond the physical world, Neiva began to create a new life for herself as a clairvoyant medium. Her journey along this path shaped the imagined world that, over time, materialized around and through her. But she did not travel alone. From the first, her sense of being guided by superhuman entities was shaped and reinforced by her interactions with a small group of social intimates, including her children, her friends and lovers, and, later, her followers.

With their confidence in her paranormal abilities, Neiva began to trust her intuitions and the wisdom she attributed to evolved spirit mentors like Mother Yara, Father White Arrow, Tiãozinho, the Tibetan monk Umahã, and others. As Aunt Neiva learned to cede her own personality to these sources of inspiration, they became intimate, familiar personages to her family members and close associates. Embodied by and voiced through Aunt Neiva, these entities gained a material reality of their own via the force of repetition: each manifested through a particular voice and manner of speaking, a posture, an energetic feel or emotional valence. Father White Arrow, for example, always spoke in parables with a detached wisdom honed of countless incarnations, whereas Mother Tildes was known for telling stories so vividly detailed that Carmem Lúcia compared them to an evening at the cinema (C. L. Zelaya 2014, 188).

Mother Yara's words, in contrast, were loving but no nonsense and salted with pragmatic advice: "Neiva, stop being ungrateful!" Carmem Lúcia recalled her admonishing Neiva when the latter complained she was tired of helping people (189). "You have no idea how much you should be grateful to these people! All of them are helping you realize your mission." Mother Yara was especially fond of moral dictums: "Do not tell lies so that your sleep is peaceful," she would say. And: "Look for the bright side of life, be optimistic." Or: "Try to climb and always hope for the best; with a hopeful heart, we shall have all the good and noble things we desire" (Sassi 1985b, n.p.).

These differences of voice, manner, and style helped endow Neiva's spirits with a presence that was augmented by other people's stories about their own encounters with this or that entity. In this way a form of social personhood was established around these otherwise invisible beings. This phenomenon is not unusual. Spirits and other supernatural entities are materialized in bodies, imagery, garments, altars, and rituals in a wide variety of Brazilian religions, from Catholic lithographs to Afro-Brazilian rituals in which the orixás are invited to inhabit the bodies of their devotees, then dressed in the appropriate ritual garments. All over Brazil and around the globe, those seeking to develop reciprocal relationships with other-than-human beings of various sorts give them offerings—a lit candle, a bit of candy, a libation poured on the ground—and even prepare sumptuous meals in their honor. The act of representing these beings in physical objects and other complex symbolizations fortifies devotees' claims about their status as independent agents apart from and outside of human beings. Mediated through material objects as well as intensely affective states, human-spirit relationships become sites where people invest their hopes and fears and express their deepest desires.

Once Neiva began to trust these sources of inspiration, her life began to change. It did not become materially or physically easier, however. If anything, her everyday life became significantly harder as she embraced her mission to help suffering humanity. But new vistas began to open to her: realities outside the limits of time and space that held possibilities unattainable on Earth. Within this vast otherworld lay ethereal realms inhabited by kind and intelligent beings dedicated to the thankless job of helping humans evolve. There were dimensions beyond matter where the recently disincarnate went to acclimate to their new, disembodied state before departing for a spirit colony appropriate to their level of evolution. There, they would continue their education, or recuperate in special hospitals and asylums, or be prepared for another incarnation on Earth in the quest for spiritual perfection.

There also were lower realms devoid of light and warmth where the truly terrible paid for the evils they had wrought while incarnated on Earth. But even here the cosmic principle of progressive evolution ruled: every spirit had the choice to go toward the light and the help necessary if they wanted it. Patrolling the interstitial zones were brave knights whose job was to release spirits from the netherworlds of torment or rescue those unwittingly trapped there. And in the most highly refined astral planes, such as the Kingdom of Zana, were dizzyingly beautiful princesses haloed in the radiance of their lovingkindness.

Inspired by these visions, Aunt Neiva and her followers were engaged in a great work of invention and synthesis: imagining a new world of human purpose guided by the principle of evolution through the practice of love, tolerance, humility, and charity. They drew on influences from a deep vein of esoteric and popular culture, or what Christopher Partridge called "occulture," combining them into something distinctly new. Creating this shared paracosm came with excitement, risk, challenge, hope, and the effervescent energy generated by working with others to advance a collective mission. Sustaining it was the community's faith in God and in Aunt Neiva. Having been initiated into the wisdom of the Great East by the Tibetan monk Umahã, Neiva was herself a living Master of Wisdom. She was Koatay 108: the seventh ray of Father White Arrow, himself the seventh ray of God. Her great mission was to bring the "doutrinador," she advised her followers, and implant the initiatory-evangelical system of the Doctrine of the Dawn, enabling them to become masters themselves.

As veteran members continually reminded me, the Valley's imagined world was not created from a preexisting blueprint to which only the Clairvoyant (and her devoted interpreter Sassi) had access. Neither did it exist as a complete whole in Aunt Neiva's mind's eye. Instead, it was revealed in bits and pieces over time, arising in "the flow of her way of knowing," Emily Pierini wrote (2020, 64). Often, the reason for something was only revealed much later, as happened with the missionary phalanxes. "First the entities directed us to make the dresses," Carmem Lúcia told me in an interview. "It was only afterwards that the organization of the phalanxes was revealed, and they arrived one by one." With the help of a dedicated circle of family, friends, patients, and followers, as well as the guiding spirits whom Aunt Neiva perceived as highly evolved Masters, the Valley of the Dawn gradually took form on the physical plane in ritual works, structures, symbols, vestments, and images. It continued to evolve and transform until Aunt Neiva's death.

Alongside the Clairvoyant and her children, one of the people who most contributed to the movement's success was Mário Sassi. As Aunt Neiva's companion and chief interpreter, Sassi brought an abiding interest in "life beyond matter," as his son Iraê described it, as well as the intellectual skills necessary to build a coherent framework for the spiritual *materia prima* that seemed to flow ceaselessly through her. Sassi's convictions about the invisible forces that infuse the human world, although unconventional, were not entirely uncommon. By the time he met Aunt Neiva, Sassi had long been immersed in a vibrant world of alternative religion, science, and healing that had been developing in Brazil since the second half of the nineteenth century. One of the key contributors to this overlapping set of discourses and practices was Kardecist Spiritism.

In the mid-nineteenth century when Allan Kardec was writing, most scientists had yet to exclude from their domain phenomena that later would be labeled "psychic," and still later, "paranormal." For Kardec and his followers, spirit mediumship offered empirical evidence of the relationship between incorporeal intelligences and human beings and thus qualified

Spiritism as a science. Kardec's work harmonized with other intellectual trends popular among Brazilian elites of the late nineteenth century like positivism, a philosophical system that regards information derived from sensory experience as the only reliable source of knowledge. For positivists, only the scientific method can produce authentic (or "positive") knowledge. Perhaps paradoxically from the perspective of the twenty-first century, the positivistic emphasis on the truth of sensory experience united scientists and Spiritists until well into the twentieth century, when the former definitively severed itself from the latter. The deep vein of positivism that runs throughout Brazil's arena of alternative religious and healing systems is a legacy of their entanglement.

Claims about the scientific status of Spiritism helped its spokespeople promote and defend the movement, which took root initially among the nation's privileged classes. Brazilian Spiritists proved to be especially adept at using mass media to disseminate their ideas to the wider public via newspapers, journals, books, and radio and television programs. Through organizations like the Brazilian Spiritist Federation, established in 1884, and its periodical *O Reformador* (The Reformer), advocates of Spiritism used a combination of reasoned argument, strategic alliances, and social connections to promote Spiritist doctrine and defend it from its critics (Giumbelli 1997, 63).

Rejecting venerable Catholic doctrines like original sin, they argued that human suffering derives from ignorance of the true nature of the self and cosmos. Knowledge and moral conduct were the true means to salvation, not blind faith. Spiritists also challenged the Catholic acceptance of inequality as God's will, reasoning that if God created souls unequal, He could not be just (Sharp 2015, 235). Instead, they argued that the human being is always progressing—both on Earth as well as after death in the spirit world or through subsequent incarnations. This fundamentally optimistic view of the human condition was congruent with modern ideas of progress, evolution, justice, and individual effort, which made it appealing to many. By the mid-twentieth century, Spiritism had firmly implanted itself in every corner of Brazil and had inspired a broad spectrum of religions, spiritual therapies, healing modalities, and philosophies (Carvalho 1994; Carpenter 1999).[1]

It also produced nationally and internationally revered mediums like Chico Xavier (1910–2002), famous for channeling messages from the dead through automatic writing ("psychography") and the author of more than 400 psychographed books, and Waldo Viera (1932–2015), founder of the movements Conscientiology and Projectiology; and Divaldo Franco (b.

1927).² Unlike her male contemporaries, Aunt Neiva faced deeply rooted misogynist attitudes that made a career as a religious leader more difficult for her. Socially, her movement could only find its full expression with the kind of male support that Mário Sassi provided. His role as Neiva's male counterpart, alongside his work as the Doctrine's theologian and intellectual spokesperson, was important for the Valley of the Dawn's internal coherence and external expansion.³ Sassi's efforts to synthesize the diverse sources of Neiva's inspiration with a metaphysical framework grounded in Western occulture helped shift the Doctrine away from Spiritism and toward something more eclectic and original.

In his book *Other Worlds: Spirituality and the Search for Invisible Dimensions*, Christopher G. White observed that when scholars talk about spiritual visionaries like Aunt Neiva as bricoleurs, "they tend to celebrate their expansive creativity, their unfettered freedom, their mix-and-match eclecticism." Often overlooked, however is an "unseen, tragic dimension to their lives."

> People who lived through these types of situations and had the courage to face them were not usually freewheeling iconoclasts who joy-fully mixed and matched traditions; they were figures who struggled to prevent their lives from collapsing and falling apart. (2018, 13)

Faced with such dissolution, some seek escape through drink or drugs, sensory indulgence, or living on the edge: experiences that dull the senses or heighten them to a razor's edge. Others fall into despair. The more self-reflective reinvent themselves, finding new causes in which to invest their energy and new narratives with which to remake their sense of self. And, rarest of all, some create new worlds altogether, drawing others into these paracosms through the sheer force of their personality or the allure and explanatory power of the alternative narratives they propose. Aunt Neiva and Mário Sassi took the latter path.

Before remaking themselves as the Clairvoyant and the Intellectual, each experienced the fragmenting of their worlds. Both were unwilling to adhere to the readymade script society had given them for a meaningful life. Both tried to find alternatives. In Neiva's case, her precocious widowhood forced her to be mother *and* father, household manager *and* bread winner, in a society that limited women of her class to the former. For his part, Sassi experienced the conventional trappings of his middle-class life as a straitjacket and longed for something greater.[4] Both went to Brasília to participate in the hopeful dream of the future and, in different ways, were disappointed. Separately, both were feeling their way toward something more: a purpose beyond themselves, a form of satisfying work connected to that purpose, a sense of possibility and promise equal to the vast yet teleology-free universe that the science of the Space Age was then revealing.

A Space Age Religion for Modern Brazil

The Doctrine that developed out of their collaboration reflects this quest: "giving anguished and suffering Man an explanation of himself and a script for his immediate life," as Sassi articulated it (2004, 3). Working together as prophetic visionary and interpreter/theologian, Aunt Neiva and Sassi drew on a kaleidoscope of familiar narratives, reinterpreting them to accord with contemporary sensibilities and values. They were engaged in a mythopoetic process, creating an imagined world as they were living it, experimenting, refining, and adapting along the way. Aunt Neiva's death ended this phase of dynamic invention, but the groundwork had been laid. The result was a Space Age religion for modern Brazil, one suited to an era in which the Earth and its human occupants no longer occupy the center of the universe but have been displaced to its margins.

It is not a historical coincidence that the Valley of the Dawn was built at the same time and in the shadow of Brasília by people who had come to the federal district to start anew. As I discuss in Chapter 4, the Valley can be seen as a satellite and a spiritual simulacrum of Brasília, an argument first articulated by James Holston (1999). Both were founded on a utopian premise: the idea of breaking with the past and its karmic baggage in order to create a different future. Both propose an idealized vision for society and a master plan for achieving it. Both construct an imagined world whose inhabitants are invited to work toward the realization of a new era characterized by equality and justice. And, albeit in different ways, both Brasília and the Valley sought to materialize certain abstract ideals and values seen as fundamental to a modern polity and a modern self. The Valley thus can be read as a dialogue with both the promise of modernity that Brasília a represented and what has turned out to be the far messier reality.

From this perspective, the Journey of the Jaguars, which recounts the saga of a vanguard of aliens sent to a primitive land to catalyse progress, is the journey of the candangos given cosmic dimensions.[5] Like all myths, it is full of dreamlike images, archetypal symbols, recurrent themes, condensations, and projections that render it open to multiple interpretations. The story's rawness requires adherents to do their own processing work, filtering the narrative through their own lives and becoming co-creators of the meanings they extract. Pulitzer Prize–winning author Douglas Hofstadter, a scholar of physics and cognitive science, contends that meaning is just a case of recursive patterns in the brain: we feel like our lives have meaning exactly when our theologies are epic representations of the lives that we ourselves have lived (Hofstadter 2007). By converting the trauma of Brasília into astral metaphors, historian Micah Oelze commented to me, Aunt Neiva and Mário Sassi enabled their community to work publicly to metabolize that trauma. "In a country with historical amnesia, where the past is rarely remembered and performed," he continued, "the Valley of the Dawn provides a way of keeping history alive, in its feeling if not in its facts" (personal communication 2022).

Today, as in Aunt Neiva's time, the Valley of the Dawn helps its followers make sense of their lives and find positive meaning in their own personal traumas. In contrast with the often difficult and unsatisfactory present, it offers a glorious past and a utopian future. It provides a form of work in which people feel that they achieve something of enduring value for themselves and others, a place where everyone has access to knowledge that leads to personal and social betterment, a community that unifies people across otherwise divisive social differences.

And, in a country where the vast majority of people consider themselves Christian, the Valley does not ask anyone to abandon that identity but rather to understand it in a new, more modern light. Aunt Neiva "took Jesus off the cross and put him back walking among us," the veteran Master Guto told Emily Pierini.

> She [rejected] the idea of sin saying that it did not exist because each one is responsible for his trajectory and actions and that God does not come to punish and blame us. She was revolutionary in this sense. She did not want mystic robots; she wanted the medium who felt moved by emotions, who cried and laughed . . . and ate beans. She did not want us to believe in her words, but she asked us to analyze and see if they suited us. I thought this was fantastic! The freedom that people have in this doctrine, where people come and go whenever they choose to do so. (Pierini 2020, 45)

In addition to the Valley's many Christian elements—images of and references to Jesus and the Virgin Mary, biblical verses, and crosses abound—the presence of pretos velhos, caboclos, and other popular spirit entities gives the movement an air of familiarity to many Brazilians. This polymorphous religious pluralism makes people feel at home: it not only reflects Brazil's religious diversity but also mirrors the religious trajectories of many Brazilians (Oliveira 2010; 2013; Pierini 2016; 2020). "The first time I came here I immediately felt at home," a twenty-four-year-old nymph named Flavia assured me in 2012. Her sister Flaviane added,

> Many people arrive here for the first time and say: "it is like I am coming home." If you come from Catholicism, if you come from Umbanda, you will find elements of those religions here, but in a more modern form. There are many cases of people who come for the first time and decide not to leave. They want to stay here because it is a doctrine like few others. It accepts all religions and welcomes people from all religions—Catholic, evangelical, Spiritist—like brothers.

Against those who dismiss the Valley of the Dawn as an escapist fantasy that provides followers with a fanciful alternative to the present, my research shows that the movement attracts members not because it offers a refuge from modern life but because it offers a different vision of modernity itself (Holston 1999). One reason that the Valley is growing worldwide is because the number of people dissatisfied by both traditional religions and modern secular society is growing (Dawson 2008).

For most people, modernity implies a continual upward trajectory of progress measured by a better life: higher standards of living, greater personal freedoms, a more just society structured around equality of opportunity rather than inherited privilege. But modernity has not always delivered on this promise. Across much of the West it has generated an economy of low-wage jobs with little security and no future, bureaucratic institutions that benefit the few at the expense of the many, and a culture of consumption, materialism, and narcissism that leaves people increasingly isolated and lonely.

By contrast, the Valley of the Dawn offers a more progressive, egalitarian version of modernity: a collective life that members find gratifying; a form of work in which people feel fulfilled; an education premised on merit, not wealth; and a system of justice that seeks reconciliation rather than punishment. "Racism, prejudice, and discrimination are big problems in Brazil," Flavia told me.

> But everyone is welcome here. It's a place that has arms open for everyone without distinction of color, or race, or sex, or money, or religion. That is the beauty of the Doctrine and that is what appealed to me. Here you see people from all over Brazil and the world working together.

Like modern capitalist labor, spiritual labor at the Valley is organized around a weekly schedule and performed by uniformed workers who have specific functions. In order to ensure maximum productivity, the Valley has instituted a complex bureaucracy of offices and procedures in which all participants have an important role to play. But in marked contrast to the real-world, capitalist economy, Valley members refuse to work for money. Healing rituals are offered freely as an expression of unconditional love and a means of the Jaguars' own karmic redemption. Any form of payment is rejected.

Thus, where modern capitalism has produced a form of labor that many experience as alienating because it is divorced from human creative self-fashioning, Valley members feel that their spiritual labors are deeply meaningful and self-transformative. As one adherent told me, "I feel very fulfilled performing this work. By living out the doctrine, you see what you can improve in your life and how you can repair the errors of the past. You see the results of your dedication and your efforts, and this is very gratifying."

The movement offers free "courses" on personal development, moral conduct, and mediumship taught by trained instructors. Educational advancement earns members a title and the right to wear specific clothing, participate in new rituals, and take on leadership duties. Regardless of aptitude or financial means, everyone at the Valley has access to knowledge that leads to self-development and opportunities for advancement.

Likewise, the community's vision of justice contrasts with contemporary criminal-justice systems that emphasize punishment and incarceration. In the Valley of the Dawn, justice means reconciliation for past harms, not retribution. Accordingly, the goal of the week-long Prisoner ritual is justice in the form of spiritual liberation for both cobrador and victim, rather than judgment, sanction, and penalization.

Taken together, these examples indicate that rather than escaping from modernity, members of the Valley of the Dawn are engaged in a complex ritual enactment of some of its major forms (Holston 1999). Although Brazil has not always lived up to the positivistic motto of "order and progress" inscribed on the national flag, the Valley has succeeded in creating for its members an orderly world structured by the principles of progress and justice, in which all are able to advance through hard work and merit.

The movement is far from being perfect or perfectly egalitarian, of course. My analysis in Chapter 6 reveals how it reproduces traditional gender norms that associate women with the nurture and care of others while granting men access to levels of power and authority over the community that are unavailable to women. Despite the Doctrine's rhetorical insistence on gender complementarity and balance, masculinity is linked systematically with autonomy and femininity with dependence in ways that reinforce women's subordination to male authority.

Consequently, the community shows a marked preference for, and actively promotes, heteronormative relationships between men and women. Unfortunately, incidents of discrimination against LGBTQ+ people are not absent, despite the community's emphasis on tolerance, unconditional love, and doctrinal conduct. For example, same-sex couples are not permitted to be married in the Temple—an important rite of passage for heterosexual couples. While I met a number of gay Jaguars, I did not encounter anyone who identified as transgender, so I cannot speak to what that experience might be like. But given the Doctrine's understanding of biological sex as the physical manifestation of an in-dwelling gender (itself considered a permanent attribute of the spirit), I can imagine that transgender folks who want to wear the garments associated with their preferred gender identity may confront resistance if that identity does not match the community's perception of them.

Materializing an Imagined World

While all religions develop specific ways of using the senses to connect the transcendent, intangible realities they propose with the material world that humans inhabit, the Valley of the Dawn is an especially rich example of this phenomenon. For Valley members, there is nothing abstract about the invisible universe "beyond matter" as Mário Sassi termed it. Rather, it is a sensually evident reality apparent in every detail of the community's material environment: visible in the sacred spaces of the temple complex; audible in hymns, emissions, and chants; conjured in symbols, vestments, and iconography; perceptible in rituals; felt in the body. The effect of materialization across multiple sensory registers is a "total synesthetic experience": a recursive feedback loop of phenomenological events through which adherents experience the community's imagined world as emphatically real.

As Aunt Neiva clearly knew, visual imagery and sensory objects are important media of communication. By endowing complex or abstract ideas with perceptual immediacy, imagery makes them more direct, comprehensible, and effective. "My clairvoyance is not enough for the world to understand our messages," Aunt Neiva confirmed. "It takes all our rituals, all our colors, the constructions, the initiations" (Sassi 1985b, 16). Whereas in her visions Aunt Neiva was unconstrained, breaking through the space-time barrier to travel to other dimensions as well as backward and forward in time, back on Earth she was limited by the materials available to her and the constant poverty that surrounded her. With great effort and considerable ingenuity, she found ways to suggest the luminous sparkle and magnetic energy fields of the ethereal worlds she perceived using bits of mirrored glass, paint, fabric, and sequins.

Over the years, Aunt Neiva relied on the talents of many community members to help her materialize the Valley's imagined world. Among them was Joaquim Vilela (b. 1950), a self-taught artist whom she consecrated official illustrator of the Doctrine sometime in the 1970s. Charged with executing paintings of the spiritual realms the Clairvoyant traversed in her visions, Vilela is responsible for much of the iconic imagery found at the Mother Temple, reproductions of which he sells in his small store on the temple grounds (see Image 9.1). He also illustrated some of the Doctrine's published materials and contributed graphic designs for the badges worn by members as part of their work uniform.[6]

Thanks to Vilela and others, the Valley of the Dawn possesses a distinctive aesthetic style reproduced in its affiliated temples worldwide. Comparable to traditions of folk or outsider art, this style is characterized by the use of readymade materials (paint, tile, fabrics), saturated colors, simple lines, and light-reflective elements like sequins, mirror, and metallic trim. Visitors tend to describe the Valley's aesthetic environment as garish or kitschy, but for adherents it functions as a vital portal between the physical world and the spiritual, linking them to dimensions otherwise imperceptible to the untrained eye: the ethereal realms of the spirit through which humans pass before they are born and after they die.[7]

254　SPIRITS OF THE SPACE AGE

Image 9.1 Official Illustrator of the Doctrine, Joaquim Vilela. Credit Márcia Alves

As people interact with the Valley of the Dawn's material culture of things (architecture, vestments, symbols, badges, images, etc.), these things are inserted into the ever-flowing process of their becoming, helping foster new configurations of thoughts, meanings, and affective states. Precisely because our sensory perceptions form the basis for our knowledge and experience of reality, it is through the activities of seeing, touching, wearing, experiencing, and interacting with a religion's created objects that its imagined world is made real for participants. Contrary to what many people think, belief is not only or even primarily a product of cognitive operations. Rather, scholar of religion David Morgan asserted, "belief happens as touching and seeing, hearing and tasting, feeling and emotion, as will and action, as imagination and intuition" (Morgan 2010a, 8).

Kátia's story is a fitting illustration. A highly accomplished, successful media professional in her forties when I first met her in 2015, Kátia expressed a deep sense of imaginative identification with the Valley of the Dawn's aesthetic and material culture. She attributed her decision to join the community to this feeling, which she variously named as enchantment, captivation, and identification. She was not alone in this: many of my informants shared similar stories about the affective power of the Valley.

"What brought me here was my transcendental heritage, my origins," Kátia said to me when I asked how she had first gotten involved with the Valley of the Dawn.

> I was on a spiritual quest. First, I was a Kardecist, then I went to Umbanda, but I did not identify with it. I thought the rituals were beautiful, but they did not touch me. One day some friends of my first husband invited us to lunch in Planaltina [a town near the Mother Temple] and at the lunch there was a singer who sang some of the Valley's hymns. And I was totally captivated by the songs. I went up to her and asked, "what is this? What are these songs? Where are they from?" And she said, "the Valley of the Dawn." I had never heard of the Valley of the Dawn, so our hosts invited us to visit and after lunch we went. They took us first to the Pyramid and, girl, I saw things. Incredible things. Enormous spiritual entities, lights, starships, everything they talk about, but at that time I did not know anything about it. I became totally, absolutely enchanted and I said, "this is it; I do not want to go anywhere else!" I saw the ritual attire, all the indumentárias, and I said, "I want to wear all of them." It was an immediate identification, immediate. And my husband said, "for the love of god, this is a madhouse, let us get

out of here." But I did not want to leave. So we went to the Temple, and when I entered it was like I was walking into a forest, like I was stepping on leaves. And in the Temple, I saw a painting of a preto velho, Father John of Enoch, and I burst into tears. This was an entity that I had incorporated in a Kardecist session, and the leader had sent it away, telling me that it was not an entity that they worked with.[8] So, I began to frequent the Temple, fighting with my entire family about it the entire time, but eventually I was initiated.

Kátia's visceral response to the Valley is noteworthy: she sees "incredible things," she feels as if she is stepping on a carpet of leaves, she bursts into tears. Her feelings and sensory impressions seem to overwhelm her. She explains this intense reaction in terms of her transcendental heritage: something in her past had been triggered and an energy began to resonate, pulling her in like a magnetic charge. She fought with her "entire family the entire time," but eventually she was initiated, realigning her life around the Valley's magnetic forcefield. When we talked, Kátia had been living in the community for several years and was happily re-married to another Valley member.

In this book I have tried to convey the various ways that the Valley of the Dawn has made sense to different people—not just intellectual sense but in terms of feelings, experiences, emotions, histories, and longings both distinct and amorphous. I have explored what adherents find compelling and meaningful about the Valley's imagined world, how they come to live within it, and how they are changed by their experiences and interactions with its material aspects, the narrative of community and self that it proposes, and the gradual education of senses that it fosters.

Like Kátia, many people are drawn to the Valley's mix of the fantastic and the familiar for reasons that cannot really be explained using logic or the language of rationality, because they derive from a different way of knowing. This way of knowing encompasses embodied feelings, sensations, associations, and perceptions that are suspect to many in the post-Enlightenment West. The words we commonly use to describe these ways of knowing—enchantment, captivation, fascination, beguilement—are themselves haunted by a ghostly metaphysical specter. All imply that one's reason has been overcome by an agency that is at once irresistible and external to the self. Valley members have various names for this spectral agency: spirits, energies, rays, forces, transcendental heritage, greater Spirituality, the Indian Space Current, descending force field.

As a scholar of religion, I have tried to explain the Valley of the Dawn in the ways that make sense to me—that is, by tracing the movement's material and intellectual history, using theoretical concepts, and seeking parallels in the familiar for what initially might seem fantastic. My goal has been to describe the Doctrine in a way that is accurate and respectful, yet scholarly and critical. At the same time, I recognize that for folks like Kátia, what is compelling about the Valley of the Dawn is precisely what cannot be understood in this way. In her words, and those of many other Jaguars, "you either feel it or you don't."

Nevertheless, the embodied feelings experienced by my interlocutors as irrefutable evidence of spiritual realities also can be understood as the product of a process of inner sense cultivation, as I argue in Chapter 5. Mediumistic development as practiced at the Valley of the Dawn is merely one way of educating the senses to perceive superhuman powers. The example of Kátia suggests that many who arrive at the Valley of the Dawn have been habituated similarly through their involvement with spirit-centered traditions like Spiritism, Umbanda, or Candomblé, or simply by virtue of growing up in a culture in which the existence of an invisible otherworld of superhuman agencies is widely accepted. The work T. M. Luhrmann and her associates provides a scholarly framework for explaining how people in many different cultures and times come to attribute unusually vivid or ambiguous sensory events to sources they perceive as wholly outside of themselves. For Luhrmann, the human propensity for imaginative absorption, refined through techniques of inner sense cultivation, provides the "scaffolding on which religions build" their imagined otherworlds (Luhrmann, Weisman, et al. 2021). The Valley's material culture of things renders its imagined world concrete in ways that, for people like Kátia, feel emotionally resonant and compelling.

A Universalizing Vision

The Valley of the Dawn also speaks to a pattern of religiosity that has been documented in many places around the world over the second half of the twentieth century: the growth of movements centered on healing, self-realization, and cosmic transformation that present themselves in the language of science yet promise direct experience of dimensions beyond its reach. Even as membership in mainstream religions is declining worldwide, these movements are flourishing, perhaps because they offer worldviews and espouse values that accord with contemporary sensibilities. The Valley provides a valuable window into this phenomenon from outside the Anglophone sphere.

It also attests to a deep undercurrent of esoteric traditions in Brazil that is widespread but remains under-researched, as José Jorge de Carvalho noted (1992, 139; 1994, 75). Despite the Valley of the Dawn's many esoteric elements, scholars have tended to classify the movement as either an "offshoot" or an especially syncretic form of Kardecist Spiritism: a "veritable sponge that absorbs and unites a host of belief systems into an original doctrine," as one researcher put it (Introvigne 2013, 189; Holston 1999, 607). However, the movement's emanationist cosmology, hierarchy of highly evolved intermediary beings, and concern with human spiritual evolution also exemplify Antoine Faivre's four intrinsic characteristics of Western esotericism (Faivre 1994). These characteristics are: (a) correspondences that link the microcosm to the macrocosm; (b) living nature, which is the comprehension of the cosmos as a complex, hierarchical being animated by a divine energy that emanates throughout all levels; (c) imagination and mediations expressed here as cosmic masters and spiritual guides whom adherents experience via imaginative perception and ritual; and (d) the experience of transmutation, an inner transformation or change of state as present-day Jaguars engage in practices aimed at redeeming their negative karma and deepening their knowledge of the principles that govern the universe (Hayes 2020a, 77).

Considering the Valley of the Dawn as an example of Western esotericism sheds light on how a transnational set of ideas with deep historical roots has interacted with local realities in Brazil, bringing that country into a scholarly conversation that has focused almost exclusively on European and North American contexts. It enables the Valley of the Dawn to be compared with other esoteric movements, past and present, and enables the identification of continuities and cross-fertilizations as well as differences.

It also clarifies much about the Valley of the Dawn itself. As Andrew Dawson put it in his survey of New Age religions in Brazil, the Doctrine's "mind-boggling abstruse cosmological system" has struck most observers as incomprehensively complex and even nonsensical (2007, 50). I myself struggled to understand the movement's obscure terms and labyrinthine theology as described by my informants in the field and in the doctrinal writings produced by Sassi and others. The scholarly work on Theosophy and Western esotericism more generally helped me see that the collaboration between the charismatic clairvoyant Aunt Neiva and her interpreter Mário Sassi created a Brazilian form of Western esotericism that transformed the local and Brazilian into something far more transcendent. Just as the humble Brazilian citizen Tiãozinho was revealed to be the Capelino Stuart, interstellar engineer and cosmic Master, esoteric literature provided an expansive framework for Aunt Neiva's visions that spoke to its local context while anchoring it in the more universalizing vision of esotericism.

* * *

Notes

Chapter 1

1. The term "solar" is used to refer to the grounds of a manor house or estate belonging to an elite or aristocratic family.
2. Due to the especially intense concentration of alternative, esoteric, and New Age communities that have emerged in and around Brasília, scholars and other observers have dubbed it the "Mystical City" or "Capital of the New Age." See Siqueira 2003 and 2016; Siqueira and Lima 2003, 144.
3. Affiliated temples vary in size and number of members. They range from small temples that basically are an extension of the house of the leader, to those in separate buildings with precarious conditions, to large temples that have initiatory works. The latter have a developed infrastructure and many members, as well as many patients (Oliveira 2013, 23).
4. In acknowledgment of the Valley's historic and cultural significance, the National Historical and Artistic Heritage Institute (IPHAN) recognized the community in 2010 as part of the federal district's intangible cultural heritage.
5. "Fancy dress party" (Datar 2012); "Fellini set" (Hess 1994, 41); "miniature theme park (Ming 2018); "poor man's Disneyland" (Moser 2008, 73); "refuge for lost souls" (Datar 2012).
6. As I detail later in this book, the priest, after several other visits and much study, felt the need "to correct that first impression" by writing an exhaustively researched and admiring profile of the group for a theological publication (367).
7. A similar understanding of worldview was articulated by Ann Taves, Egil Asprem, and Elliott Ihm (2018).
8. There are many ways to define religion and lively debates among scholars of religion about this issue and the validity of the concept itself (Nongbri 2013 provides an accessible summary of these debates and their history). The particular definition that I have offered here is useful for the project of this book, but, like all definitions of religion, it has its strengths and limitations. I offer it, therefore, as a working definition: a place to start my inquiry, rather than as capturing the definitive essence of what it purports to define.
9. "Only a scant few new religions ever garner media attention," wrote Laura Vance, a sociologist of new religions, and usually at moments of crisis or conflict. Although scandals plague established religions, "the details may seem more salacious, more novel, in the context of an unfamiliar religion, which also holds potential promise of peculiar beliefs and strange practices" (2015, 2). The Valley of the Dawn seems to be an exception to this rule, since it regularly receives media coverage. Typically, this

occurs around the time of one of its major ceremonies, which draws thousands of members from around the world to the Mother Temple every May 1 for a lengthy ceremony that begins before dawn.

10. Moore is perhaps best known for her work on the People's Temple and the events at Jonestown, Guyana, that culminated in the deaths of more than nine hundred people. Among them were two of Moore's sisters and her nephew. For a partial list of her publications, see: https://jonestown.sdsu.edu/?page_id=16580.
11. Here again, there is a great deal of scholarly debate about the definitional scope of "new religious movements," with some authors putting emphasis on period of origin and others on degree of tension with the larger social context (e.g., Melton 2004). For a comprehensive history of the study of new religious movements in academia, see: Ashcraft 2019.
12. The reference to the "beloved dead" comes from Mary Ann Clark 2014, 89. Spiritualism and Spiritism share a common origin and belief in the communication between the living and the departed but developed along slightly different paths. In Europe, the major proponent of these ideas was Allan Kardec, who used the term "spiritism" to differentiate his philosophical movement from its parent in the United States and England. Spiritualism was quite popular in the United States, peaking in the years during the Civil War when few families were untouched by the war's casualties. Historian Robert Cox cited estimates that as many as one-third of Americans were involved in Spiritualism at that time (Cox 2003, 237 fn2).
13. Silva, José Carlos Nascimento, 2010, Observações Tumará (unpublished archive of the Trino Tumará Mestre José Carlos Silva Nascimento), Brasília: Vale do Amanhecer, 93.
14. Of course, Harari is not the only scholar to make this argument. Birgit Meyer, for example, called the human imagination a "world-making device with its own reality effects" (Meyer 2015, 15). What Harari calls an "imagined order," other scholars have referred to as a "social imaginary" or simply an "imaginary" (Gaonkar 2002). The concept has a long history among contemporary philosophers and social theorists. Those that have most influenced my thinking include Cornelius Castoriadis (1987), Benedict Anderson (2006), Charles Taylor (2004), Peter Berger (1967), and Maurice Bloch (2008).
15. This description is inspired by that of Ann Taves in her book *Revelatory Events* (2016, xiii).

Chapter 2

1. At age twelve, Gertrudes had joined the family to help Neiva with the children before Raul Zelaya's premature death. The children later described her as "our mother's right arm, she was our companion, our security, she made everything seem happier amidst our difficulties" (Siqueira et al. 2010, 174 fn7).
2. Novacap was the acronym for the Companhia Urbanizadora do Nova Capital (Urbanization Company of the New Capital), created in 1956 by President Juscelino

Kubitschek. In 1958 President Kubitschek put Sayão in charge of managing the creation of the highway from Brasília to Belém, a massive undertaking that required cutting a passage through the Amazon forest. In January 1959, a mere thirty-one kilometers from the highway's destination of Belém, a massive tree cut down by one of the workers struck and killed Sayão. It was a tragic, if perhaps fitting, end to one of the nation's legendary pioneers who became known as the "opener of the wilderness" (Holston 1989, 342 fn9).

3. The description of Brasília as "intended to mirror the power and boldness that would transform the country" is taken from historian Angela de Castro Gomes's words. She characterized the period from 1930 to 1964 as a time "of a nationalism expressed through plans for a new political architecture of state institutions, visible, even, in the buildings that were supposed to house them, mirroring the power and boldness that would transform the country" (Gomes 2013, 14).

4. As Kubitschek's 1955 campaign promise put it (see Holston 1989, 84). The motto of "Fifty in Five" was based on two key initiatives for the nation's development, the construction of Brasília and the Plano de Metas (Plan of Goals), which aimed to modernize five areas: energy, food, industry, education, and transport (Skidmore 2009).

5. In 1956, approximately 250 workers contracted by Novacap arrived to begin the work of demarcating the territory. By 1957 the number of workers had increased to 2,500, and by 1958 the total working population was 28,000 people, with approximately 2,100 people arriving daily. According to the first census, in 1959, the migrant population was 55,737 people. Of these, about two-thirds were men, and most were from the states of Goiás, Minas Gerais, and Bahia (L. Oliveira 2010, 127; Santos 2016b, 156).

6. The term *candango* has a long history in Brazil. It derives from a Bantu-language term used during the colonial period to refer disparagingly to the Portuguese colonists. At the beginning of the construction of Brasília, candango retained this pejorative connotation and was used as synonym for an uneducated, itinerant worker; someone who performed unskilled menial labor; a peon. Over time, as the government depicted the workers who came to the federal district in a heroic light as modern pioneers whose work was essential to the national project of creating a modern Brazil, the term became celebratory. Eventually it referred to everyone, from workers to government officials, who moved to the federal district (Holston 1989, 209; Solomon 2019).

7. According to Holston, in 1959, 43 percent of migrants were from the northeast, and 24 percent were from the central west (principally the state of Goiás). An additional 29 percent were from the southeast (principally the state of Minas Gerais) (Holston 1989, 220, 253).

8. The population of the Free City and its surrounding areas more than tripled between 1957 and 1958, going from 2,212 inhabitants to 7,033 (Ribeiro 2008, 236). See also Epstein 1973, 76.

9. The second type of settlement consisted of construction camps authorized by Novacap but built and run by private construction companies for their employees. Finally, there were small, ad-hoc squatter settlements built "near construction sites, along the banks of creeks, and in cleared areas of the scrubland, to house migrants working low-wage jobs who couldn't afford to live in Núcleo Bandeirante" (Solomon

2019). See also Epstein 1973, chapter 3. In Novacap's original plan, the Free City was the only temporary settlement authorized to provide residence for those not lodged in the construction camps (Holston 1989, 240).

10. Since most scientists in the mid-nineteenth century had not yet excluded from their domain phenomena that later would be labeled "psychic," and still later "paranormal," this is not as strange as it might seem from the vantage point of the twenty-first century. Claims about the scientific status of Spiritism helped its spokespeople promote and defend the movement, which took root in Brazil initially among the nation's privileged classes. Brazilian Spiritists proved to be especially adept at using mass media to disseminate their ideas to the wider public via newspapers, journals, books, and radio and television programs. Through organizations like the Brazilian Spiritist Federation, established in 1884, and its periodical *O Reformador* (The Reformer), advocates of Spiritism used a combination of reasoned argument, strategic alliances, and social connections to promote Spiritist doctrine and defend it from its critics (Giumbelli 1997, 63). Eventually advocates were successful in legalizing Spiritism, which had been included among the practices outlawed by the Brazilian Penal Code of 1890, by re-classifying it as high spiritism: a "respectable doctrine," as one police report put it, focused on "evolved" European spirits and oriented around the provision of charity, education, and other noble principles (Maggie 1992, 45).

11. Spiritism differs from its North American cousin Spiritualism on several points, such as the primacy of the concept of reincarnation, which is controversial in Spiritualism according to Hess (1987; 1991a).

12. Within Kardec's system this movement is unidirectional: spirits can only progress; they cannot regress. "Spirits may remain stationary," Kardec wrote, "but they never retrograde; those who are rebellious are punished by not advancing, and by having to recommence their misused existences under the conditions suited to their nature" (Kardec 1989, 123).

13. Historian Lynn Sharp noted that most nineteenth-century Spiritists believed that these incarnations took place not only on Earth but on other planets as well (Sharp 2015, 234). The idea of a plurality of worlds was widespread at this time, and in the Spiritist version of this idea, Earth was imagined to be a fairly low-level world. Since the spirit's level of advancement determined the world into which it would be incarnated, more evolved spirits would be incarnated in worlds more evolved than Earth (Sharp 2015, 234).

14. According to Lynn Sharp, Kardec "accepted but rarely spoke about healing as one of the benefits" of Spiritism. After Kardec's death in 1869, later leaders also preferred to emphasize the movement's philosophical, doctrinal, and political possibilities. Among the rank and file, however, healing held a place of importance for many "interested in the practical applications of their newfound knowledge and beliefs" (2005, 313).

15. Franz Anton Mesmer (1734–1815) was a German-born physician who attributed illness to blockages in the flow of an invisible but vital substance he called magnetic fluid or animal magnetism. He believed that correcting imbalances of this fluid could

restore health. His treatment methods, which came to be called mesmerism, included a number of techniques including the magnetic pass. Mesmer also is credited as a forerunner of modern hypnotism.
16. Kardecism spread initially among Brazilian elites living in Rio de Janeiro in the second half of the nineteenth century. Among this segment of the population, France provided a model of the sophisticated civilization they wished to re-create in the tropics, and they eagerly adopted the latest philosophical and sartorial styles from Paris. At first, Kardec's ideas were disseminated primarily through small groups meeting in private spaces in order to discuss Spiritist tenets and receive wisdom from enlightened spirits communicated through mediums. However, Kardec also emphasized the diagnostic and therapeutic aspects of Spiritism and advocated free treatment, which helped facilitated the spread of Spiritism among the less advantaged classes. Many medical doctors were Spiritists, and many of the country's first psychiatric hospitals were founded by Spiritists. For more on the history and spread of Kardecism in Brazil, see: Aureliano and Cardoso 2015; Damazio 1994; Giumbelli 1997; Hess 1987 and 1991a; Lewgoy, 2008—among others.
17. A slightly different version of this story is recounted in Neiva's biography *My Life My Loves* (Minha Vida Meus Amores), edited by Mário Sassi (Sassi 1985, n.p.).
18. While there are lively debates about the semantic range and usefulness of the term "paranormal" term in critical analyses, I find it useful here as a broader category that can be applied to a variety of discourses centered on metaphysical claims whose empirical validity is rejected by mainstream science. As Jeffrey Kripal observed, the paranormal is also "para-scientific" because claims about empirical evidence typically are central to these discourses but lie beyond the capacity of contemporary scientific methods to measure (Kripal 2010, 9, 52). Harvey J. Irwin defines paranormal as follows: "a proposition that has not been empirically attested to the satisfaction of the scientific establishment but is generated within the non-scientific community and extensively endorsed by people who might normally be expected by their society to be capable of rational thought and reality testing" (Irwin 2009, 16–17). See also Laycock 2014 for a discussion of the paranormal as a category for religious beliefs.
19. According to Aracky Rodrigues and Francine Muel-Dreyfus, the group consisted of Neiva, her four children, a daughter-in-law (possibly Gertrudes), four other families, and forty children (2005, 239). However, Carmem Lúcia wrote in her memoir that there were approximately eighty children who lived at UESB (2014, 140).
20. The director of the federal senate, for example, later shepherded Neiva through the process of getting the appropriate state license for OSOEC's temple and orphanage. And it was through her connections with other members of the Senate that Neiva arranged government jobs for her two sons (Cunha 2008; Reis 2008).
21. There are several alternate spellings, including Humarran, Humahã, Humahan, and Umahan. In his 1977 article about the Doctrine, which was based on interviews with Aunt Neiva and Mário Sassi, Father César gave the name as Umarama, adding that "the most correct graphic transcription, which I heard from Aunt Neiva herself, would be Humahan" (1977a, 381).

22. Anthropologist James Holston reported that when he first visited the Valley of the Dawn in 1981, members lived under the constant threat of imminent eradication (Holston 1999, 610). Undeterred, Aunt Neiva predicted shortly before her death that the eradication order would be rescinded, and the land would not be flooded (1999, 610). She died before an official decision was reached, however, and in 1986 a local television report on the community's predicament began with the ominous words: "The Valley of the Dawn, the great mystical city of Brasília, will end" ("Vale do Amanhecer" 1986). Unbeknownst to the public, the governor of the federal district, José Aparecido de Oliveira (1929–2007), had dispatched engineers to study the problem, and in 1988 his government adopted a plan that saved the Valley of the Dawn from flooding.

23. Exact numbers are difficult to come by because OSOEC did not start keeping records until the 1970s and reports from outsiders vary. According to Father José Vicente César, a Catholic priest and ethnographer who studied the movement in the mid-1970s, the Valley of the Dawn had approximately 500 resident mediums in 1976 and another 15,000 registered mediums living in the surrounding area who participated in the community's ongoing schedule of spiritual works. César reported that between 50,000 and 70,000 people visited the Valley of the Dawn monthly for spiritual treatment (César 1977a). However, Ana Lúcia Galinkin, who conducted field research at the Valley of the Dawn in 1975 and 1976 for her master's thesis, reported that there were about 200 resident mediums in 1975 and a total number of about 9,000 mediums altogether (Galinkin 2008, 19). A study in 1979 cited by Arakcy Martins Rodrigues and Francine Muel-Dreyfus gave a figure of 40,000 (Rodrigues and Muel-Dreyfus 2005, 236). However, this figure probably included members who did not reside in the town surrounding the temple. In 1983, reporter Fernando Pinto of the newspaper *Correiro Brasiliense* visited the Valley and wrote that 2,000 people lived there with approximately 8,000 initiates and twenty affiliated temples (Pinto 2004, 32). American anthropologist James Holston wrote that when he first visited the Valley in 1981, "it had a resident population of about 400 people, although many times that number gathered for rituals, especially on weekends." By 1991, its resident population "grew to about 8,000, swelling to 10,000 on the weekends." Valley leadership claimed seventy affiliated temples and a total membership of about 110,000–120,000 mediums (Holston 1999, 617).

24. "We had a lot of difficulty with fabric, because the spirits she saw in her visions wore brilliant garments filled with light," Carmem Lúcia reiterated in my own 2017 interview with her. "So the first dresses we made we couldn't really achieve that look. We tried using velvet, but it was very expensive and hot. So we had this difficulty and then she saw the symbols of the Nymphs . . . But, those materials didn't exist here at the time and we realized that it couldn't be exactly the same. So, we bought glue and embellishments and glued them on the velvet. As you can imagine, that ruined the velvet forever. But that's how we did it, we obeyed and improvements came. I would go out, see a fabric, maybe Mother Yara gave me an intuition, I would buy it and bring it to her [Neiva]. And she would say, 'no, it's not like that,' or 'it's this.' And so, it began to form. The organza was difficult, because that was a material that was only used for curtains. And it was only available in pale colors and our colors are not at all pale. It

was very difficult. I went to Brasília, Goiânia, all the way to Rio searching for the right materials. I had to have many colors specially made by a factory and they would only do it if it was an order for 2,000, 3,000 meters. Not today, I do not have to do that anymore. There are places that have it, they distribute it to other stores and everything" (C. L. Zelaya 2017).

25. According to veteran members, Aunt Neiva's contacts with powerful people reached all the way to General João Baptista Figueiredo, the last of the military presidents that ruled the country following the 1964 coup d'état (1979–1985). At the time, one of Figueiredo's aides was a high-ranking Valley member through whom Figueiredo and Aunt Neiva "communicated constantly" (Cunha 2008, 60).

26. Carmem Lúcia told me that countless actors, musicians, and other pop-culture figures have visited the Mother Temple over the years (C. L. Zelaya interview 2017). Although she did not specifically recall meeting Caetano Veloso, a story prevalent among some Valley members holds that Veloso penned his 1976 song "An Indian" ("Um Índio") in homage to Father White Arrow. After spending time with Aunt Neiva, the story goes, Veloso had entered the Mother Temple and been inspired by the statue of Father White Arrow and the devotions surrounding it (see Martins 2004, 120; Hayes 2013, 64–65). About a decade later, key scenes in the telenovela "Mandala" were shot on location at the Mother Temple and aired on TV Globo between October 1987 and May 1988 (Cavalcante 2011, 12–13).

27. An acrimonious dispute between Aunt Neiva's two sons in 2009 created two separate administrative branches: OSOEC, centered at the Mother Temple outside Brasília and headed by Raul Zelaya, and CGTA (General Council of the Temples of the Dawn), led by Gilberto Zelaya and comprising many of the external temples. Despite this juridical and organizational division, however, there are few differences between the two groups in terms of beliefs and practices. However, the split did strain relationships of both sides and produced bureaucratic problems and legal wrangling over ownership of the movement's tangible and intangible resources. In 2010, OSOEC won a preliminary injunction in a civil lawsuit prohibiting the CGTA and all of its members from using any of the liturgies, symbols, and rituals pertaining to the religion, but a federal court overturned this decision in 2011. Since that time all of the temples outside of the Mother Temple have aligned themselves with either OSOEC or CGTA, although individual Valley of the Dawn members are free to cross these lines. Gilberto Zelaya's death in 2017 does not seem to have changed this arrangement. Despite these and other administrative contretemps, the movement as a whole continues to expand.

Chapter 3

1. As reported by Father José Vicente César, a Catholic priest who studied the Valley for an extended period beginning in 1976 and wrote about it for a theological publication (César 1977a, 375).
2. Galinkin reported that Sassi started a degree in philosophy at the University of São Paulo (USP) but abandoned it after two and a half years. Sassi told Galinkin

and several others that he later had enrolled in the faculty of social sciences at the University of Brasília in order to complete the degree but never did (Galinkin 2008, 55). Cací Sassi told me that her father had completed a degree in public relations at USP, but I was unable to confirm this (C. Sassi interview 2017).
3. Referencing the work of French sociologist Pierre Bourdieu (1979, 283), Arakcy Martins Rodrigues and Francine Muel-Dreyfus analyze Sassi as trapped in the classic bind of the petty bourgeoisie who occupy a contradictory and ambiguous social position, "condemned 'to all the contradictions between a condition of objective domination and a participation, in intention and will, in dominant values'" (Rodrigues and Muel-Dreyfus 2005, 243–244).
4. For a detailed discussion of these events see Salmeron 2007.
5. For a description of the dictatorship's repressive activities related to the University of Brasília and the student protest movement, see the Final Report to the Anísio Teixeira Truth and Memory Commission (Comissão Anísio Teixeira de Memória e Verdade 2015).
6. An eyewitness testified to the Anísio Teixeira Truth and Memory Commission in 2013 that he saw Abaetê handcuffed to a chair and kicked and punched by agents of the federal police in the course of his interrogation (147).
7. The reference to the "Spirit of Truth" alludes to a passage in the Biblical Gospel of John where Jesus promises his disciples that God will send them an advocate in the form of the Spirit of Truth to comfort and be with them. Although the world will not recognize this advocate, Jesus's disciples will know him for he "abides with you and will be in you" (John 14:16–17, NRSV). Edgard Armond's book *Os Exilados de Capela* cites other spirit entities, among them Chico Xavier's spirit mentor Emmanuel, as numbering among the many Spirits of Truth who have guided humanity's spiritual evolution (Armond 1987 [1940]).
8. This is a point that has been overlooked in accounts of the Valley of the Dawn that focus on Neiva's charismatic role.
9. In fact, Cací and two of her brothers became mediums at the Valley of the Dawn, and one brother lived in the community for a time.
10. "Casa Grande was a miracle of architecture and decoration," Sassi wrote. "On a standard Taguatinga lot, luckily a corner lot, was an elongated shack stretched by the four cardinal points. It was made of tiles of all kinds, wood that had already known other architectural uses, and other materials. Exactly sixty-three people lived in it, including the writer [Sassi]. Their ages ranged from one to sixty years old, of both sexes. A difference in floor height and a partition delimited the orphanage and Neiva's house" (Sassi n/d, 18).
11. There are different accounts of whether Aunt Neiva and Mário Sassi were legally married. Marcelo Reis reported that the couple's marriage was never officially recognized by the state but that veteran members recall Aunt Neiva saying that her union with Sassi had been "consecrated on the spiritual plane" (Reis 2010, 196). Iraê Sassi told me that the couple lived together but never underwent any marriage ceremony, either religious or secular (I. Sassi interview 2017). It is common in Brazil to refer to couples who live together as being married.

12. Like many of the Valley of the Dawn's publications, the original book lacks page numbers and the page number given here corresponds to a PDF copy of the book that I obtained.
13. According to historian and Valley member Marcelo Reis, who has written extensively about Aunt Neiva's life and the development of the Valley of the Dawn, Sassi "never devoted himself to one specific branch of knowledge in which he could develop his intellectual aptitudes. He seems to have focused and channeled his education and intellectual capacity in favor of Aunt Neiva's ideal" (Reis 2010, 195).
14. Christopher White called this the "scientific supernatural," which he defined as "a category of things that: 1) are either beyond nature or at its boundary and, 2) are suggested by scientific theory or empirical evidence while also at least partially eluding scientific tests, instruments, or measurements" (2018, 3).
15. Aunt Neiva's claim to have completed an esoteric apprenticeship with Umahã predates Sassi's arrival, but I believe that Sassi introduced a far more complex esoteric vocabulary and metaphysical framework into the mix. See Hayes 2020.
16. Literally, *força decrescente* means "descending force," but Valley members also use the term to refer to a system based on descending forces, so I have translated it here as descending forcefield.
17. There is some disagreement about the exact dates for the "arrival of the mestado," with some sources linking it to the first Dharman Oxinto initiation in 1973 and others with the first Elevation of Swords ritual in 1975. Guilherme Stuckert, the Valley's official photographer, recalled in an interview published in the short-lived *Jornal do Jaguar* or Journal of the Jaguar, that the mestrado arrived in 1975 with the first Elevation of Swords ritual. "It was the beginning of a whole initiatory archive brought by our Mother, Aunt Neiva, for the formation of our Doctrine" (Stuckert 2005, 7).
18. Sassi explained these events and his reasons for leave the Valley of the Dawn in a series of letters. Three of these letters are available at: http://www.valedoamanhecer.net.br/publique/news_content.php?fileName=271 (accessed March 10, 2017).
19. Author's interview with Lêda Franco de Oliveira, Sobradinho (Brazil), July 29, 2017. The movement that Sassi founded continues to this day under Lêda's direction as the Tumuchy Temple of the Spiritualist Christian Order of the Universal Light (Templo Tumuchy da Ordem Espírita Cristã da Luz Universal). Sassi's group sometimes is referred to as the Temple of the Sun by Valley of the Dawn members.
20. In an earlier publication (Hayes 2013), I erroneously gave the date of Sassi's death as 1995, following other printed sources (principally Siqueira et al. 2010). However, both Sassi's daughter Cací and his third wife Lêda confirmed to me that he actually died in December of 1994.
21. See Reis 2010a, 194–200. On Sassi's departure from the Valley see Marques 2009, 8–9. Sassi himself wrote several letters detailing his perspective on the schism, which he attributed to the other Trinos' refusal to sanction his work with the spirit of Aunt Neiva, whom Sassi claimed was being incorporated by a medium. Three of these letters written in 1990 are available under the heading "A Cisão," or "The Schism" at http://www.valedoamanhecer.net.br/publique/news_content.php?fileName=271 (accessed August 18, 2012).

Chapter 4

1. A reference to the star Capella, also known as Alpha Aurigae, visible from Earth as the brightest star in the constellation of Auriga. It is referred to almost exclusively as a planet in Valley doctrine.
2. Valley members are not alone in referring to reincarnation as the "law of cause and effect." The phrase was coined by Allan Kardec, who saw reincarnation as the mechanism through which spirits—who are endowed by God with free will—evolve toward moral perfection.
3. I am here drawing on Garry W. Trompf's notion of macrohistory as "the encapsulation of the human past in a unitary vision" (Trompf 2013, 375; Trompf 2019).
4. Although Sassi is credited as the intellectual of the Doctrine, he was not the only one in close proximity to Neiva whose recordings and memories have contributed to the community's archive. "I feel that our doctrine was brought to us gradually," veteran member Master José Carlos do Nascimento Silva wrote of his own efforts to organize Aunt Neiva's teachings, "depending on each one's understanding, and being more Science than Religion, many things were partially revealed, and we need to join the parts. It is like a huge jigsaw puzzle where the pieces were delivered, distributed to all the Jaguars. But some have the pieces that others do not" (Silva 2010, 93).
5. In a pattern common among other religions established in the nineteenth and twentieth centuries, Sassi used science as a rhetorical tool and a way to legitimate claims about the nature of reality that are not empirically verifiable. Likewise, contemporary Valley members insist that their beliefs and practices are thoroughly rational and scientifically proven. As Benjamin Zeller observed, thanks to the authority given to science in the modern world, being "scientific" is often central to the self-understanding of adherents of new religious movements. However, "their understandings of science are fluid, changing, and seldom follow rigorous academic definitions of the term" (Zeller 2011, 667). Claims about the scientific status of Spiritism helped its spokespeople promote and defend the movement, which took root initially among the nation's privileged classes. Brazilian Spiritists proved to be especially adept at using mass media to disseminate their ideas to the wider public via newspapers, journals, books, and radio and television programs. Through organizations like the Brazilian Spiritist Federation, established in 1884, and its periodical *O Reformador* (The Reformer), advocates of Spiritism used a combination of reasoned argument, strategic alliances, and social connections to promote Spiritist doctrine and defend it from its critics. See Giumbelli 1997, 63. Eventually advocates were successful in legalizing Spiritism, which had been included among the practices outlawed by the Brazilian Penal Code of 1890, by re-classifying it as High Spiritism: a "respectable doctrine," as one police report put it, focused on "evolved" European spirits and oriented around the provision of charity, education, and other noble principles (Maggie 1992, 45).
6. The Theosophical Society, founded in New York in 1875, "has been the major advocate of occult philosophy in the West and the single most important avenue of Eastern teaching to the West," as scholars J. Gordon Melton, Jerome Clark, and Aidan A. Kelly

put it in their *New Age Almanac* (Melton et al. 1991,16). According to its founders, the group's purpose was to promulgate the "wisdom" (*sophia*) of "God" (*theos*), or as Blavatsky put it "the accumulated Wisdom of the ages, tested and verified by generations of Seers" (Preston and Humphrey 2012, n.p.). On the relationship of Theosophy to Western esotericism, see also Goodrick-Clarke 2013. On Theosophy's contributions to New Age millennial movements, see Lucas 2011.

7. The reference to "cosmic U-curve" is from Trompf 2013, 376.

8. In the introduction to their edited volume *Handbook of the Theosophical Current*, Olav Hammer and Mikael Rothstein ranked the formation of the Theosophical Society as one of the most decisive events shaping Western religious history, along with the Protestant Reformation and Constantine's decision to favor Christianity (2013, 1). Despite being "one of the modern world's most important religious traditions," they wrote, Theosophy is "vastly understudied" (2).

9. In an article on Theosophy for the *Encyclopedia Brittanica*, J. Gordon Melton wrote that Theosophy inspired the creation of over a hundred esoteric movements (Melton 2020). A partial list would include the I AM Activity, the Summit Lighthouse (later called the Church Universal and Triumphant), Anthroposophy, the Aetherius Society, the Unarius Academy of Science, and many others grouped under the label of New Age movements. Many of the leaders of these movements, like Aunt Neiva and H.P. Blavatsky herself, were women. On the ways that Theosophy and related movements have promoted women's religious leadership and fostered "nonpatriarchal understandings of ultimate reality" (753), see Wessinger et al. 2006.

10. Alice Bailey (1880–1949), who was involved with the Theosophical Society for a period and wrote a number of influential books on esoteric topics, claimed to have received esoteric wisdom from a Tibetan Master named Djwal Khul, known as "The Tibetan" or D. K. According to Bailey, D. K. was the abbot of a Tibetan monastery. Although Valley of the Dawn Doctrine does not explicitly connect Aunt Neiva's Tibetan Master with D. K., Sassi wrote that Kuthumi (or Koot Hoomi, as it is more often spelled), one of the two Masters of Wisdom whom H. P. Blavatsky credited as the true founders of the Theosophical Society, was one of the guises by which Father White Arrow was known during his sojourns on Earth (Sassi 1985b). The founder of the I AM movement, Guy Ballard (1878–1939), claimed to receive regular messages from various Masters, whom he referred to as Ascended Masters of the Great White Brotherhood, beginning in 1930. Both the I AM movement and various other groups inspired by it, such as the Church Universal and Triumphant (established in 1958), promote a doctrine based on the founders' claims to have received advanced teachings from the Ascended Masters, who guide human evolution. For more on the role of the Masters in Theosophy and other groups influenced by it, see Hammer and Rothstein (eds.), 2013.

11. According to João Batista Brito Pinto (1912–1998), president of the Sociedade Teosófica no Brasil during the 1980s, the first theosophical lodge in Brazil was established in Pelotas, Rio Grande do Sul, in 1902. It was organized by members of the Spiritist Center "Love Towards God" (*Amor a Deus*) and housed there. See Pinto 1993 (1969). Brazilian scholar José Guilherme Cantor Magnani made a similar claim in

his survey of the New Age movement in Brazil (2016, 61). Given the conceptual and historical affinities between Spiritism and Theosophy, it should not be a surprise that the earliest Brazilian lodges associated with the Theosophical Society formed initially within Spiritist groups. For more intellectually inclined Spiritists, Theosophy offered an explanatory framework for understanding the immaterial dimensions and dynamics of the universe that complemented Kardec's emphasis on the wisdom of "pure and evolved" spirits. Spiritist newspapers, conferences, radio programs, and other media were an important vector through which theosophical concepts spread in Brazil throughout the twentieth century, although Theosophy as a formal movement never achieved the widespread popularity on its own.

12. According to Pinto, the first was Leadbeater's *The Other Side of Death* in 1905 (Pinto 1993 [1969], 19).
13. For many Spiritists, Theosophy offered an explanatory framework for understanding the immaterial dimensions and dynamics of the universe that complemented Kardec's emphasis on the wisdom of "pure and evolved" spirits.
14. Theosophy was not the only esoteric current that was present in Brazil whose cosmological and ontological ideas may have contributed to the Valley of the Dawn. Local communities associated with Anthroposophy, Rosicrucianism, Freemasonry, and other esoteric traditions were operating in Brazil as early as the late eighteenth century (in the case of the Freemasons) and into the early part of the twentieth century (Anthroposophy, Rosicrucianism). See Magnani 2016, 61–62.
15. Brazilian media of the 1950s and 1960s, like its American counterparts, was full of tales of flying saucers and encounters with aliens. Between 1947 and 1960, for example, *O Cruzeiro*, an influential general-interest periodical similar to *Life* magazine, ran dozens of stories about *discos voadores* or flying saucers, including reports about international and local sightings as well as interviews with people who claimed to have contact with extraterrestrials inhabiting Venus and Mars. In the decade of 1950 alone, there were fifty-eight such stories (Santos 2007; Caires 2013).
16. Desmond Leslie and George Adamski's *Flying Saucers Have Landed* (1943) was published in Brazil as *Discos Voadores* in 1957, and in 1969 Erich von Däniken's *Chariots of the Gods? Unsolved Mysteries of the Past* (1969 [1968]) was translated and published in Brazil.
17. Other scholars have termed this blend Western esotericism (Faivre 1994; Hanegraaff 1996, 1999, 2012) or metaphysical religiosity (Albanese 2007).
18. The actual star Capella is not located behind the Sun. However, George King, the founder of the Aetherius Society, also spoke of a nameless planet located behind the Sun that played a role in the mythological history of humanity (Rothstein 2003, 149). In describing Capella's location as behind the Sun, Sassi may have been trying to harmonize various esoteric sources on which he was drawing.
19. The physical nature of the Capellans makes them closer to H. P. Blavatsky's original concept of the Masters than the later Ascended Masters that developed among more theosophically oriented UFO groups.
20. The notion that highly evolved alien life forms are concerned with human progress is a recurrent theme in UFO religions and their theosophical forerunners. See

Partridge 2003. H. P. Blavatsky included among the hierarchy of Masters those who dwelled on Venus (the so-called Lords of the Flame), although they did not receive much emphasis by her or by her contemporaries. However, others, including second-generation theosophical writer Charles Leadbeater, developed the idea of Masters residing on other planets (1912). This idea is an important element in religious movements like the I AM movement, Aetherius Society, The Church Universal and Triumphant, Unarius Academy of Science, and others. Christopher Partridge argued that while there are some superficial differences between the theosophical Masters (most of whom were said to reside in Tibet) and early accounts of aliens, the similarities are striking: "both are highly spiritually evolved, morally superior, technologically advanced, benevolent beings with a deep salvific concern for a humanity bent on the destruction of the planet.... The point is that, in much UFO religion, fundamentally the same masters remain, but their location, dress, and mode of transport has been updated" (Partridge 2003, 12).

21. According to Mikael Rothstein, the founder of the Aetherius Society George King similarly claimed that extraterrestrial Space Brothers could not interact directly with uninitiated humans for "karmic reasons." See Rothstein 2013, 227.

22. Aunt Neiva's extraterrestrial experiences occurred in 1959, two years after Leslie and Adamski's *Flying Saucers Have Landed* (1943) was published in Brazil as *Discos Voadores*. However, the description of her voyages to Capella fits the model of solitary astral travel that J. Gordon Melton characterized as typical of pre-Adamski contactees, as does the fact that the Capellans are described as originating within our solar system. In Melton's survey, post-Adamski contactees said their alien visitors came from remote planets beyond our solar system. See Melton 1995, 5–7.

23. In his 1868 book *Genesis: The Miracles and the Predictions According to Spiritism*, Allan Kardec wrote that human evolution had been accelerated by beings from another planet who were "exiled on the already peopled Earth, but peopled by primitive men yet in ignorance, to whom their mission was to effect their progress by carrying among them the light of a developed intelligence . . . Their intellectual superiority proves that the world from which they came was more advanced than this Earth; but that world entering upon a new phase of progress, these spirits, by their obstinacy not placing themselves at the required heights, would have been a hindrance to the providential march of events. This is why they were expelled" (2003 [1868], 127). Second-generation theosophists like Charles Leadbeater, Annie Besant, and Alice Bailey also argued that human evolution had been jumpstarted by an extraterrestrial expedition from Venus referred to as "Lords of the Flame." The notion that the aliens had been exiled to Earth from their home planet, however, is missing in the theosophical accounts.

24. Both Xavier and Armond trace out a panorama of cosmic and human history that synthesizes Allan Kardec's ideas with theosophical teachings. In their respective books, both Xavier and Armond attempted to harmonize the theosophical vision of human evolution through root races with the biblical account of creation, relying on Kardec's notion of the "Adamic race" to do so. Both authors identified the Capellans as being the same colony of spirits "from another sphere" to which Allen Kardec refers in

his book *Genesis* as the origin of the Adamic race: "the race which has pushed all other races forward" (Kardec 2003 [1868], 124–125). Following Kardec, both claimed that the extraterrestrials were exiled to Earth from their home planet as a consequence of their misbehavior, an idea that recurs in Valley teachings.

25. The idea of advanced intelligences existing on other planets was not entirely new—most nineteenth-century Spiritists believed that incarnations took place not only on Earth but on numerous planets (Sharp 2015, 234).

26. While Sassi seems to have borrowed the Capella storyline from his Spiritist forbears, neither Xavier nor Armond refers to these extraterrestrial missionaries as Equitumans, and this term (as well as Tumuchy, which is described further on) appears to be unique to the Valley of the Dawn. In their stature and asexual means of reproduction, the Equitumans very much resemble the Lemurians, the third root race in H. P. Blavatsky's septenary schema. In essence, root races demarcate major stages within a vast, cyclical progression through which cosmic consciousness descends into matter and, reversing course, ascends again. James Santucci described root races as the "various stages experienced by the reincarnating soul or 'monad' [i.e., human entity] along an incredibly lengthy series of cyclical progressions . . . before reaching the stage of a 'perfect, septenary being,' in which consciousness is fully integrated in its operation of the 'vehicles' or 'bodies' corresponding to the seven planes of existence." Each of the seven root races (and their associated sub-races) is characterized by differing admixtures of consciousness (or spirit) and matter. See Santucci 2008, 38.

27. Valley members say that Amanto is the same spirit entity who manifested himself to Chico Xavier as Emmanuel, further underlining the importance of Xavier on the Valley's doctrine.

28. Later in the book Sassi narrated these events somewhat differently, describing the Tumuchy as "wise" Equitumans who had returned to Capella and there received new instructions from the Masters before being reincarnated on Earth in bodies that were more suited to both the terrestrial environment and their task (Sassi 1974, 219).

29. For reasons that are unclear, Valley members refer to Easter Island as Omeyocan. In Aztec mythology, Omeyocan ("the place of duality") is the highest level of heaven and the dwelling place of Ometeotl, a dual god comprised of both male and female from whom came all creation. However, I have not seen this meaning referenced in any of the Valley's doctrinal materials.

30. Sassi repeatedly emphasized the empirical reality of the Capellans and their status as "physical, concrete beings" inhabiting an alien planet of a "different constitution" than the Earth, although equally "physical [and] material" (1974, 20). Yet, the members of the Indian Space Current, like their counterparts in Umbanda and Spiritisim, are considered the spirits of former human beings who, after living and dying on Earth, have passed into a non-material, spiritual plane that is contiguous with the terrestrial plane. They are, in other words, ontologically very different from the Capellans for whom they serve as "roupagens." This ontological difference is never explicitly addressed in the Valley of the Dawn's theological corpus as far as I am aware.

31. This interpretation is not unique to the Valley but also is promulgated in Spiritism and other esoteric movements.

32. One consequence of this class stratification was that the satellite cities that sprung up in the capital's periphery increasingly were perceived as squatter camps or zones of marginality inhabited by a dangerous underclass (Holston 1989).
33. In 1967, Brasília had 90,000 inhabitants in the Plano Piloto with another 200,000 in the periphery (Rodrigues and Muel-Dreyfus 2005 [1987]).
34. The plight of the candangos is not only recorded in the memories of the migrants who experienced those events firsthand, but also embedded in the history of the word candango itself, as James Holston observed (1989, 209–216). Soon after the capital's inauguration, the government adopted the term *brasiliense* as the name for Brasília's legal residents. Candango subsequently reverted to its earlier associations with the laboring masses—more specifically the lower-class residents of satellite cities on the periphery of those who called themselves brasilienses (216). "For those who lost their jobs in the construction industries after the inauguration, as so many did," Holston wrote, "the word came to describe someone who was unemployed and excluded from the city he built" (216). Subsequently, the heroic resonances of the terms candango have reemerged again, prompted in part by the commemorations surrounding Brasília's fiftieth anniversary in 2010. See Pires 2013, 204.
35. Today, Brasília is one of the most unequal cities in the world. The United Nations ranked the city among the world's top ten most unequal cities with a Gini coefficient of 0.60 (UN-Habitat 2010, 193).
36. Over 50 percent of the population in 1950 was illiterate (Braga and Mazzeu 2017, 26, table 1).
37. By using the term "doctor," Master Manoel was referring to a fundamental, deeply rooted distinction in Brazilian society between those who perform manual labor and those who do not. "Doctors" are people who occupy a position of high social status and respect, usually based on a college education of any sort. In Holston's words, "the use of 'doctor' as a term of personal reference and address signals high respect. Among superior class equals, it signifies achieved status, usually based on university education of any sort. Among class unequals, it is used as a status marker of privileges ascribed to superior class positions." See Holston 1989, 232. During the period of Brasília's construction, Holston explained, manual laborers were expected to use the honorific "doctor" to address white-collar workers (who generally were engineers or bureaucrats but not medical doctors). In a frontier environment where traditional class markers were not always present, such formalities took on even greater significance.
38. In a pattern common among other religions established in the nineteenth and twentieth centuries, Sassi used science as a rhetorical tool and a way to legitimate claims about the nature of reality that are not empirically verifiable. Likewise, contemporary Valley members insist that their beliefs and practices are thoroughly rational and scientifically proven. As Benjamin Zeller observed, thanks to the authority given to science in the modern world, being "scientific" is often central to the self-understanding of adherents of new religious movements. However, "their understandings of science are fluid, changing, and seldom follow rigorous academic definitions of the term" (Zeller 2011, 667).

39. One of the earliest to read the Valley of the Dawn and Brasília as mimetically related was James Holston. In 1999, he proposed that both the secular city and its sacred counterpart are "homologous embodiments" of a paradigm of modernity, each offering a different understanding of the modern. What makes the Valley of the Dawn powerful for its members, he wrote, "is that it assumes as its mission a modernizing project similar in structure and origin, but not necessarily in function or performance, to the one that the state also attempts with Brasília" (Holston 1999, 624). Against Enlightenment-era notions of religion as something set apart from secular social forms, Holston argued that religious communities should be understood as one among other coeval entities, such as the state, the army, or the market, that together and simultaneously configure Brazilian modernity (1999). "They are all contemporaries," he noted, "born out of modernity. They work through commensurate situations, translating the modern conditions set loose on the land in terms of their own priorities. From this perspective, religion too may afford people an opportunity to feel modern—to express their views on modernity passionately, direct its forces, and engage its dilemmas" (614). Drawing on Holston's ideas, Patricia Pessar argued that earlier backland millenarian communities like Canudos, Contestado, Juazeiro, and Santa Brígida also can be seen as alternative forms of modernity (2004, 7).

Chapter 5

1. According to Luhrmann, the term "paracosm" was first used by Robert Silvey, an audience researcher at the BBC, to describe the private worlds that children create (Luhrmann 2018). The term itself was coined by a participant in one of Silvey's studies. Silvey later published an article about the topic with psychiatrist Stephen A. MacKeith (Silvey and MacKeith 1988).
2. A major source for this kind of language was Spiritist and esoteric literature, which were part of a broader matrix of interpenetrating, synthesizing, and overlapping discourses that adopted the language of science to describe immaterial aspects of the human organism. The field of electromagnetism seems to have been especially influential in shaping these discourses.
3. There are lively debates about how to define esotericism and the ideas, practices, and movements that can be grouped under this term have a very long and controversial history in the West. Because of this, Wouter Hanegraaff characterizes esotericism as "rejected knowledge." By this he means that esotericism centers on worldviews and ways of knowing rejected by both mainstream religions and the scientific establishment (1996; 2012). Nevertheless, esotericism has had a very important role in Western culture, influencing everything from Spiritualism to the New Age movement.
4. Although Valley members consider the doutrinador to be Aunt Neiva's supreme achievement and a form of mediumship that had not existed previously, the figure of the doutrinador echoes common Spiritist practices. The study of Kardec's work and that of other Spiritist writers is integral to most Spiritist groups, and Spiritist

mediums are expected to be familiar with doctrine. In fact, Spiritist sessions often begin with a lecture on doctrine. The practice of disobsessive healing also is central to Spiritism, as discussed in Chapter 3, and indoctrinating recalcitrant spirits is one of the major tools Spiritist use for this purpose. Nevertheless, Valley members maintain that Spiritist mediums only remove obsessing spirits from their victims, while doutrinadores, because of their initiatory training, are able to remove obsessing spirits *and* elevate them to a higher plane (Pierini 2020, 144).
5. According to Valley lore, Aunt Neiva's spirit mentors asked her to use the term apará in homage to Nossa Senhora Aparecida, Our Lady of the Apparition, who was referred to as Nossa Senhora Apará by slaves unable to pronounce her full name. Aunt Neiva said that this entity appeared to slaves during the Middle Passage, "alleviating their suffering and their pains with the force of her love" (Siqueira et al. 2010, 154).
6. The letter is available at: http://valedoamanhecer.org/doutrinador/, accessed July 25, 2018.
7. Although several thousand patients may pass through the Valley's healing rituals on a weekly basis, only a small percentage are invited to develop their mediumship. Sassi estimated it to be 1 out of every 200 patients (Silva 2004, 9). In the course of her fieldwork, Emily Pierini went through mediumistic development at the Mother Temple in 2009 and reported that there were approximately ten to fifteen new arrivals each week, a figure that roughly corresponds to the percentage given by Sassi (Pierini 2020, 154). I myself have attended the Thrones dozens of times over the years and was never invited to develop my mediumship.
8. Initially these classes were taught by Mário Sassi and Aunt Neiva but as the community grew larger, they created a system for credentialing instructors. For reasons I explain in Chapter 6, instructors are always high-ranking male doutrinadors.
9. See Pierini 2020 for a detailed explanation of the development process and its various stages.
10. See Pierini 2020, 181 for a more complete discussion of this process.
11. Although the Brazilian constitution guarantees all citizens a public education, higher education continues to be the prerogative of the few. According to researchers there are two major reasons for this. The first is that there simply are not enough openings to meet the demand. The second is that the entire system of public higher education functions in a way that benefits the wealthy. Students attending public universities pay no tuition, but the competitiveness of the nationwide entrance exam (*vestibular*) ensures that the majority of them come from families able to afford higher-quality, private high schools. As a result, public universities in Brazil serve a population that is wealthier and whiter than the national average (Ristoff 2014).
12. Some of these doctor spirits are well known in Brazil, like Dr. Fritz and Dr. André Luiz, and even have been recognized by international Spiritist organizations. Chico Xavier, one of the most celebrated mediums of the twentieth century, penned several books whose authorship he attributed to Dr. André Luiz. Xavier did not perform psychic surgeries, although other mediums do. On the phenomena of spiritual surgeries in Brazil, see Greenfield 1991; 2008. Perhaps the most notorious Brazilian Spiritist medium today is John of God (João Teixeira de Faria), who performed hundreds of

minor surgeries using such instruments as kitchen knives, scissors, and scalpels while allegedly possessed by a doctor spirit. After multiple women came forward accusing him of sexual assault, he turned himself into the Brazilian police in 2018 and is now in prison. On John of God, see Rocha 2009; 2017.
13. Pierini describes the process of mediumistic development as a form of "embodied, intuitive, conceptual, performative, and intersubjective learning" (2020).
14. According to the Doctrine, pretos velhos are actually highly evolved spirits of light who manifest in the more familiar form of humble black slaves in order to put patients at ease. Beloved in Umbanda circles for their gentle counsel, succor, and folksy wisdom, the preto velho's roots in romanticized caricatures of colonial white supremacy has not diminished their emotional power for many people, black and white alike. But pretos velhos also speak to and embody unsettled questions about race and power, as Lindsay Hale observed and can occasionally model defiance and resistance as well as humility (1997).
15. For a more complete discussion of the spiritual development process and the various levels through which it proceeds, see Pierini 2020, 152–159.
16. With the exception of two ritual works, the Trono Milenar and the Abatá das Missionárias.
17. This fully realized environment is re-created to a greater or lesser degree of fidelity in affiliated temples, some of which have many of the large, outdoor ritual structures found at the Mother Temple.

Chapter 6

1. Extract from a letter written by Aunt Neiva dated April 9, 1981. Reproduced in Silva n.d., "Mulher."
2. A kind of supernatural substance produced by the body.
3. This is a pattern that I myself also noted.
4. The exception is that women can command the Abatá ritual as part of their missionary phalanx.
5. Aunt Neiva's letters circulate widely in different official and unofficial publications, collections, and blogs. This letter is reproduced in *Vale do Amanhecer* blog, http://valedoamanhecerbrasil.blogspot.com/2009/09/carta-tia-neiva-variadas-cartas.html. Last accessed November 12, 2021.
6. José Carlos de Nascimento Silva quoted in Siqueira, Reis, et al. 2010, 261.
7. There are several digitized versions of this book available online, and page numbers differ. However, Emily Pierini reported that in temples outside of the Valley's headquarters, the "great majority of incorporation mediums were men" (2013, 49).
8. In March of 2014, the president of the Valley's Mother Temple determined after consulting Aunt Neiva's writings that Sun Nymphs and Moon Nymphs could work together in certain spiritual works as long as they had reached the highest ranks available to women. However, many Valley members continue to feel that it is not appropriate.

9. Since the Valley collapses sex and gender, the community considers disembodied spirits to be either male or female.
10. After Aunt Neiva's death, a twenty-second phalanx was established for the wives of the presidents of external temples, who play an important role coordinating the affairs of the temple.
11. Letter of Aunt Neiva, May 17, 1978. Reproduced in Souza 2000, "Obrigações de um Adjunto." It is worth noting that the term *cavalheiro* (gentleman) is closely related to *cavaleiro* (knight).
12. See, for example, Master Kazagrande's blog post "Sexo e Doutrina" (Kazagrande 2012).
13. New religious movements often propose arrangements of gender, sexuality, and family structures that diverge from the mainstream, such as plural marriages, freedom of sexual expression, acceptance of LBGTQ+ people, non-traditional family structures, and so forth. For this reason, they often face public resistance of various sorts that can flare into violence. It is possible that the Valley of the Dawn's heteronormativity helped the community avoid this.
14. In their article exploring the Doctrine's appeal among Brazilian immigrants to the United States, Manuel Vásquez and José Claudio Souza Alves argued that this gendered division of spiritual labor "cosmicized" the relationship between Aunt Neiva and Mário Sassi by transposing it to a transcendent spiritual realm (Vásquez and Alves 2013, 320).

Chapter 7

1. Author's interview with Peter Owen Jones, July 8, 2020.
2. OSOEC asks visitors not to photograph or video the Thrones in order to protect the privacy of the mediums working there who incorporate obsessor and sofredor spirits. Valley officials told me that Owen Jones's camera crew had ignored this request and filmed the Thrones from a distance using the camera's zoom function.
3. The phrase *pronto socorro espiritual* or spiritual emergency room also is used.
4. From what I have seen, this number is somewhat inflated but not entirely off base. Given that healing rituals also are performed at the movement's network of affiliated temples, the total number of people treated by Valley mediums doubtless is much higher. However, there is no systematic effort to keep track of the total number of patients visiting each temple. Emily Pierini estimated that approximately four thousand mediums and patients participate in the daily healing rituals at the Mother Temple each week (2013, 14).
5. The central role that healing plays within diverse religious traditions in Brazil leads anthropologist Sidney Greenfield to assert that treating human affliction is the main product on offer within the "Brazilian religious marketplace" (2006, 100–101). In his analysis, Brazilians move from one religion to another in the quest for healing, affiliating with a particular community only if their needs are met. Within this transactional dynamic, affiliation serves as a kind of "payment" in exchange for a service. Thus, a single individual may participate in diverse and competing religions over his

or her lifetime. While the quest for healing explains some patterns of religious affiliation in Brazil, Pierini argues that it does not hold for the Valley of the Dawn. Patients who are invited to develop their mediumship seldom do so out of a sense of gratitude for the help they have received, she writes. Rather, developing one's mediumship typically is motivated by a far more complex calculus involving the trajectory of a person's life and "the question of healing being perceived as 'evidence or 'confirmation' of the spirit world's intervention in a person's life and, thus, of having been given the opportunity to become the means, oneself, through which this intervention is made possible for others" (2020, 212).
6. Only a small number of patients are invited to develop their mediumship at the Valley. Sassi reported a figure of one in every 200 patients (2004, 9).
7. Richard Shweder offered a similar definition of suffering as "disvalued and unwanted states of body, mind, and spirit" (Shweder 1997, 121).
8. Similarly, Emily Pierini characterized the Valley's ultimate mission as aiming "to transform suffering via hope and faith and develop in the patient an awareness of their own forces" (Pierini 2020, 128).
9. Or, as James Holston said more poetically, "these abominations imprison the spirits of their victims in walls of hatred and link them to the souls of their oppressors through a web of mutual affliction" (1999, 621).
10. Salve Deus is a ubiquitous salutation used throughout the Valley as a greeting and a farewell, or to indicate agreement or a shift in conversational topic. It is liberally interspersed in everyday life as well as in more formal discourse and is a distinctive element within the Valley's vernacular. The first thing one sees from the roadway that connects the Valley to the outside world is "Salve Deus" written in large concrete letters on a hill that rises over the temple complex.
11. The idea of the sevenfold nature of human beings and the universe is found in Theosophy and other schools of esoteric thought.
12. There are a total of seven healing rituals performed in the Temple and an additional two outside of the Temple that patients may attend. Readers interested in the details of each may consult Pierini (2020).
13. The complete title in Portuguese is: *Nosso Lar: A Vida no Mundo Espiritual* (Xavier 1944). It is the first in a series of books with the same name, which translates to *Our Home: Life in the Spiritual World*. A popular English translation was published under the title *The Astral City: The Story of a Doctor's Odyssey in the Spirit World*.
14. A movie version of *Nosso Lar* written and directed by the Brazilian filmmaker Wagner de Assis was the top-selling film when it debuted in Brazil in 2010 ("'Nosso Lar' lidera bilheterias no Brasil" 2010).
15. David Hess argued compellingly that the highly organized spiritual world described in *Our Home* can be read as both a reflection and critique of the Estado Novo, Getúlio Vargas's paternalistic dictatorship then dominating Brazil (Hess 1991, 34–35). The Estado Novo was established in 1937 and ended in 1945 when the Brazilian military encircled the presidential palace and forced Vargas to renounce the presidency. Subsequently, democratic elections were re-established, and Vargas was elected for another term in 1951.

16. Holston reported that the 1981 vision occurred during his first period of fieldwork at the Valley. Over the course of the next year, he wrote, "the prophetess and her associates transposed that vision into ritual" (1999, 621).
17. Because Zack could not speak Portuguese, Valley officials assigned him a special instructor who spoke English. He was part of a small number of English-speaking foreigners who were attending the Valley's development classes in 2015. With the exception of Zack, the others originally had travelled to Brazil to see John of God, the famous Brazilian spirit healer. They were staying in Abidiânia, the small town in the state of Goiás where John of God's healing center is located. They were introduced to the Valley by an Australian woman who owned a guest hostel in Abidiânia and had been initiated at the Valley, which is about three hours away by car. With the exception of Zack, who was staying at the Valley, the group would come to the Mother Temple on Sundays in order to participate in the development classes and then return to Abidiânia. In 2018, John of God turned himself into police following a cascade of sex abuse allegations against him and was sentenced to prison in 2019, where he remains. As of this writing, his healing center, Casa de Dom Inacio, continues to operate.
18. According to Zack, the cleansing sessions had not been authorized by OSOEC, so he was hesitant to go into too much detail about them.
19. Zack's description suggests Mihaly Csikszentmihalyi's concept of flow as a state in which the individual becomes so involved in a task that their actions and awareness merge in a state of effortless absorption (Csikszentmihalyi 1990).
20. This also is the key insight of narrative medicine or narrative-based medicine (NBM), a discipline that emerged to address some of the failures of biomedicine, especially as it was subsumed within a commodified system of healthcare (Charon 2001; 2008).

Chapter 8

1. This material culture is reproduced on a smaller scale in affiliated temples around the world.
2. As Kristina Wirtz explained, Bakhtin's chronotope is "productive of subjectivity itself in grounding our experience of temporal and spatial relationships, which themselves structure our experience of being and sociality" (Wirtz 2016, 344).
3. Not all kabbalistic rituals are directed at recuperating the Jaguars' past karma. However, for the sake of simplicity I will limit my discussion here to those that do.
4. This version of the story was recounted to me in 2012 by one of Aunt Neiva's early converts who today occupies a position of authority in the movement's hierarchy and is held in great esteem among community members. Interview with Mestre Caldeira, Adjunto Yumatã, Vale do Amanhecer, May 2012. It closely follows the narrative that Aunt Neiva herself gave of the origins of the "Turigano ritual in a letter of October 21, 1984 ("Origens do Turigano"). See also Valley member Gilmar Santos' blog entry "Jaguar: O Espírito Espartano" (Santos 2021).

5. More precisely, *canto* can be translated as "song" in English. However, given their usage within the context of the Valley of the Dawn, I have opted to translate it as "chant" since cantos are recited in rituals, not sung.
6. According to Aunt Neiva, upon her liberation the exiled queen left Greece and went to a palace in the Nile delta, where she dedicated her life to healing others. This story is the narrative framework for another Valley ritual called Cruz do Caminho or Cross of the Way.
7. Other sources describe Pythia's mission more explicitly as "preparing that world for the arrival of Jesus." The *Dicionário do Vale* (Dictionary of the Valley), for example, notes that "through the charms of Pythia, those kings accepted the idea of the One God, the God of Love, preparing the people for Christianity" (Souza 2000, "Pytia").
8. Some Valley members associate Apollo with Father White Arrow.
9. At another level, we can read the Turigano ritual as coded message about gender in which the force of masculinity represented by King Leonidas (and his Valley stand-in Trino Arakém)—the greatest warrior of them all—submits to the feminine force represented by Pythia (aka Aunt Neiva). Pythia/Aunt Neiva's message is transformative: she is the one who "spiritualizes" the ancient Spartans, reorienting them away from material power and godlessness to the pursuit of spiritual evolution under the "transcendent law" of Apollo (aka Jesus/doutrinador). So great is her spiritual power (indexed by the drums beating by themselves) that even the mightiest warrior of Western history, King Leonidas, must recognize it. Love triumphs over warmongering.
10. The indivisibility of time and space is central to the concept of chronotope, however, for the purposes of my analysis I have found it expedient to discuss them separately.
11. At that time, the inner walls were lined with framed images of various supernatural entities recognized as spiritual mentors, including Knights, Missionary Guides, Ministers, Caboclos, and Pretos Velhos. After the building was remodeled in 2017, many of these images were removed, and the benches were replaced by seats lining the interior perimeter.
12. This is the first portion of the chant, which includes an additional stanza.
13. The Minister Japuacy was originally represented on Earth by his Adjunct, Master Valdemar Ferreira. After Ferreira's death, another high-ranking master became the representative of Master Ferreira and inherited the chant. At the time of this interview (2015), it had been passed on to Master João Nunez.
14. Simiromba is an "initiatic" title for Father White Arrow. The Doctrine teaches that spiritual forces are organized into a pyramidal system (força decrescente or descending forcefield) headed by a spirit of the highest level of illumination. Each of these pyramids is referred to as an Oracle. The Oracle that governs the Doctrine of the Dawn is the Oracle of Simiromba, which is headed by Father White Arrow. For this reason, he often is referred to as Simiromba or the Simiromba of God (Kazagrande 2011, 292).
15. It was a struggle to translate the dress of the luminous beings that Aunt Neiva saw in her visions into the material world. "We had a lot of difficulty with fabric, because the missionary guides she saw in her visions wore brilliant garments filled with light,"

Carmem Lúcia told me in a 2017 interview: "So the first dresses we made we couldn't really achieve that look. We tried using velvet, but it was very expensive and hot. So, we had this difficulty and then she saw the symbols of the Moon Nymph, the shiny Sun Nymph. But those materials didn't exist here at the time, and we realized that it couldn't be exactly the same. So, we bought glue and embellishments and glued them on the velvet. As you can imagine, that ruined the velvet forever. But that's how we did it, we obeyed, and improvements came. I would go out, see a fabric, maybe Mother Yara gave me an intuition, I would buy it and bring it to her [Neiva]. And she would say, 'no, it's not like that,' or 'it's this.' And so, it began to form. The organza was difficult, because that was a material that was only used for curtains. And it was only available in pale colors and our colors are not at all pale. It was very difficult. I went to Brasília, Goiânia, all the way to Rio searching for the right materials. I had to have many colors specially made by a factory and they would only do it if it was an order for 2,000, 3,000 meters. Not today, I don't have to do that anymore. There are places that have it, they distribute it to other stores and everything."

16. The Grega phalanx is one of three open to women between the ages of twelve and eighteen (the other two are the Mayas and Nityamas).
17. Emily Pierini used the term "transhistorical self" to get at the same idea (2020, 81).
18. That this style characterized not only the government buildings of the Greek polis, but also its pagan temples suggests, at least to those alert to such things, that the authority of the American state is grounded ultimately in some power greater than human.
19. As a builder himself, former United States president Donald Trump knew the importance of the signifying power of architecture. In an executive order issued Monday December 21, 2020, the Trump administration announced a project to promote neoclassical architecture in federal buildings. George Washington and Thomas Jefferson "sought to use classical architecture to visually connect our contemporary Republic with the antecedents of democracy in classical antiquity," the order stated, "reminding citizens not only of their rights but also their responsibilities in maintaining and perpetuating its institutions." Trump's order was controversial and many on the left criticized his desire to "make federal buildings beautiful again" (and there are principled reasons for doing so). Nevertheless, Trump clearly was aware of the ability of the neoclassical style to conjure abstract ideals associated with a national mythology.

Chapter 9

1. According to the most recent census for which religion data is available (IBGE 2010), Spiritism is the third largest religion in Brazil with approximately 3.8 million followers (https://cidades.ibge.gov.br/brasil/pesquisa/23/22107). However, because the census only counts people who identify as Spiritist, not people who engage with Spiritism in some way, it underestimates Spiritism's wider influence in Brazil. It does show that compared to other religions, Spiritists tend to have greater education levels (60% have at least eleven years of education) and greater incomes.

2. For an English-language introduction to the cultural significance of Chico Xavier in Brazil, see Premack 2015.
3. Also important to the movement's expansion was the work of Neiva's eldest son Gilberto Zelaya in developing and overseeing the establishment of external temples outside of the Mother Temple.
4. In their analysis of the Valley of the Dawn, sociologists Arakcy Martins Rodrigues and Francine Muel-Dreyfus argued that the founders and members of the Valley share the social and psychological experience of rupture, dislocation, and uprooting, and they inhabit an ambiguous social position of participating in worlds in which they feel they do not entirely belong. Sassi, they noted, came from a working-class background and tried to be middle class but was unhappy and felt like an imposter to some degree. Similarly, many contemporary Valley members work as functionaries and in the service industry in Brasília, where they are exposed to upper-class life or corridors of power but do not fully belong or are invisible there. See Rodrigues and Muel-Dreyfus 2005 (1987).
5. Historian Micah Oelze made this observation to me in a personal communication, August 2022. This paragraph is inspired by his remarks and draws on some of his language.
6. For more on Vilela, his art, and his role at the Valley of the Dawn, see Hayes 2019a and Hayes 2019b.
7. Writer Julian Dibbels offered an especially acute description of the Valley's built environment as "monumental modernism" taken "on a long detour through the aesthetic of the miniature golf course" (1992).
8. This is not uncommon. I heard similar stories many times over the years of my research. Emily Pierini described how Italians undergoing mediumistic development at a temple in Italy reported having seen or even incorporated entities cultivated at the Valley like pretos velhos without knowing who or what these spirits represented. See Pierini 2020, 168–169.

Bibliography

Scholarly Literature

Albanese, Catherine. 2007. *A Republic of Mind and Spirit: A Cultural History of American Metaphysical Religion.* New Haven, CT: Yale University Press.

Anderson, Ben. 2009. "Affective Atmospheres." *Emotion, Space and Society* 2: 77–81.

Anderson, Benedict. 2006 (1983). *Imagined Communities: Reflections on the Origin and Spread of Nationalism.* New York: Verso.

Aubree, Marion, and François Laplantine. 1990. *La Table, le Livre et les Esprits. Naissance, évolution et actualité du mouvement social spirite entre France et Brésil.* Paris: J.C. Lattès.

Ashcraft, W. Michael. 2019. *A Historical Introduction to the Study of New Religious Movements.* London: Routledge.

Aureliano, Waleska de Araújo, and Vânia Zikán Cardoso. 2015. "Spiritism in Brazil: From Religious to Therapeutic Practice." In *Handbook of Spiritualism and Channeling*, edited by Cathy Gutierrez, 275–293. Leiden: Brill.

Bakhtin, Mikhail M. 1981. "Forms of Time and of the Chronotope in the Novel: Notes toward a Historical Poetics." In *The Dialogic Imagination: Four Essays*, edited by Michael Holquist, translated by Caryl Emerson and Michael Holquist, 84–258. Austin: University of Texas Press.

Barnes, Jennifer. 2015. "Fanfiction as Imaginary Pplay: What Fan-Written Stories Can Tell Us about the Cognitive Science of Fiction." *Poetics* 48: 69–82. https://doi.org/10.1016/j.poetic.2014.12.004.

Berger, Peter L. 1967. *The Sacred Canopy: Elements of a Sociological Theory of Religion.* Garden City, NY: Doubleday and Company, Inc.

Berger, Peter L., and Thomas Luckman. 1967 (1966). *The Social Construction of Reality: A Treatise in the Sociology of Knowledge.* New York: Penguin Press.

Bloch, Maurice. 2008. "Why Religion Is Nothing Special but Is Central." *Philosophical Transactions of the Royal Society B* 363 (1499): 2055–2061, February 21. https://doi.org/10.1098/rstb.2008.0007.

Bourdieu, Pierre. 1979. *La distinction: critique sociale du jugement.* Paris: Les Editions de Minuit.

Braga, Ana Carolina Linhares, and Francisco José Carvalho Mazzeu. 2017. "O analfabetismo no Brasil: lições da história." *Revista on line de Política e Gestão Educacional* 21 (1): 24–46. https://periodicos.fclar.unesp.br/rpge/article/view/9986.

Brown, Diana, and Mario Bick. 1987. "Religion, Class, and Context: Continuities and Discontinuities in Brazilian Umbanda." *American Ethnologist* 14 (1): 73–93.

Caires, Luiza. 2013. "Discos voadores: imprensa e debate público no Brasil dos anos 1940–50." *Especial* (USP on-line magazine), June 20. http://www5.usp.br/28778/discos-voadores-imprensa-e-debate-publico-no-brasil-dos-anos-1940-50/.

Camargo, Cândido Procópio Ferreira de. 1961. *Kardecismo e umbanda: uma interpretação sociológica*. São Paulo: Livraria Pioneira Editora.
Carpenter, Robert. 1999. "Esoteric Literature as Microcosmic Mirror of Brazil's Religious Marketplace." In *Latin American Religions in Motion*, edited by Chrisitan Smith and Joshua Prokopy, 235–260. New York: Routledge.
Carvalho, José Jorge de. 1992. "Características do fenômeno religioso na sociedade contemporânea." In *O impacto da modernidade sobre a religião*, edited by Maria Clara Lucchetti Bingemer, 133–195. São Paulo: Loyola.
Carvalho, José Jorge de. 1994. "O encontro de velhas e novas religiões." In *Misticismo e novas religiões*, edited by Alberto Moreira and Renée Zicman, 67–98. Petrópolis: Vozes.
Carvalho, José Jorge de. 1999. "Um Espaço Público Encantado: Pluralidade Religiosa e Modernidade no Brasil." *Série Antropologia* 249: 1–22.
Carvalho, José Jorge de. 2000. "An Enchanted Public Space: Religious Plurality and Modernity in Brazil." In *Through the Kaleidoscope: The Experience of Modernity in Latin America*, edited by Vivian Schelling, 275–296. London: Verso.
Castilho, Denis. 2012. "A Colônia Agrícola Nacional de Goiás (CANG) e a Formação de Ceres—GO—Brasil." *Élisée - Revista De Geografia Da UEG* 1 (1): 117–139.
Castoriadis, Cornelius. 1987 (1975). *The Imaginary Institution of Society*, translated by Kathleen Blarney. Cambridge, MA: M.I.T. Press.
Cavalcante, Carmen Luisa Chaves. 2000. *Xamanismo no Vale do Amanhecer: O Caso da Tia Neiva*. São Paulo: Annablume.
Cavalcante, Carmen Luisa Chaves. 2011. *Dialogias no Vale do Amanhecer: Os Signos de um Imaginário Religioso*. Fortaleza, Ceará: Expressão Gráfica Editora.
César, Father José Vicente. 1977a. "O Vale do Amanhecer: Parte I." *Atualização: Revista de Divulgação Teológica Para o Cristão de Hoje* 95/96: 367–391. Belo Horizonte: Editora o Lutador.
César, Father José Vicente. 1977b. "O Vale do Amanhecer: Parte II." *Atualização: Revista de Divulgação Teológica Para o Cristão de Hoje* 95/96: 451–507. Belo Horizonte: Editora o Lutador.
César, Father José Vicente. 1978. "O Vale do Amanhecer: Parte III." *Atualização: Revista de Divulgação Teológica Para o Cristão de Hoje* 97/98: 58–73. Belo Horizonte: Editora o Lutador.
Charon, Rita. 2001. "Narrative Medicine: A Model for Empathy, Reflection, Profession, and Trust." *JAMA: The Journal of the American Medical Association* 286 (15): 1897–1902. https://doi.org/10.1001/jama.286.15.1897.
Charon, Rita. 2008. *Narrative Medicine: Honoring the Stories of Illness*. New York: Oxford University Press.
Chesnut, Andrew. 2003. *Competitive Spirits: Latin America's New Religious Economy*. New York: Oxford University Press.
Clark, Mary Ann. 2014. "Spirit is Universal: Development of Black Spiritualist Churches." In *Esotericism in African American Religious Experience: "There Is a Mystery"...*, edited by Stephen Finley, Margarita Guillory, and Hugh Page Jr., 86–101. Leiden: Brill.
Comissão Anísio Teixeira de Memória e Verdade. 2015. "Relatório da Comissão Anísio Teixeira de Memória e Verdade." Acervo Memória e Direitos Humanos da Universidade Federal de Santa Catarina (UFSC). https://www.memoriaedireitoshumanos.ufsc.br/items/show/653.
Cox, Robert S. 2003. *Body and Soul: A Sympathetic History of American Spiritualism*. Charlottesville: University of Virginia Press.

Csikszentmihalyi, Mihaly. 1990. *Flow: The Psychology of Optimal Experience*. New York: Harper and Row.
Damazio, Sylvia. 1994. *Da elite ao povo: Advento e expansão do espiritismo no Brasil*. Rio de Janeiro: Bertrand Brasil.
Datar, Rajan. 2012. "The Valley of the Dawn—Brazil's Refuge for Lost Souls." *BBC Fast Track*, November 1. http://news.bbc.co.uk/2/hi/programmes/fast_track/9762166.stm.
Dawson, Andrew. 2008. "New Era Millenarianism in Brazil." *Journal of Contemporary Religion* 23: 269–283.
Dawson, Andrew. 2016 (2007). *New Era—New Religions: Religious Transformation in Contemporary Brazil*. New York: Routledge.
Dibbell, Julian. 1992. "Tropical Millennium: The Cult (and Cults) of Brasília." Juliandibbell.com, http://www.juliandibbell.com/texts/brasilia.html.
Ellwood, Robert, and Catherine Wessinger. 1993. "The Feminism of 'Universal Brotherhood': Women in the Theosophical Movement." In *Women's Leadership in Marginal Religions: Explorations Outside the Mainstream*, edited by Catherine Wessinger, 68–87. Urbana: University of Illinois Press.
Engler, Steven. 2012. "Umbanda and Africa." *Nova Religio* 15 (4): 13–35.
Engler, Steven. 2020. "Umbanda: Africana or Esoteric?" *Open Library of Humanities* 6 (1): 1–36. https://doi.org/10.16995/olh.469.
Epstein, David G. 1973. *Brasília, Plan and Reality: A Study of Planned and Spontaneous Urban Development*. Berkeley: University of California Press.
Faivre, Antoine. 1994. *Access to Western Esotericism*. Albany: State University of New York Press.
Fonseca, Isabel. 2007. "A Clarividente Neiva." In *Jornalistas literários: narrativas da vida real por novos autores brasileiros*, edited by Sergio Vilas Boas, 223–268. São Paulo: Summus.
Freitas, Wagner Abadio de, and Marcelo de Mello. 2014. "A colônia agrícola nacional de Goiás e a redefinição nos usos do território." *Sociedade e Natureza* 26 (3): 471–482.
Galinkin, Ana Lúcia. 2008. *A Cura no Vale do Amanhecer*. Brasília: TechnoPolitik.
Gaonkar, Dilip Parameshwar. 2002. "Toward New Imaginaries: An Introduction." *Public Culture* 14 (1): 1–19.
Giumbelli, Emerson. 1997. *O cuidado dos mortos. Uma história da condenação e legitimação do espiritismo*. Rio de Janeiro: Arquivo Nacional.
Gomes, Angela de Castro. 2013. *Olhando para dentro: 1930–1964*. Coleção Histórias do Brasil Nação 1808–2010. Vol. 4. Rio de Janeiro: Editora Objetiva.
Goodrick-Clarke, Nicholas. 2013. "Western Esoteric Traditions and Theosophy." In *Handbook of the Theosophical Current*, edited by Olav Hammer and Mikael Rothstein, 261–307. Leiden: Brill.
Greenfield, Sidney M. 1991. "Hypnosis and Trance Induction in the Surgeries of Brazilian Spirit Healer-mediums." *Anthropology of Consciousness* 2 (3–4): 20–25.
Greenfield, Sidney M. 2008. *Spirits With Scalpels: The Cultural Biology of Religious Healing in Brazil*. Walnut Creek, CA: Left Coast Press.
Grigori, Pedro. 2017. "Criação do reservatório Lago São Bartolomeu estava prevista nos anos 1970." *Correiro Braziliense*, November 20. https://www.correiobraziliense.com.br/app/noticia/cidades/2017/11/20/interna_cidadesdf,642033/lago-sao-bartolomeu-em-brasilia.shtml.
Hahn, Robert A. 1995. *Sickness and Healing: An Anthropological Perspective*. New Haven, CT: Yale University Press.

Hale, Lindsay. 1997. "Preto Velho: Resistance, Redemption, and Engendered Representations of Slavery in a Brazilian Possession Trance Religion." *American Ethnologist* 24 (2): 392–414.

Hale, Lindsay. 2009. *Hearing the Mermaid's Song: The Umbanda Religion in Rio de Janeiro*. Albuquerque: University Of New Mexico Press.

Hammer, Olav, and Mikael Rothstein, eds. 2013. *Handbook of the Theosophical Current*. Leiden: Brill.

Hanegraaff, Wouter. 1996. *New Age Religion and Western Culture: Esotericism in the Mirror of Secular Thought*. Leiden: Brill.

Hanegraaff, Wouter. 1999. "Some Remarks on the Study of Western Esotericism." *Theosophical History* 7 (6): 223–232.

Hanegraaff, Wouter. 2012. *Esotericism and the Academy: Rejected Knowledge in Western Culture*. Cambridge: Cambridge University Press.

Hartenthal, Mariana von. 2019. "Peter Scheier and Marcel Gautherot: Brasília Lyric and Epic." *Sophia Peer Review Journal* 4 (1): 119–133. https://doi.org/10.24840/2183-8976_2019-0004_0001_15.

Hayes, Kelly E. 2011. *Holy Harlots: Femininity, Sexuality, and Black Magic in Brazil*. Berkeley: University of California Press.

Hayes, Kelly E. 2013. "Intergalactic Space-Time Travelers: Envisioning Globalization in Brazil's Valley of the Dawn." *Nova Religio* 16 (4): 63–92.

Hayes, Kelly E. 2018. "Where Men Are Knights and Women are Princesses: Gender Ideology in Brazil's Valley of the Dawn." In *Irreverence and the Sacred: Critical Studies in the History of Religions*, edited by Hugh B. Urban and Greg Johnson, 197–226. Oxford: Oxford University Press.

Hayes, Kelly E. 2019a. "I Am a Psychic Antenna: The Art of Joaquim Vilela." *Black Mirror* 2: 144–177.

Hayes, Kelly E. 2019b. "Joaquim Silva Vilela" profile. *Religious and Spiritual Movements and the Visual Arts, World Religions and Spirituality Project*. https://wrldrels.org/2019/11/04/joaquim-silva-vilela/.

Hayes, Kelly E. 2020a. "Western Esotericism in Brazil: The Influence of Esoteric Thought on the Valley of the Dawn." *Nova Religio* 23 (3): 60–85.

Hayes, Kelly E. 2020b. "Brazilian Mystics Say They're Sent by Aliens to Jump Start Human Evolution but Their Vision for a More Just Society Is Not Totally Crazy." *The Conversation*, April 29. https://theconversation.com/brazilian-mystics-say-theyre-sent-by-aliens-to-jump-start-human-evolution-but-their-vision-for-a-more-just-society-is-not-totally-crazy-132730.

Hayes, Kelly E. 2021. "Spirits of the Space Age: The Valley of the Dawn as a UFO Religion," In *Handbook of UFO Religions*, edited by Benjamin Zeller, 425–451. Leiden: Brill.

Hayes, Kelly E. 2022. "The High Magic of Jesus Christ: Materializing Secrets in Brazil's Valley of the Dawn." In *The Routledge Handbook of Religion and Secrecy*, edited by Paul C. Johnson and Hugh Urban, chapter 17. London: Routledge.

Hess, David J. 1987. "The Many Rooms of Brazilian Spiritism." *Luso-Brazilian Review* 24 (2): 15–34.

Hess, David J. 1991a. *Spirits and Scientists: Ideology, Spiritism, and Brazilian Culture*. University Park: Penn State University Press.

Hess, David J. 1991b. "On Earth as It Is in Heaven: Reading Spiritist Otherworldly Ethnographies." In *Toward Socio-Criticism: Selected Proceedings of the Conference*

"Luso-Brazilian Literatures, A Socio-Critical Approach," edited by Roberto Reis, 55–65. Tempe: Arizona State University at Tempe, Center for Latin American Studies.
Hess, David J. 1994. *Samba in the Night: Spiritism in Brazil*. New York: Columbia University Press.
Hojo, Adam, and Adam Galinsky. 2012. "Enclothed Cognition." *Journal of Experimental Social Psychology* 48 (4): 918–925.
Holston, James. 1989. *The Modernist City: An Anthropological Critique of Brasília*. Chicago: University of Chicago Press.
Holston, James. 1999. "Alternative Modernities: Statecraft and Religious Imagination in the Valley of the Dawn." *American Ethnologist* 26 (3): 605–631.
Hofstadter, Douglas. 2007. *I Am a Strange Loop*. New Work: Basic Books.
Houtman, Dick, and Birgit Meyer, eds. 2012. *Things: Religion and the Question of Materiality*. New York: Fordham University Press.
Hui, Bryant, Jacky Ng, Erica Berzaghi, Lauren Cunningham-Amos, and Aleksandr Kogan. 2020. "Rewards of Kindness? A Meta-Analysis of the Link Between Prosociality and Well-Being." *Psychological Bulletin* 146 (12): 1084–1116. https://doi.org/10.1037/bul0000298.
Instituto Brasileiro de Geografia e Estatística (IBGE). 2010. *Censo Demográfico: População residente por religião*. IBGE. https://cidades.ibge.gov.br/brasil/pesquisa/23/22107.
Inagaki, Tristen K., Kate Bryne Haltom, Shosuke Suzuki, Ivana Jevtic, Erica Hornstein, Julienne E. Bower, and Naomi I. Eisenberger. 2016. "The Neurobiology of Giving Versus Receiving Support." *Psychosomatic Medicine* 78 (4): 443–453. https://doi.org/10.1097/PSY.0000000000000302.
Introvigne, Massimo. 2013. "The Vale do Amanhecer: Healing and Spiritualism in a Globalized Brazilian New Religious Movement." *Sociologia, Revista da Faculdade de Letras da Universidade do Porto* 26: 189–200.
Irwin, Harvey J. 2009. *Psychology of Paranormal Belief: A Researcher's Handbook*. Hertfordshire, UK: University of Hertfordshire.
Johnston, Sarah Iles. 2021. "How Faith Happens." *LA Review of Books*, March 14. https://lareviewofbooks.org/article/how-faith-happens/.
Kardec, Allan. 2003 (1868). *Genesis: The Miracles and the Predictions According to Spiritism*. New York: Spiritist Alliance for Books.
Kaufman, Scott Barry. 2021. "The Science of Spiritual Narcissism." *Scientific American Mind* 32 (2): 17. https://www.scientificamerican.com/article/the-science-of-spiritual-narcissism/.
Kish, Stephen J. 2008. "Pharmacologic Mechanisms of Crystal Meth." *Canadian Medical Association Journal* 178 (13): 1679–1682. https://doi.org/10.1503/cmaj.071675.
Kleinman, Arthur. 2020 (1988). *The Illness Narratives: Suffering, Healing, and the Human Condition*. New York: Basic Books.
Kripal, Jeffrey J. 2010. *Authors of the Impossible: The Paranormal and the Sacred*. Chicago: University of Chicago Press.
Lafer, Celso. 2002. *JK e o Programa de Metas (1956–1961): Processo de planejamento e sistema politico no Brasil*. Rio de Janeiro: FGV.
Lambek, Michael. 2002. *The Weight of the Past: Living with History in Mahajanga, Madagascar*. New York: Palgrave Macmillan.
Laycock, Joseph. 2014. "Approaching the Paranormal." *Nova Religio* 18 (1): 5–15.
Laycock, Jospeh. 2015. *Dangerous Games: What the Moral Panic over Role-Playing Games Says about Play, Religion, and Imagined Worlds*. Berkeley: University of California Press.

Leslie, Desmond, and George Adamski. 1943. *Flying Saucers Have Landed*. New York: British Book Centre.
Lévi-Strauss, Claude. 1955. "The Structural Study of Myth." *The Journal of American Folklore* 68 (270): 428–444.
Lévi-Strauss, Claude. 1966. *The Savage Mind*. Chicago: University of Chicago Press.
Lewgoy, Bernardo. 2008. "A transnacionalização do Espiritismo Kardecista Brasileiro: Uma discussão inicial." *Religião e Sociedade* 28 (1): 84–104.
Lewis, James. 2003. *Legitimating New Religions*. New Brunswick, NJ: Rutgers University Press.
Lima, Gersilene Oliveira de. 2019. "Os Sentidos da Experiência Religiosa nas Narrativas de Missionárias Nityamas, Gregas e Mayas: Um Mergulho no Universo do Vale do Amanhecer." PhD diss., Universidade Federal do Ceará.
Lincoln, Bruce. 1989. *Discourse and the Construction of Society: Comparative Studies of Myth, Ritual, and Classification*. New York: Oxford University Press.
Lincoln, Bruce. 2013. "Reflections on the Reflections of Messrs. Junginger, Arvidsson, Albinus, and Ullucci." *Method and Theory in the Study of Religion* 25: 209–219.
Lispector, Clarice. 1992. "Five Days in Brasília." In *The Foreign Legion: Stories and Chronicles*, translated by Giovanni Ponteiro, 136–140. New York: New Directions Publishing.
Lucas, Philip C. 2011. "New Age Millennialism." In *The Oxford Handbook of Millennialism*, edited by Catherine Wessinger, 567–586. New York: Oxford University Press.
Lucchetti, Alessandra Lamas Granero, Giancarlo Lucchetti, Frederico Camelo Leão, Mario Fernando Prieto Peres, and Homero Vallada. 2016. "Mental and Physical Health and Spiritual Healing: An Evaluation of Complementary Religious Therapies Provided by Spiritist Centers in the City of São Paulo, Brazil." *Culture, Medicine and Psychiatry* 40 (3): 404–21. httpd://doi.org/10.1007/s11013-015-9478-z.
Luhrmann, T. M. 2020a. *How God Becomes Real: Kindling the Presence of Invisible Others*. Princeton, NJ: Princeton University Press.
Luhrmann, T. M. 2020b. "T.M. Luhrmann on Small Acts of Real-Making." https://press.princeton.edu/ideas/tm-luhrmann-on-small-acts-of-real-making.
Luhrmann, T. M. 2018. "World's Apart." In *The Minds of Others: The Art of Persuasion in the Age of Trump*, by David Bromwich, Garth Greenwell, Hanif Abdurraqib, Kelly Clancy, Laila Lalami, Mychal Denzel Smith, and T. M. Luhrmann. *Harper's Magazine* 336: 27–36. https://harpers.org/archive/2018/02/the-minds-of-others/2/.
Luhrmann, T. M. 2012. "Imagining God." *Psychology Today*, December 16. https://www.psychologytoday.com/us/blog/when-god-talks-back/201212/imagining-god.
Luhrmann, T. M., Kara Weisman, et al. 2021. "Sensing the Presence of Gods and Spirits across Cultures and Faiths." *Proceedings of the National Academy of Sciences (PNAS)* 118 (5): 1–8. https://doi.org/10.1073/pnas.2016649118.
Maggie, Yvonne. 1992. *Medo do feitiço: Relações entre magia e poder no Brasil*. Rio de Janeiro: Arquivo Nacional.
Magnani, José Guilherme Cantor. 2016. "The New Age Movement and Urban Shamanism in Brazil." In *New Age in Latin American: Popular Variations and Ethnic Appropriations*, edited by Angela Renée de la Torre Castellanos, María Cristina del Refugio Gutiérrez, and Nahayeilli Juárez-Huet, 60–88. Leiden: Brill.
Marques, Erich Gomes. 2008. "Ritual e Gênero no Vale do Amanhecer." Unpublished paper from the conference *Fazendo Gênero 8—Corpo, Violência e Poder*, 1–7.

Florianapolis, Brazil, August 25–28. http://www.wwc2017.eventos.dype.com.br/fg8/sts/ST30/Erich_Gomes_Marques_30.pdf.

Marques, Erich Gomes. 2009. "Os Poderes do Estado no Vale do Amanhecer: Percursos Religiosos, Práticas Espirituais e Cura." MA thesis, University of Brasília.

Martins, Maria Cristina de Castro. 2004. "O Amanhecer de Uma Nova Era: Um Estudo da Simbiose Espaço Sagrado/Rituais do Vale do Amanhecer." In *Antes do Fim do Mundo: Milenarismos e Messianismos no Brasil e na Argentina*, edited by Leonarda Musumeci, 119–143. Rio de Janeiro: Editora UFRJ.

McLaren, Kevin. 2016. "Pharaonic Occultism: The Relationship of Esotericism and Egyptology, 1875–1930." MA thesis, California Polytechnic State University.

Mello, Glaúcia Buratto Rodrigues de. 2004. "Os peregrinos ecléticos cristãos." *Cadernos de Campo* 12 (12): 25–40.

Melton, J. Gordon. 1995. "The Contactees: A Survey." In *The Gods Have Landed: New Religions from Other Worlds*, edited by James R. Lewis, 1–13. New York: State University of New York Press.

Melton, J. Gordan. 2004. "An Introduction to New Religions." In *The Oxford Handbook of New Religious Movements*, edited by James R. Lewis, 16–35. New York: Oxford University Press.

Melton, J. Gordan. 2020. "Theosophy." *Encyclopedia Brittanica*. https://www.britannica.com/topic/theosophy (accessed May 11, 2021).

Melton, J. Gordan, Jerome Clark, and Aidan A. Kelly, eds. 1991. *New Age Almanac*. Detroit, MI: Gale.

Meyer, Birgit. 2015. *Sensational Movies: Video, Vision, and Christianity in Ghana*. Berkeley: University of California Press.

Ming, Ye Charlotte. 2018. "Meet the Worshipers Who Believe They're Aliens in Human Form." *National Geographic*, September 5. https://www.nationalgeographic.com/culture/2018/09/religion-psychic-medium-extraterrestrial-sunrise-dawn-valley-brasilia-brazil.

Moore, Rebecca. 2018. "Cult, New Religious Movement, or Minority Religion?" *Erraticus*, August 29. https://erraticus.co/2018/08/29/cult-new-religious-movement-minority-religion/.

Moreira-Almeida, Alexander, and Joan Koss-Chioino. 2009. "Recognition and Treatment of Psychotic Symptoms: Spiritists Compared to Mental Health Professionals in Puerto Rico and Brazil." *Psychiatry* 72 (3): 268–83. https://doi.org/10.1521/psyc.2009.72.3.268.

Morgan, David, ed. 2010a. *Religion and Material Culture: The Matter of Belief*. New York: Routledge.

Morgan, David. 2010b. "The Material Culture of Lived Religions: Visuality and Embodiment." In *Mind and Matter*, edited by Johanna Vakkari, 14–31. Helsinki: Society of Art History. https://materialreligions.blogspot.com/2014/09/the-material-culture-of-lived-religions.html.

Moser, Benjamin. 2008. "Cemetery of Hope: Brasília at 50." *Harper's Magazine* 316 (1892): 67–74. January 18. https://harpers.org/archive/2008/01/cemetery-of-hope/.

Motta, Rodrigo Patto Sá. 2014. *As universidades e o regime militar: cultura política brasileira e modernização autoritária*. Rio de Janeiro: Zahar.

Nongbri, Brent. 2013. *Before Religion: A History of a Modern Concept*. New Haven, CT: Yale University Press.

Oliveira, Amurabi Pereira. 2010. "Imaginário e construção da realidade: um olhar sobre as visualidades do Vale do Amanhecer." *Cultura Visual* 13: 71–83.

Oliveira, Amurabi Pereira. 2013. "Os caboclos e pretos velhos do Vale do Amanhecer." *Ciências da Religião—História e Sociedade* 11 (2): 14–38.
Oliveira, Daniela de. 2007. "Visualidades em foco: Conexões entre a cultura visual e o Vale do Amanhecer." MA thesis, Federal University of Goiás.
Oliveira, José Aparecido de. 1991. *JK: O Estadista do Desenvolvimento*. Brasília: Memorial JK.
Oliveira, Luiz Antônio Pinto de. 2010. "Em 1959, o censo experimental na alvorada de Brasília." In *Veredas de Brasília: expedições geográficas em busca de um sonho*, edited by Nelson de Castro Senra, 123–136. Rio de Janeiro: IBGE.
Orsi, Robert. 2003. "Is the Study of Lived Religion Irrelevant to the World We Live In?" *Journal for the Scientific Study of Religion* 42 (2): 169–174.
Orsi, Robert. 2005. *Between Heaven and Earth: The Religious Worlds People Make and the Scholars Who Study Them*. Princeton, NJ: Princeton University Press.
Palmié, Stephan, and Charles Stewart. 2016. "Introduction: For an Anthropology of History." *Hau: Journal of Ethnographic Theory* 6 (1): 207–236.
Partridge, Christopher. 2003. "Understanding UFO Religions and Abduction Spiritualities." In *UFO Religion*, edited by Christopher Partridge, 3–44. London: Routledge.
Partridge, Christopher. 2004. *The Re-enchantment of the West*, Vol. 1: *Alternative Spiritualities, Sacralization, Popular Culture, and Occulture*. New York: T&T Clark International.
Partridge, Christopher. 2005. *The Re-Enchantment of the West*, Vol. 2: *Alternative Spiritualities, Sacralization, Popular Culture, and Occulture*. New York: T&T Clark International.
Partridge, Christopher. 2014. "Occulture is Ordinary." In *Contemporary Esotericism*, edited by Egil Asprem and Kennet Granholm, 113–133. New York: Routledge.
Partridge, Christopher. 2015. "Channeling Extraterrestrials: Theosophical Discourse in the Space Age." In *Handbook of Spiritualism and Channeling*, edited by Cathy Gutierrez, 390–417. Leiden: Brill. https://doi.org/10.1163/9789004264083_019.
Pessar, Patricia R. 2004. *From Fanatics to Folk: Brazilian Millenarianism and Popular Culture*. Durham, NC: Duke University Press.
Pew Research Center. 2013. *Brazil's Changing Religious Landscape*. July 18, 1–11. Washington, DC: Pew Research Center's Religion and Public Life Project. http://www.pewforum.org/2013/07/18/brazils-changing-religious-landscape/.
Pew Research Center. 2015. *Seven Key Changes in the Global Religious Landscape*. Washington, DC: Pew Research Center's Religion and Public Life Project.
Pierini, Emily. 2013. "The Journey of the Jaguares: Spirit Mediumship in the Brazilian Vale Do Amanhecer." PhD diss., University of Bristol.
Pierini, Emily. 2016. "Becoming a Jaguar: Spiritual Routes in the Vale do Amanhecer." In *Handbook of Contemporary Religions in Brazil*, edited by Steven Engler and Bettina Schmidt, 225–232. Leiden and Boston: Brill.
Pierini, Emily. 2020. *Jaguars of the Dawn: Spirit Mediumship in the Brazilian Vale do Amanhecer*. New York: Berghahn Books.
Pinto, Francisco. 2004. *Memórias de um Reporter*. Brasília: Thesaurus Éditora.
Pinto, João. 1993 (1969). "Breve Histórico da Teosofia no Brasil: Desde os Seus Primórdios Até a Fundação da Seção Nacional da Sociedade Teosófica, em 1919." *Boletim do CIBLA (Círculo Blavatsky)*. Porto Alegre, Rio Grande do Sul (Junho): 19–22.

Pires, Larissa. 2013. "Gender in the Modernist City: Shaping Power Relations and National Identity with the Construction of Brasilia." PhD diss., University of Iowa.

Premack, Laura. 2015. "Dead Man Talking: Brazil's Spiritist Redefine Religion." *Boston Review*, April 13. https://bostonreview.net/articles/laura-premack-dead-man-talking-brazil-spiritism/.

Preston, Elizabeth, and Christmas Humphrey, eds. 2012 (1966). *An Abridgement of the Secret Doctrine, by H.P. Blavatsky*. Wheaton, IL: Quest Books.

Promey, Sally M., ed. 2014. *Sensational Religion: Sensory Cultures in Material Practice*. New Haven, CT: Yale University Press.

Queiroz, Larissa Maria de. 2015. "Indumentárias de Falanges Femininas no Vale do Amanhecer: Uma Etnografia no Templo de Eusébio, Ceará, Brasil." MA thesis, Universidade de Salamanca (Salamanca, Spain).

Rebhun, Linda-Anne. 1994. "Swallowing Frogs: Anger and Illness in Northeast Brazil." *Medical Anthropology Quarterly* 8 (4): 360–382.

Reis, Marcelo. 2008. "Tia Neiva: A Trajetória de Uma Líder Religiosa e Sua Obra, O Vale do Amanhecer (1925–2008)." PhD diss., University of Brasília.

Reis, Marcelo. 2010a. "Tia Neiva: Traços de um Itinerário Existencial." In *Vale do Amanhecer: Inventário Nacional de Referências Culturais*, edited by Deis Siqueira, Marcelo Reis, Jairo Zelaya Leite, and Rodrigo M. Ramasotte, 163–231. Brasília: Superintendência do IPHAN no Distrito Federal.

Ribeiro, Gustavo Lins. 2008. *O Capital da Esperança: A Experiencia dos Trabalhadores na Construção de Brasilia*. Brasília: Editora UnB.

Ristoff, Dilvo. 2014. "O novo perfil do campus brasileiro: uma análise do perfil socioeconômico do estudante de graduação." *Avaliação* 19 (3): 723–747. https://doi.org/10.1590/S1414-40772014000300010.

Rocha, Cristina. 2009. "Seeking healing transnationally: Australians, John of God and Brazilian Spiritism." *The Australian Journal of Anthropology* 20: 229–246.

Rocha, Cristina. 2017. *John of God: The Globalization of Brazilian Faith Healing*. New York: Oxford University Press.

Rodrigues, Arakcy Martins, and Francine Muel-Dreyfus. 2005 (1987). "Reencarnações: Notas de Pesquisa sobre uma Seita Espírita de Brasília." In Arakcy Martins Rodrigues, *Indivíduo, Grupo e Sociedade: Estudos de Psicologia Social*, 233–260. São Paulo: Editora USP.

Rodrigues, Joice Meire. 2011. "Ninfas e Jaguares: uma interrogação feminista sobre o universo religioso do Vale do Amanhecer." PhD diss., Pontifícia Universidade Católica de São Paulo.

Rodrigues, Marly. 1994. *A Decada de 50: Populismo e Metas Desenvolvimentistas no Brasil*. São Paulo: Atica.

Rothstein, Mikael. 2003. "The Idea of the Past, the Reality of the Present, and the Construction of the Future: Millenarianism in the Aetherius Society." In *Encyclopedic Sourcebook of UFO Religions*, edited by James R. Lewis, 143–156. Amherst, NY: Prometheus Books.

Rothstein, Mikael. 2013. "Mahatmas in Space: The Ufological Turn and Mythological Materiality of Post-World War II Theosophy." In *Handbook of the Theosophical Current*, edited by Olav Hammer and Mikael Rothstein, 217–236. Leiden: Brill.

Rubinstein, Murray. 2019. "New Religious Movement." *Encyclopedia Britannica*, February 25. https://www.britannica.com/topic/new-religious-movement.

Ruether, Rosemary Radford. 2005. "Androcentrism." In *Encyclopedia of Religion*, 2nd edition, edited by Lindsay Jones, Mircea Eliade, et al, 334–337. Detroit, MI: Macmillan Reference.
Salmeron, Roberto Aureliano. 2007. *A universidade interrompida: Brasília 1964–1965.* 2nd edition. Brasília: Ed.UnB.
Santos, Altierez Sebastião dos. 2016a. "As narrativas religiosas do Vale do Amanhecer." MA thesis, Universidade Metodista de São Paulo.
Santos, Altierez Sebastião dos. 2016b. "O elemento espacial na iconografia do Vale do Amanhecer: os signos de uma nova cosmologia na religião." *Revista Eletrônica Correlatio* 15 (2): 151–169.
Santos, Altierez Sebastião dos. 2018. "A narrativa religiosa do Vale do Amanhecer e a vocalização dos excluídos." *Convenit Internacional* 26: 39–54.
Santos, Rodolpho Gauthier Cardoso dos. 2007. "Imaginário e representação: A história dos discos voadores e seres extraterrestres no Brasil." Paper presented at the XXIV Simpósio Nacional da História, São Leopardo, Rio Grande do Sul, July. http://anais.anpuh.org/wp-content/uploads/mp/pdf/ANPUH.S24.0476.pdf.
Santos, Vagner dos, Gelya Frank, and Ana Mizue. 2020. "Candangos: Occupational Reconstruction as a Tool to Understand Social Problems and Transformative Action in the Utopian City of Brasília." *Cadernos Brasileiros de Terapia Ocupacional* 28 (3): 765–783. https://doi.org/10.4322/2526-8910.ctoAO2061.
Santucci, James A. 2008. "The Notion of Race in Theosophy." *Nova Religio* 11 (3): 37–63.
Shweder, Richard A., Nancy C. Much, Manamohan M. Mahapatra, and Lawrence Park. 1997. "The Big Three of Morality (Autonomy, Community, Divinity) and the Big Three Explanations of Suffering." In *Morality and Health*, edited by Allan Brandt and Paul Rozin, 119–172. New York: Routledge.
Sharp, Lynn L. 2005. "Popular Healing in a Rational Age: Spiritism as Folklore and Medicine." *Proceedings of the Western Society for French History* 33: 308–324.
Sharp, Lynn L. 2015. "Reincarnation: The Path to Progress." In *Handbook of Spiritualism and Channeling*, edited by Cathy Guttierez, 219–247. Leiden: Brill. https://doi.org/10.1163/9789004264083_012.
Silvey, Robert, and Stephen MacKeith. 1988. "The Paracosm: A Special Form of Fantasy." In *Organizing Early Experience: Imagination and Cognition in Childhood*, edited by Delmont C. Morrison, 173–197. Amityville, New York: Baywood Publishing Company.
Siqueira, Deis. 2003. *As novas religiosidades no Ocidente: Brasília, cidade mística.* Brasília: Editora UnB/FINATEC.
Siqueira, Deis. 2016. "Unconventional Religiosities and the New Age in Vale do Amanhecer (Valley of the Dawn), Brasilia." In *New Age in Latin America: Popular Variations and Ethnic Appropriations*, edited by Angela Renée de la Torre Castellanos, María Cristina del Refugio Gutiérrez, and Nahayeilli Juárez-Huet, 243–264. Leiden: Brill.
Siqueira, Deis, and Ricardo Barbosa de Lima, eds. 2003. *Sociologia das adesões: Novas religiosidades e a busca místico-esotérica na capital do Brasil*. Rio de Janeiro: Garamond.
Siqueira, Deis, Marcelo Reis, Jairo Zelaya Leite, and Rodrigo M. Ramasotte. 2010. *Vale do Amanhecer: Inventário Nacional de Referências Culturais*. Brasília: Superintendência do IPHAN no Distrito Federal.
Smith, Emily Esfahani. 2012. "Let's Give Chivalry Another Chance." *The Atlantic*, December 10. http://www.theatlantic.com/sexes/archive/2012/12/lets-give-chivalry-another-chance/266085/ (accessed September 1, 2015).

Smith, William, ed. 1873. *"Leonidas I": A Dictionary of Greek and Roman Biography and Mythology*. London: John Murray. http://www.perseus.tufts.edu/hopper/text?doc=Perseus:text:1999.04.0104:entry=leonidas-i-bio-1&highlight=leonidas%2Ci (accessed April 30, 2022).

Solomon, David Nunes. 2019. "Brasília and the Populist Frontier." *Places Journal*, October. https://doi.org/10.22269/191008 (accessed December 1, 2022).

Stuckrad, Kocku von. 2015 (2005). *Western Esotericism: A Brief History of Secret Knowledge*, translated and with a foreword by Nicholas Goodrick-Clarke. 2nd edition. New York: Routledge.

Taves, Ann. 2016. *Revelatory Events: Three Case Studies of the Emergence of New Spiritual Paths*. Princeton, NJ: Princeton University Press.

Taves, Ann, Egil Asprem, and Elliott Ihm. 2018. "Psychology, Meaning Making, and the Study of Worldviews: Beyond Religion and Non-religion." *Psychology of Religion and Spirituality* 10 (3): 207–217. https://doi.org/10.1037/rel0000201.

Taylor, Charles. 2004. *Modern Social Imaginaries*. Durham, NC: Duke University Press.

Trompf, Garry. 2013. "Theosophical Macrohistory." In *Handbook of the Theosophical Current*, edited by Olav Hammer and Mikael Rothstein, 375–403. Leiden: Brill.

Trompf, Garry. 2019. "Gnostics and Temporality: From Myth to Macrohistory." In *The Gnostic World*, edited by Garry W. Trompf, Gunner B. Mikkelsen, and Jay Johnston, 43–59. New York: Routledge.

"UFO Airport." 2009. *Around the World in 80 Faiths*. Episode 7: Latin America, Faith 69. BBC, January 2.

UN-Habitat. 2010. *State of the World's Cities 2010/2011—Cities for All: Bridging the Urban Divide*. Nairobi, Kenya: United Nations Human Settlements Programme.

Vance, Laura. 2015. *Women in New Religions*. New York: New York University Press.

Vásquez, Manuel A., and José Cláudio Souza Alves. 2013. "The Valley of Dawn in Atlanta, Georgia: Negotiating Gender Identity and Incorporation in the Diaspora." In *The Diaspora of Brazilian Religions*, edited by Cristina Rocha and Manuel Vásquez, 313–338. Leiden: Brill.

Von Däniken, Erich. 1969 (1968). *Chariots of the Gods? Unsolved Mysteries of the Past*, translated by Michael Heron. New York: G.P. Putnam's Sons.

Wessinger, Catherine, ed. 1993. *Women's Leadership in Marginal Religions: Explorations Outside the Mainstream*. Urbana: University of Illinois Press.

Wessinger, Catherine. 2000. *How the Millennium Comes Violently: From Jonestown to Heaven's Gate*. New York: Seven Bridges Press.

Wessinger, Catherine. 2020. *Theory of Women in Religions*. New York: New York University Press.

Wessinger, Catherine, Dell DeChant, and William Michael Ashcraft. 2006. "Theosophy, New Thought, and the New Age Movements." In *The Encyclopedia of Women and Religion in North America*, edited by Rosemary Skinner Keller and Rosemary Radford Ruether, 753–767. Bloomington: Indiana University Press.

White, Christopher. 2018. *Other Worlds: Spirituality and the Search for Invisible Dimensions*. Cambridge, MA: Harvard University Press.

Wirtz, Kristina. 2016. "The Living, the Dead, and the Immanent: Dialogue across Chronotopes." *Hau: Journal of Ethnographic Theory* 6 (1): 343–369.

Wollock, Jennifer G. 2011. *Rethinking Chivalry and Courtly Love*. Santa Barbara: Praeger.

Zeller, Benjamin. 2010. "Extraterrestrial Biblical Hermeneutics and the Making of Heaven's Gate." *Nova Religio* 14 (2): 34–60.

Zeller, Benjamin. 2011. "At the Nexus of Science and Religion: UFO Religions." *Religion Compass* 5 (11): 666–674.

Spiritist and Valley of the Dawn Publications and Media

Conceito de Doutrina do Amanhecer. n.d. Vale do Amahecer: self-published encyclopedia.
Manual de Instruções. 2008. Planaltina: Obras Sociais da Ordem Espiritualista Cristã.
Manual das Dharman Oxinto. n.d. Vale do Amanhecer: self-published pamphlet.
Acioly, Romulo. 2018. "Iniciação é o primeiro passo." *Vale do Amanhecer* blog, February 19. https://salvedeus.com.br/?p=5582 (consulted October 1, 2020).
Armond, Edgard. 1987 (1940). *Os Exilados da Capela: Esboço Sintético da Evolução Espiritual no Mundo*. São Paulo: Editora Aliança.
Betinho. 2005. "O Mestre Humahan." *Jornal do Jaguar* 1 (2): 4.
Betinho. 2006. "Nós, Os Ciganos . . ." *Jornal do Jaguar* 2 (6): 6.
Chiarotto, Antonio Claudio. n.d. *Templo Puemar do Amanhecer—Brasil* blog. http://puemardoamanhecer.blogspot.com/.
Chiarotto, Antonio Claudio. 2013. "Polaridade." *Templo Puemar do Amanhecer—Brasil* blog. http://puemardoamanhecer.blogspot.com/2013/09/polaridade.html.
Cunha, Francisco R. 2008. *Memórias de um Seguidor de Tia Neiva*. Brasília: self-published book.
Damião, Itamir. 2004. *Apostila de Recepção*. Vale do Amanhecer: self-published pamphlet.
José, Ivanildo. n.d. *Blog do Vale do Amanhecer da Cidade de Téofilo Otoni-MG*. http://temploabavano.blogspot.com/2010/03/templo-abavano-totoni-mg.html.
Kazagrande. n.d. *Exílio do Jaguar* Blog. https://www.exiliodojaguar.com.br.
Kazagrande. 2010. "Escrava??" *Exílio do Jaguar* blog. https://www.exiliodojaguar.com.br/2010/03/escrava_31.html.
Kazagrande. 2011. *O Centurião*. n.p.: self-published book.
Kazagrande. 2012. "Sexo e Doutrina."*Exílio do Jaguar* blog. https://www.exiliodojaguar.com.br/2012/03/sexo-e-doutrina.html.
Leite, Jairo Oliveira Junior. 2005. "Tia Neiva: Um exemplo de vida, de amor e de fé." *Jornal do Jaguar* 1 (1): 4.
Lucena, Bálsamo Álvares do Brasil de, ed. 1992. *Tia Neiva: Autobiografia Missionária*. Planaltina: Obras Sociais da Ordem Espiritualista Cristã.
Moura, Marcello Henrique Dias de, et al. 2010. *Guia Prático de Desenvolvimento de Doutrinadores*. n.p.: self-published pamphlet.
Patricio, Cristiano. 2012. "1º de Maio dia do Doutrinador." *Inconfidências* blog, May 1. http://ministroabazo.blogspot.com/2012/05/1-de-maio-dia-do-doutrinador.html (accessed June 17, 2022).
Reis, Marcelo. 2010b. "Heranças Transcendentais." *Jornal do Jaguar* 10: 5.
Santos, Gilmar. 1994. Interview with Mário Sassi. November. https://youtu.be/SkPevoc6Np0 (accessed April 14, 2018).
Santos, Gilmar. 2012. "Uma Reflexão sobre Nossa Doutrina," *Doutrina do Amanhecer— Um Salto para Outras Dimensões* blog. https://valedoamanheceradoutrinadetianeiva.blogspot.com/2012/10/uma-reflexao-sobre-nossa-doutrina.html (accessed September 2020).
Santos, Gilmar. 2021. "Jaguar: O Espírito Espartano." *Portal do Jaguar* blog, March 21. https://portaldojaguar.com/jaguar-o-espirito-espartano/ (accessed May 30, 2022).

Sassi, Mário. n.d. *Sob os Olhos da Clarividente*. Brasília: Editora Vale do Amanhecer.
Sassi, Mário. 1972. *No Limiar do Terceiro Milênio*. Brasília: Editora Vale do Amanhecer.
Sassi, Mário. 1974. *2000: A Conjunção de Dois Planos*. Brasília: Editora Vale do Amanhecer.
Sassi, Mário. 1977. *Instruções Práticas para os Médiuns*, 7 volumes. Brasília: Editora Vale do Amanhecer.
Sassi, Mário. 1985a. *Partida Evangélica: Apostila para Distribuição entre os Médiuns*. Brasília: Editora Vale do Amanhecer.
Sassi, Mário, ed. 1985b. *Minha Vida, Meus Amores, Autobiografia de Tia Neiva*. Brasília: Editora Vale do Amanhecer.
Sassi, Mário. 1986. "Tiãozinho e Justininha." In *Pequenas Histórias: Sob os Olhos da Clarividente*, edited by Mário Sassi, n.p. Brasília: Editora Vale do Amanhecer.
Sassi, Mário. 2004 (1979). *O Que é o Vale do Amanhecer*. Brasília: Editora Vale do Amanhecer.
Silva, José Carlos do Nascimento. n.d. *Observações Tumará*. Self-published document.
Silva, José Carlos do Nascimento. 1998. "Transcendentalidade da Doutrina do Amanhecer." Lecture given at the First Seminar of the Temples of the Dawn, Ipatinga, Minas Gerais, Brazil, August 15.
Silva, José Carlos do Nascimento. 2001. *O Evangelho do Jaguar*. Planaltina: Vale do Amanhecer.
Silva, José Carlos do Nascimento, ed. 2004. *O Que é o Vale do Amanhecer: Uma pequena síntese da história, atividades e localização, no tempo e no espaço, do movimento doutrinário da Ordem Espiritualista Cristã, em Brasília, no Vale do Amanhecer* (based on work edited by Mário Sassi in 1979). Planaltina: Vale do Amanhecer.
Souza, José Donato de. n.d. *Compêndio de Cartas da Tia Neiva*. Self-published document.
Souza, Marcos Antônio de. 2000. *Dicionário do Vale*. Self-published dictionary.
Stuckert, Guilherme. 2005. "O nascimento da Estrela Candente." *Jornal do Jaguar* 1 (1): 7.
Zelaya, Carmem Lúcia. 2009. *Os Símbolos na Doutrina do Vale do Amanhecer: Sob os Olhos da Clarividente*. Vale do Amanhecer: Tia Neiva Publicações.
Zelaya, Carmem Lúcia. 2014. *Neiva: Sua Vida pelos Meus Olhos*. Brasília: Coronário.
Zelaya, Neiva Chaves. 1999. *Cartas Abertas Minhas e de Meu Mestre Umahã*. Vale do Amanhecer: Editora Vale do Amanhecer.
"'Nosso lar' lidera bilheterias no Brasil pela segunda semana seguida." 2010. G1—Globo.com, September 13. http://g1.globo.com/pop-arte/noticia/2010/09/nosso-lar-lidera-bilheterias-no-brasil-pela-segunda-semana-seguida.html (accessed September 19, 2020).
Xavier, Francisco Cândido. 1939. *A Caminho da Luz: História da Civilização à Luz do Espiritismo, ditada pelo espírito Emmanuel*. São Paulo: Editora FEB.
Xavier, Francisco Cândido. 1944. *Nosso Lar: A Vida no Mundo Espiritual*. Rio de Janeiro: Federação Espírita Brasileira.

Index

For the benefit of digital users, indexed terms that span two pages (e.g., 52–53) may, on occasion, appear on only one of those pages.

Note: Tables and figures are indicated by *t* and *f* following the page number

ajanãs, 160–62
alternative religions, 8–9, 18, 24, 84, 245. *See also* new religions
animal magnetism, 82, 112, 147–48, 264–65n.15
aparás, 114–15, 117*f*, 119, 121, 124, 125, 152–53, 155*f*, 159
Apollo, 17–18
Arana Amarela spirit, 167–68, 167*f*
Ascended Masters, 271n.10, 272n.19
aspirant (first stage) of mediumship, 120–27
astral planes, 45, 51–52, 82, 111–12, 137, 162, 244. *See also* spiritual planes
Atzingen, Moema Quadros von, 58–59, 61–62, 65–66
Aunt Neiva
  autobiography, of, 19
  Capellans and, 85–91
  Chief Tupinambá and, 40, 45, 46–47
  in Cidade Ecléctica, 37–38
  clairvoyance of, 26–27, 216–17, 242, 247–48, 253
  death, 76–77, 248
  early life, 27–30
  Father White Arrow and, 44–50, 47*f*, 68, 78–81
  in Free City, 31–33, 32*f*
  gender ideology of, 144–47
  interplanetary education, 85–88
  introduction to, 1, 6–7
  Lady of Space and, 39–40
  mediumship of, 6, 38–44
  mestrado completion, 51–53
  Mother Yara and, 39–40, 45–46, 195, 243, 266–67n.24, 280n.15

  Night Owls work, 74–77
  nomadic existence, 30–31
  overview, 20–25, 242–48
  psychiatric help, 40–42
  relationship with Sassi, Mário, 22
  selflessness of, 11, 163–64
  spirit culture and, 38–41
  Tiãozinho and, 94–97, 96*f*
  truck driving career, 29–30, 29*f*
  tuberculosis, 51–52
  Umahã and, 51–52, 73, 83, 110–11, 243, 244–45, 269n.15
  vanity of, 144–45, 146*f*
  visionary mission, 15–16, 103–5
  visions/waking dreams, 33–34, 253
auras, 39–40, 82, 95, 195, 196, 211
authentic religion, 7, 9
authoritarianism, 19, 27–28, 64
automatic writing (psychography), 246–47

Berger, Peter, 44
beyond matter, 37, 81, 244, 245, 252–53
biomedicine, 187–88, 281n.20
Blavatsky, Helena P., 82–83
branquinha (little white) uniform, 121, 122*f*
Brazilian Spiritist Federation, 246
Brasília, 4, 6, 15–16, 21, 31–33, 47–48, 50, 51, 53, 56, 60–61, 65, 97-100, 103, 104, 119, 211, 242, 248-249, 262*f*, 262n.2, 263n3–5, 263n.6, 275n.33, 275n.34, 275n.35, 275n.38, 276n.39, 284n.3

caboclo, 40, 49, 79–80, 84–85, 88, 93, 106–7, 112, 121, 125, 138, 250
candango (migrant worker), 21, 97–103

Capellans, 26–27, 85–91
Capella (Mother Planet), 80, 88–91
Carlos, Antônio, 5–6, 185, 186, 190–91, 216
Carvalho, José Jorge de, 36, 258
Catholicism, 6, 11, 36, 38–39, 54, 57–58, 61, 93–94, 163, 166–67, 184–85, 194, 243–44, 246, 250
César, José Vicente, 54
chakras, 82, 124, 128, 152
chanting, 234–39
charismatic leaders, 9, 10, 12, 37–38, 43, 77, 83, 144, 258–59, 268n.8
Chaves, Senhor Antônio de Medeiros, 27–28
Chief Tupinambá (Cacique Tupinambá), 40, 45, 46–47
Christianity, 9–10, 12, 13. *See also* Catholicism
Christic System, 13, 79–80, 92, 93–94, 128, 192
chronotropic regimes, 219–22
Cidade Ecléctica (Eclectic City), 37–38
clairvoyance of Aunt Neiva, 26–27, 216–17, 242, 247–48, 253
classifications *(classificações)*, 119–20, 161
cobradores (debt-collectors), 189, 192–93, 202–4, 207
conscious transport, 45, 86
Consecration of the Centúria *(Consagração de Centúria)*, 134–38, 135*f*, 136*f*
conventional medicine, 5, 186
cosmic masters, 84–85, 88, 93–95, 97, 258–59
cosmic U-curve, 82
countercultural, 12, 70–71
cult debate, 9–11

Darger, Henry, 107
debt-collector spirits. See *cobradores*
descending forcefield *(força decrescente)*, 73, 269n.16, 282n.14
development *(desinvolvimento)* sessions, 36
Dharman Oxinto initiation *(iniciação Dharman Oxinto)*, 127–32, 163–64
disadvantaged classes *(classes desfavorecidas)*, 186–87
Discourse and the Construction of Society (Lincoln), 156
disincarnation, 35

disobsession rituals, 191–94
doctrinal conduct, 11–13, 104–5, 171–72, 173, 228, 229, 230, 252
Doctrine of the Dawn, 11–13, 56, 73, 74, 81, 120, 144, 185, 221–22, 242, 244–45, 248–52, 282n.14
Dona Júlia, 39
doutrinadores, 73, 114–15, 116*f*, 121, 152–53, 154*f*, 159, 276–77n.4. *See also* indoctrination medium

Eclectic City. *See* Cidade Ecléctica
Eclectic Spiritualist Universal Brotherhood (Fraternidade Eclética Espiritualista Universal), 37–38
ectoplasm, 82, 112–13, 148, 152–53, 189–90, 192, 193, 203
egalitarianism, 104–5, 250–51, 252
Elevation of Swords *(Elevação de Espadas)* step, 132
emplacado mediums, 126–27
enclothed cognition, 140
energetic currents, 194–96
Equitumans, 15, 88–91, 92, 227, 274n.26, 274n.28
escravas, 161
esoteric movements, 110, 258, 271n.9
esoteric traditions, 12, 82, 110, 128, 258, 272n.14
etheric plane, 26, 86
existential meaning in suffering, 208–13
extraterrestrial, 12, 22, 23–24, 58–59, 78–79, 80, 82–85, 88, 93, 95, 272n.15, 273n.21, 273–74nn.22–26, 273n.23, 273–74nn.24–25, 274n.26

fan fiction, 107–8
Father White Arrow, 44–50, 47*f*, 68, 78–81, 93
feminine plexus, 148–49, 159–61, 172
First Master Jaguar Sun Tumuchy. *See* Sassi, Mário
First Mistress Sun Jaguar *(Primeira Mestra Sol Jaguar)*, 159
flying saucers *(discos voadores)*, 83–84, 85–86, 272n.15
folk healers, 6, 38–39
folk medicine, 188
força decrescente, 73, 269n.16, 282n.14
Francis of Assisi (Saint), 121

Franco, Divaldo, 246–47
free will, 8–9, 10, 51, 120, 180, 190, 270n.2
Froes, Adevaldo Sampaio, 72–73, 75, 76

gendered ideology
  ajanãs, 160–62
  androcentrism of, 172–77
  binary system of, 147–52
  escravas, 161
  feminine plexus, 148–49, 159–61, 172
  indumentárias and, 74, 132, 134f, 139, 162–72, 236–38, 255–56
  magnetic force, 144, 148, 149, 151–52, 153, 168, 256
  mediumship as binary system, 152–60, 153t, 156t
  Moon Masters, 152–60, 161, 176
  Moon Nymphs, 156–59, 158f, 160, 161–62, 174–76, 278n.8, 282–83n.15
  overview of, 144–47, 149t, 151t
  phalanxes, 162–72
  Sun Masters, 152–60, 161–62, 176
  Sun Nymphs, 156–59, 157f, 160, 176, 278n.8, 282–83n.15
gnosticism, 88, 93, 220
The Gospel According to Spiritism (Kardec), 45
Gospel of Jesus Christ, 5–6, 12, 214–15
Goulart, João, 64
Great East, 110–11, 244–45
Great Initiates, 73, 76–77, 110, 128, 132, 137, 166
Great Masters, 104
guia missionária (missionary guide), 166–67, 167f, 168–70, 236, 282–83n.15

habitual practice, 141
Hahn, Robert, 23, 187
Hanna, Michel (Trino Sumanã), 76
Harari, Yuval Noah, 142
healing
  biomedicine, 187–88, 281n.20
  cobradores (debt-collectors), 192–93, 202–4, 207
  disobsession rituals, 191–94
  energetic currents, 194–96
  existential meaning in suffering, 208–13
  folk healers, 6, 38–39
  folk medicine, 188

free rituals, 251
karma and, 199–201
obsessores (obsessors) spirits, 37, 126, 181, 184, 191–93, 198–99, 209–10, 212, 279n.2
Prisão (Prison ritual), 202–8, 205f
Thrones ritual, 178–84, 197–99, 197f
transformation and, 213–15
universal emergency room, 184–87
unwanted conditions of the self, 187–91
Hinduism, 7, 220
Hofstadter, Douglas, 248–49
Holston, James, 55, 98, 119, 203, 206, 248
Homo Deus (Harari), 142
How God Becomes Real: Kindling the Presence of Invisible Others (Luhrmann), 107
human suffering, 12, 13, 36, 172, 183–85, 187, 188–89, 194, 246

imagined order, 16–20, 24–25, 142, 262n.14
imagined places, 229–39, 252–57
imagined world, 8, 14–18, 22, 23, 56, 106–08, 110-111, 127, 138–139, 141–144, 147, 153, 166, 176, 177, 215, 243, 245, 248, 252–253, 255–256, 257
Incandescent Star (Estrela Candente), 3–4, 5f, 88–89, 230
Indian Space Current, 110–11, 114, 115–17, 124–25, 186, 256, 274n.30
indoctrination medium, 76, 113, 152–53, 156, 193. *See also* doutrinadores
indumentárias, 74, 132, 134f, 139, 162–72, 236–38, 255–56
initiatory key *(chave iniciática),* 114
initiatory steps in mediumship, 126–28
intelligent consciousness, 82–83
interplanetary education, 85–88

Jaguars spirit tribe, 78–81, 79f, 91–93. *See also* Journey of the Jaguars
Jesus
  Christic System, 13, 79–80, 92, 93–94, 128, 192
  emulating teachings of, 79–80
  Gospel of Jesus Christ, 5–6, 12, 214–15
  living gospel of, 13, 214–15
  in Mother Temple, 3, 3f
  reconfigured in *Conjunction,* 93–95
  resurrection of, 7

Journey of the Jaguars, 22, 78–81, 103–4, 106–7, 248–49. *See also* Jaguars spirit tribe
Juventude Operária Católica, 57–58

kabbalistic rituals, 221–22
Kardec, Allan, 35–37, 45, 82
Kardecism Spiritism, 6, 11, 35–37, 44, 49–50, 57–58, 60–61, 82, 112, 245, 255–56, 258, 265n.16
karma
　healing and, 199–201
　Kardec on, 35
　Lady of Space and, 39–40
　liberation from, 13, 248
　physicality and, 12–13
　redemption from, 13, 80
　Turigano ritual and, 222–29
Kaufman, Scott Barry, 214
kindlings, 108–10, 138–40
Kleinman, Arthur, 187
Kubitschek, Juscelino, 31, 59–60, 99

Lady of Space, 39–40
Law of Assistance, 45–46, 102, 113, 128, 153, 167–68, 185, 200, 201, 206
Law of Charity, 207
Leadbeater, Charles W., 83
legitimate religions, 9, 10
Leite, Jairo Zelaya, 80–81, 148
Lévi-Strauss, Claude, 103–4, 124–25
LGBTQ+ discrimination, 252
Lincoln, Bruce, 156
linha de passe, 38
Lispector, Clarice, 99–100
living gospel of Jesus, 13, 214–15
lost souls, 7, 45, 198–99
Love Towards God (Amor a Deus), 83
lower-level spirits, 13, 43, 112
Lucas, George, 107
Luckmann, Thomas, 44
Luhrmann, T. M., 8, 22, 24–25, 106–10

magnetic fluid, 82, 152, 264–65n.15
magnetic force, 144, 148, 149, 151–52, 153, 168, 256
magnetic pass, 35–36, 264–65n.15
Mahatmas, 82–83

mantric hymns, 194–95
masters *(mestres)*
　Ascended Masters, 271n.10, 272n.19
　in binary system, 147–52
　cosmic masters, 84–85, 88, 93–95, 97, 258–59
　defined, 2–3
　Great Masters, 104
　Mahatmas, 82–83
　Moon Masters *(Mestres Lua)*, 152–60, 161, 176
　planetary master, 78–79, 88, 93, 104
　Sun Masters *(Mestres Sol)*, 152–60, 161–62, 176
Masters of Wisdom, 82–83, 148–49
master teaching master *(mestre ensinando mestre)*, 119
material culture, 22–25, 54–55, 184, 216, 218, 219, 227, 236–38, 239, 241, 255, 257
mediumization *(mediunização)*, 118, 200
mediums/mediumship
　aparás, 114–15, 117f, 119, 121, 124, 125, 152–53, 159
　aspirant (first stage), 120–27
　Aunt Neiva as, 6, 38–44
　as binary system, 152–60, 153t, 156t
　clothing/uniforms of, 128, 129f, 130f, 131f, 132, 133f, 134f
　conceptualization of, 112–13
　Consecration of the Centúria, 134–38, 135f, 136f
　culture of, 38–41
　development of, 115–20, 141–42
　Dharman Oxinto initiation, 127–32, 163–64
　Elevation of Swords step, 132
　emplacado mediums, 126–27
　indoctrination medium, 76, 113, 152–53, 156, 193
　initiatory steps, 126–28, 142
　kindlings, 108–10, 138–40
　semi-conscious, 114, 147
　unconscious, 114
Melton, J. Gordon, 72
mental illness, 5, 36, 42, 100–1, 186–87
merit *(merecimento)*, 106–7, 199, 200, 201, 202–3

INDEX 303

Mesmer, Franz, 35–36
mesmerism, 35–36, 82, 264–65n.15
mestrado, 51–53, 73–74
metaphysics/metaphysical, 12, 13, 21–22, 65–66, 80, 82, 84–85, 87, 93, 104, 118, 126–27, 152, 188, 234, 246–47, 265n.18
Moon Masters *(Mestres Lua),* 152–60, 161, 176
Moon Nymphs *(Ninfas Lua),* 156–59, 158f, 160, 161–62, 174–76, 278n.8, 282–83n.15
Morgan, David, 216
Moser, Benjamin, 1
Mother Neném (Mãe Neném), 44–50
Mother Planet (Capella), 80, 88–91
Mother Yara, 39–40, 45–46, 195, 243, 266–67n.24, 280n.15, 282–83n.15
Muel-Dreyfus, Francine, 66
Mundos Negros (Dark Worlds), 168

National Agricultural Colony of Goiás (CANG), 28
New Age movements, 4, 7, 14, 23–24, 74, 93, 104, 258–59, 271–72n.11
new religions, 8–9, 18, 24, 84, 245. *See also* alternative religions
new religious movements (NRMs), 7, 11–12, 18, 23, 72, 83, 262n.11, 270n.5, 275n.38, 279n.13
Night Owls work, 74–77
Nunez, João, 100–1, 102–3
nymphs *(ninfas)*
  in binary system, 147–52
  defined, 2–3
  Moon Nymphs *(Ninfas Lua),* 156–59, 158f, 160, 161–62, 174–76, 278n.8, 282–83n.15
  Sun Nymphs *(Ninfas Sol),* 156–59, 157f, 160, 176, 278n.8, 282–83n.15

obsessão, 34
obsessores (obsessors) spirits, 37, 126, 181, 184, 191–93, 198–99, 209–10, 212, 279n.2
occultural cosmology, 84–85
occulture, 84, 244–45, 246–47
Olcott, Henry Steel, 82

Oliveira, José Aparecido de, 55–56
Oliveira, Maria de. *See* Mother Neném (Mãe Neném)
orixá, 89, 93, 243–44
OSOEC. *See* Social Works of the Christian Spiritualist Order
Other Worlds: Spirituality and the Search for Invisible Dimensions (White), 247
Our Home (Nosso Lar) (Xavier), 200–1
Owen-Jones, Peter, 178–84, 189

paracosms/paracosmic, 106–10
paranormal, 22, 42, 58–59, 84, 87, 163–64, 243, 245–46, 264n.10, 265n.18
parascientific, 42
Partridge, Christopher, 84–85, 244–45
past lives, 23, 31, 36, 39–40, 106–7, 150–51, 162–63, 189, 199, 216–17, 227, 228, 235
patriarchal norms, 21, 27–28, 144
perispirit, 82
phalanxes, 162–72, 245
physicality, 12–13, 88–89, 148
Pierini, Emily, 42–43, 138–39, 240
Pilgrims, 94
Pimental, Lúcia, 100–1
Pira (Pyre), 195–96, 196f
planetary master, 78–79, 88, 93, 104
plausibility structure, 44
positivism, 245–46, 251–52
preto velho spirit, 40, 49, 115–17, 125, 138, 180, 197, 198–99, 207, 255–56, 278n.14
Prisão (Prison ritual), 202–8, 205f
psyche, 42
Pyramid, significance of, 230–33, 231f, 232f

rays *(raios),* 91
reality effects, 18, 262n.14
realness experiences, 140–43
reincarnation, 7, 12–13, 35, 39–40, 79–80, 82, 83, 148–49, 203, 240, 264n.11, 270n.2
Ribeiro, Darcy, 59–60
Rodrigues, Arakcy Martins, 66
Rodrigues, Joice Meire, 140
root race, 82, 273–74n.24, 274n.26

roots *(raizes)*, 91
Rosicrucianism, 57–58, 61, 272n.14
roupagens, 112, 121, 274n.30
rules of engagement, 141

Sabatoviks, Nestor (Trino Arakém), 76
Sassi, Abaetê, 65
Sassi, Cací, 57–62, 60f, 65, 68–69
Sassi, Iraê, 61, 65, 70
Sassi, Mário
  alternate universes and intelligences, 83–84
  Atzingen, Moema Quadros von and, 58–59, 61–62
  Aunt Neiva and, 22, 54–55, 57, 62–63, 67–74, 69f, 101–2
  beyond matter terminology, 37, 81, 244, 245, 252–53
  Capellans, 85–91
  on doutrinadors, 114–15
  esoteric and spiritual studies of, 81–84
  as First Master Jaguar Sun Tumuchy, 67–70
  influence of, 245
  introduction to, 19–20, 21–22, 57–61, 60f
  Jaguars spirit tribe and, 78–81, 79f, 91–93
  karma and, 202
  on mediumship, 113, 115, 152–53, 199–200
  Night Owls work, 74–77
  occultural cosmology, 84–85
  personal and professional life, 63–67
  science and, 71–74, 81
  visionary mission, 103–5, 184–85
  waning influence, 76–77
Sayão, Bernardo, 31, 50–51
self-knowledge, 12, 74, 104–5, 190, 199, 212–13, 229, 239, 240
selflessness, 11, 35, 163–64
semi-conscious mediumship, 114, 147
seventh ray, 244–45
shared reality, 17–18
Shweder, Richard, 178, 188
sickness *vs.* disease, 187
Silva, José Carlos do Nascimento, 75
The Social Construction of Reality (Luckmann, Berger), 44
Social Works of the Christian Spiritualist Order (OSOEC), 4, 12, 19–20, 50–56. *See also* Valley of the Dawn
Solar dos Médiuns (Medium's Estate), 3–4, 4f
Space Age religion, 4, 12, 248–52
Space Brothers, 273n.21
spacecraft, 3–4, 26–27, 83–84, 88–89, 97
spirit guides, 4, 6, 34, 40, 46, 49, 84–85, 95, 134–35, 167, 171
Spiritist Union of Father White Arrow (União Espiritualista Seta Branca) (UESB), 44–50, 46f
spirit mediumship, 38–41
Spirit of Truth, 57, 65–66, 68, 268n.7
spirits of light, 13, 40, 112, 114, 121, 124–25, 197, 203, 224, 278n.14
spiritual classification. *See* classifications
spiritual disequilibrium, 112–13
spiritual healing, 5–7, 46–48, 61–62, 74, 138
spiritualized science, 104
spiritual narcissism, 214
spiritual planes. *See also* astral planes
  energies from, 139–40, 218–19
  etheric plane, 26, 86
  evolution to, 111–12, 114, 193, 203, 268n.11
  force of, 168
  harmony with, 118, 148
  indoctrination medium and, 113
  instructions from, 72–73, 102
  Kingdom of Zana and, 236
  life on, 19
  lyrics and music from, 194–95
  Moon Nymph and, 161
  positive intention and, 183
  proximity to, 45, 112, 150, 152
  structure of, 126–27, 135–37
  travels to, 138
spiritual quadrant *(quadra espiritual)*, 216–17
spiritual sensitivity, 6, 36, 148, 176
Stuckrad, Kocku von, 110
subtle energies, 82, 112
suffering spirit *(sofredor)*, 125, 178
Sun Masters *(Mestres Sol)*, 152–60, 161–62, 176

INDEX

Sun Nymphs *(Ninfas Sol)*, 156–59, 157*f*, 160, 176, 278n.8, 282–83n.15
supernatural, 6, 8, 36, 71–72, 94–95, 123, 141, 148, 176–77, 183–84, 195, 220, 243–44, 269n.14

Taguatinga, 49, 50, 51, 53, 62, 65–66, 99, 268n.10
terrestrial existence, 12–13, 88–89, 148
Theosophy, 82, 83–84, 148–49, 258–59, 271nn.8–10, 271–72nn.11–14, 280n.11
Third Millennium, 6, 12, 13, 26, 68, 80, 86, 90–91, 92–93, 95, 234, 235–36
Thrones ritual, 178–84, 197–99, 197*f*
Tiãozinho (Sebastião Quirino de Vasconcelos), 94–97, 96*f*
Tolkien, J. R. R., 107
trabalhos iniciáticos (initiatory works), 73–74
transcendental heritage *(herança transcendental)*
 chanting and, 234–39
 chronotropic regimes, 219–22
 imagined places and, 229–39
 introduction to, 23
 of Jaguars, 92
 overview of, 23, 216–19
 past lives, 23, 31, 36, 39–40, 106–7, 150–51, 162–63, 189, 199, 216–17, 227, 228, 235
 Pyramid significance, 230–33, 231*f*, 232*f*
 Turigano ritual, 222–29
transcendentalism, 12–13
transformation and healing, 213–15
Trinos Triada Presidentes, 68, 76
tuberculosis, 51–52
Tumuchy, Great, 89–91. *See also* Father White Arrow
Tupinambá, Chief, 40, 45, 46–47. *See also* Father White Arrow
Turigano ritual, 222–29
2000: The Conjunction of Two Planes (2000: A Conjuncão de Dois Planos) (Sassi), 62–63, 68, 84–85, 88

UFO religions, 23–24, 272–73n.20
Umahã (Buddhist monk), 51–52, 73, 83, 110–11, 243, 244–45, 269n.15

Umbanda tradition, 6, 36, 38–41
unconscious mediumship, 114
universal emergency room *(pronto socorro universal)*, 1–9, 23, 184–87, 193
universal energies, 111–12, 189
University of Brasília, 59–60, 63–65, 267–68n.2
unwanted conditions of the self, 187–91
utopia, 4, 97, 99–100, 102, 103, 104–5, 201, 248, 249

Valley of the Dawn
 Christic System, 13, 79–80, 92, 93–94, 128, 192
 cult debate over, 9–11
 doctrinal conduct in, 11–13, 104–5, 171–72, 173, 228, 229, 230, 252
 Doctrine of the Dawn, 11–13, 56, 73, 74, 81, 120, 144, 185, 221–22, 242, 244–45, 248–52, 282n.14
 entrance to, 1–2, 2*f*
 experiences of realness, 140–43
 free will in, 8–9, 10, 51, 120, 180, 190, 270n.2
 language and metaphor, 110–12
 overview, 1–9, 14–16, 20–25, 53–56, 103–5
 as psychic ecosystem, 4
 as Space Age religion, 248–52
 universalizing vision, 257–59
vanity of Aunt Neiva, 144–45, 146*f*
veterans *(veteranos)*, 20
vibration, 110, 112, 121, 124–25, 166–67, 171, 182, 184, 192, 196, 207
vibrational field, 82
vibratory planes, 86
Viera, Waldo, 246–47
Vilas-Boas, António, 83–84
Vilela, Joaquim, 253, 254*f*
Virgin Mary, 11, 250

Wessinger, Catherine, 7, 9–10
Western esotericism, 24, 82, 258–59
White, Christopher G., 247
White Current of the Great East, 110–11
woman-founded religions, 24

Xavier, Francisco (Chico), 45, 141, 200–1, 246–47

Yokaanam, Master, 37–38

Zelaya, 5–6, 12, 214–15
Zelaya, Carmem Lúcia
   gendered ideology of Aunt Neiva, 163
   healing mission, 186
   mediumship and, 128, 139–40
   on Mother Neném (Mãe
      Neném), 44–45
   on Mother Yara, 243
   ritual vestments, 55
   Spiritism and, 36–37, 43–44
   Umbanda mediumship and, 38–41
   vanity of Aunt Neiva, 144–45
Zelaya, Gilberto (Trino Ajarã), 55, 76
Zelaya, Neiva Chaves. *See* Aunt Neiva
Zelaya, Raul Alonso, 28, 37, 144–45, 197
Zeus, 17–18
zone of exclusion, 99

Printed in the USA/Agawam, MA
February 6, 2024

860710.007